Reframing Organizations

Reframing Organizations

Artistry, Choice, and Leadership

SECOND EDITION

Lee G. Bolman

Terrence E. Deal

JOSSEY-BASS
A Wiley Company
San Francisco

Published by

JOSSEY-BASS
A Wiley Company
350 Sansome St.
San Francisco, CA 94104

www.josseybass.com

Copyright © 1997 by John Wiley & Sons, Inc.

Jossey-Bass is a registered trademark of John Wiley & Sons, Inc.

Jossey-Bass books and products are available through most bookstores. To contact
Jossey-Bass directly, call (888) 378-2537, fax to (800) 605-2665, or visit our website
at www.josseybass.com.

Substantial discounts on bulk quantities of Jossey-Bass books are available to
corporations, professional associations, and other organizations. For details and
discount information, contact the special sales department at Jossey-Bass.

We at Jossey-Bass strive to use the most environmentally sensitive paper stocks available to
us. Our publications are printed on acid-free recycled stock whenever possible, and our
paper always meets or exceeds minimum GPO and EPA requirements.

Library of Congress Cataloging-in-Publication Data

Bolman, Lee G.
    Reframing organizations: artistry, choice, and leadership / Lee G. Bolman,
Terrence E. Deal.—2nd ed.
        p.   cm.—(The Jossey-Bass business & management series) (The Jossey-Bass
higher and adult education series)
    Includes bibliographical references and index.
      ISBN 0-7879-0822-3 (HC: alk. paper).—ISBN 0-7879-0821-5 (PBK: alk. paper)
      1. Management. 2. Organizational behavior. 3. Leadership. I. Deal, Terrence E.
II. Title. III. Series. IV. Series: The Jossey-Bass higher and adult education series.
HD31.B6135   1997
658.4'063—dc21   96-53592
                                                                    CIP

SECOND EDITION
HB Printing 10 9 8 7 6 5 4 3
PB Printing 10 9 8 7

A joint publication in
The Jossey-Bass Business & Management Series
and
The Jossey-Bass Higher and Adult Education Series

Contents

15   Integrating Frames for Effective Practice   265
16   Reframing in Action: Opportunities and Perils   280
17   Reframing Leadership   294
18   Reframing Change: Training, Realigning,
      Negotiating, Grieving   318
19   Reframing Ethics and Spirit   340
20   Bringing It All Together: Change and Leadership
      in Action   354
21   Epilogue: Artistry, Choice, and Leadership   377

      References   381
      Name Index   403
      Subject Index   410

Preface

This is the third release of a work that began in 1984 as *Modern Approaches to Understanding and Managing Organizations,* reappeared seven years later as *Reframing Organizations,* and has since been translated into multiple languages. We're grateful to readers around the world who have told us the book gave them ideas that make a difference, ideas they use every day at work and elsewhere.

It is time for an update, and we're gratified to be back by popular demand. Organizations and the leadership challenges they pose have been changing faster than ever in recent years, and scholars have been running hard to stay abreast. This edition tries to capture the end-of-century frontiers of both knowledge and art.

The four-frame model, with its view of organizations as factories, families, jungles, and temples, remains intact as the conceptual heart of the book. But much has changed. We have extensively revised our discussion of organizational structure to include the new structural forms proliferating in response to developments in technology and the global economy. In our survey of human resource management, we have added a discussion of the changing employment contract and updated other developments at the human resource frontier. We have added new case material and research findings to our discussion of organizational politics and symbols. We have added two entirely new chapters. One examines the relationship among ethics, soul, and spirit in organizations. The second uses a case that we have used before (Robert F. Kennedy High School) in a new context: to explore the reframing process in action.

There is new material throughout, but the book as a whole is shorter. We worked zealously to track down and expunge every redundant sentence, marginal concept, or extraneous example. At the same time, we've tried to keep it fun. Organizational life is an endless source of examples as entertaining as they are instructive, and we've sprinkled them throughout the text. We apologize to anyone who finds that an old favorite fell to the cutting room floor, but we think most readers will find the book an even clearer and more efficient read.

As always, our primary audience is managers and future managers. We have tried to answer the question, What do we know about organizations and leadership that is genuinely important and useful to practitioners? We have striven to present a large, complex body of theory, research, and practice as clearly and simply as possible, without watering it down or offering simplistic views on how to solve every managerial problem. We try not to offer solutions but rather to suggest more powerful and provocative ways of thinking about organizations' opportunities and pitfalls.

We continue to focus on both management *and* leadership. Leading and managing are different, but both are important. When organizations are overmanaged but underled, they eventually lose any sense of spirit or purpose. Poorly managed organizations with strong charismatic leaders may soar briefly only to crash shortly thereafter. Malpractice can be as damaging and unethical for managers and leaders as for physicians. Myopic managers or overzealous leaders usually harm more than just themselves. The challenges of modern organizations require the objective perspective of managers as well as the brilliant flashes of vision and commitment that wise leadership provides. We need more people in managerial roles who can find simplicity and order amid organizational confusion and chaos. We need versatile and flexible leaders who are artists as well as analysts, who can reframe experience to discover new issues and possibilities. We need managers who love their work, their organizations, and the people whose lives they affect. We need leaders and managers who appreciate management as a moral and ethical undertaking. We need leaders who combine hardheaded realism with passionate commitment to larger values and purposes. We hope to encourage and nurture such qualities and possibilities.

As in the past, we have tried to provide a clear and readable synthesis, integrating major theoretical traditions in the field. We concentrate mainly on what organization theory says that is important and useful for practice. We have drawn on examples in every sector and around the globe. Historically, organization studies has been divided into several intellectual camps, often isolated from one another. Works that seek to provide a comprehensive overview of organization theory and research often drown in social science jargon and abstraction and have little to say to practitioners. We try to find a balance between misleading oversimplification and unhelpful complexity.

Most work in organization theory has focused almost exclusively on either the private *or* the public sector but not both. Managers need to understand similarities and differences among all types of organizations. The public and private sectors are increasingly intertwined. Public administrators who regulate airlines, nuclear power plants, or pharmaceutical companies face the problem of "indirect management" every day. They struggle to influence the behavior of organizations over which they have very limited authority. Private firms need to manage their relationships with multiple levels of government. The situation is even more complicated for managers in multinational companies who have to cope with the subtleties of governments with very different systems and traditions. Across sectors and cultures, managers often harbor narrow, stereotypical conceptions of government that impede effectiveness on both sides. We need common ground and a shared understanding that can help strengthen public and private organizations in the United States and throughout the world. Dialogue between public and private, domestic and multinational organizations has become increasingly important. Because of their wide applicability, the frames concept provides an ecumenical language for the exchange.

The idea of *reframing* continues to be a central theme. Throughout the book, we show how the same situation can be viewed in at least four different ways. Part Six features a series of chapters on reframing critical organizational issues such as leadership, change, and ethics. Two chapters are specifically devoted to reframing real-life situations.

We also continue to emphasize artistry. Overemphasizing the rational and technical side of organizations often contributes to their decline or demise. Our counterbalance emphasizes the importance of art in both management and leadership. Artistry is neither exact nor precise. The artist interprets experience, expressing it in forms that can be felt, understood, and appreciated. Art allows for emotion, subtlety, and ambiguity. An artist reframes the world to give us a deeper understanding of what is and what might be. In modern organizations, quality, commitment, and creativity are highly valued but often hard to find. They can be developed and encouraged by leaders or managers who embrace the expressive side of their work.

Outline of the Book

Part One, "Making Sense of Organizations," tackles a perplexing question about management: Why is it that smart people so often do dumb things? Chapter One explains why: managers often misunderstand the situation they're in. They have not learned how to reframe, using multiple lenses to get a better reading of what they're up against and what they might do about it. Chapter Two presents a famous case, the destruction of a Korean Airlines jet plane by the Soviet Air Force, to show how managers' everyday theories can lead to catastrophe in the complicated world of modern organizations. It explains the basic factors that make organizational life complicated, ambiguous, and unpredictable; discusses common fallacies in managerial thinking; and spells out criteria for effective approaches to diagnosis and action.

Part Two, "The Structural Frame," has been updated to describe the rapid evolution of flatter, more flexible forms (networks, spiderwebs, and the like) and to analyze the strengths and limitations of the reengineering movement. Chapter Three describes basic issues managers need to consider in designing a structure to fit the organization's goals, tasks, and context. It shows why different organizations—such as Harvard University and McDonald's—need very different structures to be effective in their respective environments. Chapter Four explains major structural pathologies and pitfalls. It provides guidelines for aligning structures to situations and presents several contemporary cases illustrating successful structural change. Chapter Five shows that structure is a key to high-performing teams.

Part Three, "The Human Resource Frame," includes new material on the changing employment relationship and updates best practices in human resource management. Chapter Six focuses on the relationship between organizations and human nature. It shows how managers' practices and assumptions about people can lead either to alienation and hostility or to commitment and high motivation. It contrasts two different strategies for achieving effectiveness: working "lean and mean" and investing in people. Chapter Seven provides an overview of practices that build a more motivated and committed workforce—including participative management, job enrichment, self-managing work groups, organizational democracy, organization development, and quality initiatives. Chapter Eight presents a case example of interpersonal conflict to illustrate how managers create either effective or ineffective relationships. It also discusses how groups can increase their effectiveness by attending to group process, including informal norms and roles, interpersonal conflict, leadership, and decision making.

Part Four, "The Political Frame," has new material on the organizational environment as a political ecosystem and features new cases as well. Chapter Nine analyzes the tragic loss of the space shuttle *Challenger*, illustrating the power of political dynamics in decision making. It shows how scarcity and diversity lead to conflict, bargaining, and games of power, and it differentiates constructive and destructive political dynamics. Chapter Ten illustrates the basic skills of the constructive politician: diagnosing political realities, setting agendas, building networks, negotiating, and making choices that are both effective and ethical. Chapter Eleven highlights organizations as arenas for political contests and as agents influencing broader social, political, and economic trends. The story of Ross Johnson and history's biggest leveraged buyout explores the intersection of politics both inside and outside organizations.

We explore the symbolic frame in Part Five. Chapter Twelve spells out the basic symbolic elements in organizations: myths, metaphors, stories, humor, play, rituals, and ceremonies. It defines organizational culture and shows its central role in shaping performance. The power of symbol and culture are illustrated in organizations as diverse as Volvo France, the U.S. Congress, and Nordstrom department stores. Chapter Thirteen reveals how organizational structures, activities, and events serve as secular theater, expressing our fears and joys, arousing our affect, and kindling our spirit. It shows how organizational structures and processes, such as planning, evaluation, and decision making, are often more important for what they *express* than for what they *do*. Chapter Fourteen uses the case of a computer development team to show what leaders and group members can do collectively to build a culture that bonds people together in pursuit of a shared mission. Initiation rituals, specialized language, group stories, humor and play, and ceremonies all combine to transform diverse individuals into a cohesive team with purpose, spirit, and soul.

Part Six, "Improving Leadership Practice," focuses on the implications of the frames for central issues in managerial practice, including leadership, change, and ethics. Chapter Fifteen shows how managers can blend the frames to improve their own personal effectiveness. It looks at organizations as multiple realities and provides guidelines for aligning frames with different situations. Chapter Sixteen presents four different scenarios, or scripts, derived from the frames. It applies the scenarios to a challenging case of a young manager whose first day in a new job turns out to be far more challenging than she expected. The discussion illustrates how leaders can expand their options and enhance their effectiveness by considering alternative approaches to a situation. Chapter Seventeen discusses limitations in traditional views of leadership and provides a more comprehensive view of leadership and how it works in organizations. It summarizes and critiques current knowledge on the characteristics of leaders, showing that the frames generate distinctive images of effective leaders as architects, servants, advocates, and prophets. Chapter Eighteen describes four fundamental issues that arise in any change effort: individual needs, structural alignment, conflict, and loss. It uses cases of successful and unsuccessful change to document key strategies, such as training, realignment, creating arenas, and using symbol and ceremony.

Chapter Nineteen is new to this edition. It discusses four ethics emerging from the frames (excellence, caring, justice, and faith). It argues that leaders can build more ethical organizations through gifts of authorship, love, power, and significance. Chapter Twenty provides an integrative treatment of the reframing process. It takes a troubled school administrator through a weekend of reflection on critical difficulties he faces. The chapter shows how reframing can help managers move from feeling confused and stuck to a renewed sense of clarity and confidence. The epilogue, Chapter

Twenty-One, describes strategies and characteristics future leaders will require. It explains why they will need an artistic combination of conceptual flexibility and commitment to core values. Efforts to prepare future leaders need to focus as much on spiritual as on intellectual development.

January 1997   Lee G. Bolman
                                                                 Kansas City, Missouri
                                                                 Terrence E. Deal
                                                                 Nashville, Tennessee

Acknowledgments

We noted in our first book, "Book writing often feels like a lonely process, even when an odd couple is doing the writing." This uncommon pair keeps getting older and, some would say, even odder. Yet the process seems less lonely because of our close friendship and our contact with many other colleagues and friends. The best thing about teaching is that you learn so much from your students. Students at Harvard, Vanderbilt's Peabody College, and the University of Missouri–Kansas City have continued to provide valuable criticism, challenge, and support. We wish we could thank personally all of the leaders and managers from whom we have learned so much in seminars, workshops, and consultations. Their experience and wisdom are the foundation and touchstone for our work.

As in the past, we owe much to our colleagues. Thanks again to all who helped us in the two prior editions—your contribution still lingers in this work. But we particularly want to mention those who have made more recent contributions. For some reason, Deal has experienced more turnover in his teacher colleagues. They have included recently Ellen Goldring and Robert Crowson, whose conceptual and structural emphasis reinforced our commitment to social science traditions.

We have learned much from collaboration with a number of teaching fellows and graduate assistants. At Peabody, we have benefited at the graduate level from the counsel and assistance of Brad Gray and Nathaniel Bray. Those who have shared the challenge and diligence of teaching organizational theory and behavior to undergraduates include Nathaniel Bray, Paul Gleason, Brad Gray, Char Gray, Jeff Kenyon, Paul Ransdel, Amanda Stubblefield, and Roy Williams. Nathaniel and Amanda also pitched in to help us locate references in the final stages of the manuscript. At the University of Missouri–Kansas City, we are grateful for the help of Gurpreet Singh and Angela Khurana.

We also wish we could thank all the colleagues and readers in the United States and around the world who have provided valuable comments and suggestions, but the list is long and our memories keep getting shorter. Elena Granell de Aldaz of the Institute for Advanced Study of Management in Caracas collaborated with us on the development of a Spanish-language adaptation of *Reframing Organizations.* We are proud to consider her a valued colleague and a wonderful friend. Bob Marx, of the University of Massachusetts, deserves special mention as a charter member of the frames family. Bob's interest in the frames, creativity in developing teaching designs, and eye for video material have aided our teaching immensely. Peter Frost at the University of British Columbia has also been a continuing source of ideas, support, and inspiration. Bill Eddy, dean of the Bloch School at the University of Missouri–Kansas City, gets special thanks for nurturing an environment that helps scholarship flourish. Dick Heimovics and Bob Herman, also at the Bloch School, have enriched our ideas through their remarkably creative research on leadership in the nonprofit sector. Tom Johnson, longtime friend and colleague, has continued to be a source of new applications of the frames. Tom Brewer, a gifted Saturn manager, provided insightful assistance about teaming in one of our country's finest manufacturing operations. We're very grateful to Vanderbilt's Ellie Shick for her help in publicizing our work. Others to whom our debt is particularly clear include Chris Argyris, Pat Arnold, Sam Bacharach, Cliff Baden, Warren Bennis, Estella Bensimon, Al Bertani, Don Bowen, Pat Bower, Barbara Bunker, Tom Burks, Ellen Castro, Sharon Conley, Joseph Cox, Donna Culver, Linton Deck, Judy Doktor, Max Elden, Alice Farling, Bill Jenkins, Ralph Kilmann, Rick Mann, Linda Martinez, Jack Mayer, Grady McGonagill, John Meyer, Larry Michaelsen, Jerome Murphy, Harrison Owen, Kent Peterson, Sharon Rallis, Fernando Reimers, David Renz, Michael Sales, Mary Jane Saxton, Dick Scott, Ed and Beth Smith, Kit Taylor, Marilyn Taylor, Phyllis Thompson, Peggy Umanzio, Joan Vydra, and Karl Weick. Thanks again to Dave Brown, Tim Hall, Todd Jick, Bill Kahn, Phil Mirvis, and Barry Oshry of the Brookline Circle, now well into its second decade of searching for joy and meaning in lives devoted to the study of organizations.

Outside the United States, we are grateful to Rolf Kaelin, Cüno Pumpin, and Peter Weisman in Switzerland, Ilpo Linko in Finland, Craig Collins (author of the DDB Bank case in Chapter Eighteen) in Belgium, Tom Case in Brazil, Einar Plyhn and Haakon Gran in Norway, Peter Normark and Dag Bjorkegren in Sweden, and H.R.H. Prince Philipp von und zu Liechtenstein.

Closer to home, we owe more than we can say to Nancy Gray and Homa Aminmadani, without whom our sanity and health would be significantly diminished. Homa's Persian elegance and extraordinary determination continue to wrest about as much efficiency from Deal as possible, given the material she's had to work with for more years than she likes to admit. She is becoming a legend around the world for her attention to detail, her negotiating skills, and her extraordinary caring and compassion, despite working for someone who is, she is sure, a "legend in his own mind." Nancy Gray has achieved remarkable results since taking on the challenge of bringing a modicum of order and sanity to Bolman's professional functioning. We also continue to be grateful for the long-term support and friendship of Linda Corey, who still holds down the fort at Harvard.

The six Bolman children—Edward, Shelley, Lori, Scott, Christopher, and Bradley—all continue to enrich their father's life and contribute to his growth. He still wishes that he could give them as much as they have given him. Janie Deal has delighted her father in becoming a fascinating and independent young woman. Her hopes that advancing years would temper her father's outrageousness have not yet been fully realized; she is still waiting for his maturity and wisdom to come to full flower—particularly now that he is a card-carrying member of the AARP. He is eager to see what she will eventually become.

We dedicate the book to our wives, who have earned more credit and appreciation than we can ever give them. Joan Gallos, Lee Bolman's spouse and closest colleague, combines intellectual challenge and critique with support and love. She has been an active collaborator in the development of our ideas, and her teaching manual for the previous edition was a trailblazing model for the genre. Her contributions have become so integrated into our own thinking that we are no longer able to thank her for all the ways that the book has gained from her wisdom and insights.

Sandy Deal's training enables her to approach the field of organizations with a distinctive and illuminating slant. Her concentration on individual and family therapy has helped us make some even stronger connections to the field of clinical psychology. (We are skeptical, though, that she ever really said, "I don't need to bring my work home because it's waiting there for me.") Sandy is a delightful partner whose love and support over the long term have made all the difference. She is a rare combination of courage and caring, intimacy and independence, responsibility and playfulness.

To Joan and Sandy, thanks again. As the years accumulate, we love you even more.

L. G. B.
T. E. D.

The Authors

LEE G. BOLMAN holds the Marion Bloch Missouri Chair in Leadership at the Bloch School of Business and Public Administration, University of Missouri–Kansas City. He received a B.A. (1962) in history and a Ph.D. (1968) in administrative sciences, both from Yale University. Bolman's interests lie at the intersection of leadership and organizations, and he has published numerous articles, chapters, and cases. Bolman has been a consultant to corporations, public agencies, universities, and public schools in the United States, Asia, Europe, and Latin America. For twenty years, he taught at the Harvard Graduate School of Education, where he also chaired the Institute for Educational Administration and the School Leadership Academy. He has been director and board chair of the Organizational Behavior Teaching Society and director of the National Training Laboratories.

Bolman lives in Kansas City, Missouri, with his wife, Joan Gallos; the two youngest of his six children, Chris and Brad; and their Dalmatian, Vincent Van Gogh of KCMO.

TERRENCE E. DEAL is professor of education at Peabody College of Vanderbilt University. Before joining Peabody, he served on the faculties of the Stanford University Graduate School of Education and the Harvard Graduate School of Education. He received his B.A. degree (1961) from LaVerne College in history, his M.A. degree (1966) from California State University at Los Angeles in educational administration, and his Ph.D. degree (1972) from Stanford University in education and sociology. Deal has been a policeman, public school teacher, high school principal, district officer administrator, and university professor. His primary research interests are in organizational symbolism and change. He is the author of fifteen books, including the best-seller *Corporate Cultures* (with A. A. Kennedy, 1982).

He has published numerous articles on change and leadership. He is a consultant to business, health care, military, educational, and religious organizations both domestically and abroad. He lectures widely and teaches in a number of executive development programs.

Bolman and Deal first met in 1976 when they were assigned to co-teach a course on organizations in the same Harvard University classroom. Trained in different disciplines on opposite coasts, they disagreed on almost everything. It was the beginning of a challenging but very productive partnership. They have written a number of other books together, including *Leading with Soul: An Uncommon Journey of Spirit* (1995). Their books have been translated into multiple languages for readers in Asia, Europe, and Latin America.

For five years, Bolman and Deal also codirected the National Center for Educational Leadership, a research consortium of Harvard, Vanderbilt, and the University of Chicago.

The authors appreciate hearing from readers and welcome comments, questions, suggestions, or accounts of experiences that bear on the ideas in the book. Stories of success, failure, or puzzlement are all welcome. Readers can contact the authors at the following addresses:

Lee Bolman
Bloch School—UMKC
5100 Rockhill Road
Kansas City, Missouri 64113
lbolman@cctr.umkc.edu

Terry Deal
Box 514, Peabody College
Vanderbilt University
Nashville, Tennessee 37203

Part One

Making Sense of Organizations

Chapter One

Introduction

The Power of Reframing

For a century, Sears was America's largest and most successful retailer—until Wal-Mart forged ahead in the 1980s. How did Sears's leadership not see Wal-Mart coming? Was the view obscured from atop America's tallest building, Chicago's Sears Tower? What about IBM, long the world's largest and most admired computer firm, endowed with an unparalleled collection of patents, products, and scientists? How could such an excellent company misjudge changes in its industry so much that it ceded first place in minicomputers to Digital Equipment in the 1970s and then fumbled away leadership in personal computers to Intel and Microsoft a decade later? When General Motors's market share plummeted in the 1980s, how difficult was it to figure out that the world's largest car company had lost touch with its customers? Yet when someone asked GM's CEO, Roger Smith, what went wrong, all he could say was, "I don't know. It's a mysterious thing" (Loomis, 1993, p. 41). These profoundly important questions confront every manager and organization. A look at Roger Smith's well-publicized career offers important clues about what needs to be learned.

Shortly after becoming GM's chief executive in 1981, Smith was hailed as a bold and visionary leader. Six years later, he ruefully admitted, "I'm not as smart as people said a few years ago, and not as dumb as they say now" (Smith, 1987, p. 26). *Business Week* ran a cover story under the title "General Motors: What Went Wrong—

Eight Years and Billions of Dollars Haven't Made Its Strategy Succeed" (Hampton and Norman, 1987).

In 1979, General Motors earned $3.5 billion on sales of $63 billion and held nearly half the American car market. Earnings hit $4.5 billion in 1984 and $4.8 billion in 1988, yet GM's market share and Roger Smith's reputation declined steadily during the decade. In 1987, Ford earned more than General Motors for the first time in sixty years.

Described by one author as a "shrill-voiced accountant with the ego of a prima-donna" (Sherman, 1994, p. 75), Smith was parodied as an insensitive bureaucrat in the film *Roger and Me.* One of his first decisions as CEO was to kill a design for a new small car, a dubious move at a time when high-quality compact cars from Japan were gnawing off large chunks of GM's market share. Smith's commitment to rational thinking and financial logic convinced him that technology and automation would propel the company into a better future. It didn't turn out that way.

Ironically, it was the same Roger Smith who overruled opposition from his executive team to launch New United Motors Manufacturing, Inc. (NUMMI), a joint venture with Toyota. Under Toyota management, NUMMI reopened a failed and strife-torn GM plant in California, rehired the same workforce, and became a people-friendly, teamwork-dominated operation producing cars of higher quality than any other GM factory. Smith was also the godfather of Saturn, though much of Saturn's success occurred because it departed from his initial vision of an organization built around robotics and computers (Lee, 1988, pp. 242–243). Saturn's management team concluded that better people management was even more important than new technology. The team created a nonbureaucratic environment that set new standards in enlightened relationships with employees (Deal and Jenkins, 1994). The emotion-packed rollout of Saturn's first car found Roger Smith at the wheel, looking more like a small boy at a birthday party than the famously aloof and unemotional CEO. One Saturn worker commented after the ceremony, "I loathed Roger Smith. Yet I clapped and cheered ten minutes for the man" (Sherman, 1994, p. 206).

Smith's tenure at the helm of General Motors illustrates a basic management challenge: How do you know if what you see is what's really there? How do you avoid championing the wrong strategy or tackling the wrong problem? Even well-trained professionals make devastating mistakes. Consider the crew of a jet airliner, taking off from New York City. Noting surprisingly high airspeed readouts, the puzzled crew attributed them to unusual updrafts. They did not realize that before takeoff they had missed a crucial checklist item: turning on heaters to prevent freeze-up in the airspeed indicators. So the pilot kept easing back on the throttles to get the speed down. When the control stick began to shake, the crew interpreted it as a "Mach buffet"—an indication they were approaching the speed of sound. It was actually a stall warning. These were professional pilots, trained to know the difference in a highly technical environment. But by the time the crew members recognized their error, their aircraft was plunging to the ground, hopelessly out of control. Plane and crew were both destroyed. The costs of misreading a situation can be dire—in an airplane, a business, or government.

The challenge of finding the right way to frame our world has always been difficult, but it has become overwhelming in the turbulent and complicated world of the late twentieth century. Forms of management and organization serviceable a few years back are now obsolete. Sérieyx (1993) calls it the organizational big bang: "The information revolution, the globalization of economies, the proliferation of events that undermine all our certainties, the collapse of the grand ideologies, the arrival of the CNN society which transforms us into an immense, planetary village—all these shocks have overturned the rules of the game and suddenly turned yesterday's organizations into antiques" (pp. 14–15).

Many observers described Roger Smith as a brilliant manager with a wealth of ideas. Smith's frame was not wrong, just incomplete. As a result, the world's largest corporation stumbled through the 1980s with a dated and truncated vision. NUMMI and Saturn, two domains where Smith apparently shifted his perspective, were GM's only visionary initiatives in that decade.

The aim of this book is help managers and leaders enrich the ideas and approaches they bring to their work. Too often, psychic prisons prevent seeing old problems in a new light or finding more promising tools to work on perennial challenges. Effectiveness deteriorates when managers and leaders cannot *reframe*. When they don't know what to do, they do more of what they know. This helps explain a number of unsettling reports from the managerial front lines:

- Corporate strategic plans almost always forecast double-digit growth, but few companies achieve that target, and half the companies in the Fortune 1000 shrank between 1983 and 1993 (Gertz and Baptista, 1995).
- Hogan, Curphy, and Hogan (1994) estimate that one-half to three-quarters of all American managers are, in their assessment, incompetent.
- A study by CSC Index (cited in Gertz and Baptista, 1995) found that fewer than one-third of reengineering initiatives met or exceeded their goals (and the same could be said for almost any other popular business improvement scheme, including total quality management and strategic planning).

Small wonder that so many corporate veterans nod assent to Scott Adams's admittedly unscientific "Dilbert principle": "the most ineffective workers are systematically moved to the place where they can do the least damage—management" (1996, p. 14).

The ability to reframe experience enriches and broadens a leader's repertoire. It is a powerful antidote to self-entrapment. Expanded options help managers generate creative responses to the broad range of issues they encounter every day, as well as the haunting challenges that keep coming back. We cannot count the number of times managers have told us that they handled a particular problem the "only way" it could be done. Such statements betray a failure of both imagination and courage. It may be comforting to think that failure was unavoidable and we did all we could. But it can be enormously liberating for managers to realize there is *always* more than one way to respond to *any* organizational problem or dilemma. Managers are imprisoned only to the extent that their palette of ideas is impoverished.

This lack of imagination—Langer (1989) calls it "mindlessness"—is a major cause of the shortfall between the reach and the grasp of so many organizations—the empty chasm between dreams and reality, between noble aspirations and disappointing results. Such gaps are painfully acute in a world in which organizations dominate so much of our lives.

Virtues and Drawbacks of Organized Activity

The first humanlike primates appeared on earth about twelve million years ago. During most of the time since, our ancestors were hunters and gatherers. Humans evolved in a vastly simpler social context than today's. Only the last ten or fifteen thousand years have seen the emergence of institutions more complex than small, nomadic communities. Large organizations came to dominate the social landscape even more recently. There was little need for professional managers when people managed their own affairs. Today, things are very different: "A century and a half of technological evolution has produced communication and transportation technologies that make our entire planet a global marketplace. Industrial technologies, beginning with the steam engine, have led to larger and larger factories to produce products for that marketplace. The changes mean that today's executives deal with thousands of interdependent relationships—linkages to people, groups, or organizations that have the power to affect their job performance. And the diversity of goals, opinions, and beliefs among these players is typically enormous" (Kotter, 1985, pp. 22–23).

The proliferation of complex organizations has made almost every human activity a collective one. We are born, raised, and educated in organizations. We work in them and rely on them for goods and services. We learn in schools and universities. We play sports in teams. We join clubs and associations. Many of us will grow old and die in hospitals or nursing homes. We build organizations because of what they can do for us. They produce consumer goods, bring entertainment into our homes, provide education and health care, and deliver the mail.

All too often we experience the darker side. Organizations often frustrate and sometimes exploit people. Too often, products are flawed, students don't learn, patients stay sick, and policies make things worse instead of better. Many organizations infuse work with so little meaning that jobs have little value beyond a paycheck. Almost everyone, every day, receives services or goods from someone who obviously doesn't care.

NASA, the same organization that put a man on the moon, launched America's ill-fated space shuttle *Challenger*. Around the world, schools are blamed for social ills, universities are said to close more minds than they open, and government agencies are criticized for red tape and rigidity. The sarcastic phrase "good enough for government work" reflects widespread cynicism about the performance of public agencies. But the private sector has its own problems. Automakers recall faulty cars, baby food producers apologize for adulterated fruit juice, and software companies deliver bugs and "vaporware." Industrial accidents dump chemicals, oil, toxic gas, and radioactive materials into the air and water. Corporate greed and insensitivity create havoc for lives and communities. The bottom line: we are hard pressed to manage organizations so that benefits regularly exceed costs.

Strategies for Improving Organizations: The Track Record

We have certainly tried to make organizations better. Legions of managers go to work every day with that hope in mind. Authors and consultants spin out a steady flow of new answers and solutions. Policymakers develop laws and regulations to guide organizations on the correct path.

The most basic change strategy is to improve management and leadership. Modern mythology promises that organizations will work splendidly if they are well managed. Managers are supposed to have the big picture and be responsible for their organization's overall health and productivity. Unfortunately, they have not always been equal to the task, even when armed with computers, information systems, flowcharts, quality programs, and a panoply of other tools and techniques. They go forth with this rational arsenal to try to tame our wild and primitive workplaces. Yet in the end, irrational forces often prevail.

When managers cannot solve problems on their own, they often hire consultants. The number and variety of consultants today are overwhelming. Most have a specialty: reengineering, quality, mergers, strategy, human resource management, information technology, executive search, outplacement, training, organization development, and many more. For every managerial question or issue there is a consultant willing to offer assistance—at a price.

For all their sage advice and remarkable fees, consultants have yet to solve all the pressing problems plaguing businesses, public agencies, military services, hospitals, and schools. Sometimes the consultants are more hindrance than help. More than a few managers wish that the Hippocratic injunction ("Above all else, do no harm") applied as much to consultants as to physicians. Meanwhile, consultants grouse about clients' failure to implement their insights.

When managers and consultants fail to get organizations on track, government frequently jumps in with legislation and regulation. Constituents badger elected officials to "do something" about a variety of ills: pollution, dangerous products, hazardous working conditions, and chaotic schools, to name a few. Governing bodies respond by making "policy." But policies regularly go awry as they meander from the legislative floor to the targeted problems. A sizable body of research documents the continuing saga of perverse ways in which policy implementation distorts policymakers' intentions (Bardach, 1977; Elmore, 1978; Pressman and Wildavsky, 1973).

Difficulties surrounding each strategy for improving organizations are well documented. Exemplary intentions produce more costs than benefits. Problems outlast solutions. It is as if tens of thousands of hardworking, highly motivated pioneers keep hacking away at a swamp that continues to produce new growth faster than anyone can clear the old. Someday there may be a clearing, and the swamp might be drained. The basic purpose of this book is to help the pioneers improve the odds.

There are reasons for optimism. Organizations have changed about as much in the past ten years as in the previous fifty. To survive, they had to. Revolutionary changes in technology, the rise of the global economy, and shortened product life cycles have spawned a flurry of activity to design more fluid and more flexible organizational forms. These efforts have spawned a bewildering variety of labels: networks (Chaize, 1992), virtual organizations, adhocracies (Mintzberg, 1979), atomized organizations (Deal and Kennedy, 1982), spider plants (Morgan, 1993), PALs (Kanter, 1989), and many others. These new forms can be seen in network organizations like the French packaging giant Carnaud et Metal Box. CEO Jean-Marie Descarpentries said his approach to management was simple: "You catalyze toward the future, you trust people, and they discover things you never would have thought of" (Aubrey and Tilliette, 1990, p. 142). New organization models are also in evidence in companies like Ben and Jerry's (the socially conscious ice-cream people) or Saturn (the automobile producer with a soul)—both are passionate about core values and create familylike bonds among employees and customers.

The electronics industry has bred an array of innovative forms visible in firms like Intel, the king of microprocessors, and software powerhouse Microsoft. These and many other firms provide dramatic models of corporate success. Yet there are still too many failures. This book is intended to help leaders and managers improve the odds for themselves as well as their organizations.

Theory Base

Managers, consultants, and policymakers draw, formally or otherwise, on a variety of theories in efforts to change or improve organizations. Yet only in the past few decades have social scientists devoted much time or attention to developing ideas about how organizations work (or why they often fail). In the social sciences, several major schools of thought have evolved, each with its own concepts and assumptions and its own view of how to bring social collectives under control.

Each tradition claims a scientific foundation. But theories easily become theologies, preaching a single, parochial scripture. Each theory offers its own version of reality and its own vision of the future. Each also offers a range of techniques for reaching the promised land. Modern managers encounter a cacophony of voices and visions. Consider an executive browsing in the management section of her local bookstore on a brisk Fall day in 1996. She is worried about her company's flagging performance and about the chance that her job might disappear next.

The bright red spine of *Reengineering the Corporation* (Hammer and Champy, 1993) catches her eye. She's heard of reengineering—for a while everyone was talking about it. But she isn't quite sure what it is. Scanning the book, she is drawn to phrases like "radical redesign of business processes" and "dramatic improvements in performance." She reads on: "It is no longer necessary or desirable for companies to organize their work around Adam Smith's division of labor. Task-oriented jobs in today's world of customers, competition, and change are obsolete. Instead companies must organize around process" (pp. 27–28). "Once a real work process is reengineered, the shape of the organizational structure required to perform the work will become apparent" (pp. 40–41).

"Sounds good," the executive thinks to herself, "but a little mechanistic." Then she spots another bright red book: Robert Waterman's *What America Does Right* (1994). It talks about people, relationships, and how truly effective companies respond to the needs of their workforce: "Organizing to meet your own people's needs seems a simple enough idea. It isn't. It means understanding what motivates people, and aligning culture, systems, structure, people and leadership attention toward things that are inherently motivating. It's a radical departure from management convention. The old (and still very pervasive) dictum says that the job of the managers is to tell people what to do. My research says that the managers' job is to lead. Leaders recognize and act on the idea that the needs of the business and the needs of people are inextricably linked" (pp. 17–18).

"Nice," she thinks, "but idealistic. Let's look for something a little more down to earth." She finds Jeffrey Pfeffer's *Managing with Power* (1992) and browses the chapter headings: "Where Does Power Come From?" "Timing Is (Almost) Everything," "Changing the Structure to Consolidate Power," "Even the Mighty Fall: How Power Is Lost." She flips through it, reading: "Unless we are willing to come to terms with organizational power and influence, and admit that the skills of getting things done are as important as the skills of figuring out what to do, our organizations will falter and fall behind. The problem is, in most cases, not an absence of insight or organizational intelligence. Instead, the problem is passivity" (p. 12). "This is why power and influence are not the organization's last dirty secret, but the secret of success for both individuals and their organizations" (p. 345).

"He's talking reality," she tells herself, "but he's too cynical. Isn't there something a little more uplifting?" She spots Max DePree's *Leadership Jazz* (1992). Again she scans the chapter titles: "Finding One's Voice," "A Key Called Promise," "God's Mix," "The Gift of Change." She skims a few passages: "An organization's cultural harmony is fragile. I'm talking about the sweet music that emanates from diverse and productive groups of people. Leaders certainly have a hand in creating the atmosphere where this kind of harmony can exist, but they don't direct it or mandate it or control it" (p. 44). "I think about management in two categories, scientific and tribal. The tribal is certainly the most important and, while palpable, is quite difficult to grasp and nurture. Tribal implies membership. . . . It can illuminate for us meaningful connections to our ancestors and elders" (p. 70).

Had the executive visited another store in another year, she might have encountered different books but a similar range of opinions. Our purpose in this book is to sort through the multiple voices competing for managers' attention. In the process, we have consolidated major schools of organizational thought into four perspectives. There are many ways to label such perspectives.[1] We have chosen the label *frames*. Frames are both windows on the world and lenses that bring the world into focus. Frames filter out some things while allowing others to pass through easily. Frames help us order experience and decide what to do. Every manager, consultant, or policymaker relies on a personal frame or image to gather information, make judgments, and determine how best to get things done. Goran Carstedt, the talented executive who championed the turnaround of Volvo's French division in the 1980s, put it this way: "The world simply can't be made sense of, facts can't be organized, unless you have a mental model to begin with. That theory does not have to be the right one, because you can alter it along the way as information comes in. But you can't begin to learn without some concept that gives you expectations or hypotheses" (quoted in Hampden-Turner, 1992, p. 167).

Artistic managers like Carstedt learn fluidly because they are able to frame and reframe experience, sorting through the tangled underbrush to find solutions to problems. A critic once commented to Cézanne, "That doesn't look anything like a sunset." Pondering his painting, Cézanne responded, "Then you don't see sunsets the way I do." Like Cézanne, leaders need to find new ways to see things. They must also articulate and communicate their vision so others can also learn to shift perspectives.

Frames also become tools, each with its strengths and limitations. The wrong tool gets in the way. The right one makes a job easier. One or two tools may suffice for simple jobs but not for more complex undertakings. Managers who master the hammer and expect all problems to behave like nails find organizational life confusing and frustrating. The wise manager, like a skilled carpenter or an experienced cook, will want a diverse collection of high-quality implements. Experienced managers also understand the difference between possessing a tool and knowing how to use it. Only experience and practice bring the skill and wisdom to use tools well.

Kurosawa's film *Rashomon* recounts the same event through the eyes of several witnesses. Each tells a very different story. Organizations are filled with people who have different interpretations of what is happening and what should be happening. Each version contains a glimmer of truth, but each is a product of the prejudices and blind spots of its maker. No single story is comprehensive enough to make an organization truly understandable or manageable. Effective managers need multiple tools, the skill to use each of them, and the wisdom to match frames to situations.[2]

Our goal is usable knowledge. We have sought ideas powerful enough to capture the subtlety and complexity of life in organizations yet simple enough to be useful. Our distillation has drawn much from the social sciences—particularly from sociology, psychology, political science, and anthropology. Thousands of managers and scores of organizations have also been our mentors. They helped us sift through the social science research to identify ideas that work in practice. We have sorted the insights drawn from both research and practice into four major perspectives, or frames, used both by academics and practitioners to make sense of organizations. The four frames that we first described in the early 1980s (Bolman and Deal, 1984) have since been adopted by other organizational scholars (including Bergquist, 1992; Birnbaum, 1988, 1992; Dunford, 1992). The worried executive earlier in the chapter, seeking revelation in a bookstore, rediscovered the same four perspectives.

The first book she found, *Reengineering the Corporation* (Hammer and Champy, 1993), extends a long tradition that treats the factory as the metaphor for organization. Drawing from sociology and management science, the *structural frame* emphasizes goals, specialized roles, and formal relationships. Structures—commonly depicted by organization charts—are designed to fit an organization's environment and technology. Organizations allocate responsibilities to participants ("division of labor") and create rules, policies, procedures, and hierarchies to coordinate diverse activities. Problems arise when the structure does not fit the situation. At that point, some form of reorganization is needed to remedy the mismatch.

Our executive next encountered *What America Does Right* (Waterman, 1994), with its focus on the relationship between organizations and people. The *human resource frame,* based particularly on ideas from psychology, sees an organization as much like an extended family, inhabited by individuals who have needs, feelings, prejudices, skills, and limitations. They have a great capacity to learn and sometimes an even greater capacity to defend old attitudes and beliefs. From a human resource perspective, the key challenge is to tailor organizations to people—to find a way for individuals to get the job done while feeling good about what they are doing.

Pfeffer's *Managing with Power* (1992) is a contemporary example of the *political perspective,* rooted particularly in the work of political scientists. It sees organizations as arenas, contests, or jungles. Different interests compete for power and scarce resources. Conflict is rampant because of enduring differences in needs, perspectives, and lifestyles among various individuals and groups. Bargaining, negotiation, coercion, and compromise are part of everyday life. Coalitions form around specific interests and change as issues come and go. Problems arise when power is concentrated in the wrong places or is so broadly dispersed that nothing gets done. Solutions arise from political skill and acumen—as Machiavelli suggested centuries ago in *The Prince* ([1514] 1961).

Finally, our executive encountered DePree's *Leadership Jazz* (1992), with its emphasis on symbolic forms like story, metaphor, and music. The *symbolic frame,* drawing on social and cultural anthropology, treats organizations as tribes, theaters, or carnivals. It abandons the assumptions of rationality more prominent in the other frames. It sees organizations as cultures, propelled more by rituals, ceremonies, stories, heroes, and myths than by rules, policies, and managerial authority. Organization is also theater: actors play their roles in the organizational drama while audiences form impressions from what they see onstage. Problems arise when actors play their parts badly, when symbols lose their meaning, when ceremonies and rituals lose their potency. We rebuild the expres-

Table 1.1.   Overview of the Four-Frame Model.

	Frame			
	Structural	*Human Resource*	*Political*	*Symbolic*
Metaphor for organization	Factory or machine	Family	Jungle	Carnival, temple, theater
Central concepts	Rules, roles, goals, policies, technology, environment	Needs, skills, relationships	Power, conflict, competition, organizational politics	Culture, meaning, metaphor, ritual, ceremony, stories, heroes
Image of leadership	Social architecture	Empowerment	Advocacy	Inspiration
Basic leadership challenge	Attune structure to task, technology, environment	Align organizational and human needs	Develop agenda and power base	Create faith, beauty, meaning

sive or spiritual side of organizations through the use of symbol, myth, and magic.

The overview of the four-frame model in Table 1.1 shows that each of the frames has its own image of reality. You may be drawn to one or two frames and repelled by others. Some frames may seem clear and straightforward while others seem puzzling. As you learn to apply all four, you should develop greater appreciation and deeper understanding of organizations. Galileo discovered this when he devised the first telescope. Each lens that he added contributed to a more accurate image of the heavens. Successful managers take advantage of the same truth. They reframe until they understand the situation at hand.

This claim has stimulated a growing body of research. Dunford and Palmer (1995) found that management courses that taught multiple frames had significant positive effects over both the short and the long term—in fact, 98 percent of their respondents rated reframing as helpful or very helpful, and about 90 percent felt it gave them a competitive advantage. Another series of studies has shown that the ability to use multiple frames is associated with greater effectiveness for managers and leaders (Bensimon, 1989, 1990; Birnbaum, 1992; Bolman and Deal, 1991, 1992a, 1992b; Heimovics, Herman, and Jurkiewicz Coughlin, 1993, 1995; Wimpelberg, 1987).

Multiframe thinking requires movement beyond narrow and mechanical thinking. Table 1.2 presents two distinctive ways of approaching management and leadership. One is a rational-technical approach that emphasizes certainty and control. The other is

Table 1.2.   Expanding Managerial Thinking.

How Managers Think	*How Managers Might Think*
They often have a limited view of organizations (for example, attributing almost all problems to individuals' flaws and errors).	They need a holistic framework that encourages inquiry into a range of significant issues: people, power, structure, and symbols.
Regardless of a problem's source, managers often choose rational and structural solutions: facts, logic, restructuring.	They need a palette that offers an array of options: bargaining as well as training, celebration as well as reorganization.
Managers often value certainty, rationality, and control while fearing ambiguity, paradox, and "going with the flow."	They need to develop creativity, risk taking, and playfulness in response to life's dilemmas and paradoxes, focusing as much on finding the right question as the right answer, on finding meaning and faith amid clutter and confusion.
Leaders often rely on the "one right answer" and the "one best way"; they are stunned at the turmoil and resistance they generate.	Leaders need passionate, unwavering commitment to principle, combined with flexibility in understanding and responding to events.

a more expressive, artistic conception that encourages flexibility, creativity, and interpretation. The first sees managers as mechanics. The second sees them as leaders and artists. Managers who master the ability to reframe report a liberating sense of choice and power. They are able to develop unique alternatives and novel ideas about what their organization needs. They are better attuned to people and events around them. They are less often startled by organizational perversity, and they learn to anticipate the turbulent twists and turns of organizational life. The result is managerial freedom—and more productive, humane organizations.

Artistry is neither exact nor precise. Artists interpret experience and express it in forms that can be felt, understood, and appreciated by others. Art allows for emotion, subtlety, ambiguity. An artist reframes the world so that others can see new possibilities. Modern organizations often rely too much on engineering and too little on art in their search for attributes like quality, commitment, and creativity. Art is not a replacement for engineering but an enhancement. Artistic leaders and managers help us see beyond today's reality to forms that release untapped individual energies and improve collective performance. The leader as artist relies on images as well as memos, poetry as well as policy, reflection as well as command, and reframing as well as refitting.

Notes

1. Among the possible ways of talking about frames are schemata or schema theory (Fiedler, 1982; Fiske and Dyer, 1985; Lord and Foti, 1986), representations (Frensch and Sternberg, 1991; Lesgold and Lajoie, 1991; Voss, Wolfe, Lawrence, and Engle, 1991), cognitive maps (Weick and Bougon, 1986), paradigms (Gregory, 1983; Kuhn, 1970), social categorizations (Cronshaw, 1987), implicit theories (Brief and Downey, 1977), mental models (Senge, 1990), and root metaphors. We follow Goffman (1974) in using the term *frame*.
2. A number of management scholars (including Allison, 1971; Bergquist, 1992; Birnbaum, 1988; Elmore, 1978; Morgan, 1986; Perrow, 1986; Quinn, 1988; Quinn, Faerman, Thompson, and McGrath, 1996; and Scott, 1981) have made similar arguments for a multiframe approach to organizations.

Chapter Two

Simple Ideas,
Complex Organizations

Early in the morning of August 31, 1983, Kim Eui Donz, a Korean Airlines flight engineer, entered the cockpit of KAL Flight 007. His responsibility was to program the inertial navigation system (INS) to direct the automatic pilot on a 4,100-mile flight from Anchorage to Seoul. Routinely, he entered the plane's position into the computer. Unknowingly, his entry was ten degrees off; he noted the plane's position as W139 instead of W149. A warning light blinked on when he entered the incorrect position, but he thought the computer had malfunctioned. That ten-degree error programmed the INS to believe that the plane was starting from a position some three hundred miles *east* of Anchorage. The error should have been caught. Elaborate cross-checking is built in to the work of airline pilots, but pilots are human—and humans sometimes take shortcuts. The aircraft commander, Captain Chun, revised his flight plan at the last minute, and the crew had to rush through its routine flight checks.

The Anchorage control tower cleared Flight 007 to proceed directly to the Bethel checkpoint, and Captain Chun switched on the INS without verifying the settings. After takeoff, air traffic control gave the flight a more direct route to save time and fuel. But the new route bypassed Bethel, the last checkpoint before the plane flew over water on a route with no checkpoints until it reached Asia. The crew and passengers were now en route to an unknown destination. Even then, the error might still have been detected if Captain Chun had stayed on the flight deck. But after turning off the seat belt sign, he went back to the first-class cabin to mix with dignitaries and talk to deadheading KAL pilots.

The "finger error" of ten degrees put the plane on a course similar to that flown by American reconnaissance flights near Soviet airspace. Each reconnaissance mission probed the perimeter of the Soviet border and then veered off. To Soviet radar, the KAL plane looked like a routine and familiar blip until it did the unexpected. Instead of turning away, the plane crossed the border into Soviet territory. Now another human organization came into play— the Soviet Air Defense Force. When radar operators could not identify the intruding aircraft, four interceptors were deployed. Soviet commanders were thrown into panic and confusion. An unidentified intruder was as dangerous as it was puzzling. If this was a reconnaissance plane, why wasn't it turning away? Still unable to identify Flight 007, they scrambled more fighters. The flight was now well inside Soviet airspace, on a course that would take it between two major Soviet air bases.

At 3:12 A.M., Lieutenant Colonel Gennadi Osipovich flew his SU-15 fighter right alongside KAL 007. He was initially surprised to see flashing lights— unprecedented for a U.S. reconnaissance plane. He was even more surprised to discover a Boeing civilian aircraft. Osipovich told ground control about the lights, and two senior Russian officers speculated that the intruder might be a passenger plane. But Osipovich never mentioned that he had identified a Boeing 747. "They did not ask me," he said later [Gordon, 1996, p. A6]. In his mind, it had to be a spy mission, and he expected both a hero's welcome and a substantial cash bonus for destroying the enemy target. But time was short— KAL 007 would soon leave Soviet airspace. Ordered to force KAL 007 to land, Osipovich concluded radio was useless, because the foreign pilots would not speak Russian. He flashed his lights and fired more than five hundred cannon rounds as a signal—but the shells contained no tracers and were invisible. There was no response. At 3:26 A.M., less than half a minute before KAL 007 was to exit Soviet airspace, Osipovich fired two missiles. He reported to ground control, "The target is destroyed." Two hundred sixty-nine people fell to their deaths [Hersch, 1986; Gordon, 1996; Witkin, 1993].

The ensuing outrage produced charges and countercharges. Was the plane on an American spy mission? Had the Russians intentionally shot down a civilian aircraft? The KAL Flight 007 incident is a dramatic version of an old story—human error leading to tragedy. If we look deeper, though, we find another source of error— systems breakdowns. Korean Airlines had systems to prevent human errors. The systems failed. It had additional procedures to detect and correct errors that did occur. These also failed. Similar patterns appear in many other well-publicized disasters: nuclear accidents at Chernobyl in the Ukraine and at Three Mile Island in the United

States, the 1995 collapse of a department store in Seoul. Each illustrates a similar chain of error, miscommunication, and misguided actions.

The spate of theories to paint John F. Kennedy's assassination as a conspiracy suggests that we often prefer to believe that a dramatic and bizarre event must be the product of extraordinary antecedents. But the KAL tragedy can be traced to ordinary processes that occur routinely in and between organizations. Error and chaos are the everyday stuff of managerial life. Many errors are insidious because they are subtle or even invisible. A good example is the following case, a true story disguised to protect both the innocent and the guilty.

> Helen Demarco arrived in her office to find a clipping from a local newspaper. The headline read, "Osborne Announces Plan." Paul Osborne had arrived two months earlier as Amtran's new chief executive. His mandate was to "revitalize, cut costs, and improve efficiency." After twenty years of service, Demarco had achieved a senior management position at Amtran. She had not yet talked directly with Osborne, but her boss reported directly to him. Like other long-term employees, Demarco waited with curiosity and apprehension to learn what the new chief would do. She was startled when she read the newspaper account of Osborne's plan. It made technical assumptions that related directly to her area of expertise. She knew that Osborne was a manager, not a technical expert. She saw immediately that the new plan contained fatal technical flaws. "If he tries to implement this, it'll be the worst management mistake since the Edsel," she thought to herself.
>
> Two days later, Demarco and several colleagues received a memo instructing them to form a committee and begin work on the revitalization plan. When the group met, everyone agreed the plan was "crazy."
>
> "What do we do?" someone asked.
>
> "Why don't we just tell him it won't work?" said one hopeful soul.
>
> "He's already gone public! You want to tell him his baby is ugly?"
>
> "Not me. Besides, he already thinks a lot of us are deadwood. If we tell him it's no good, he'll just think we're defensive."
>
> "Well, we can't just go ahead with it. It's bound to fail!"

"That's true," said Demarco thoughtfully. "But what if we tell him we're conducting a study of how to implement the plan?"

Her suggestion was overwhelmingly approved. The group told Osborne the study was starting. They were even given a substantial budget to support the "research." No one mentioned the study's real purpose: to find a way to kill the plan without alienating Osborne.

Over time, the group developed a strategy. They assembled a lengthy, technical report, filled with graphs, tables, and impenetrable jargon. The report offered Osborne two options. Option A, his original plan, was presented as technically feasible but phenomenally expensive—well beyond anything Amtran could possibly afford. Option B, billed as a "modest downscaling" of the original plan, was much more affordable.

When Osborne pressed the group to explain the huge cost difference between the two proposals, he received a barrage of technical jargon and quotations from the charts. No one mentioned that if Osborne penetrated the smoke screen, he would see that even Option B offered very few benefits at a very high cost.

Osborne argued and pressed for more information. He finally agreed to proceed with Option B. Since the plan took several years to implement, Osborne had moved on before it was fully operational. In fact, the "Osborne plan" was widely described as an extraordinary innovation proving once again Paul Osborne's ability to revitalize ailing organizations.

Helen Demarco came away from the experience with deep feelings of frustration and failure. The Osborne plan, in her view, was a wasteful mistake, and she had knowingly participated in the charade. "But," she rationalized to herself, "I really didn't have much choice. Osborne was determined to go ahead. It would have been career suicide to try to stop him."

In fact, Demarco did have other choices; there are always alternatives in any managerial quandary. Tragedies occur because managers cannot foresee the issues, are unaware of their options, or lack the artistry and skill to chart a different course. Helen Demarco, Paul Osborne, and the crew of KAL Flight 007 all thought they were performing effectively. They were tripped up in part by human fallibility, but they were misled as well by a limited understanding of the circumstances. The first step in managerial wisdom and artistry is to understand the situation you face.

Properties of Organizations

Human organizations can be exciting and challenging places, as they are often depicted in management texts and corporate annual reports. But they are as likely to be snake pits as rose gardens (Schwartz, 1986). Assuming that they are only one or the other distorts reality. Managers need to be mindful of several basic characteristics that provide opportunities for the wise as well as traps for the unwary.

Organizations are complex. Organizations are populated by people, and our ability to understand and predict human behavior is still limited. Interactions among many different individuals, groups, and organizations get complicated in a hurry. The transactions in the flight crew of KAL Flight 007 suggest some of the intricacies that arise even in relatively simple systems like a three-person cockpit. Larger organizations have a bewildering array of people, departments, technologies, goals, and environments. The complexity is compounded even further when a number of different organizations are involved. In the case of KAL Flight 007, disaster resulted from a chain of events within and among several separate systems. Almost anything can affect anything else in collective activity. Permutations produce complex, causal knots that are very hard to disentangle. Osborne probably never understood the real story of what happened to his plan. Even after exhaustive investigation, our understanding of what really happened to KAL Flight 007 is still woven from conjecture and supposition. We may never know the real story.

Organizations are surprising. What you expect is often stunningly different from what you get. Paul Osborne saw his plan as a bold leap forward. Helen and her group thought it was an expensive albatross. If Helen was right, Osborne actually made matters *worse* by trying to change them. He might have produced better results by leaving things alone.

The solution to yesterday's problem often creates future impediments to getting anything done, and it may even create new possibilities for disaster. Think of the procedural hurdles and bureaucratic obstacles often created after a disaster such as Flight 007 or the loss of the space shuttle *Challenger.* A friend of ours was the president of a chain of retail stores. In the firm's early years, he had a problem with two sisters who worked in the same store. To prevent this sort of thing from recurring, he established a nepotism policy that prohibited two members of the same family from working for the company. Years later, two of his employees met at work, fell in love, and began to live together. The president was stunned when they asked if they could get married without being fired. Taking action in an organization is like shooting a wobbly cue ball into a large and complex array of self-directed billiard balls. So many balls bounce off one another in so many directions that it is hard to know how things will look when everything settles down.

Organizations are deceptive. They defy expectations and then camouflage surprises. The Soviet Air Defense Force wanted to hide its surprise and confusion for fear of revealing critical strategic weaknesses. Helen Demarco and her colleagues did their best to ensure that Paul Osborne never learned that their "research" was a holding action and their "technical report" was mostly artful camouflage.

It is too easy to attribute Demarco's deception to a character flaw or a personality disorder. In fact, she disliked deception and regretted doing it. Yet she believed she had no other choice. Sophisticated managers know that what happened to Paul Osborne happens routinely in organizations. Even though the new quality initiative might be flawed or the new product doomed, subordinates often clam up. Challenging the authority of a KAL captain would violate a strong core value of East Asian cultures. It is a taboo a first officer or flight engineer will often honor even when facing catastrophe. Such sensitivity to one's place in the formal pecking order is not confined to Asia. People in almost any culture are reluctant to offend superiors. They often feel the boss would not listen or might even punish them for being resistant or insubordinate. A friend who occupies a senior position in a large government agency put it simply: "Communications in organizations are rarely candid, open, or timely."

Organizations are ambiguous. Complexity, unpredictability, and deception add up to a lot of ambiguity. Figuring out what is really happening in businesses, hospitals, schools, or public agencies is difficult. Even if we think we know what is happening, it is hard to know what it means or what to do about it. Helen Demarco was never sure how Paul Osborne really felt, how receptive he would be to other points of view, or how much he was willing to compromise. She and her peers heightened ambiguity by trying to keep Osborne in the dark. As the KAL case shows, when you incorporate additional organizations—or cultures—to the human equation, the level of ambiguity can become overwhelming.

Ambiguity comes from a number of sources. Sometimes information is incomplete or vague. Sometimes the same information is interpreted in a variety of ways by different people. At other times, ambiguity is deliberately created to hide problems or avoid conflict. Much of the time, events and processes are so complex, scattered, and uncoordinated no one can fully understand—let alone control—what is happening. Exhibit 2.1, adapted from McCaskey (1982), lists some of the most important sources of organizational ambiguity.

Organizational Learning

An environment filled with complexity, surprise, deception, and ambiguity makes it easier to go crazy than to learn. Yet an increasingly turbulent, rapidly changing environment requires contemporary organizations to learn better and faster just to survive. Michael Dell, founder and CEO of Dell Computer Corporation, explained it this way: "In our business, the product cycle is six months, and if you miss the product cycle, you've missed the opportunity. In this business, there are two kinds of people, really: the quick and the dead" (Farkas and De Backer, 1996).

With the stakes so high, organizational learning has become a topic of increasing urgency. A decade or so back, some scholars still debated whether the idea even made sense: Could organizations learn, or was learning something only individuals can do? That debate died out as scholars and practitioners regularly noted instances in which individuals learned and organizations didn't, or vice versa. Complex firms like Microsoft, Toyota, or British Airways have "learned" capabilities as a system that go far beyond the knowledge of any individual. Yet individuals within a system can and often do learn things that the system does not. In the late 1980s and early 1990s, for example, even senior officials in China recognized that the nation was heading in two contradictory directions at once, pro-

Exhibit 2.1. Sources of Ambiguity.

We are not sure what the problem is. Definitions of the problem are vague or competing, and any given problem is intertwined with other messy problems.

We are not sure what is really happening. Information is incomplete, ambiguous, and unreliable, and people disagree on how to interpret the information that is available.

We are not sure what we want. We have multiple goals that are unclear or conflicting. Different people want different things, leading to political and emotional conflict.

We do not have the resources we need. Shortages of time, attention, or money make a difficult situation even more chaotic.

We are not sure who is supposed to do what. Roles are unclear, there is disagreement about who is responsible for what, and things keep shifting as players come and go.

We are not sure how to get what we want. Even if we agree on what we want, we are not sure (or we disagree) about how to make it happen.

We are not sure how to determine if we have succeeded. We are not sure what criteria to use to evaluate success. Or if we do know the criteria, we are not sure how to measure them.

Source: Adapted from McCaskey (1982).

moting capitalism on the economic front while defending communism in the political arena. It was clear that something had to change for China to avert cataclysm, yet the system continued down the same path, acting as if there were no problem. The phenomenon can be summed up this way: "Individually we know we're headed for a cliff, but collectively we don't know how to change course."

At least two major perspectives on organizational learning have emerged. One view, exemplified in the work of Peter Senge (1990) and Barry Oshry (1995), focuses on the mental models that humans use to make sense out of organizational complexity. Both Senge and Oshry argue that learning fails because humans apply simplistic mental models to complicated systems. They are like the blind men and the elephant in the old Sufi parable—each sees a part, but no one sees the whole. Studying only the elephant's trunk or tail gives a poor understanding of the animal. Conversely, "splitting an elephant in half does not produce two small elephants"

(Senge, 1990, p. 66). Senge and Oshry differ noticeably, however, in the kinds of organizational complexity that they emphasize. Oshry emphasizes organizational power dynamics, whereas Senge focuses on structural and environmental forces.

Senge sees a core learning dilemma in organizations: "We learn best from our experience, but we never directly experience the consequences of many of our decisions" (1990, p. 23). Organizations violate one of our basic expectations: that cause and effect will be reasonably close to one another (Cyert and March, 1963; Senge, 1990). When we see a problem, we expect the solution to be close by. If sales are down, for example, we look at the sales force. In complex systems, though, cause may be nowhere near effect, solutions may be far removed from the problem, and feedback may be delayed or misleading. At home, you flip the switch and the light goes on. In organizations, you flip the switch and nothing happens. Or nothing happens until long after you leave the room. Or the switch eventually causes a toilet to flush in a building ten miles away, but you are still in the dark, and so is the surprised user of the toilet. Neither of you realizes that causality is circular, and the flushing toilet starts a new causal chain that eventually comes back to haunt you. You will not understand what is going on—and you won't know what to do about it—until you learn to see the system.

Senge emphasizes the value of "system maps," visual diagrams that clarify how a system works. Consider "Chainsaw Al" Dunlap, CEO of the Scott Paper Company in the early 1990s. Dunlap was proud of his nickname and his turnaround at Scott: profits and market value rose substantially on his watch. He did this by slashing the head count and cutting such frills as research and development. He rarely talked about Scott's steady loss of market share during his tenure (Byrne, 1996). There are many examples in organizations and in life of actions that produce short-term improvements but create much more serious long-term problems. A systems model might look like Figure 2.1.

The strategy might be cutting the training budget to improve short-term profitability, drinking martinis to relieve stress, offering big rebates to get customers to buy now, or borrowing from a loan shark to pay back your gambling debts. In each case, the strategy seems to work in the short term, and the long-term costs become apparent only much farther down the road.

Figure 2.1.   Systems Model with Delay.

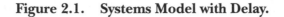

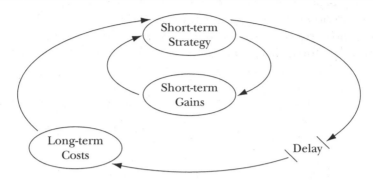

Oshry (1995) makes the same basic point, that people have trouble seeing systems, but emphasizes asymmetric relationships: relationships between tops and bottoms or vendors and customers. When we are at the top of an organization, for example, we lose track of what it is like to be in the middle or at the bottom. We do not see that system dynamics are producing a "dance of blind reflex" (p. 54). In this dance, for example, top managers feel overwhelmed by complexity, responsibility, and overload. They are chronically disappointed in middle management's lack of initiative and creativity. Middle managers, meanwhile, feel torn up by conflicting signals and pressures. Top managers tell them to take risks, then punish them for making mistakes. Their subordinates and bosses tug them in opposite directions, and they feel confused and weak. Workers feel vulnerable, unappreciated, and oppressed: "They give us lousy jobs with lousy pay, they order us around all the time but never tell us what's really going on, and then they wonder why we don't love our work." If you do not see the dance, says Oshry, you continue to play your part blindly, unaware of any other option.

Oshry and Senge both make a similar point: when we do not understand system dynamics, we get trapped into cycles of blaming and self-defense: the enemy is always out there, and problems are always caused by someone else. This same theme appears in another perspective on organizational learning, exemplified in the work of Chris Argyris and Donald Schön (1978, 1996). Argyris and Schön focus less on system dynamics and more on individual and group defenses. Senge's learning paradox is that we don't learn from experience because we don't see the consequences of our actions. Argyris and Schön describe a different paradox: "The actions we take to promote productive organizational learning actually inhibit deeper learning" (1996, p. 281). Our actions are counterproductive because we try to solve problems without discussing the undiscussable or running afoul of organizational taboos. Like Helen Demarco, we look for solutions that won't make us vulnerable. We ignore "sensitive" issues, no matter how important, and cover up the fact that we are ignoring them. Such strategies often seem to work in the short run but eventually create a double bind: to get a better solution, we have to face the issues we have ducked, but that will reveal the cover-up. Facing that double bind, Demarco and her colleagues chose to pile camouflage on top of camouflage. The consequence, say Argyris and Schön, is escalating games of deception that make it more and more difficult for organizations to recognize and correct their most significant errors and difficulties.

Coping with Ambiguity and Complexity

All of the work on organizational learning converges around the basic idea that our ability to make sense out of a complicated and ambiguous world depends very much on the frames, or mental models, that we bring to the task. When an event is clear and unambiguous, it is not hard for people to agree on what is happening. Determining if a train is on schedule, if a plane landed safely, or if a clock is keeping accurate time is easy enough. But most of the important issues confronting managers are not so clearcut. Harold Geneen, former chief executive of the American conglomerate International Telephone and Telegraph (ITT), used to hound his subordinates for the "unshakable facts" (Deal and Kennedy, 1982). But solid facts are hard to find. Will a reorganization work? Was a meeting successful? Why did a decision made by consensus not work? When issues are complex and evidence is incomplete, individuals make judgments or interpretations. Their judgments depend on their expectations, beliefs, and values. What we assume to be facts are often social interpretations, largely based on what we expect and want our world to be like.

The powerful influence of social interpretation was revealed in a classic experiment on perception. Subjects were asked to identify playing cards projected rapidly on a screen. The color of some cards was reversed, so people were seeing a red nine of clubs or a black jack of hearts. They usually reinterpreted reversed cards to make them "right"—the red club became either a black club or a red heart. When people were given more time, many became uncomfortable. They knew that something was wrong but had trouble pinpointing what it was. Some could not determine what was amiss no matter how much time they were given. The experiment provides dramatic evidence of just how much people's perspectives determine what they see. One's internal world is as important as what is outside—sometimes more so. Given the fuzzy realities of everyday life, it is hardly surprising that people try to make the world conform to their internal maps.

Managers regularly face an unending series of puzzles or "messes." In order to act without creating more problems, they must first establish what is happening. Then they must proceed to a deeper level: asking, "What is *really* going on here?" This important step in reading a situation is often overlooked. Managers form superficial analyses and leap on the solution nearest at hand or most in vogue. Market share declining? Try strategic planning. Customer complaints? Put in a quality program. Profits down? Time to reengineer or downsize.

A better alternative is to probe more deeply to pinpoint what is *really* going on. Sometimes more careful assessment shows that we have a problem. Often we find that we are caught on the horns of a dilemma. The first possibility stimulates the search for a satisfactory solution. The second requires a choice based on values and ethics— or enough patience to wait until things change on their own.

Suppose that you consult a physician with symptoms of a fever and a runny nose. You would probably not be happy to hear your doctor say, "Let me call around and see what others are doing." Physicians are trained to find recognizable patterns in presenting symptoms. A bacterial infection is treatable with antibiotics, but the normal prescription for a virus—which means roughly that the doctor does not know much more than you do—is "Rest, drink plenty of liquids, and call me in a week if things don't clear up." It is just as crucial for managers to make the right diagnosis. Flight 007 vividly demonstrates the costs of acting without knowing what is really going on.

The ideas, or theories, we carry with us determine whether a given situation is confusing or clear, meaningful or cryptic, a paralyzing disaster or a learning experience. Theories are essential because of a simple but very basic fact about human perception: there is simply too much happening in any situation for us to attend to everything. To help us understand what is going on and to take action, our theories do two things: (1) they tell us what is important and what can be safely ignored, and (2) they group many different bits of information into patterns or concepts.

To a nonpilot, the cockpit of a jet airliner is a confusing array of controls, switches, and gauges. Yet an experienced pilot knows in a glance a great deal about the aircraft's status. Pilots learn a set of patterns that group a lot of information into a few manageable chunks. It takes many hours to learn the concepts, but once learned, they can be used with ease, speed, and, usually, accuracy. In the same way, experienced managers often size up a situation very rapidly, decide what needs to be done, and move on. Their intuition and skill are based on extensive prior learning of effective patterns of thought and action.

It takes time and effort to learn these patterns. Helen Demarco's experience provided her with a set of theories for making sense of Paul Osborne's behavior and for deciding how to respond. Because she read the situation through only one frame, she could see no other options. Giving up a theory sacrifices our investment in learning it. Our theories shield us from confusion, uncertainty, and anxiety. We get anxious and stuck when we have tried every lens we know, and nothing works. We are caught in a dilemma: holding on to old patterns is ineffective, but developing new ones is expensive. Changing old frames takes time and effort. It is also risky—it might lead to further erosion of our confidence and effectiveness.

This dilemma exists even if we are not aware of flaws in our current theory. The card experiment shows how a theory can block recognition of its own errors. An extensive body of research documents the many ways that individuals interpret reality to protect their existing belief systems (see, for example, Garland, 1990; Kühberger, 1995; and Staw and Hoang, 1995). Heath and Gonzalez

(1995) found that decision makers use interaction with others not so much to gain new information as to strengthen the justification for their current thinking. Their research suggests that interaction makes people more confident without producing any improvement in the quality of their decisions.

Most of us recognize that mental maps influence how we interpret the world around us. Less widely understood is the Pygmalion effect—what we expect is what we get. Rosenthal and Jacobson (1968) studied schoolteachers who were told that certain students in their classes were "spurters"—students who were "about to bloom." The so-called spurters had been chosen at random but still made above-average gains on achievement tests during the school year. They really *did* spurt. Somehow the teachers' expectations were communicated to and assimilated by the students.

Extensive research on the "framing effect" (Kahneman and Tversky, 1979) shows how powerful subtle cues can be. Relatively modest changes in how a problem or decision is framed can have a dramatic impact on how people respond (Shu Li and Adams, 1995; Gegerenzer, Hoffrage, and Kleinbölting, 1991). Decision makers, for example, tend to respond more favorably to an option that has a "70 percent chance of success" than one that has a "30 percent chance of failure," even though they are statistically identical. Similar Pygmalion effects have been replicated in countless reorganizations, new product launches, and new approaches to performance appraisal.

Common Fallacies in Organizational Diagnosis

We have asked a number of students and managers to develop diagnoses of cases like KAL Flight 007 and Helen Demarco. Most of them use one of three limited perspectives.

Most common is the *people-blaming approach*. This view explains everything in terms of individual characteristics. Problems are caused by bad attitudes, abrasive personalities, neurotic tendencies, or incompetence. People with this view may label Paul Osborne authoritarian and Helen Demarco "gutless" for not standing up to her boss. They blame the Flight 007 disaster on the flight engineer's incompetence or the callousness of the Russian military. As children, we all learned that it was important to assign blame for every broken toy, stained carpet, or wounded sibling. Pinpointing who is at fault is comforting. In one stroke it resolves ambiguity, explains mystery, and makes clear what must be done next: punish the guilty.

When it is hard to single out a guilty person, a popular alternative is to *blame the bureaucracy*. Whatever went wrong happened because the organization was too bureaucratic—or too disorganized. If it's disorganized, it should develop a rational, clearcut set of procedures and role expectations. The problem between Helen Demarco and Paul Osborne could have been averted if roles were clear and everyone behaved rationally. Tragedies such as Flight 007 can be prevented if we verify cockpit procedures and make sure pilots fly "by the book." The problem is that all those rules and regulations are what we dislike about bureaucracy. They inhibit freedom and flexibility. They stifle initiative and generate oceans of red tape. Then the solution is to "free up" the system so that red tape and rigid rules do not stifle creativity and bog things down. But many organizations vacillate ceaselessly between being too loose and too tight.

The third fallacy attributes problems to a *thirst for power*. From this viewpoint, Paul Osborne and Helen Demarco were both playing games. The winner is whoever is the most adroit—or the most treacherous. Organizations are jungles full of predators and prey. Problems arise from political game playing and petty bickering. The only solution is to play the game better than your opponents.

Each of these three approaches is based on a partial truth. Blaming people points to the perennial importance of individual differences. Some problems *are* caused by personal characteristics: rigid bosses, slothful subordinates, bumbling bureaucrats, greedy union members, insensitive elites. Much of the time, though, faulting people gives us simplistic answers that block us from seeing systems and offer little help, even if they are partly right. If, for example, the problem is someone's personality, what do we do? Even psychiatrists find it difficult to alter personality, and firing everyone with a less than ideal persona is rarely a viable solution.

The overly rational, blame-the-bureaucracy perspective starts from a reasonable assumption: organizations are created to achieve certain goals. They are most effective when the goals and policies are clear (but not excessive), jobs are well defined (but not *too* well), control systems are in place (but not oppressive), and employees behave reasonably and prudently. Disagreements between Helen Demarco and Paul Osborne should be resolved through discussion and careful consideration of the facts. If people always behaved that way, organizations would presumably work a lot better than most of them do.

The problem with the rational perspective is it is very good at explaining how organizations should work but very poor at explaining why they often do not. Managers who cling to the rational perspective get discouraged and frustrated when confronted by intractable and irrational forces. Year after year, we witness the introduction of new control systems, we hear of new studies and new ways to reorganize, we are dazzled by new management consultants and the latest management methods. Yet the same problems persist, seemingly immune to every rational cure we devise.

The thirst-for-power view also points to some enduring features of organizations. Helen Demarco and Paul Osborne actually do have different self-interests and sources of power. Demarco is a career employee with a stake in protecting her status. She can afford to take a long-term view. An unrealistic crash program that fails could hurt her career. Osborne's situation is different. He came with a mandate for change—the sooner the better. A ten-year program will not enhance his reputation as a leader who gets results. He needs a dramatic and visible initiative that promises big improvements quickly.

The dog-eat-dog perspective provides a plausible analysis of why the situation turned out the way it did. Demarco and her colleagues played their cards adeptly and, apparently, achieved a significant victory. But neither Demarco nor Osborne wants political games to dominate decision making. In that sense, both lost. The thirst-for-power view offers no hope of preventing such tragedies.

Each of these commonly used perspectives points to important phenomena but is incomplete and oversimplified. All lead to a false sense of clarity and optimism. Surprises, complexities, and ambiguities of organizational life require more powerful and more comprehensive approaches. Determining what is really going on requires more sophisticated lenses than many managers currently possess. It also requires the flexibility to look at organizations from more than one angle.

In Western cultures, particularly, there is a tendency to embrace one theory or ideology and to try to make the world conform. If it works, we persist in our view. If discrepancies arise, we try to rationalize them away. If people challenge our view, we ignore them or put them in their place. Only poor results over a long period of time call our theories into question. Even then we might simply entrench ourselves in a new worldview, triggering the cycle again.

In Japan, there are four major religions, each with its own beliefs and assumptions: Buddhism, Confucianism, Shintoism, and Taoism. Though the religions are very different in their history, traditions, and basic tenets, many Japanese feel no need to choose only one. They use them all, taking advantage of the strengths of each for suitable purposes or occasions. The four organizational frames can play a similar role for managers in modern organizations. Rather than portraying the field of organizational theory as fragmented, we present it as pluralistic. Seen this way, the field provides a varied assortment of lenses for viewing organizations. Each theoretical tradition is helpful. Each has blind spots. The ability to shift from one conceptual lens to another helps redefine situations so that they become manageable. The ability to reframe situations is one of the most powerful capacities of great artists. It can be equally powerful for managers.

Summary

Because organizations are complex, surprising, deceptive, and ambiguous, they are formidably difficult to understand and manage. Our theories and images determine what we see, what we do, and what we accomplish. Perspectives too simple or too narrow become fallacies that cloud rather than illuminate managerial action. The world of most managers and administrators is a world of messes: complexity, ambiguity, value dilemmas, political pressures, and multiple constituencies. For managers whose images blind them to this messy reality, it is a world of frustration and failure. For those with better theories and the capacity to use their theories with skill and grace, it is a world of excitement and possibility. In succeeding chapters, we will examine four perspectives, or frames, that have helped managers and leaders find clarity and meaning amid the confusion of organizational life. We cannot guarantee your success as a manager or a change agent. We believe, though, that you can improve the odds in your favor with an artful appreciation of each of the four frames and how they can be used to understand and influence what's really going on.

Part Two

The Structural Frame

| Getting Organized

Many of us remember the black-and-white classic *Modern Times*. The film features Charlie Chaplin as a production worker who tightens bolts on the stream of widgets passing by him on the assembly line. From a remote corner office, the big boss determines the pace of work and transmits orders to a manager, who controls the line's speed. A foreman hovers over Charlie and his colleagues, cajoling and keeping them on task. A camera in the rest room pressures workers not to waste time.

Specialized tasks, sequential work, close supervision, and top-down directives cluster in a widely accepted image of organizational structure. But this familiar stereotype does not prepare us for the emerging modern factory: still structured, but in a dramatically different way. Case in point: within a few years of start-up, Saturn Corporation was building some of the best cars in the world. The speed of the assembly line was shaped by a shared concern for quality. Any worker could stop the line if a problem arose. Much of the work was done in self-managed teams. Collective decisions determined working conditions. All workers were cross-trained in a variety of specialized skills. Strategic decisions were made with the union president at the table. His office was in the suite next to Saturn's chief executive. Saturn is one of many examples of radically different structural forms emerging in the late twentieth century.

Origins of the Structural Perspective

The structural view has two main intellectual sources. The first is the work of industrial analysts who wanted to design organizations for maximum efficiency. The most prominent of these researchers,

Frederick W. Taylor (1911), was the father of time-and-motion studies and an approach he labeled "scientific management." Taylor broke tasks into minute parts and retrained workers to get the largest payoff from each motion and each second spent at work. Another group of theorists who contributed to the scientific management approach included Henri Fayol ([1919] 1949), Lyndall Urwick (1937), and Luther Gulick (Gulick and Urwick, 1937). Their work led to principles focused on specialization, span of control, authority, and delegation of responsibility.

The second branch of structural ideas is rooted in the work of the German economist and sociologist Max Weber. Weber wrote around the turn of the twentieth century, when formal organization was a relatively new phenomenon. Patriarchy, rather than rationality, was still the customary organizing principle. Patriarchal organizations had a father figure, a single individual with almost unlimited power, who could reward, punish, promote, or fire on personal whim. Seeing the evolution of new models of organization in late-nineteenth-century Europe, Weber sought to conceptualize "monocratic bureaucracy" as an ideal form that maximized norms of rationality. His model outlined several major features of bureaucracy: (1) a fixed division of labor, (2) a hierarchy of offices, (3) a set of rules governing performance, (4) separation of personal from official property and rights, (5) technical qualifications for selecting personnel (not family ties or friendship), and (6) employment as primary occupation and long-term career.

After World War II, Weber's work was rediscovered by organization theorists and spawned a substantial body of theory and research. Blau and Scott (1962), Perrow (1986), and Hall (1963), among others, contributed significantly to the extension of the bureaucratic model. Their work examined the relationships among the elements of structure, looked closely at why organizations choose one structure rather than another, and analyzed the impact of structure on morale, productivity, and effectiveness.

Structural Forms and Functions

Structure is a blueprint for the pattern of expectations and exchanges among internal players (executives, managers, employees) and external constituencies (such as customers and clients). Like an animal's skeleton or a building's framework, structural form both enhances and constrains what organizations can accomplish. The alternative design possibilities are infinite, limited only by human preferences and capacities. We often assume that people prefer structures with more choices and latitude (Leavitt, 1978), but this is not always the case. A study by Moeller (1968), for example, explored the effects of structure on morale in two school systems. One was structured loosely and encouraged wide participation in decision making. The other was tightly controlled with a centralized hierarchy and a clear chain of command. Moeller found the opposite of what he expected: faculty morale was higher in the district with tighter structure. Adler and Borys (1996), citing research showing both positive and negative effects of structure, argue that the type of structure is as important as the amount. There are good rules and bad ones. Formal structure has a positive impact on morale when it helps us get our work done. It has a negative impact when it gets in our way or simply makes it easier for management to control us. Stereotypical images of machine bureaucracy confuse "two very different kinds of machine—machines designed to de-skill work and those designed to leverage users' skills" (p. 69).

The structural perspective is not inherently as machinelike or inflexible as many often believe. Structures in stable environments will often be hierarchical and rules-oriented. But recent years have witnessed remarkable inventiveness in designing structures to emphasize flexibility, participation, and quality. Dramatic changes in technology and the business environment have rendered old structures obsolete at an unprecedented rate, spawning a resurgence of interest in organizational design. Pressures of globalization, competition, technology, customer expectations, and workforce dynamics are causing organizations worldwide to rethink and redesign structural patterns. A swarm of items compete for managers' attention: money, markets, people, and technological competencies, to name a few. But a significant amount of time and attention must be devoted to social architecture. "How a firm organizes its efforts can be a source of tremendous competitive advantage, particularly in times where premiums are placed on flexibility, adaptation, and the management of change" (Nadler, Gerstein, and Shaw, 1992, p. 3).

The assumptions of the structural frame reflect a belief in rationality and a faith that the right formal arrangements minimize problems and increase quality and performance. Where the human resource perspective emphasizes the importance of changing people (through training, rotation, promotion, or dismissal), the structural perspective focuses on designing a pattern of roles and relationships that will accomplish collective goals as well as accommodate individual differences.

Six assumptions undergird the structural frame:

1. Organizations exist to achieve established goals and objectives.
2. Organizations work best when rationality prevails over personal preferences and external pressures.
3. Structures must be designed to fit an organization's circumstances (including its goals, technology, and environment).
4. Organizations increase efficiency and enhance performance through specialization and division of labor.
5. Appropriate forms of coordination and control are essential to ensuring that individuals and units work together in the service of organizational goals.
6. Problems and performance gaps arise from structural deficiencies and can be remedied through restructuring.

Basic Structural Tensions

Two design issues lie at the heart of social architecture: how to allocate work and how to coordinate different roles and units after responsibilities have been parceled out. Division of labor—or differentiation—is the cornerstone. Every living system finds a way to create specialized roles. Consider an ant colony: "Small workers . . . spend most of their time in the nest feeding the larval broods; intermediate-sized workers constitute most of the population, going out on raids as well as doing other jobs. The largest workers. . . have a huge head and large powerful jaws. These individuals are . . . soldiers; they carry no food but constantly run along the flanks of the raiding and emigration columns" (Topoff, 1972, p. 72).

Like ants, humans long ago discovered the virtues of specialization. A job (or position) constrains behavior by prescribing what an individual is to do—or not do—to accomplish a task. Prescriptions take the form of job descriptions, procedures, or rules (Mintzberg, 1979). Formal constraints can be burdensome, leading to apathy, absenteeism, and resistance (Argyris, 1957, 1964), but they help ensure predictability, uniformity, and reliability. If manufacturing standards, airline maintenance, hotel housekeeping, or prison sentences were left solely to individual discretion, problems of quality and equity would abound.

Once an organization specifies positions or roles, managers face the second set of key decisions: how to group them into working units. There are several basic options (Mintzberg, 1979):

1. Functional groups based on *knowledge or skill*, as in the case of a university's academic departments or in the classic industrial arrangement: research, engineering, manufacturing, marketing, and finance.
2. Units created on the basis of *time*, as by shift: day shift, swing shift, graveyard shift.
3. Groups organized by *product:* detergent versus bar soap, widebody versus narrow-body aircraft.
4. Groups established around *customers or clients*, as in hospital wards created around patient type (pediatrics, intensive care, or maternity) or computer sales departments organized by customer (corporate, government, education, individual).
5. Groupings around *place or geography*, such as regional offices for corporations or government agencies.
6. Grouping by *process:* a complete flow of work, like "the order fulfillment process. This process flows from initiation by a customer order, through the functions, to delivery to the customer" (Galbraith, 1993, p. 34). Organization by process attained new prominence from the 1990's reengineering movement (Hammer and Champy, 1993).

Creating different roles and units provides the benefits of specialization but inevitably creates problems of coordination and control. Each operation tends to focus on its own priorities and go its own way. The result is *suboptimization*, an emphasis on achieving unit goals rather than the overall mission. As a result, integrated efforts become fragmented, and performance suffers. Successful organizations employ a variety of methods to coordinate individual and group efforts and to link them with desired goals. Coordination and control are achieved in two primary ways: *vertically,* through top-down devices, and *laterally*, through meetings, committees, coordinating roles, or network structures.

Vertical Coordination

Higher levels coordinate and control the work of subordinates at lower levels through devices like authority, rules and policies, and planning and control systems.

Authority

The most basic and most ubiquitous method of linking efforts of individuals, units, or divisions is "the boss"—someone in a position of formal authority. Authorities—executives, managers, and supervisors—are formally charged with keeping activities aligned with goals. They control activity by making decisions, resolving conflicts, solving problems, evaluating performances and output, and distributing rewards and sanctions. A chain of command is a hierarchy of managerial and supervisory strata, each with legitimate power to shape and direct the behavior of those in lower levels. It works best when authority is both endorsed by subordinates and authorized by superiors (Dornbusch and Scott, 1975).

Rules and Policies

Rules, policies, and standard operating procedures limit discretion and help ensure predictability and uniformity. Rules govern conditions of work and specify standard processes for carrying out tasks, handling personnel issues, and relating to the external environment. One purpose is to minimize "particularism" (Perrow, 1986)—the intrusion of personal or political forces unrelated to organizational goals—and to ensure that similar situations will be handled uniformly. A citizen's complaint about a tax bill is supposed to be handled the same way, whether the issue is brought forward by a prominent politician or by a shoe clerk. Once a situation is defined as one where a rule applies, the course of action is clear, straightforward, and almost automatic.

Commercial airline pilots typically fly in different crews every month. Because interdependence is high and mistakes are critical, standard operating procedures govern all significant aspects of their work. All pilots are extensively trained in the procedures. So long as they follow the rules, actions of crew members mesh. If not, disaster may follow. A significant percentage of aviation accidents occur after someone violated standard operating procedures. More than one airplane has crashed on takeoff simply because the crew neglected a required checklist item.

Planning and Control Systems

Reliance on planning and control systems has mushroomed since the dawn of the computer era. Retailers, for example, need to know what's selling and what isn't. It used to take months to find out; point-of-sale terminals now provide information instantly. Information about performance against plan and budget flows freely up and down the hierarchy, greatly enhancing management's ability to control performance and outcomes.

Mintzberg (1979) distinguishes two major approaches to control and planning. *Performance control* imposes outcome objectives (for example, "increase sales by 10 percent this year") without specifying how the results are to be achieved. Performance control both measures and motivates and works best when things are reasonably clear. It is less successful when goals are ambiguous, hard to measure, or of dubious relevance. A notorious example was the use of "body counts" by the U.S. Army as a measure of combat effectiveness in Vietnam. Field commanders became obsessed with "getting the numbers up," regardless of whether the numbers of enemies killed were accurate or reflected any real military progress.

Action planning specifies decisions and actions to be carried out in a particular way within a specified time frame: "increase this month's sales by conforming to a companywide sales pitch" (Mintzberg, 1979, pp. 153–154). Action planning is most useful when it is easier to assess *how* a job is done than to measure whether the objectives were actually achieved. This is often true of service jobs. The McDonald's Corporation has very clear specifications for how counter employees are to greet customers (for example, with a smile and a cheerful welcome). The intended outcome is customer satisfaction, but it is easier to monitor the employees' behavior than the customers' reactions.

Lateral Coordination

Though efficient, vertical coordination is not always effective. People's behavior is often remarkably untouched by commands, rules, or systems. Lateral techniques—formal and informal meetings, task forces, coordinating roles, matrix structures, and network organizations—emerge to fill the void. Lateral forms of coordination are typically less formalized and more flexible than authority-bound systems and rules. They are often simpler and quicker as well.

Meetings

Informal communication and formal meetings are cornerstones of lateral coordination. All organizations have regular meetings. Boards confer to make policy. Executive committees gather to make strategic decisions. In some government agencies, review committees (referred to as "murder boards") convene to examine proposals from lower-level officials. Formal meetings provide much of the lateral coordination in relatively simple, stable organizations—for example, a railroad with a predictable market or a manufacturer with a stable product.

Task Forces

As organizations become more complex, technologies grow in sophistication, and environments become more turbulent, the demand for lateral communication mushrooms. Additional coordination devices are needed. Task forces assemble when new problems or opportunities require collaboration of a number of different specialties or functions. High-technology firms rely heavily on project teams to coordinate development of new products or services.

Coordinating Roles

To augment the efforts of formal groups, coordinating roles or units arise, using persuasion and negotiation to help others integrate their work. A product manager in a consumer goods company, responsible for the overall performance of a laundry detergent or a low-fat snack, spends much of her time interacting with different people and units critical to the product's success: research, manufacturing, marketing, sales. For example, Cooper Industries grew dramatically in the 1980s and 1990s by aggressively cultivating crosscutting manufacturing expertise. It created a coordinating unit, a SWAT team of manufacturing experts, to spread production know-how across Cooper's various business units (Farkas and De Backer, 1996, pp. 100–101).

Matrix Structures

Beginning in the 1960s, many organizations in complex environments developed matrix structures that spelled out crosscutting coordination responsibilities. By the mid-1990s, Asea Brown Boveri (ABB), the electrical engineering giant, had grown to encompass some 1,300 separate companies and more than two hundred thousand employees around the globe. ABB maintained a very small corporate headquarters (less than two hundred people) in Zürich, Switzerland, where CEO Percy Barnevik rarely spent more than a day or two a week (often Saturday and Sunday). The energetic Barnevik spent much of his time in an airborne office traveling around ABB's far-flung empire ("The ABB of Management," 1996). To hold this complex collection of businesses together, ABB had a matrix structure that crisscrossed approximately one hundred countries with about sixty-five business sectors (Rappaport, 1992). Each of the subsidiary companies reported to both a country manager (Sweden, Germany, and so on) and a sector manager (power transformers, transportation, and the like). The design carried the inevitable risk of tension and conflict between sector and country managers. ABB tried to create structural glue at the top with a small executive coordinating committee (thirteen individuals from eight countries), an elite cadre of some five hundred global managers, and a policy of doing business in English, even though it was a second language for the majority of ABB's employees. Variations on ABB's structure—a matrix with business or product lines on one side and country or region on the other—are common in global corporations.

Networks

Beginning in the 1980s, the proliferation of microcomputers spawned explosive growth of computer networks—everything from small local networks to the Internet. These powerful new lateral communication devices often supplanted vertical coordination strategies and spurred the development of network structures both within and between organizations (Steward, 1994). Powell, Koput, and Smith-Doerr (1996) describe the mushrooming of "interorganizational networks" in rapidly developing fields like biotechnology, where knowledge is complex and widely dispersed and no single organization can go it alone. They give an example of work on Alzheimer's disease that was developed by thirty-four scientists from three corporations, a university, a government laboratory, and a private research institute.

Ghoshal and Bartlett (1990) argue that many large global corporations have evolved into interorganizational networks. In such firms, horizontal linkages among many units around the globe supplement and sometimes supplant vertical coordination. Such firms are multicentric: initiatives and strategy emerge from many places and take shape through a variety of partnerships and joint ventures.

Every lateral coordination strategy has strengths and weaknesses. Formal and informal meetings provide opportunities for dialogue and decisions but may absorb excessive amounts of time and energy. Task forces provide a vehicle for creativity and integration around specific problems but may divert attention from ongoing operating issues. The effectiveness of coordinators who span boundaries of different organizational units is heavily dependent on their skills and credibility. Matrix structures provide a continuing source of lateral linkage and integration but are notorious for creating conflict and confusion. Digital Equipment CEO Robert Palmer blamed the company's matrix for delaying by several years the company's badly needed shift from minicomputers to PCs—competitors moved ahead while Digital debated (Dwyer, Engardio, Schiller, and Reed, 1994). The self-organizing network's bias toward decentralization, teaming, cross-functional, and cross-geographical work makes it well attuned to conditions of complexity and change (Steward, 1994). But networks are inherently difficult for any one person or group to control, and evolution produces vipers as well as orchids—there is no guarantee that we will like all the outcomes these systems produce.

The optimal blend of vertical and lateral strategies depends on the unique coordination challenges in any given situation. Vertical coordination is generally superior when environments are stable, tasks are predictable and well understood, and uniformity is crucial. Lateral communications work best for complex tasks performed in turbulent, fast-changing environments. Every organization must either find a design that works or reorganize—or ultimately it will fail. Consider the contrasting structures of two highly successful organizations: McDonald's and Harvard University.

McDonald's and Harvard: A Structural Odd Couple

McDonald's first Indian restaurant, and its first in the world with no beef on the menu, opened Sunday in New Delhi with a traditional Hindu ceremony and a rush of enthusiastic customers. O. P. Sahani, a seventy-five-year-old retired civil servant, came all the way from Vrindavan, ninety miles south, to show his support for McDonald's efforts to do business with India. "They have not brought raw materials from overseas," Sahani said, proudly wearing a red-and-yellow McDonald's cap.

Other customers didn't seem all that interested in the fact that the mutton for Maharaja Macs came from Indian sheep, the potatoes for the fries from Indian farms, and the Coke from an Indian bottler. The menu also featured rice-based Vegetable Burgers patties—flavored with peas, carrots, red pepper, beans, coriander, and other spices. Sahani, a vegetarian who was the first customer, praised the Vegetable Burgers but had one word of advice for the owners: "It was nice, but you require some improvement in the chips," he said, describing the fries as "too soft" [Associated Press, 1996].

McDonald's, the company that made the Big Mac a household word, has been enormously successful. It dominates the fast-food business. McDonald's has a relatively small staff at its world headquarters outside Chicago. The vast majority of its employees are spread across the world in thousands of local outlets. Despite its size and geographic reach, McDonald's is a highly centralized, tightly controlled organization, and most major decisions are made at the top.

The managers and employees of McDonald's restaurants have limited discretion about how to do their jobs. Much of their work is controlled by technology—machines time french fries and measure soft drinks. Cooks are not expected to develop creative new versions of Big Macs or Quarter Pounders (although the Egg McMuffin and other innovations were created by local franchises). The parent company has powerful systems to ensure that food and service conform to standard specifications. A Big Mac tastes virtually the same whether it is purchased in New York or Los Angeles, Hong Kong or Moscow. Guaranteed standard quality inevitably limits the discretion of people who own and work in individual outlets. Creative departures from standard product lines are neither encouraged nor tolerated except when a new item is being tested for adoption across the local outlets.

Historically, McDonald's made little effort to offer special products in different markets. The McDonald's on the Champs Élysées in Paris makes little effort to conform to French culinary style. But the new mutton burgers and vegetable nuggets in New Delhi indicate that globalization is forcing even McDonald's to broaden its standard menu.

Harvard University is also highly successful. Like McDonald's, it has a very small administrative group at the top, but in most other respects the two organizations are structured very differently. Even though Harvard is much more geographically concentrated than McDonald's, it is significantly more decentralized. Virtually all of Harvard's activities occur within a few square miles of Boston and Cambridge, Massachusetts. Most employees are housed in the university's several schools: Harvard College (the undergraduate school), the graduate Faculty of Arts and Sciences, and various professional schools. Each school has its own dean and its own endowment and, in accordance with Harvard's philosophy of "every tub on its own bottom," largely controls its own destiny.

Harvard is one of few universities in which different faculties choose to operate on different academic calendars. The fall semester in the law and business schools usually begins a week or two earlier than in the schools of government or education. Each school has a large measure of fiscal autonomy and responsibility for its own budget. Individual professors also have enormous autonomy and discretion. In many schools, they have almost unlimited control over what courses they teach, what research they do, and what, if any, university activities they pursue. Faculty meetings are often sparsely attended. When a dean or a department head wants a fac-

Table 3.1.   Structural Imperatives.

Dimension	Structural Implications
Size and age	Complexity and formalization increase with size and age.
Core process	Core processes or technologies must align with structure.
Environment	Stable environments reward simpler structure; uncertain, turbulent environments require more complex, adaptable structure.
Strategy and goals	Variations in clarity and consistency of goals require appropriate structural adaptations.
Information technology	Information technology permits flatter, more flexible, and more decentralized structure.
Nature of the workforce	More educated and professional workers need and want greater autonomy and discretion.

ulty member to chair a committee or offer a new course, the request is more often a humble entreaty than an authoritative command.

The contrast between McDonald's and Harvard is particularly strong at the level of service delivery. No one expects individual personalities to influence the quality of McDonald's hamburgers. But everyone expects each course at Harvard to be the unique creation of an individual professor. Two different schools might offer courses with the same title, covering entirely different content with widely divergent teaching styles.

Structural Imperatives

Why do McDonald's and Harvard have such radically different structures? Is one more effective than the other? Or has each organization evolved a structural design that fits its circumstances? Every organization needs to respond to a generic set of structural parameters (outlined in Table 3.1). An organization's size, age, core process, environment, strategy and goals, information technology, and workforce characteristics combine to dictate social architecture. Each must be taken into account in designing a workable structure.

Size and Age

An organization's size and age affect the shape and character of its structure. Unless growth (or downsizing) is matched with corresponding adjustments in roles and relationships, problems inevitably arise. Small, entrepreneurial organizations typically have very simple, informal structural arrangements. Over time, particularly if the organization gets larger, pressures for efficiency and discipline push toward greater formalization and complexity (Greiner, 1972; Quinn and Cameron, 1983). If carried too far, this process ultimately leads to the suffocating bureaucratic rigidity often seen in large, mature organizations.

In the beginning, McDonald's was not the complex, standardized, tightly controlled company that it is today. It began as a single hamburger stand in San Bernardino, California, owned and managed by the McDonald brothers, who virtually invented the concept of "fast food." It was phenomenally successful. The brothers tried to expand by selling franchise rights to others, with little success. They were making more money than they needed, disliked travel, and had no other family. If they had more money, said one brother, "we'd be leaving it to a church or something, and we didn't go to church" (Love, 1986, p. 23).

The concept took off when Ray Kroc came into the picture. Kroc had achieved only modest business success selling milk shake machines to restaurants. When he began to get calls from people who wanted to buy whatever milk shake mixer the McDonalds were using, he decided to pay a call on the McDonald brothers. As soon as he saw their original stand, Kroc realized the possibility of building a great business: "Unlike the homebound McDonalds, Kroc had traveled extensively, and he could envision hundreds of large and small markets where a McDonald's could be located. He understood the existing food services businesses, and understood how a McDonald's unit could be a formidable competitor" (Love, 1986, pp. 39–40). Kroc persuaded the McDonald brothers to let him take over the franchising effort. The rest is history.

Core Process

Structure has to be built around an organization's core process for transforming raw materials into finished products. Every organization has a central process, or core technology, with at least three elements: raw materials, activities that transform raw materials into desired ends, and underlying beliefs about the cause-and-effect relations that link materials, activity, and outcome (Dornbusch and Scott, 1975).

Technologies vary in clarity, predictability, and effectiveness. Assembling a Big Mac is a relatively routine and programmed activity. The task is clear, most of the potential problems are known in advance, and the probability of a successful outcome is high. McDonald's relatively simple technology allows it to function successfully with mostly vertical coordination.

In contrast, Harvard's two core processes—research and teaching—are much more complex and unpredictable. Teaching objectives are usually complicated and amorphous. Unlike hamburger buns, students are active agents. Their needs and skills vary widely; their moods fluctuate in response to the weather, the time of day, and the season of the year. Their preoccupation with extracurricular activities is a fact of life. Which teaching strategies will yield desired outcomes is more a matter of faith than one of fact. Even if students could be molded in predictable ways, it would be hard to know which molds are best, since mystery surrounds what knowledge and skills they will need in future. Feedback is slow or absent: professors rarely learn much about what, if any, benefits students derived from their course in later years. This complex technology is a key source of Harvard's highly decentralized, loosely coordinated structure.

Because structure must align with an organization's core process, significant technical change implies structural change (Barley, 1990), but existing structures often hinder adaptation. In recent decades, differential ability to integrate new technologies has become fateful for firms' effectiveness and survival (Henderson and Clark, 1990). This means that new entrants often have an advantage over established firms in exploiting new technologies. Existing firms are tempted to force-fit new technology into the current structure. When high-strength, low-alloy steel was introduced into the manufacture of automobiles in the 1970s, for example, one firm's engineers were slow to realize that traditional methods would not work with new materials (Henderson and Clark, 1990). The firm fell behind other firms less hindered by structural inertia.

Environment

Although organizations employ strategies to buffer internal activities from external fluctuations and interference, the environment is still a potent force. It provides raw materials and receives products and services. Stable, mature businesses—such as railroads or postal departments—deal with relatively homogeneous, stable, and predictable environmental influences. As a result, they can successfully use simpler organizational forms. Organizations with rapidly changing technologies or markets—such as high-technology electronics firms—cope with much higher degrees of uncertainty. New state-of-the-art products may be obsolete in six months or less.

Uncertainty and turbulence press organizations to develop more sophisticated architectural forms. New specialties and roles are required to deal with emerging problems. More specialized and diversified structures require more elaborate, flexible approaches to vertical and lateral coordination. Uncertain environments demand high levels of flexibility and adaptability. Many traditional managers, steeped in the tradition of the pyramid, struggle to adapt to strange new forms. In these, structural design is more emergent than prescribed, chains of command are flat rather than multilayered, and coordination arises mainly from a dense network of horizontal relationships rather than from top-down decisions (Chaize, 1992; Sérieyx, 1993).

All organizations are dependent on their environment, but some are more dependent than others. Public schools, for example, have low power with respect to external constituencies and struggle to get resources they need. Small size, powerful competitors, well-organized external constituencies, limited flexibility, and scarcity of resources tend to increase dependence. An organization such as Harvard University is insulated from its environment by its size, elite status, and large endowment. Harvard can afford to offer low teaching loads, generous salaries, and substantial autonomy to its faculty. A small college with serious financial pressures is likely to have tighter controls, higher workloads, and limited discretion in using its funds.

Strategy and Goals

Strategic decisions are oriented to the future and are concerned with long-term direction (Chandler, 1962). Most organizations, particularly in the business world, devote considerable effort to developing strategy: "the determination of long-range goals and objectives of an enterprise, and the adoption of courses of action and allocation of resources necessary for carrying out these goals" (p. 13).

Goals of varying specificity are embedded in strategy. In firms, goals like profitability, growth, and market share are relatively specific and easy to measure. That is one reason that McDonald's can structure its resources so tightly. Goals in educational and human services organizations are typically much more diffuse—"producing educated men and women" or "improving individual well-being." That is another reason that Harvard adopts a more decentralized, loosely integrated system of roles and relationships.

Goals vary in number and complexity. McDonald's goals are fewer, less complex, and less controversial than Harvard's. Uncertainty and conflict over goals are typically much higher in public agencies, universities, and schools. To complicate matters further, stated goals are not the only, or even the most important, goals an organization pursues. Westerlund and Sjostrand (1979) suggest a variety of others:

- Honorific goals—fictitious goals that credit the organization with desirable qualities
- Taboo goals—actual goals not talked about
- Stereotypical goals—goals that any reputable organization should have
- Existing goals—goals quietly pursued even though inconsistent with the organization's stated values and self-image

To understand the linkages among goals, structure, and strategy, one has to look beyond formal statements of purpose. Schools, for example, are often criticized because their structure does not always align with the goal of scholastic achievement. But schools have other, less visible goals. One is character development. Another is the "taboo" goal of certification and selection: schools channel students into different tracks and sort them into different careers. Still a third goal is custody and control—keeping kids off the streets and out from underfoot. Finally, schools often herald honorific goals like excellence. Strategy and goals shape structure, but the process is often complex and subtle.

Information Technology

Computers and new technologies they have spawned are revolutionizing both the amount of available information and the speed at which it moves from place to place. Information once available only to top-level or middle managers is now easily accessible and widely shared, making it possible to move decisions closer to the action.

The implications of improved technology for the design of organizations are far-reaching. Information is a central determinant of structure. Galbraith (1973) defines uncertainty as the difference between the information an organization has and the information it needs at a given time and place. As uncertainty increases, more information is needed to make decisions—information that may be hard to get. Organizations then have two choices: reduce the need for information or increase the capacity to process information (Galbraith, 1973). Organizations can reduce the need for information by creating slack resources or by establishing self-contained units that work independently.

Before the proliferation of personal computers, information technology (IT) was centralized and controlled by specialists. Mainframes could do things previously impossible, but coordinating user needs with IT offerings was often a very frustrating and time-consuming process for both sides. The spread of personal computers on managers' desks created a slack resource (more computing power than users needed) that often reduced the need to coordinate. Linking desktop machines to one another opened new possibilities for structuring organizations as networks or "complex adaptive systems" (Waldrop, 1992, p. 145). Such systems are assemblies of loosely connected units, or agents, each with its own agenda.

Control is dispersed and emerges from a bottom-up series of interactions among many different agents, all pursuing their own interests and needs, rather than from headquarters's edicts (Chaize, 1992; Holland, 1995; Waldrop, 1992). These characteristics can be found in systems as diverse as prairies, cities, economies, and the Internet.

Microsoft's development of its Windows NT operating system, one of the most complex pieces of software ever written, provides an example of a network in action. The product had to work as a unified whole, yet more than two hundred developers in dozens of small units were organized "right on the edge of chaos" (Zachary, 1994, p. 107). Each had its own goals and working style. Many developers never talked to one another, and some didn't even like one another. Reporting relationships were "a crazy quilt, not a hierarchy. Formal reporting lines were often ignored" (p. 108). What held it together? Basically, a requirement set down by the boss, David Cutler. After the first year, he decreed, programmers had to "eat their own dog food" (p. 1) by developing NT on computers operating under NT itself. A daily "build" stitched the operating system together electronically (Cusumano and Selby, 1995). Initially, developers were stunned at the poor quality of the "dog food" they had to consume—the system crashed all the time. But they learned immediately if their latest code were defective or crashing into someone else's. There were powerful incentives to find problems and fix them. One spur was Cutler's authoritative harangue: "If you break the build, your ass is grass, and I'm the lawnmower" (Zachary, 1994, pp. 129–130). Even more important was an emerging appreciation for interdependence and contributions to the whole. If your code broke the build, your pride suffered and you jeopardized everyone else's ability to get on with the work.

Innovations and investments in information technology make flatter structures inevitable. "Only five years ago it was treated as sensational news when I pointed out that the information-based organization needs far fewer levels of management than the traditional command-and-control model. By now a great many—maybe most—American companies have cut management levels by one-third or more. But the restructuring of corporations—middle-sized ones as well as large ones, and, eventually, even smaller ones—has barely begun" (Drucker, 1989, p. 20).

People: Nature of the Workforce

Human resource requirements have changed dramatically in recent decades. Many lower-level jobs now require high levels of skill. A better-educated workforce expects and sometimes demands more discretion in daily work routines. Increasing specialization of knowledge has professionalized many functions. Professionals often know more than their supervisors about technical aspects of their work. Socialized to expect autonomy, they prefer reporting to professional colleagues. Lawyers who report to engineers, or engineers who report to lawyers, often question their boss's competence to evaluate their work.

Changes in the workforce put additional pressure on traditional hierarchical forms. Combined with changes in technology and increasing emphasis on symbolic approaches to organizational control, dramatically different structural forms are emerging. Deal and Kennedy (1982) predicted the emergence of the atomized or network organization—small, autonomous, often geographically dispersed work groups tied together by information systems and organizational symbols. Drucker makes a similar observation in noting that businesses will increasingly "move work to where the people are, rather than people to where the work is" (1989, p. 20).

The many forces affecting structural design often combine to create a complicated mix of challenges and tensions. In many cases, the questions are complex. It is not simply a matter of deciding, for example, whether we should be hierarchical and centralized like McDonald's or flat and decentralized like Harvard. Many organizations find that they have to do both and somehow accommodate the structural tensions involved.

Beginning in the 1980s, New York–based Citibank bet a large chunk of its future on consumer banking outside the United States, particularly in Asia and the Pacific Rim (Hansell, 1996). Serving consumers in places as diverse as Australia, Hong Kong, India, Indonesia, Malaysia, the Philippines, and Singapore requires coping with a confusing melange of cultures, governments, competitors, and business climates. At the same time, a key element of the bank's strategy was to develop a consistent, global brand name and image: "Citibank is working to make its outposts as consistent as McDonald's restaurants, with the offerings, advertising images and branch décor identical from country to country" (Hansell, 1996, p. 12). The idea was that Citibank customers should be able to go anywhere in the world and find an automatic teller machine that spoke their language and provided the same services they found at home. But that strategy inevitably carried great risks: "No company can operate effectively on a global scale by centralizing all key decisions and then farming them out for implementation. It doesn't work. The conditions in each market are too varied, the nuances of competition too complex, and the changes in climate too subtle and too rapid for long-distance management. No matter how good they are, no matter how well supported analytically, the decision-makers at the center are too far removed from individual markets and the needs of local customers" (Ohmae, 1990, p. 87).

The challenge was to globalize and localize at the same time: centralizing functions like product development and computer services while finding and developing managers around the globe who had the resources and flexibility to respond to local conditions.

Summary

The structural frame looks beyond individuals to examine the social context of work. Though sometimes equated with red tape, mindless memos, and rigid bureaucrats, the structural approach is broader and more subtle than that. It encompasses the freewheeling, loosely structured entrepreneurial task force as well as the more tightly controlled railway company or the postal department. When structure is overlooked, organizations often misdirect energy and resources. For example, massive training programs to solve problems that have more to do with structure than people never work out and waste money.

Organizations divide work by creating a variety of specialized roles, functions, and units. They must then tie the different elements together by means of both vertical and horizontal methods of integration. There is no one best way to organize. The right structure depends on an organization's goals, strategies, technology, and environment.

Organizations operating in simpler and more stable environments are likely to employ less complex and more centralized structures. They rely on authority, rules, and policies as the primary vehicles for coordinating the work. Organizations operating in rapidly changing, turbulent, and uncertain environments need much more complex and flexible structures. Understanding the complexity of organizational contexts and the variety of structural possibilities can help create structures that work for, rather than against, both people and the purposes of organizations.

Chapter Four

Structuring and Reengineering

If there is an appropriate structural design for every situation, how does a manager choose the right one? One possibility is to bring in a consultant.

> Tomorrow in Manhattan, Harvard Business School professor Michael Porter and McGraw-Hill president Joseph Dionne will share the dais at a World Management Council forum [titled] "Managing Innovation." The setting—and the pairing—is ironical, as Michael Porter is the architect of a costly and ruinous restructuring of McGraw-Hill. After reading Porter's best-selling management manual, *Competitive Strategy,* Dionne invited the wispy-haired HBS *wunderkind* to devise a strategy for pumping new life into the moribund, billion-dollar publishing giant. In 1984, Porter suggested a sweeping reorganization of the company, which had been divided up into book, magazine, and financial services divisions, into twenty-one "market focus" segments. But Porter's scheme backfired. The elaborate mixmastering of McGraw-Hill assets cost hundreds of staffers their jobs, but has fallen far short of management's expectations. Revenues in 1988 grew only 3.8 percent to $1.8 billion, trailing the rate of inflation. McGraw-Hill is no longer a leader in trade magazine publishing, an industry it once dominated [Beam, 1989].

The divisions that performed best were those reorganized least. A McGraw-Hill executive commented ruefully, "Market focus was the atom [bomb] that blew the company apart. It was like our first

59

whiff of coke, this seductive idea that the solution to our problems could be found inside the company, by reorganizing the pieces. Now, when things are going badly, we reorganize" (Beam, 1989).

Structural Dilemmas

Finding a satisfactory arrangement of roles and relationships is an ongoing, universal struggle. Rather than responding to well-defined problems with clearcut solutions, most managers confront enduring structural dilemmas: tough trade-offs with no easy answers.

• *Differentiation Versus Integration.* The tension between allocating work and coordinating it once it has been distributed creates a classic dilemma. The more complex a role structure, with lots of people doing many different things, the harder it is to integrate it all into a focused, tightly coupled enterprise. As complexity grows, organizations require more sophisticated—and more costly—coordination strategies.

• *Gaps Versus Overlaps.* When key responsibilities are not clearly assigned, important tasks fall through the cracks. Conversely, roles and activities can overlap, creating conflict, wasted effort, and unintended redundancies.

• *Underuse Versus Overload.* When employees have too little work, they become bored and get in other people's way. In one physician's office, for example, clerical staff were able to complete most of their tasks during the morning. After lunch, they filled their time talking to family and friends. As a result, the office's telephone lines were constantly busy, making it difficult for patients to schedule appointments. Meanwhile, nurses were swamped with clients and routine paperwork. Too busy for informal talk with patients, they were often brusque and curt. Patients complained about impersonal care. A better structural balance was accomplished by reassigning many of the nurses' clerical duties to office staff.

• *Lack of Clarity Versus Lack of Creativity.* When employees are unclear about what they are supposed to be doing, they often shape their roles around personal preferences instead of organizational goals. But when responsibilities are overdefined, people conform in a "bureaupathic" way to prescribed roles. They rigidly follow their job description regardless of how much the service or product suffers.

• *Excessive Autonomy Versus Excessive Interdependence.* When efforts of individuals or groups are too autonomous, people come to feel isolated and unsupported. Schoolteachers typically work in isolation, rarely seeing other adults. In contrast, when units and roles are too tightly linked, people are distracted from work and waste time on unnecessary coordination. One reason that IBM lost its early lead in the personal computer business was that new initiatives required so many approvals—from both levels and divisions—that new products were overdesigned and late to market.

• *Too Loose Versus Too Tight.* A critical structural challenge is holding an organization together without holding it back. When structure is too loose, people go their own way or get lost, with little sense of what others are doing. Structures that are too tight stifle flexibility and cause people to spend much of their time trying to get around the system.

• *Diffuse Authority Versus Overcentralization.* In some situations, no one knows who has authority over what. The resulting confusion limits individual initiative and creates conflict. At the other extreme, too many layers of authority pull decisions so far from their source that decision making is sluggish and clumsy. Northwest Airlines and Scandinavian Air Systems both reduced passenger complaints significantly by giving front-line personnel more discretion to respond on the spot to passengers' frustrations.

• *Goalless Versus Goalbound.* In some situations, few people know what the goals are; in others, people cling to goals long after they have become irrelevant or outmoded.

• *Irresponsible Versus Unresponsive.* When people abdicate their responsibilities, performance suffers. However, adhering too rigidly to policies or procedures has the same effect. In public agencies, "street-level bureaucrats" (Lipsky, 1980) who deal with the public are often asked, "Could you do me this favor?" or "Couldn't you bend the rules a little bit in this case?" Turning down every request, no matter how reasonable, alienates the public and perpetuates images of bureaucratic rigidity and red tape. But overaccommodating agency workers create problems of inconsistency and favoritism.

Recognizing structural dilemmas is a recurrent management challenge. Achieving the right balance is tied closely to an organization's total situation: current environment, workforce, technology, and past structural commitments.

Structural Configurations

Structural design rarely starts from scratch. Managers search for options among existing blueprints in experience or in the popular literature. Mintzberg and Helgesen offer two examples.

Mintzberg's Fives

As the two-dimensional lines and boxes of the conventional table of organizations have become increasingly obsolete, students of organizational design have developed a variety of new images of structure. One influential example is Mintzberg's five-sector "logo," depicted in Figure 4.1. At the base of Mintzberg's hierarchical image is the *operating core,* consisting of people who perform the basic work. The core consists of manufacturing, service, professional, or other workers who produce or provide products or services to customers or clients: teachers in schools, assembly-line workers in factories, physicians and nurses in hospitals, and flight crews in airlines.

Directly above the operating core is the *administrative component:* managers who supervise, control, and provide resources for the operators. School principals, factory foremen, and other first-line supervisors fulfill this role. At the top of Mintzberg's picture is the strategic apex, where senior managers focus on the outside environment, determine the mission, and provide the grand design. In school systems, the strategic apex includes superintendents and school boards. In corporations, the apex is home to senior executives and the board of directors.

Two more components sit alongside the administrative component. The *technostructure* houses specialists and analysts who standardize, measure, and inspect outputs and processes. Quality control departments in industry, audit departments in government agencies, and flight standards departments in airlines perform such technical functions. The *support staff* performs tasks that support or facilitate the work of others. In schools, for example, the support staff includes nurses, secretaries, custodians, food service workers, and bus drivers.

Using this blueprint, Mintzberg (1979) derived five basic structural configurations: simple structure, machine bureaucracy, professional bureaucracy, divisionalized form, and adhocracy. Each creates a unique set of management challenges.

Figure 4.1.   Mintzberg's Model.

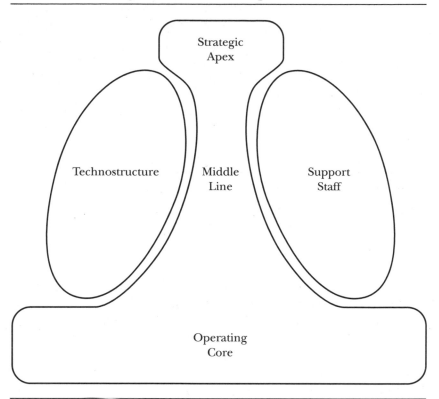

Source: Mintzberg, H. *The Structuring of Organizations.* Upper Saddle River, N.J.: Prentice Hall, 1979, p. 20. Copyright © 1979. Reprinted by permission of Prentice Hall, Upper Saddle River, N.J.

Simple Structure

A simple structure has only two levels: the strategic apex and an operating level (see Figure 4.2). Coordination is accomplished primarily through direct supervision, as in a small mom-and-pop operation. Either mom or pop constantly monitors what is going on and exercises total authority over daily operations.

Start-up companies typically begin with simple structures. William Hewlett and David Packard began their business in a garage; General Electric had its humble beginnings in Thomas Edison's laboratory. The virtues of simple structure are its flexibility and adaptability—one person directs the entire operation. But virtues

Figure 4.2.   Simple Structure.

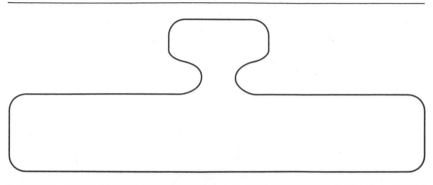

Source: Mintzberg, H. *The Structuring of Organizations.* Upper Saddle River, N.J.: Prentice Hall, 1979, p. 307. Copyright © 1979. Reprinted by permission of Prentice Hall, Upper Saddle River, N.J.

can become vices. Authorities block as well as initiate change, punish capriciously as well as reward handsomely. A boss too close to day-to-day operations is easily distracted by immediate problems, neglecting long-range strategic decisions.

Machine Bureaucracy

McDonald's is a classic machine bureaucracy: important decisions are made at the strategic apex; day-to-day operations are controlled by managers and standardized procedures. Unlike simple hierarchies, machine bureaucracies have large support staffs and technostructure, with many layers between apex and operating levels (see Figure 4.3).

For routine tasks, such as making hamburgers or manufacturing automotive parts, machine bureaucracy is enormously efficient and effective. A key challenge is how to motivate and satisfy workers in the operating core. People tire quickly of repetitive work and standardized procedures. Yet providing too much creativity and personal challenge in a McDonald's outlet could undermine consistency and uniformity—two keys to the company's success.

Like other machine bureaucracies, McDonald's deals constantly with tensions between local managers and headquarters. Middle managers are heavily influenced by local concerns and tastes. Top

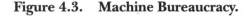

Figure 4.3.   Machine Bureaucracy.

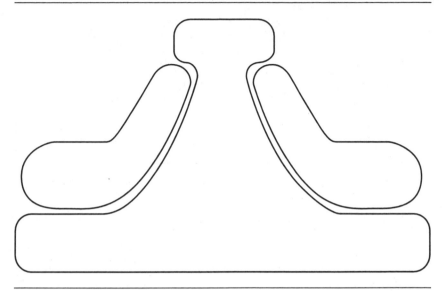

Source: Mintzberg, H. *The Structuring of Organizations.* Upper Saddle River, N.J.: Prentice Hall, 1979, p. 325. Copyright © 1979. Reprinted by permission of Prentice Hall, Upper Saddle River, N.J.

exccutives, aided by analysts, rely more on generic and abstract information and pursue corporatewide concerns. As a result, solutions from the top may not always match the needs of individual units. McDonald's moderates tensions by allowing individual restaurants to experiment with new ideas. As noted in the previous chapter, the Egg McMuffin was developed by a local franchisee who hoped to enlarge his market by serving breakfast. Breakfast is now standard across the chain. Permitting experimentation stimulates innovation, the lack of which is one of machine bureaucracy's classic weaknesses.

Professional Bureaucracy

Harvard University provides a glimpse into the inner workings of a professional bureaucracy (see Figure 4.4). Its operating core is large relative to its other structural parts—particularly the technostructure. Few managerial levels exist between the strategic apex and

Figure 4.4.   Professional Bureaucracy.

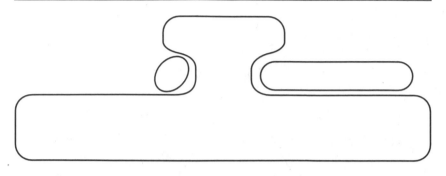

Source: Mintzberg, H. *The Structuring of Organizations.* Upper Saddle River, N.J.: Prentice Hall, 1979, p. 355. Copyright © 1979. Reprinted by permission of Prentice Hall, Upper Saddle River, N.J.

professors, creating a flat and decentralized profile. Control relies heavily on professional training and indoctrination. Professionals are insulated from formal interference, freeing them to use their expertise. Though producing many benefits, this arrangement leads to problems of coordination and quality control. Tenured professors, for example, are largely immune to formal sanctions. As a result, universities have to find other ways to deal with incompetence and irresponsibility.

Professional bureaucracies respond slowly to changes in the environment. Waves of reform typically produce little impact because professionals often view change in their surroundings as an annoying distraction from their work. The result is a paradox: individual professionals may be at the forefront of their specialties while the institution as a whole changes at a glacial pace. Professional bureaucracies regularly stumble when they try to rationalize the operating core. Requiring Harvard professors to follow standard teaching methods would be more likely to harm performance than to improve it.

Divisionalized Form

In divisionalized structures (see Figure 4.5), the bulk of the work is done in quasi-autonomous units—campuses in a multicampus university, specialties in large multispecialty hospitals, or divisions

Figure 4.5.   Divisionalized Form.

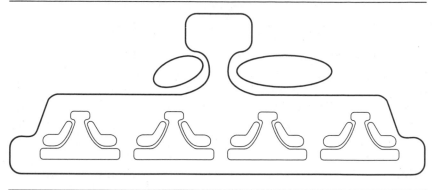

Source: Mintzberg, H. *The Structuring of Organizations.* Upper Saddle River, N.J.: Prentice Hall, 1979, p. 393. Copyright © 1979. Reprinted by permission of Prentice Hall, Upper Saddle River, N.J.

in Fortune 500 companies (Mintzberg, 1979). One of the oldest businesses in the United States, the Berwind Company, houses divisions in a variety of businesses: manufacturing, financial services, real estate, and land management. Each division serves a well-defined market and supports its own functional units. Division presidents are accountable to the corporate office in Philadelphia for specific results: profits, sales growth, and return on investment. As long as they deliver, the divisions have relatively free rein. Philadelphia manages the strategic portfolio and allocates resources based on its assessment of market opportunities.

Divisionalized structures offer economies of scale, ample resources, and responsiveness without undue economic risks, but they create other tensions. One is a cat-and-mouse game between headquarters and divisions. Headquarters wants tighter oversight while divisional managers try to evade corporate controls:

> Our top management likes to make all the major decisions. They think they do, but I've seen one case where a division beat them. I received . . . a request from the division for a chimney. I couldn't see what anyone would do with a chimney, so I flew out for a visit. They've built and equipped a whole plant on plant expense orders. The chimney is the only indivisible item that exceeded the $50,000 limit we put on plant expense orders. Apparently they learned that

a new plant wouldn't be formally received, so they built the damn thing. I don't know exactly what I'm going to say [Bower, 1970a, p. 189].

Another risk in the divisionalized form is that headquarters may lose touch with operations. As one manager put it, "Headquarters is where the rubber meets the air." Divisionalized enterprises become unwieldy unless goals are measurable and reliable vertical information systems can be designed (Mintzberg, 1979).

Adhocracy

Adhocracy is a loose, flexible, self-renewing organic form tied together mostly through lateral means (see Figure 4.6). Usually found in diverse, freewheeling environments, adhocracy functions as an "organizational tent," exploiting benefits that structural designers traditionally regarded as liabilities. "Ambiguous authority structures, unclear objectives, and contradictory assignments of responsibility can legitimize controversies and challenge traditions. . . . Incoher-

Figure 4.6.   Adhocracy.

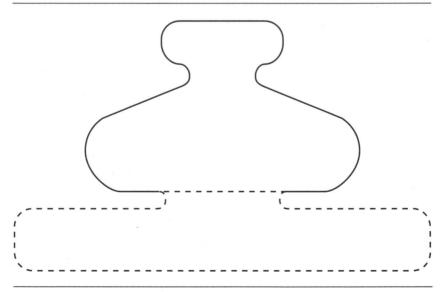

Source: Mintzberg, H. *The Structuring of Organizations.* Upper Saddle River, N.J.: Prentice Hall, 1979, p. 443. Copyright © 1979. Reprinted by permission of Prentice Hall, Upper Saddle River, N.J.

ence and indecision can foster exploration, self-evaluation, and learning" (Hedberg, Nystrom, and Starbuck, 1976, p. 45).

Ad hoc structures are most often found in conditions of turbulence and rapid change. Examples include advertising agencies, think-tank consulting firms, and the recording industry. In the 1970s and 1980s, Digital Equipment Corporation (DEC) was a well-known pioneer of adhocracy: "In many ways [DEC] is a big company in small company clothes. It doesn't believe much in hierarchy, rule books, dress codes, company cars, executive dining rooms, lofty titles, country club memberships, or most trappings of corpocracy. It doesn't even have assigned parking spots. Only the top half-dozen executives have sizable offices. Everyone else at the company headquarters in Maynard, Mass., makes do with dinky doorless cubicles" (Machan, 1987, p. 154).

Digital's structural arrangements helped make it the world leader in minicomputers but became more problematic when the rise of personal computers dramatically altered Digital's market environment. "They flew so high and crashed so hard," said one observer, because "at DEC, the internal mattered so much. They spent their lives playing with each other" (Johnson, 1996). Like every structural form, adhocracy creates its own set of managerial issues.

Helgesen's Web of Inclusion

Mintzberg's five-sector imagery adds a new dimension to the conventional line-staff organization chart but still retains much of the traditional image of structure as a top-down pyramid. Helgesen argues that the idea of hierarchy is primarily a male-driven image, quite different from versions created by female executives: "The women I studied had built profoundly integrated and organic organizations in which the focus was on nurturing good relationships; in which the niceties of hierarchical rank and distinction played little part; and in which lines of communication were multiplicitous, open, and diffuse. I noted that women tended to put themselves at the center of their organizations rather than at the top, thus emphasizing both accessibility and equality, and that they labored constantly to include people in their decision-making" (Helgesen, 1995, p. 10).

Helgesen coined the expression "web of inclusion" to describe an architectural form more circular than hierarchical. The web builds from the center out. The web's architect works much like a spider, spinning new threads of connection and reinforcing existing strands. The web's center and periphery are interconnected. Action in one place ripples across the entire configuration, forming "an interconnected cosmic web in which the threads of all forces and events form an inseparable net of endlessly, mutually conditioned relations" (Fritjof Capra, quoted in Helgesen, 1995, p. 16). As a consequence, weaknesses in either the center or the periphery of the web undermine the strength of the organic network.

Helgesen's concept started to take form while she was an assistant at the *Village Voice*, a Greenwich Village alternative newspaper. Dan Wolf, the editor, ran a very lean operation: no fact checkers, department heads, or consultants and only a few assistants. Missing entirely were formal staff meetings, memos, and a rational chain of command. The only visible source of information was a centrally located corkboard to which staff affixed a variety of notices and scribbled responses. Yet for all the supposed ambiguity and chaos, communication at the *Voice* was excellent. Wolf was at the center of the communication hub, readily accessible in his centrally located office. Anyone could walk through his door, no appointment needed. An agenda was unnecessary—just talk about whatever was on your mind. Most operational details were delegated to the paper's four editors. Wolf invited people to lunch on a regular basis—to eat, talk, and get to know one another. Everyone, irrespective of role or level, was included in an ongoing dialogue, characterized as "fractious togetherness." The architecture of the *Voice* was an organically connected web rather than a clearly defined pyramid. It had a recognizable, well-understood structure, observable in its employees' daily behavior.

Generic Issues in Restructuring

Restructuring efforts need to take account of tensions specific to each structural configuration. Consultants and managers often apply general principles without recognizing key differences across architectural forms. Restructuring an adhocracy is radically different from restructuring a machine bureaucracy. Reweaving a web is a far cry from tinkering with a professional bureaucracy. Subjecting radically different organizations to the same organizing logic is a surefire recipe for the kind of difficulty that Michael Porter experienced in his work with McGraw-Hill.

Mintzberg's imagery, for example, suggests general principles to guide restructuring across a range of circumstances. Each of the major components of his model exerts its own pressures. Restructuring triggers a multidirectional tug-of-war that eventually determines the shape of the structure. Unless the various pulls are acknowledged and managed effectively, the result may be a catastrophe.

The strategic apex tends to exert centralizing pressures. Through commands, rules, or less obtrusive means, top managers continually try to develop a unified mission or strategy. Deep down, they long for a simple structure they can control. By contrast, middle managers tend to pull the organization toward balkanization. Navy captains, school principals, department heads, and bureau chiefs become committed to their own domain. It is their job to protect and enhance their unit's interests. Tensions between centripetal forces from the top and centrifugal forces from middle management are especially prominent in divisionalized structures but are critical issues in any restructuring effort.

The technostructure exerts pressures to standardize—analysts want to measure and monitor the organization's progress against well-defined criteria. Depending on the circumstances, they counterbalance (or complement) top administrators who want to centralize and middle managers who seek greater autonomy. Technocrats feel most at home in the machine bureaucracy.

The support staff pulls in the direction of greater collaboration. Its members usually feel happiest when authority is given to small work units. There they can influence, directly and personally, the shape and flow of everyday decisions. They prefer adhocracy. Meanwhile, the operating core seeks to control its own destiny and minimize influence from the other components. Its members often look outside—to unions or to their professional colleagues—for support.

Attempts to restructure must acknowledge natural tensions among various components. Depending on the configuration—simple structure, machine bureaucracy, professional bureaucracy, divisionalized form, or adhocracy—different components will have more or less influence on the final outcome. In a simple structure, the boss undoubtedly has the edge. In machine bureaucracies, the technostructure and strategic apex possess the most clout. In professional bureaucracies, chronic conflict between administrators and professionals is the dominant tension, while members of the technostructure play an important role in the wings. In the adhocracy, a number of different actors can play pivotal roles in shaping the emerging structural patterns.

Beyond internal negotiations lurks a more pivotal issue. A workable structure is ultimately a function of how well it fits an organization's environment and technology. Natural selection weeds out the field, determining survivors and victims. It is always a poker game among the major players to negotiate a structure that meets the needs of each component and still works in the organization's environment.

Pressures for Restructuring

Miller and Friesen (1984) studied a sample of both successful and troubled firms to identify structural patterns that worked and those that did not. Firms in trouble typically fell into one of three configurations:

1. *Impulsive firms*—fast-growing organizations, controlled by one individual or a few top people in which structures and controls have become too primitive and the firm is increasingly out of control. Profits may fall precipitously, and survival may be at stake.
2. *Stagnant bureaucracies*—older, tradition-dominated organizations with obsolete product lines. A predictable and placid environment has lulled everyone to sleep, and top management is slavishly committed to old ways. Information systems are too primitive to detect the need for change. Lower-level managers feel ignored and alienated. Many old-line corporations and public bureaucracies fit here.
3. *Headless giants*—loosely coupled, feudal organizations. The administrative core is weak, and most of the initiative and power resides in autonomous departments or divisions. With no real strategy or leadership at the top, the firm is adrift. Collaboration is minimal because departments compete for resources. Decision making is reactive and crisis-oriented.

Miller and Friesen (1984) found that even in organizations in trouble, structural change is episodic: long periods of time with little change are followed by major restructuring. A stable structure helps maintain internal consistency and protect the existing equilibrium but risks becoming increasingly maladaptive. Eventually, the gap widens so much that a major overhaul is inevitable. Restructuring, in this view, is like spring cleaning: we accumulate debris over months or years until we are finally forced to face up to the mess.

The pressures that lead to restructuring include the following:

- *The environment shifts.* At American Telephone & Telegraph, a shift from regulation to competition required a massive reorganization of the Bell System.
- *Technology changes.* The aircraft industry's shift from piston to jet engines profoundly affected the relationship between engine and airframe. Some established firms faltered because they underestimated the complexities; Boeing rose to lead the industry because it understood them (Henderson and Clark, 1990).
- *Organizations grow.* DEC thrived with a very informal and flexible structure during the company's early years, but the same structure produced major problems when DEC grew into a multibillion-dollar corporation.
- *Leadership changes.* Reorganization is often the first initiative of new leaders, even when it is not clear that it is needed.

Restructuring and Reengineering: Three Case Examples

In the early 1990s, reengineering rose to prominence as an umbrella concept for a set of emerging trends in structural thinking: "When a process is reengineered, jobs evolve from narrow and task oriented to multidimensional. People who once did as they were instructed now make choices and decisions on their own instead. Assembly-line work disappears. Functional departments lose their reason for being. Managers stop acting like supervisors and behave more like coaches. Workers focus more on customers' needs and less on their bosses'. Attitudes and values change in response to new incentives. Practically every aspect of the organization is transformed, often beyond recognition" (Hammer and Champy, 1993, p. 65).

The process of reengineering and the results it produces vary significantly. One survey by CSC Index (cited in Gertz and Baptista,

1995) found that fewer than one-third of reengineering initiatives met or exceeded their goals. Some have been catastrophic, including a notorious example at the American long-haul bus company, Greyhound Van Lines. As the company came out of bankruptcy in 1991, a new management team announced a major reorganization, with sizable cuts in staffing and routes and the development of a new, computerized reservation system. The new initiative played very well on Wall Street, where the company's stock soared, but very poorly on Main Street, where customer service and the new reservations system both collapsed. Rushed, underfunded, and insensitive to both employees and customers, it was a textbook example of how not to reengineer. Eventually, Greyhound's stock crashed, and management was forced out. One observer noted wryly, "They reengineered that business to hell" (Tomsho, 1994, p. A1). But reengineering has also produced examples of notable success, and we discuss three of them in the following paragraphs. The first, from Citibank, dates to the 1970s, well before the term *reengineering* was applied to structural change yet in anticipation of many of its principles.

Citibank's Back Room

The "back room" at Citibank—the department that processes checks and other financial instruments—was in trouble when John Reed took charge in 1970 (Seeger, Lorsch, and Gibson, 1975). Productivity was disappointing, errors were frequent, and expenses were rising almost 20 percent every year. Reed soon determined that the area needed dramatic structural change. Traditionally, it was viewed as a service for the bank's customer-contact offices, though it was structured as a machine bureaucracy. Reed decided to think of it not as a support function but as a factory: an independent, high-volume production facility. To implement this concept, he imported high-level executives from the automobile industry. One was Robert White, who came from Ford Motor Company to become the primary architect of a new structure and systems for the back room. White arrived with a strong faith in top-down management: "We use a pass/fail system as a management incentive. A manager passes or fails in terms of the objectives he himself has set within the top-down framework. He is rewarded, or not rewarded, accordingly. No excuses or rationalization of events beyond one's control are accepted" (Seeger, Lorsch, and Gibson, 1975, p. 3).

White began by developing a "phase one action plan" that called for cutting costs, putting in new computer systems, and developing a financial control system capable of both forecasting and measuring performance. In effect, the strategy retained the machine bureaucracy but tightened it. After phase one was implemented, White concluded that "we hadn't gone back to the basics enough. We found that we did not really understand the present processes completely" (Seeger, Lorsch, and Gibson, 1975, p. 8). What followed was an intensive, detailed study of how the back room's processes worked. White and his associates developed a detailed flowchart that covered the walls of a room. They realized that the current structure was, in effect, one very large, functional pipeline. Everything flowed into "preprocessing" at the front end of the pipe, then to "encoding," and on through a series of functional areas until it eventually came out at the other end. Reed and White decided to break the pipe into several smaller lines, each carrying a different "product" and each supervised by a single manager with responsibility for an end-to-end process. The key insight was to change the structure from machine bureaucracy to a divisionalized form.

White also instituted extensive performance measures and tight accountability procedures:

> We currently measure 69 different quality indicators, and we are meeting the standards 87 percent of the time. When a given indicator is met or beaten consistently, we tighten the standard; we expect to continue this process indefinitely. We have defined 129 different standards for time lines, and we expect that number to continue to grow. Today, we are meeting 85 percent of those standards. Moreover, we also continually tighten these standards as soon as they can be consistently met. I think it is fair to say that our service performance has improved greatly since we began to hold costs flat— if for no other reason than that we really know what we are doing [Seeger, Lorsch, and Gibson, 1975, p. 8].

Not surprisingly, this demanding, top-down approach produced fear and loathing among many old-timers in the back room and nearly led to rebellion. As Mintzberg's model predicts, the technical core strongly resisted this major intrusion. Reed and

White decided to implement the new structure virtually overnight, and the short-term result was chaos and a major breakdown in the system. It took two weeks to get the system functioning normally and five months to recover from the problems generated by the transition. But once past that crisis, the new system led to a dramatic improvement in operating results: production was up, and costs and errors were down. The back room was unexpectedly making a major contribution to corporate profitability.

The basic concepts behind restructuring the back room are not new. The change from a large, functional bureaucracy to a divisionalized form had first occurred in the 1920s at General Motors and Du Pont. By the 1970s, it had become the dominant form for large organizations. What was unusual was to take the basic concept of a divisionalized organization and apply it to the back room of a bank. Reed and White did not, in fact, begin with that in mind. It emerged from their intense mapping of the existing processes and recognition that dramatic change was possible.

Kodak's Black-and-White Division

The Citibank restructuring was strongly driven from the top down and focused primarily on internal efficiencies. This has been true of many, but by no means all, reengineering efforts. A more recent example from Eastman Kodak began with a push from the top but put much greater emphasis on customers and on empowering employees at multiple levels.

Kodak traces its origins to the late 1880s when George Eastman began to manufacture wooden boxes capable of capturing one hundred personal images on film. He also conceived of an innovative "no fuss, no muss" way to process the pictures: just send the whole box back to Kodak. Kodak processed the pictures, reloaded the camera, and shipped it back to the customer.

A century later, Kodak was a giant in trouble. Its name and film were known around the world, but the company had been rocked by intense competition, high costs, declining customer satisfaction, threats of a hostile takeover, and low employee morale. At a top management meeting in 1989, Kodak's normally gentle, soft-spoken CEO, Colby Chandler, wielded a machete to hack a wooden lectern to pieces. The message was clear and dramatic: Kodak needed fundamental change, and its functional, "stovepipe" structure had to give way to an organization based on process—a seamless flow from raw materials to finished products (Hammer and Champy, 1993).

Kodak chose to reorganize into six flows, one of which was black-and-white film. Implementation was to begin immediately, and any laggard operations would be shut down. In the black-and-white division, a group of executives focused on creating three streams: graphics, health sciences, and solvent coatings. All other areas (financial services, human resources, and engineering support) would be "dedicated" to supporting the flows.

One of the first tasks was to create performance measures and standards for the flows (productivity, inventory, waste, quality, conformance to specifications). With the operating flow as the center of attention, managers and supervisors became coaches and cheerleaders. Frequent informal meetings provided opportunities to air concerns and identify problems. Employees were encouraged to develop local visions and determine priorities and improvement plans for everything from reducing inventory and cutting waste to establishing relationships with suppliers and speeding delivery time. "In the old days, there wasn't much real interaction between the people on the shop floor and the product engineers. When you needed a repair or a modification, you called MEMO [the Manufacturing, Engineering and Maintenance Operation]. No one ever encouraged you to figure out ways to solve problems yourself" (Frangos, 1993, p. 108).

While the overall flow focused on satisfying external customers, each step in the process emphasized satisfying internal customers and building cooperation among employees. Cross-functional teams began to achieve breakthroughs in quality and cost reduction. "We demonstrated that the internal customers can focus their energy on a common problem" (Frangos, 1993, p. 110).

Two years after the restructuring was launched in the black-and-white division, performance standards were being surpassed, the division was one of the company's shining stars in terms of profitability, and it was widely heralded as one of the company's best places to work. The division's new title, "Team Zebra," summarized the structural transformation. The zebra was selected as a symbol because "every zebra is unique. No two zebras' stripes are the same—kind of like fingerprints. They also run in herds. Being animals that are preyed upon, they understand that to the extent they can stay together, they can defend themselves from lions and other predators. In fact, predators probably have a hard time distinguishing the individuals from the mass of black and white stripes. . . . We also need to band together as part of a team—when we're operating in synch, we baffle the competition" (Frangos, 1993, p. 126).

Beth Israel Hospital

When Joyce Clifford assumed duties as Beth Israel's director of nursing, she found a top-down structure common in today's hospitals:

> The nursing aides, who had the least preparation, had the most contact with the patients. But they had no authority of any kind. They had to go to their supervisor to ask if a patient could have an aspirin. The supervisor would then ask the head nurse, who would then have to ask a doctor. The doctor would ask how long the patient had been in pain. Of course the head nurse had absolutely no idea, so she'd have to track down the aide to ask her, and then relay that information back to the doctor. It was ridiculous, a ludicrous and dissatisfying situation, and one in which it was impossible for the nurse to feel any satisfaction at all. The system was hierarchical, fragmented, impersonal, and [overmanaged] [Helgesen, 1995, p. 134].

Within units, the responsibilities of nurses were highly specialized: some were assigned to handling medications, others to monitoring vital signs, and still others to taking blood pressure readings. Add to the list specialized housekeeping roles—bedpan, bedmaking, and food services—and an individual patient's day was filled with interruptions from a multitude of virtual strangers. No one really knew what was going on with the patient.

With the support and cooperation of Mitchell Rabkin, Beth Israel's progressive CEO, Clifford instituted a major structural change: from a pyramid with nurses at the bottom to an inclusionary web with nurses at the center. The concept was called primary nursing. Each primary nurse assumes responsibility for the care of a specific patient. The nurse takes information when the patient is admitted, develops a comprehensive plan, assembles a team to provide round-the-clock care, and lets the family know what to expect. A nurse manager sets goals for the unit, deals with budget and administrative matters, and makes sure that primary nurses have ample resources to provide quality care.

The primary nurse's role assures a central point for information about the patient's progress. As the primary nurse assumed more responsibility, connections with physicians and other hospital workers had to be revised. Instead of simply carrying out the orders of physicians, the primary nurse became a professional partner—attending rounds and participating as an equal in treatment decisions. Housekeepers reported to primary nurses rather than to housekeeping supervisors. The same housekeeper was assigned to make a patient's bed, attend to the patient's hygiene, and deliver trays. Laundry workers provided clean items on demand rather than in a once-a-day delivery. Beth Israel's inclusivity web was further strengthened by sophisticated technology that gave all points of the network easy access to patient information and administrative data.

Primary nurses themselves performed a variety of tasks for a single patient. Rather than being seen as menial undesirable work, for example, bedmaking became an opportunity to evaluate a patient's condition and assess how well a treatment plan is working.

At the center of all patient care at Beth Israel, Joyce Clifford linked the various intersecting points of the inclusive web: "A big part of my job is to keep nurses informed on a regular basis of what's going on out there—what the board is doing, what decisions are confronting the hospital as a whole, what the issues are in health care in this country. I also let them know that I'm trying to represent what the nurses here are doing—to our vice-presidents, to our board, and people in the outside world, . . . to the nursing profession and the health care field as a whole" (Helgesen, 1995, p. 158).

No one knows whether more reorganization efforts succeed than fail, but the percentage of failures is high. The Kodak, Citibank, and Beth Israel efforts were successful where others failed because they followed several basic principles of successful structural change. First, they developed a new conception of the organization's goals and strategies. Second, they carefully studied the existing structure and process so that they understood how things worked. Many efforts at structural change fail because they start from an incomplete picture of current processes. Third, they designed the new structure in light of changes in goals, technology, and environment. Finally, they experimented, retaining things that worked and discarding things that did not.

Summary

At any given moment, an organization's structure represents its resolution of an enduring set of organizational dilemmas: Are we too loose or too tight? Are employees underworked or overwhelmed? Are we too rigid, or do we lack standards? Do people spend too much or too little time coordinating with one anther? Structure also represents a resolution of contending claims of different groups within the organization. Mintzberg differentiates five major components in organizational structure: the strategic apex, the middle management, the operating core, the technostructure, and the support staff. Different configurations of these components lead to different organizational forms: simple structure, machine bureaucracy, professional bureaucracy, divisionalized form, and adhocracy. Helgesen adds the web of inclusion.

A given resolution of structural tensions may be right for a particular time and circumstance, but changes in the organization and its environment will eventually require some form of structural adaptation. Restructuring is a powerful but high-risk tool for organizational change. In the short term, it almost invariably produces confusion, resistance, and even a decline in effectiveness. Success or failure in the long run depends on how well the new model aligns the organization with its environment, task, and technology and on the effectiveness of the processes for putting the new structure in place. Effective restructuring requires both a microscopic view of typical structural problems as well as an overall, topographical sense of structural options.

Chapter Five

Organizing Groups and Teams

Teams play a vital role in cultures around the world. Bowling teams, soccer teams, baseball teams, SWAT teams, and fundraising teams absorb participants' energy, raise morale, and provide an outlet for competitive spirit. For spectators, sports teams of all kinds provide drama, exhilaration, and a common cultural focal point. Every four years, for example, the world's athletes gather to compete in the Olympic Games. It is a spectacle that captures universal attention and unites people of diverse and even warring countries for a period of time. Teams have also assumed a prominent role in the workplace. Leadership teams, design teams, quality teams, and many other forms are replacing the individualistic, Lone Ranger, "I'll do my own job, thank you" attitude that hampered the ability of many organizations to compete in the global marketplace.

Much of the work in large organizations is now done in work groups or teams. When these units work well, they elevate the performances of ordinary individuals to extraordinary heights. When teams malfunction, as they often do, they erode the potential contributions of the most talented members. The athletic world is replete with stories of underdogs stealing championships from a collection of better players who were not a better team.

Although the world of work relies more and more on teamwork, it often lacks a solid grasp of what makes a team work. "Most executives advocate teamwork. And they should. Teamwork represents a set of values that encourages listening and responding constructively to views expressed by others, giving each other the benefit of the doubt, providing support, and recognizing the interests and achievements of others. Such values help teams perform, and they also promote individual performance as well as the performance of an entire organization. But teamwork values by themselves are not exclusive to teams, nor are they enough to ensure team performance" (Katzenbach and Smith, 1993, p. 112). One of the key ingredients of any top-performing team is an effective structure of roles and relationships focused on attaining common goals.

A High-Performing Commando Unit

During the Second World War, an unusual U.S. Army commando team compiled a distinctive record. It successfully accomplished every mission it was assigned, including extremely high-risk, behind-the-lines operations. It had one of the lowest rates of battle-related deaths or injuries of any U.S. military unit. A research team was charged with finding out what made the unit so successful. Were the enlisted men and officers especially talented? Had their training been longer or more intensive than normal? Or was the group just plain lucky?

Researchers pinpointed the reason for the group's success: its ability to reconfigure depending on the situation. Planning for missions, the group functioned democratically. Anyone, irrespective of specialty or rank, could volunteer ideas and make suggestions. Decisions were reached by consensus, and the strategy for an engagement was approved by the group as a whole. The unit's planning structure resembled that of a research and development team or a creative design group. Amorphous roles and a flat hierarchy encouraged participation, creativity, and productive conflict. Battle plans reflected the best ideas of the entire group.

Executing the plan was another story. The group's structure changed from a loose, creative confederation to a well-defined, tightly controlled chain of command. Each individual had a specific assignment. Tasks had to be done with split-second precision. The commanding officer had sole responsibility for operational decisions and changes in the plan. Everyone else obeyed orders without question, though the others might offer suggestions if time permitted. In battle, the group relied on the traditional military structure: clearcut responsibilities, decisions made at the top and executed by the rank and file.

The group's ability to tailor its structure to circumstances provided the best of two worlds. Participation encouraged creativity, ownership, and understanding of the battle plan. Authority, accountability, and clarity enabled the group to function with speed and efficiency during the operation.

Like all organizations, small groups must arrange people vertically and laterally to deal with the immediate task and environment. In the case of the commando unit, strategic structural changes won battles and saved lives.

Tasks and Linkages in Small Groups

The commando team's experience is consistent with what we have learned from several decades of research on small work groups. In dealing with tasks, groups have a number of structural options. The one they choose—or the one that evolves—must allow members to pool individual contributions successfully without creating pathologies that often plague small groups. Tasks vary in clarity, predictability, and stability. The relationship between tasks and structure is the same for small groups as for larger organizations. As we learned in Chapter Four, complex tasks present different challenges than simple tasks. Planning a commando mission or doing open-heart surgery is very different from painting a house or performing an appendectomy.

Simple tasks align with simple structures—clearly defined roles, simple forms of interdependence, and coordination by plan or command. More complicated projects generally require more complex structures—flexible roles, reciprocal interdependence, and coordination by lateral relationships and mutual feedback. When situations become exceptionally ambiguous and fast-paced, particularly in cases where time is a factor, more centralized authority often works best. Otherwise the group is unable to make decisions quickly enough. Until a group finds a workable structure, performance and morale suffer—and troublesome pathologies multiply.

Finding the right group structure is always challenging. It requires careful consideration of a number of situational variables, some of which are ambiguous or hard to assess:

1. What are we trying to accomplish?
2. What needs to be done?

3. Who should do what?
4. How should we make decisions?
5. Who is in charge?
6. How do we coordinate efforts?
7. What do individual members care about most—time, quality, participation?
8. What are the special skills and talents of each group member?
9. What is the relationship between this group and others?
10. How will we determine success?

   To illustrate design options, small group research has identified several basic structural configurations in five-member teams.
The first is a one-boss arrangement—one person has authority over
others (see Figure 5.1). Information and decisions flow from the
top. Group members provide information to and communicate
primarily with the official leader rather than with one another.
Although this arrangement is efficient and fast, it works best with
relatively simple and straightforward tasks. More complicated situations snarl things unless the boss has unusual levels of skills,
expertise, and energy. Subordinates quickly become frustrated
when directives they receive are slow or ill-suited to their work.

Figure 5.1.   One Boss.

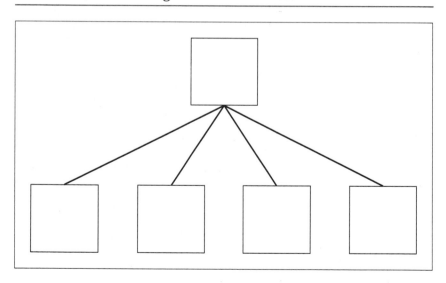

Figure 5.2.   Dual Authority.

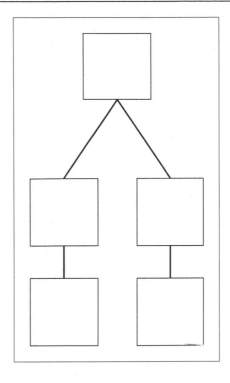

A second option is to create a second management level (see Figure 5.2). Two members are given authority over specific areas of the group's work. Information and decisions flow through them. This arrangement works when a task is divisible. It reduces the span of control of the person in charge, allowing greater concentration on mission, strategy, or the group's relationships with higher-ups. But adding a new management layer limits access of lower levels to higher-ups and may eventually erode morale and performance. With added layers, communication is more difficult, and it often takes more time to get things done.

Another possibility is to create, in effect, a simple hierarchy, with a middle manager who reports to the boss and who in turn supervises and communicates with other group members (see Figure 5.3). This frees the person at the apex to focus on mission and external relations while operational details are left to the second

Figure 5.3.   Simple Hierarchy.

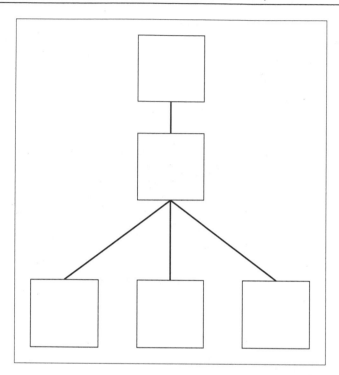

in command. Though this further limits access to the top, it can be more efficient than a dual-manager arrangement. At the same time, friction between operational and top-level managers is commonplace and can lead to attempts by Number 2 to usurp Number 1's position.

A fourth possibility is a circle network where information and decisions flow sequentially from one group member to another (see Figure 5.4). Each person can add to or modify whatever comes around. This configuration is more egalitarian and simplifies communication. Each team member has to worry about communicating with only two others. Transactions are therefore easier to manage. But one weak link in the chain can undermine the entire enterprise, and the circle can bog down with complex tasks that require more reciprocity.

Figure 5.4.   Circle.

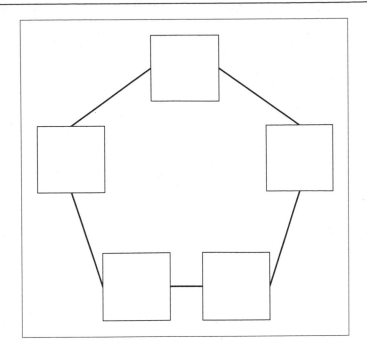

A final possibility is to create what small group researchers call the all-channel or star network (see Figure 5.5). This design is similar to Helgesen's "web of inclusion." It creates multiple connections so that each team member can talk to anyone else. Information flows freely; decisions require touching multiple bases. Morale in all-channel networks is usually very high. The arrangement works well when tasks are amorphous or complicated. It can also be slow and relatively inefficient. Team members need well-developed communication skills. They must also enjoy participation, tolerate ambiguity, embrace diversity, and manage conflict.

In small groups, such as school boards, families, task forces, or leadership teams, many day-to-day problems are caused by poorly understood or inappropriate structural forms. Creating effective teamwork requires a design of roles and relationships well suited to the situation.

Figure 5.5. All-Channel Network.

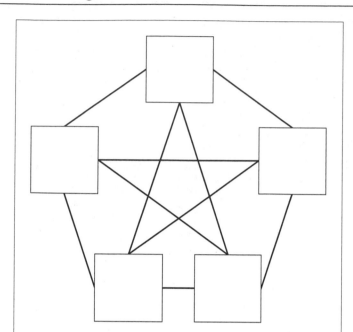

Teamwork and Interdependence

In the world of organized sports, different games call for unique patterns of differentiation and coordination. How closely team members depend on one another—levels of interdependence— vary widely from sport to sport. Because of this, team structures are not alike (Keidel, 1984). Teams, like organizations, need to be aligned with the task at hand. Social architecture is remarkably different for baseball, football, and basketball teams. Unique patterns of differentiation, interdependence, and coordination are required for each.

Baseball

As Pete Rose once noted, "Baseball is a team game, but nine men who meet their individual goals make a nice team" (Keidel, 1984 p. 8). Baseball teams are loosely integrated confederations. Individual efforts are mostly independent, seldom involving more than two or three players at a time. Particularly on defense, players are separated from one another by significant distances. Because of the differentiated, loosely linked nature of a baseball team, very little coordination is required among the various positions. The pitcher and catcher must each know what the other is going to do, and at times, infielders must have an idea of how others will act, particularly in the case of a double play or "squeeze" situation. Most managerial decisions are tactical, normally involving individual substitutions or actions. Managers come and go without seriously disrupting the team's playing ability. Players can be transferred from one team to another with relative ease. Newcomers can carry out responsibilities without significant adjustments.

John Updike summed it up very well: "Of all the team sports, baseball, with its graceful intermittence of action, its immense and tranquil field sparsely salted with poised men in white, its dispassionate mathematics, seemed to be best suited to accommodate, and be ornamented by, a loner. It is an essentially lonely game" (Keidel, 1984, pp. 14–15).

Football

American football is a different story. Compared to a baseball team, players perform in close proximity to one another. Linemen and offensive backs can hear and often see or touch one another. Each play involves every player on the field. Efforts are sequentially linked. Actions of linemen pave the way for the movements of backs; a defensive team's field position becomes the starting point for the offense, and vice versa. In transitions from offense to defense, specialty platoons play a pivotal role (Keidel, 1984). Unlike baseball, the efforts of individual players are tightly coordinated. George Allen, coach of the Washington Redskins, put it this way: "A football game is a lot like a machine. It's made up of parts. If one part doesn't work, one player pulling against you and not doing his job, the whole machine fails" (Keidel, 1984, p. 9).

Because of the interdependence among parts, a football team must be well integrated, a situation achieved mainly through planning and hierarchical control. The primary units of coordination are the offensive, defensive, and specialty platoons, each with its own coordinator. Under the direction of the head coach, the team uses scouting reports and other surveillance to develop a strategy or game plan in advance. During the game, strategic decisions are typically made by the head coach. Tactical decisions are made by assistants or by designated players on either offense or defense (Keidel, 1984).

A football team's systemic characteristics make it hard to swap players from one team to another. Irv Cross of the Philadelphia Eagles once remarked, "An Eagles player could never make an easy transition to the Dallas Cowboys; the system and philosophies are just too different" (Keidel, 1984, p. 15). Coaches are not easily replaced. Tom Landry, Vince Lombardi, and Don Shula led their Cowboys, Packers, and Dolphins teams to many victories over the years. Their success was rooted significantly in their ability to create a well-coordinated team from available talent. Unlike baseball, sound strategy and tightly meshed execution are necessary ingredients in winning at football (Keidel, 1984).

Basketball

Basketball players perform in even closer proximity than football players. In quick, rapidly moving transitions (if any at all), offense becomes defense—with the same players. Efforts of basketball players are highly reciprocal; each player depends on the efforts of all others. Every player may be involved with any of the other four. Anyone can handle the ball or attempt to score.

Basketball teams require high levels of mutual adjustment. Everyone is on the move, often in a spontaneous rather than predetermined direction. A successful basketball season depends heavily on a flowing relationship among team members who "read" and anticipate one another's moves. Players who are together a long time develop a sense of what each will do in various circumstances. A team of newcomers experiences difficulty in adjusting to individual predispositions or quirks. Keidel (1984) notes that coaches serve as integrators whose periodic interventions reinforce team cohesion. They help players coordinate laterally. Unlike baseball teams, basketball teams cannot function as a collection of individual stars. Unlike football, there are no platoons. Basketball is wholly a group effort. After a talented group of Philadelphia 76ers lost to a more cohesive Portland Trailblazers team, Bill Bradley commented, "Maybe someday a team will have so much individual fire power that on that alone it can win a championship. It hasn't happened yet" (Keidel, 1984, p. 12).

Determinants of Successful Teamwork

Successful teamwork is not governed by a universal set of principles applicable across the board. The right structure depends on what a team is trying to do. All games are not the same, nor are tasks and environments in different settings the same. Keidel (1984) suggests several important questions in determining an appropriate structural design:

1. What is the nature and degree of task-related interaction among unit members?
2. What is the geographic distribution of unit members?
3. Given a group's objectives and constraints, where does autonomy reside?
4. How is coordination achieved?
5. What words best describe the required structure—conglomerate, mechanistic, or organic?
6. What sports expression metaphorically captures the task of management—filling out the line-up card, preparing the game plan, or influencing the game's flow?

Outside the field of sports, even within the same organization, team structures vary. As an example, a senior research manager in a pharmaceutical firm observed a structural progression in the discovery and development of a new drug: "The process moves through three distinct stages. It's like going from baseball to football to basketball" (Keidel, 1984, p. 11). In basic research, individual scientists work independently to develop a body of knowledge. As in baseball, individual efforts are the norm. Once identified, a promising drug passes from developmental chemists to pharmacy researchers to toxicologists. If the drug receives preliminary federal approval, it moves to clinical researchers for experimental tests. These sequential relationships are reminiscent of play sequences in football. In the final stage—"new drug application"—physicians, statisticians, pharmacists, pharmacologists, toxicologists, and chemists work closely and reciprocally to win final approval from the Food and Drug Administration. Their efforts resemble the closely linked and flowing patterns of a basketball team (Keidel, 1984).

Team Structure and Top Performance

The commando team whose exemplary performance was linked to the group's social architecture is not an isolated example. Team performance in general is tied to how well a group matches task and structure. Katzenbach and Smith (1993) interviewed hundreds of people on more than fifty different teams in developing their book *The Wisdom of Teams*. Their sample encompassed thirty enterprises in diverse settings (including Motorola, Hewlett-Packard, Operation Desert Storm, and the Girl Scouts). They drew a clear distinction between undifferentiated "groups" and sharply focused "teams": "A team is a small number of people with complementary skills who are committed to a common purpose, set of performance goals, and approach for which they hold themselves mutually accountable" (p. 112).

High-Performing Teams

Katzenbach and Smith's research highlights the importance of structure to exemplary team performance. They noted six distinguishing characteristics of high-performing teams.

1. *High-performing teams shape purpose in response to a demand or an opportunity placed in their path, usually by higher management.* Top managers clarify the team's charter, rationale, and challenge while providing flexibility for the team to work out specific goals and plans of operation. By giving a team clear authority and then staying out of the way, management releases collective energy and creativity.

2. *High-performing teams translate common purpose into specific, measurable performance goals.* Purpose outlines the mission, but successful teams take the additional step of recasting purpose into specific and measurable performance goals: "If a team fails to establish specific performance goals or if those goals do not relate directly to the team's overall purpose, team members become confused, pull apart, and revert to mediocre performance. By contrast, when purpose and goals are built on one another and are combined with team

commitment, they become a powerful engine of performance" (Katzenbach and Smith, 1993, p. 113). Specific goals define collective "work products," facilitate clear communication and constructive conflict, keep the team focused on getting results, and provide a yardstick for gauging small wins along the way.

3. *High-performing teams are of manageable size.* Katzenbach and Smith (1993) fix the optimal size for an effective team somewhere between two and twenty-five people: "Ten people are far more likely than fifty to work through their individual, functional, and hierarchical differences toward a common plan and to hold themselves jointly accountable for the results" (p. 114).

4. *High-performing teams develop the right mix of expertise.* The structural frame stresses the critical link between specialization and expertise. Effective teams seek out the full range of necessary technical fluency: "Product development teams that include only marketers or engineers are less likely to succeed than those with the complementary skills of both" (Katzenbach and Smith, 1993, p. 115). In addition, exemplary teams find and reward expertise in problem solving, decision making, and interpersonal skills to keep the group focused, on task, and free of debilitating personal squabbles.

5. *High-performing teams develop a common commitment to working relationships.* "Team members must agree on who will do particular jobs, how schedules will be set and adhered to, what skills need to be developed, how continuing membership in the teams is to be earned, and how the group will make and modify decisions" (Katzenbach and Smith, 1993, p. 115). Effective teams take the time to explore who is best suited for a particular task as well as how individual roles will come together. How structural clarity is achieved varies from team to team, but it takes more than an organization chart that identifies general roles and pinpoints one's place in the official hierarchy. Most teams require a more detailed understanding of who is going to do what and how people relate to each other in carrying out diverse tasks. One possibility is to use responsibility charting (Galbraith, 1977). Responsibility charting provides a framework and a language for hammering out how people will work together. For a given task, responsibility is assigned to the individual or group with overall accountability. The next step is to outline how that role relates to others on the team. Does someone need to approve the actions of the responsible person? Are there people who

need to be consulted? Are there others who must be kept informed? Whatever form it takes, an effective team "establishes a social contract among members that relates to their purpose and guides and obligates how they will work together" (Katzenbach and Smith, 1993, p. 116).

6. *Members of high-performing teams hold themselves collectively accountable.* Pinpointing individual responsibility is crucial to a well-coordinated effort, but effective teams find ways to hold the collective accountable. "Teams enjoying a common purpose and approach inevitably hold themselves responsible, both as individuals and as a team, for the team's performance" (Katzenbach and Smith, 1993, p. 116).

A focused, cohesive structure is a foundation for high-performing teams. Even highly skilled people zealously pursuing a shared mission will falter and fail if group structure continually generates confusion and frustration.

Saturn: The Story Behind the Story

The Saturn Corporation's top performance in achieving high quality, consumer satisfaction, and customer loyalty has been widely recognized. What is the secret of the company's success? Very often credit is given to its sophisticated technology or its enlightened approach to managing people. Both are important. On the technology side, Saturn makes extensive use of computers and deploys robots for many repetitive or dangerous jobs. Its human resources practices emphasize training, conflict management, and extensive employee participation. Yet it is too easy to overlook Saturn's distinctive team structure as an important element of its achievements.

Companywide, Saturn employees are granted authority to make decisions within a few and flexible guidelines. Restrictive rules and ironclad, top-down work procedures were left behind as the company moved away from what employees call the "old world" of General Motors.

Early in the company's history a new manager imported from General Motors was walking the line and noticed an assembly worker standing beside a pile of parts. He asked the employee why the parts were not being used. The worker replied that they did not meet quality standards. The manager ordered him to use the parts anyway. The worker refused. "Very quickly the UAW president and a top manager came to the scene. They flat out told [the manager] that things aren't done that way here at Saturn and that he'd better learn his job. To which the manager replied, 'What is my job?' The union president retorted, 'That's for you to discover'" (Deal and Jenkins, 1994, p. 244).

At Saturn, engineers and assembly-line workers work together to solve problems and design manufacturing processes. Relationships between UAW (United Automobile Workers) and Saturn management are cordial and cooperative, governed by an official agreement one page in length.

Most of the actual assembly of the Saturn automobile is done by teams. One hundred fifty-five production teams of eight to fifteen cross-trained, highly interdependent workers put the car together on a half-mile-long assembly line. The old system of sequential, repetitive efforts by isolated individuals is a thing of the past. Saturn has created "a work environment where people provide leadership for themselves and others. It is cooperation and self and team management that make Saturn tick. Problems are solved by people working together—they are not kicked upstairs for others to solve" (Deal and Jenkins, 1994, p. 230).

Across the subassembly groups—body systems, power train, and general assembly, operating in three shifts, twenty-four hours a day—Saturn teams exemplify the successful profile from *Wisdom of Teams*. The design of the car, corporate values, and quality standards are passed down from the executive suite. But each team translates broad objectives into measurable performance goals. Teams are empowered to deal with budget, safety procedures, ergonomics, vacations, time off, and other matters. In effect, each team manages its own business within general guidelines. An employee in body systems describes how it works on her team: "The working conditions are like running your own business. We decide when the shifts are, who starts where, break and eating times, and vacation schedules" (Deal and Jenkins, 1994, p. 242).

Saturn teams are of manageable size and are generally staffed with people who have the right mix of expertise to handle all aspects of the team's tasks. When necessary, additional expertise can be borrowed from other teams through a process called augmentation.

Saturn teams design their own working relationships. Prior to the beginning of a shift, team members confer in a team center for five or ten minutes. They determine the day's rotation. A team of ten people has ten jobs to do and typically rotates through jobs, unless a job involves heavy lifting or stress. If so, rotation occurs more frequently. Every week the plant shuts down, providing teams an opportunity to review quality standards, budget, safety, and the ergonomics of assembly. A WUC (work unit counselor) is designated as official team leader. These people typically rise through the ranks to assume the role. To demonstrate how much responsibility teams assume to define working relationships, an interior design team eliminated sixteen team jobs. In looking for ways to trim costs, the team identified an inefficient practice—walking too far to pick up parts for the assembly. Moving the parts closer to the line eliminated the extra distance but also made the extra positions unnecessary. The team—including those eventually moved to other positions at Saturn—made decisions about which positions would be eliminated.

Group accountability is also an accepted way of life for Saturn teams. People watch the numbers every day. At least $10,000 in salary is put at risk each year. When the company meets its performance objectives, everyone benefits. When it does not, everyone shares the loss.

Everyone at Saturn admits that things are not perfect. But there is general agreement that teams are learning from mistakes and constantly refining the structure of teamwork.

Summary

Every group will evolve structure as its members work together, but the design may or may not be effective. Though they are often blamed on individuals, many classic team problems arise from ill-fitting structures. Conscious attention to structure and roles can make an enormous difference in a group's performance. Many teams never learn the lesson of the commando team: vary the structure in response to changes in task and circumstance. A task force that meets to study a problem and develop a report will go through several phases, each calling for different patterns of roles, linkages, and interdependence. Loose, nonhierarchical forms may work extremely well in the early phases of goal setting and brainstorming, particularly if the group has enough time to work through the inevitable challenges in getting a new group started on any task.

Later phases of report writing and editing may require a more centralized and differentiated structure.

When a group encounters the inevitable vicissitudes of group life—such things as overload, conflict, confusion, communication gaps, or bungled handoffs—the members often pin the blame on each other. Few groups are blessed with flawless members, but many will find that it is much easier and more profitable to restructure the team than to reconstruct each member's personality.

Part Three

The Human Resource Frame

Chapter Six

People and Organizations

Home from the Korean War, David Swanson took a job with American consumer products giant Procter & Gamble. His joy in landing a good civilian job was short-lived. He was discouraged to find that P&G managed its production plants much as the U.S. Army managed combat units, with a strong emphasis on rank, command, and top-down control. The results were debilitating: militant unions, deep-seated mistrust, perennial labor-management antagonism. During a strike at one P&G plant, managers flown in as replacement workers never got beyond the airport. It was surrounded by union members in pickup trucks carrying shotguns. Swanson felt there must be a better way.

Swanson studied at MIT with Professor Douglas McGregor, one of few Americans in the 1950s who believed that workers actually *wanted* to be productive. McGregor felt that workers would be highly productive if management was smart enough to align jobs with workers' needs. Swanson retained him as a consultant to design a new P&G plant in Augusta, Georgia. They built the plant as an "open system" featuring then radical innovations: communication of both good and bad news, self-managing teams, and a peer-controlled pay system. The experiment became a huge success. "By the mid-1960s, and by almost any productivity measure Swanson and his colleagues could think of, Augusta was 30 percent more productive than any other P&G plant" (Waterman, 1994, p. 41).

McGregor's early efforts helped lay the foundation of the human resource frame. This perspective regards people's skills, attitudes, energy, and commitment as vital resources capable of either making or breaking an enterprise. We all know that organizations can be alienating, dehumanizing, and frustrating. Such conditions waste talent, distort lives, and sometimes convince individuals to fight back, devoting most of their time and effort to beating the system.

The human resource frame champions another possibility—that organizations can also be energizing, productive, and mutually rewarding. This possibility exists despite the widespread image of organizations as oppressive places dominated by callous and selfish bosses who care only about accumulating money and power. In Franz Kafka's novel *The Trial,* for example, the protagonist faces a mysterious, impersonal, unpredictable, and hostile system that destroys people at will, seemingly for no reason. Countless books and films follow Kafka's lead. There is a grain of contemporary truth in these fictional accounts. Waves of layoffs and downsizing in the 1980s reinforced workers' vulnerability in the face of economic and political forces over which they had little control. Sacrificing jobs for profits reinvigorated age-old images of insensitive and heartless organizations. America's fastest-growing cartoon strip in the early 1990s was "Dilbert," whose white-collar, cubicle-class hero wanders mindlessly through an office landscape of incompetent bosses, bureaucratic inertia, and corporate doublespeak.

Is the workplace really this bleak across the board? Are individuals simply pawns, sacrificed to collective purposes and casually cast aside when no longer needed? Is there hope that work will ever fully engage people's talent and energy? Such questions have intensified with globalization and the growth in size and power of modern institutions. How can people find freedom and dignity in a world dominated by economic fluctuations and an emphasis on short-term results? Answers are not easy. They require a sensitive understanding of people and their symbiotic relationship with organizations. The human resource frame is built on core assumptions that highlight this linkage:

1. Organizations exist to serve human needs rather than the reverse.
2. People and organizations need each other: organizations need ideas, energy, and talent; people need careers, salaries, and opportunities.
3. When the fit between individual and system is poor, one or both suffer: individuals will be exploited or will exploit the organization—or both will become victims.

4. A good fit benefits both: individuals find meaningful and satisfying work, and organizations get the talent and energy they
need to succeed.

People always want to know, "How well will this place fulfill my
needs?" Organizations universally ask, "How do we find and retain
people with the skills and attitudes needed to do the work?" This
chapter first examines the human side of organizations, how people's needs are satisfied or frustrated at work. Then we look at the
changing employment contract and its impact on both people and
organizations.

Human Needs

The concept of need is controversial. Some theorists argue that the
idea is too vague and refers to something difficult to observe. Others
say that whatever needs people might have are so variable and so
strongly influenced by the environment that the concept provides
little help in explaining how they behave (Salancik and Pfeffer,
1977). Despite this academic skepticism, needs are a central element in everyday psychology. Most parents worry about the needs
of their children, politicians pride themselves on responding to
needs of their constituents, and many managers try to meet the
needs of their workers. Common sense tells us that needs are important but is less clear about what they are.

A horticultural analogy may help clarify matters. Gardeners
know that every plant has "needs." Certain combinations of temperature, moisture, soil conditions, and sunlight allow any plant to
grow and flourish. Within their design limits, plants do their best
to get what they need. They orient leaves sunward to get more light
or sink roots deeper to get more water. A plant's capabilities generally increase with maturity. Highly vulnerable seedlings become
more self-sufficient as they grow (better able to fend off insects and
competition from other plants). These capabilities decline as the
plant nears the end of its life cycle.

Human needs are similar. Conditions or elements in the environment allow people to survive and evolve. Needs for oxygen, water,
and food are clear. The idea of universal psychic needs is more controversial. Many psychologists argue that certain psychological needs

are basic to being human (Maslow, 1954; McClelland, 1985; White 1960). Others argue that people are so shaped by environment, socialization, and culture that it is fruitless to talk about universal psychic needs.

In extreme forms, both nature and nurture arguments mislead us. No degree in psychology is needed to know that people are capable of enormous amounts of learning and adaptation and that they are influenced by their surroundings. Nor do we need advanced training in biology to recognize that many individual differences are present at birth. Genes determine so many physical characteristics that it is surprising so many proponents of the nurture view are wedded to their argument that behavioral differences are *always* caused by environmental factors.

An emerging consensus sees human behavior as resulting from the interplay between heredity and environment. Genes determine initial potential and predispositions. Subsequent learning profoundly modifies and sometimes reverses the original instructions. The nature-nurture seesaw suggests a more powerful way of thinking about human needs. A need can be defined as a genetic predisposition to prefer some experiences over others. Needs energize and guide behavior and vary in strength at different times. We enjoy the company of others yet sometimes want to be alone. Since the genetic instructions cannot anticipate all the situations an individual will encounter, both the form and the expression of each person's needs will be significantly modified by experiences after birth.

What Needs Do People Have?

The existential psychologist Abraham Maslow (1954) developed one of our most influential theories about needs. He started with the notion that people are motivated by a variety of wants, some more fundamental than others. The desire for food dominates the lives of the chronically hungry, but other motives drive people with enough to eat. Maslow grouped human needs into five basic categories, arrayed in a hierarchy:

1. Physiological (needs for oxygen, water, food, physical health, and comfort)
2. Safety (to be safe from danger, attack, and threat)

3. Belongingness and love (needs for positive and loving relationships with other people)
4. Esteem (to feel valued and to value oneself)
5. Self-actualization (needs to develop to one's fullest, to actualize one's potential)

In Maslow's view, basic needs for physiological well-being and safety are "prepotent"—they have to be satisfied first. Once lower needs are satisfied, individuals are motivated by higher needs of belongingness, esteem, and self-actualization. The order is not ironclad. Parents may sacrifice themselves for their children, and martyrs sometimes give their lives for a cause. Maslow believed that such reversals occurred when lower needs had been so well satisfied early in life that they receded into the background later on.

Attempts to validate Maslow's theory have proved inconclusive (Alderfer, 1972; Lawler and Shuttle, 1973; Schneider and Alderfer, 1973). The skimpy evidence has turned many academics skeptical, but Maslow's view is still widely accepted and enormously influential among managers. Take, for example, the advice that Federal Express's *Manager's Guide* offers employees: "Modern behavioral scientists such as Abraham Maslow . . . have shown that virtually every person has a hierarchy of emotional needs, from basic safety, shelter, and sustenance to the desire for respect, satisfaction, and a sense of accomplishment. Slowly these values have appeared as the centerpiece of progressive company policies, always with remarkable results" (Waterman, 1994, p. 92).

Theory X and Theory Y

David Swanson's professor, Douglas McGregor (1960), built on Maslow's theory by adding another central idea: that managers' assumptions about people tend to become self-fulfilling prophesies. McGregor argued that most managers harbor so-called Theory X assumptions—a set of beliefs advocating that subordinates are passive and lazy, have little ambition, prefer to be led, and resist change. Most conventional management practices, in his view, were built on either hard or soft versions of Theory X. The hard version emphasizes coercion, tight controls, threats, and punishments. Over time, it generates low productivity, antagonism, militant unions, and subtle sabotage. Soft versions of Theory X try to avoid conflict and satisfy everyone's needs. The usual result is superficial harmony with undercurrents of apathy and indifference. Either hard or soft Theory X approaches become self-fulfilling: if you treat people as if they're lazy and need to be directed, they conform to your expectations. Old-line managers often pointed to years of experience proving that Theory X was the only way to get anything done because workers "are never satisfied" and "just don't seem to give a damn."

McGregor argued a different view, which he called Theory Y. Maslow's hierarchy of needs provided the foundation:

> We recognize readily enough that a man suffering from a severe dietary deficiency is sick. The deprivation of physiological needs has behavioral consequences. The same is true—although less well recognized—of deprivation of higher-level needs. The man whose needs for safety, association, independence, or status are thwarted is sick just as surely as the man who has rickets. And his sickness will have behavioral consequences. We will be mistaken if we attribute his resultant passivity, his hostility, his refusal to accept responsibility to his inherent human nature. These forms of behavior are symptoms of illness—of deprivation of his social and egoistic needs [McGregor, 1960, pp. 35–36].

Theory Y's key proposition is that "the essential task of management is to arrange organizational conditions so that people can achieve their own goals best by directing their efforts toward organizational rewards" (McGregor, 1960, p. 61). If individuals find no satisfaction in their work, management has little choice but to rely on Theory X and external control. Conversely, the more that managers align organizational requirements with employee self-interest, the more they can rely on the Theory Y principle of self-direction.

Personality and Organization

Like his contemporary McGregor, Chris Argyris (1957, 1964) also saw a basic conflict between human personality and the way in which organizations are typically structured and managed. Argyris argued that people have basic "self-actualization trends"—akin to plants' efforts to reach their biological potential. From infancy into adulthood, people advance from dependence to independence, from a narrow to a broader range of skills and interests. They move from a short time perspective (interests quickly developed and quickly forgotten, with little ability to anticipate the future) to much longer term horizons. The child's impulsivity and limited self-knowledge are replaced by more mature levels of self-awareness and self control.

Like McGregor, Argyris felt that organizations often treated workers like children rather than adults—a view eloquently expressed in a film mentioned earlier, Charlie Chaplin's *Modern Times.* In one scene, Chaplin's character works furiously on an assembly line, trying to tighten bolts on every piece that goes past. His time perspective can be measured in seconds. Skill requirements are minimal; he has almost no control over the pace of his work. An efficiency "expert" uses Chaplin as the guinea pig for a new machine designed to feed him lunch while he continues to tighten bolts. It goes haywire and begins to assault Chaplin with food. The film's message is clear—industrial organizations treat workers as much like infants as possible.

Argyris saw person-structure conflict built into traditional principles of organizational design and management. The structural concept of task specialization defines jobs as narrowly as possible to improve efficiency. But the rational logic often backfires. Consider the experience of autoworker Ben Hamper. As a child, he was first introduced to life on the automobile assembly line. His personal account of what it was like captures a story many other American workers could tell:

> I was seven years old the first time I ever set foot inside an automobile factory. The occasion was Family Night at the old Fisher Body plant in Flint where my father worked the second shift. If nothing else, this annual peepshow lent a whole world of credence to our father's daily grumble. The assembly line did indeed stink. The noise was very close to intolerable. The heat was one complete bastard. . . .
>
> After a hundred wrong turns and dead ends, we found my old man down on the trim line. His job was to install windshields using this goofy apparatus with large suction cups that resembled an octopus being crucified. A car would nuzzle up to the old man's work area and he would be waiting for it, a cigarette dangling from his lip, his arms wrapped around the windshield contraption as if it

might suddenly rebel and bolt off for the ocean. Car, windshield. Car, windshield. Car, windshield. No wonder my father preferred playin' hopscotch with barmaids [Hamper, 1992, pp. 1–2].

Following in his father's and grandfather's footsteps, Ben Hamper became an autoworker. He soon discovered a familiar pattern. Though his career began twenty years after Argyris and McGregor questioned the fallacies of traditional management techniques, little had changed. Hamper held down a variety of jobs, each as mindless and repetitious as the next. "The one thing that was impossible to escape was the monotony. Every minute, every hour, every truck, and every movement was a plodding replica of the one that had gone before" (Hamper, 1992, p. 41).

Specialization, as we saw in Chapter Three, calls for a clear chain of command to coordinate discrete jobs. Bosses direct and control people at lower levels, potentially encouraging passivity and dependence, conditions Argyris considered fundamentally in conflict with the needs of healthy human beings. The conflict worsens as one moves down the hierarchy—more mechanized jobs, more directives, and tighter controls. As people mature, the conflict intensifies. Argyris argued that employees inevitably look for ways to respond to these frustrations. He identified six of them.

1. *They withdraw—through chronic absenteeism or simply by quitting.* Ben Hamper chronicled many examples of absenteeism and quitting, including his friend Roy, who lasted only a couple of months:

My pal Roy was beginning to unravel in a real rush. His enthusiasm about all the money we were makin' had dissipated and he was having major difficulty coping with the drudgery of factory labor. He wallowed in the slow-motion injustice of the time clock. His job, like mine, wasn't difficult. It was just plain monotonous. . . .

The day before he quit, he approached me with a box-cutter knife sticking out of his glove and requested that I give him a slice across the back of the hand. He felt sure this ploy would land him a few days off. Since slicing Roy didn't seem like a solid career move, I refused. Roy went down the line to the other workers where he received a couple of charitable offers to cut his throat, but no dice on the hand. He wound up sulking back to his job. After that night, I never saw Roy again [Hamper, 1992, pp. 40, 43].

2. *They stay on the job but withdraw psychologically, becoming indifferent, passive, and apathetic.* Like many other workers, Ben Hamper didn't want to quit, so he looked for ways to cope with the tedium. His favorite was to "double up" by making a deal with another worker to take turns covering each other's job. This way it was even possible to work half a day and still receive full pay:

> What a setup. Dale and I would both report to work before the 4:30 horn. We'd spend a half hour preparing all the stock we'd need for the evening. At 5:00, I would take over the two jobs while Dale went to sleep in a makeshift cardboard bed behind our bench. He'd stuff some plugs into his ears, crawl into his bed, and often be sound asleep before I had even finished my first truck. I'd work the jobs from 5:00 until 9:24, the official lunch period. When the line stopped, I'd give Dale's cardboard coffin a good kick. It was time for the handoff. I would give my ID badge to Dale so that he could punch me out at quitting time [Hamper, 1992, p. 61].

If doubling up didn't work, workers invented other diversions like Rivet Hockey (kicking rivets as hard as possible into a coworker's foot or leg) or Dumpster Ball (kicking cardboard boxes high enough to clear a dumpster). And if games weren't enough, there was always alcohol: "Drinking right on the line wasn't something everyone cared for. But plenty did, and the most popular time to go snagging for gusto was the lunch break. As soon as that lunch horn blew, half of the plant put it in gear, sprinting out the door in packs of three or four, each pointed squarely for one of those chilly coolers up at one of the nearby beer emporiums" (Hamper, 1992, p. 56).

3. *They resist by restricting output, deception, featherbedding, or sabotage.* Hamper (1992) reports what happened when the company removed a popular foreman because he was "too close to his work force" (p. 205):

> With a tight grip on the whip, the new bossman started riding the crew. No music. No Rivet Hockey. No horseplay. No drinking. No card playing. No working up the line. No leaving the department. No doubling-up. No this, no that. No questions asked.
>
> No way. After three nights of this imported bullyism, the boys had had their fill. Frames began sliding down the line minus parts. Rivets became cross-eyed. Guns mysteriously broke down. The

repairmen began shipping the majority of the defects, unable to keep up with the repair load.

Sabotage was drastic, but it got the point across and brought the new foreman back into line. The boss's strong-arm tactics had engendered an equally strong reaction from workers. To succeed, the foreman had to fall into step. Otherwise, he would be replaced and the cycle would start anew.

4. *They try to climb the hierarchy to better jobs.* The problem with upward mobility as a way out is there often aren't enough "better" jobs to go around. Many workers are reluctant to take promotions anyway. Hamper (1992) reports what happened to a coworker who tried to crack down after he was promoted to foreman: "For the next eight days, we made Calvin Moza's short-lived career switch sheer hell. Every time he'd walk the aisle, someone would pepper his steps with raining rivets. He couldn't make a move without the hammers banging and loud chants of "suckass" and "brown snout" ringin' in his ears. He got everything he deserved. There was simply no room for pity when dealing with a hypocrite who was about as pure as freshly driven snot" (p. 208).

Hamper himself was lucky: he'd started to moonlight as a writer during one of the periodic layoffs punctuating his automaking career. Styling himself "The Rivethead," he wrote a column about factory life from the inside. His writing eventually led to a best-selling book. Most of his buddies weren't nearly as fortunate.

5. *They form groups (such as labor unions) to redress the power imbalance.* Argyris cautioned, however, that unions would probably be managed much like factories. In the long run, employees' sense of powerlessness would not change. Ben Hamper, like most autoworkers, was a union member, yet the union is largely invisible in his accounts of life on the assembly line. He rarely sought union help and even less often got any. Nothing in the labor agreement protected workers from boredom, frustration, or feeling powerless.

6. *They socialize their children to believe that work is unrewarding and hopes for advancement are slim.* Hamper's account of life on the line provides a vivid illustration for Argyris's contention that organizations treat adults like children. The company made halfhearted efforts to do otherwise: they assigned an employee to wander through the plant dressed in costume as "Howie Makem, the Quality Cat."

(Howie was mostly greeted with groans, insults, and an occasional flying rivet.) Message boards were plastered with inspirational words like "Riveting is fun." A usually invisible plant manager would give an annual speech promising to get around more to talk to workers. All this hypocrisy took its toll: "Working the Rivet Line was like being paid to flunk high school the rest of your life. An adolescent time warp in which the duties of the day were just an underlying annoyance. No one really grew up here. No pretensions to being anything other than stunted brats clinging to rusty monkeybars. The popular diversions—Rivet Hockey, Dumpster Ball, intoxication, writing, rock 'n' roll—were just reinventions of youth. We were fumbling along in the middle of a long-running cartoon" (Hamper, 1992, p. 185).

Researchers in the 1960s began to note that children of farmers grew up believing that hard work paid off, while children of urban blue-collar workers did not. As a result, many U.S. companies, such as Saturn, began to move facilities away from old industrial states like Michigan (where Ben Hamper worked) to more rural states like North Carolina and Tennessee in search of employees who still embodied the "work ethic." Argyris predicted, however, that industry would eventually demotivate even the most committed workforce unless management practices changed.

Argyris and MacGregor formed their views on observations of American organizations in the 1950s and 1960s.[1] Since then, investigators everywhere have documented similar conflicts between people and organizations. Orgogozo (1991), for example, contended that French management practices regularly caused workers to feel humiliation, boredom, anger, and exhaustion "because they have no hope of being recognized and valued for what they do" (p. 101). She depicted relations between superiors and subordinates in France as tense and distant because "bosses do everything possible to protect themselves from the resentment that they generate" (p. 73).

Early on, ideas of the human resource frame were often overlooked or ignored by scholars and practicing managers. The frame's influence has grown with the realization that misuse of human resources is bad for profits as well as for people. Legions of consultants, managers, and researchers have pursued answers to the vexing human problems of organization. In the process, they have developed a range of strategies for improving the fit between individuals and organizations. These will be discussed in depth in Chapter Seven.

Human Capacity and the Changing Employment Contract

The symbiotic relationship between individuals and organizations has evolved in response to changes in the needs and capabilities of both. Human resource pioneers focused primarily on aligning organizations to people in a world of old-line bureaucracies and relatively stable employment. The other side of this coin is how individuals align and realign their needs and skills to their workplace. Both sides of the person-organization relationship have become problematic as a result of dramatic trends pushing organizations simultaneously in two very different directions.

On the one hand, global competition, rapid technical change, and shorter product life cycles have produced a turbulent, intensely competitive environment that places an enormous premium on being "free, fast, and facile": "*Free* means having components (work units and people) that are autonomous and able to respond to problems and opportunities in market segments. *Fast* means having the capability to assess and respond quickly to these situations. *Facile* means being able to change thinking practices and established routines in the light of new information or developments" (Mirvis and Hall, 1996, p. 74).

Handy (1993) sees organizations adopting a "shamrock" form with three clusters of people: (1) a core group of managers and professionals with skills and capacities critical to the enterprise; (2) the basic workforce, "increasingly working part-time or in shifts to provide the necessary flexibility" (p. 366), and (3) a "contractual fringe" of people who do work that can be done more cheaply by outsiders. In the 1990s, more and more organizations have turned to downsizing, outsourcing, and reliance on part-time and temporary employees to cope with business fluctuations. In 1996, Volkswagen opened a new manufacturing plant in Brazil with 80 percent of the workforce employed by subcontractors. Volkswagen's CEO described it as a "dream factory" that would revolutionize auto manufacturing (Schemo, 1996, p. C1). Analysts disagreed whether the new factory was lean or merely mean. Even in Japan, traditional notions of lifetime careers began to erode in the face of "a bloated work force, particularly in the white collar sector, which proved to be an economic drag prolonging [Japan's] economic troubles" (WuDunn, 1996, p. 8). Around the world, employees looking for career advice encountered a set of new mantras:

Job security is dead.

There is no guarantee of employment, only of employability.

Everyone is self-employed (Hakim, 1994).

If you're searching for excellence, become excellent at searching for new jobs (Paul Hirsch, cited in Kanter, 1989).

Focus on learning and credibility rather than promotions (Kanter, 1989).

Meanwhile, some of the same global forces are also pushing in a different direction—toward a growing dependence on well-trained human capital. Organizations have become much more complex as a consequence of globalization and shifts to an information-intensive economy. More decentralized structures—like the networks discussed in Chapter Three or the spiderwebs described in Chapter Four—are proliferating in response to complexity and turbulence. These new configurations depend on higher levels of skill, intelligence, and commitment across a broader spectrum of employees. A network of decentralized decision nodes is a blueprint for disaster if decision makers lack the capacity or the desire to make sensible choices. Skill requirements have been changing so fast that individuals are hard pressed to keep up. The result is a troubling gap: organizations struggle to find people who bring the skills and qualities that they need while individuals with yesterday's skills face dismal job prospects. "The evidence is that skill problems in the U.S. work force are widespread and growing. Moreover, there is little evidence that U.S. employers, for the most part, are doing what is required to address this problem" (Pfeffer, 1994, p. 17).

The shift from a production-intensive to an information-intensive economy is not helping to close the gap. There used to be far more jobs that involve making *things*. In the first three decades after World War II, high-paying work in developed nations was heavily concentrated in blue-collar work (Drucker, 1993). These jobs generally required little formal training and few specialized skills but provided pay and benefits to sustain a reasonably comfortable and stable lifestyle. No more. Blue-collar workers accounted for more than one-third of the U.S. workforce in the late 1970s; by the mid-1990s, the percentage had dropped to less than one-fifth and was still declining (Handy, 1989; Drucker, 1993). Production jobs that survive often require much higher skill levels. When U.S. automobile manufacturers began to replace retiring older workers in the mid-1990s, they emphasized quick minds more than strong bodies and put applicants "through a grueling selection process that emphasized mental acuity and communication skills" (Meredith, 1996, p. 1).

Trying to increase both flexibility and employee skills simultaneously creates an increasingly vexing human resource dilemma. Should organizations seek flexibility and adaptability (through a downsized, outsourced, part-time workforce) or commitment and loyalty (through a long-term commitment to people)? Should they seek high skills (by hiring the best and training them well) or low costs (by hiring the cheapest and investing no more than necessary)?

Lean and Mean: More Benefits Than Costs?

Advantages of a smaller, more flexible workforce seem compelling: lower costs, higher efficiency, and greater flexibility in responding to fluctuations in the business cycle. Many economists and business analysts argued that U.S. competitive success in the 1980s was directly related to corporate willingness to shed unnecessary staff (Lynch, 1996). For some companies, it has worked well: "The formula of cutting staff and investing heavily in computerized equipment has paid off particularly in manufacturing, which enjoys a much greater productivity growth rate—more than 3 percent a year on average in the 1990s—than business as a whole. General Electric is a winner. So is the Chrysler Corporation. . . . Chrysler made 1.72 million cars in the United States [in 1995], the same as in 1988, but with 9,000 fewer workers. The departure of those workers meant that the remaining 93,700 produced more cars per hour" (Uchitelle, 1996, p. 1).

Yet even when downsizing works, it risks trading short-term gains for long-term decay. As mentioned in Chapter Two, "Chainsaw Al" Dunlap became a hero of the downsizing movement during his tenure as chief executive of Scott Paper, where he more than doubled profits and market value. His strategy? Cut people—half the managers, half of research and development, and a fifth of blue-collar workers. For good measure, he told managers not to get involved in community activities, eliminated all corporate contributions to charity, and moved company headquarters from Philadelphia (where it had been for more than a century) to Boca Raton, Florida (where Dunlap had a new home). Financial outcomes were impressive, but employee morale sank and Scott lost market share in every major product line. Dunlap did not stay around long enough to find out if he had sacrificed Scott's future for short-term gains. After less than two years on the job, he sold the company to its biggest competitor and walked away with almost $100 million for his efforts. On the same day that officials in Boca Raton received Dunlap's request for a $156,000 incentive grant for job creation, Scott's new owners announced that the Boca Raton headquarters would close (Byrne, 1996).

Companies eliminated millions of jobs in the 1980s and 1990s, many in middle management (Uchitelle and Kleinfeld, 1996; Pennar, 1996), yet firms found benefits elusive or nonexistent. A survey by the American Management Association found that less than half of the companies that downsized in the early 1990s went on to report higher profits subsequently (Gertz and Baptista, 1995). Gertz and Baptista (1995) found that cost cutting almost never led to profitable growth. Conversely, another survey found that stability rather than major change was characteristic of 90 percent of firms that outperformed the average in their industries over a ten-year period ("Fire and Forget," 1996). Markels and Murray (1996) reported that downsizing too often turned into "dumbsizing": "Many firms continue to make flawed decisions—hasty, across-the-board cuts—that come back to haunt them, on the bottom line, in public relationships, in strained relationships with customers and suppliers, and in demoralized employees." In shedding staff, firms too often found that they had also sacrificed knowledge, skill, and loyalty (Reichheld, 1993, 1996).

Downsizing and outsourcing also have a corrosive effect on employees' motivation and commitment. A 1996 poll found that 75 percent of U.S. workers felt that companies had become less loyal to their employees and 64 percent felt that employees were less loyal to their companies (Kleinfeld, 1996). Workers reported that the mood in the workplace was angrier and colleagues were more competitive. The resultant cynicism was palpable in many places. When Chemical Bank and Chase Manhattan went through a difficult merger in the mid-1990s, management tried to allay anxiety by publishing a periodic newsletter. Many employees found it "saccharine and platitudinous" (Kleinfeld, 1996, p. 8), and some skeptics began distributing their own more candid updates. One mock memo, ostensibly from the chief executive, offered the following answers to "frequently asked questions" (Kleinfeld, 1996, p. 8):

Q: Why am I being laid off, why is my career in ruins, why can't I sleep at night?
A: Your largely insignificant life is being sacrificed to bring into existence the best banking and financial services company in the world, bar none, without equal, post no bills, void where prohibited.
Q: When will I know if I'm being laid off?
A: You, you, you. Is that all you care about, you? Please understand that we need to think about "us," which probably doesn't include you. It's about time you started thinking about the greater whole, buddy. It should be an honor to be laid off.

All this foment has implications for both people and systems. For individuals, an age of downsizing and insecurity has personal and social costs: low wages, minimal benefits, job insecurity, stress, and burnout. Pfeffer (1994) and Lawler (1996) argue that a skilled and motivated workforce is a powerful source of strategic advantage precisely because few employers invest the time and resources to develop a cadre of committed, talented employees. The most successful company in the U.S. airline industry in the 1980s and 1990s, Southwest Airlines, had no particular advantage in terms of what it paid its employees but had an enormous cost advantage over its competitors because its highly committed workforce was far more productive. Competitors tried to imitate Southwest's approach but found that "the real difference is in the effort South-west gets out of its people. That is very, very hard to duplicate" (Labich, 1994, p. 52).

Investing in People

The picture is not altogether bleak, however. Many successful organizations have embraced creative and powerful ways to align individual and organizational needs. All these reflect core assumptions of the human resource frame and advocate treating the workforce as an investment rather than a cost. Waterman (1994) argues that a pervasive characteristic of high-performing companies is doing a better job of understanding and responding to the needs of both employees and customers. As a result, they attract better people who are motivated to do a superior job. The downward spiral now takes a more positive upward spin.

Ewing Kauffman grew a pharmaceutical business begun in a Kansas City basement into a multibillion-dollar company (Morgan, 1995). His approach was heavily influenced by his personal experiences as a young pharmaceutical salesman:

> I worked on straight commission, receiving no salary, no expenses, no car, and no benefits in any way, shape, or form—just straight commission. By the end of the second year, my commission amounted to more than the president's salary. He didn't think that was right, so he cut my commission. By then I was Midwest sales manager and had other salesmen working for me under an arrangement whereby my commission was three percent of everything they sold. In spite of the cut in my commission, that year I still managed to make more than the president thought a sales manager should make. So this time he cut the territory, which was the same as taking away some of my income. I quit and started Marion Laboratories.
>
> I based the company on a vision of what it would be. When we hired employees, they were referred to as "associates," and they shared in the success of the company. Once again, the two principles that have guided my entire career, which were based on my experience working for that very first pharmaceutical company, are these: "Those who produce should share in the profits," and "Treat others as you would be treated" [Kauffman, 1996, p. 40].

Few managers in 1950 shared Kauffman's faith, and there are still many skeptics in the human resource frame's assumptions half a century later. An urgent debate is under way about the future of the relationship between people and organizations. Some visions are apocalyptic: the "end of the job," a massive underclass of underemployed and unemployed, increasing polarization and social unrest (Rifkin, 1995). A more optimistic scenario depicts a continuing increase in the number of the world's organizations that recognize the importance of human assets and find their own version of Ewing Kauffman's principles for success.

Ben Hamper's employer, General Motors, began to recognize the challenge in the late 1960s at a time when the company's profits were declining even though sales were increasing. Just as Argyris and McGregor predicted, human resource issues were becoming increasingly expensive and difficult to manage. In 1972, GM's new plant at Lordstown, Ohio, became a notorious site of conflict between the individual and the system. Lordstown was GM's newest and most automated plant when it opened in 1970. It focused on sophisticated technology, rather than new approaches to engaging employees. A year later, new managers, brought in because the plant had failed to achieve production targets, added fuel to employee foment by eliminating people rather than fixing the people problems. They downsized the workforce and increased the workload of the employees who remained. Wages and benefits for survivors were excellent, but the grievance rate soon soared, from five hundred complaints a year to more than five hundred a month. Employee sabotage slowed or stopped the assembly line multiple times, and the local union finally voted to strike over working conditions. One of the major issues was "doubling up." Cars moved down the line at a rate of one hundred per hour, meaning that each worker normally had about thirty-six seconds to perform one job. Doubling up cut that to eighteen seconds. That was a fast pace, but like Ben Hamper, many employees preferred working faster with an occasional break to facing another car every half-minute all day long. Management tried to eliminate the practice for fear it would produce inferior work.

When employees were interviewed about the strike vote, they said that wages were not the issue: "The job pays good, but it's driving me crazy." "It's just like the army. No, it's worse than the army, 'cause you're welded to the line. You just about need a pass to piss."

After a costly wildcat strike at Lordstown, GM began to get the message. In 1973, three years after the strike, GM and the United Automobile Workers (UAW) signed a contract establishing the joint union-management National Committee to Improve the Quality of Working Life. Subsequently, GM joined Procter & Gamble and a growing list of corporations worldwide that invested heavily in improving human resource management (Maccoby, 1981; Kanter, 1983; Lawler, 1986; Deal and Jenkins, 1994). The results at GM and elsewhere have sometimes been dramatic. We will discuss some of the successes—and failures—in Chapter Seven, where we explore the state of the art in managing human assets.

Summary

The human resource frame stresses the relationship between people and organizations. Organizations need people (for their energy, effort, and talent), and people need organizations (for the many intrinsic and extrinsic rewards they offer), but their needs are not always well aligned. When the fit between people and organizations is poor, one or both suffers: individuals may feel neglected or oppressed, and organizations sputter because individuals withdraw their efforts or even work against organizational purposes. Conversely, a good fit benefits both: individuals find meaningful and satisfying work, and organizations get the talent and energy they need to succeed.

Global competition, turbulence, and rapid change have heightened an old organizational dilemma: Is it better to be lean and mean or to invest in people? A variety of strategies to reduce the workforce—downsizing, outsourcing, use of temporary and part-time workers—have been widely applied to reduce costs and increase flexibility. They risk a loss of talent and loyalty that leads to organizations that are mediocre, even if flexible. Emerging evidence suggests that downsizing has often produced disappointing results. Many highly successful organizations have gone in a different direction—investing in people on the premise that a highly motivated and skilled workforce is a powerful competitive advantage.

Note

1. Argyris, Maslow, McGregor, and their contemporaries built on a tradition with roots going back well into the nineteenth century. In *Capital*, Karl Marx (1887) posited his own version of a fundamental conflict between individual and organization. "The capitalist gets rich, not like the miser, in proportion to his personal labour and restricted consumption, but at the same rate as he squeezes out the labour-power of others, and enforces on the laborer abstinence from all life's enjoyments." Marx did not foresee the twentieth-century discovery that conflict and exploitation are fundamental issues in *organization*. That these problems were at least as severe in communist societies is illustrated by a joke popular among Soviet workers in the 1980s: "We pretend to work, and they pretend to pay us."

Chapter Seven

Improving Human Resource Management

Separated by centuries, Bill Gates (born in Seattle, 1955) and David Owen (born in Wales, 1771) never met but had much in common. Both were wildly successful entrepreneurs before the age of thirty. Both exploited the day's hot technology: software for Gates, spinning mills for Owen. Both were highly controversial. Gates, founder of Microsoft, the software powerhouse, was widely envied and feared for his wealth and his take-no-prisoners approach to competition. Owen was bitterly loathed and attacked for being the only capitalist of his time to conclude that it was not good for *business* to have eight-year-olds working thirteen-hour shifts in factories. At his knitting mill in New Lanark, Scotland, which he bought in 1799, Owen took a new approach:

> Owen provided clean, decent housing for his workers and their families in a community free of controllable disease, crime, and gin shops. He took young children out of his factory and put them in a school he founded. There he invented preschool, day care, and the brand of progressive education that stresses learning as a pleasurable experience (along with the first adult night school). . . .
> The entire business world was shocked when he prohibited corporal punishment in his factory and dumbfounded when he retrained his supervisors in humane disciplinary practices. While giving his workers an extremely high standard of living compared to other workers of the era, Owen was making a fortune at New Lanark. This conundrum drew twenty thousand visitors between 1815 and 1820 [O'Toole, 1995, pp. 201, 206].

Owen anticipated the growing importance of human capital and tried to convince fellow capitalists that investing in people could produce an even greater return than investing in machinery. Eager to spread his heretical philosophy, Owen left New Lanark and entered the political arena. He thereafter encountered continual frustration, ending, ultimately, in failure. Though he attracted a number of admirers (including Thomas Jefferson, Ralph Waldo Emerson, and Karl Marx), the business world rejected his ideas *in toto.* He was portrayed as a wild radical whose ideas would hurt the very people he hoped to help (O'Toole, 1995).

Owen was well ahead of his time: it was another century before many business leaders came to understand that investing in people was a key to organizational effectiveness. In the 1990s, waves of restructuring and downsizing raised age-old questions about the relationship between individuals and organizations. A number of persuasive reports suggested that Owen was right (Collins and Porras, 1994; Deal and Jenkins, 1994; Farkas and De Backer, 1996; Kotter and Heskett, 1992; Lawler, 1996; Levering and Moskowitz, 1993; Pfeffer, 1994; Waterman, 1994). Long-term business success centers on investing in employees and responding to their needs. Each report had a different emphasis, but all highlighted basic strategies for human resource management, summarized in Table 7.1.

Building a Human Resource Philosophy

Many, if not most, organizations either lack an explicit human resource philosophy or ignore the one they claim to have. Yet business success may hinge on a thoughtful, explicit philosophy of how to treat people. Federal Express explains its philosophy in the company's *Manager's Guide:* "Take care of our people; they in turn will deliver the impeccable service demanded by our customers who will reward us with the profitability necessary to secure our future. People-Service-Profit, these three words are the very foundation of Federal Express." These might be little more than words if FedEx were not so diligent about reinforcing its philosophy in practice. Managers are rated annually by subordinates on a leadership index that contains questions such as how well the manager helps subordinates, listens to their ideas, and respects them. Managers with subpar scores have to repeat the process in six months—a distinc-

Table 7.1.   Basic Human Resource Strategies.

Human Resource Strategy	Practices
Develop a long-term human resource philosophy	Build the philosophy into the corporate structure and incentives.
	Develop measures of human resource management.
Invest in people	Hire the right people and reward them well.
	Provide job security.
	Promote from within.
	Train and educate.
	Share the wealth (through gain sharing, ESOPs, employee ownership, and other means).
Empower employees and redesign their work	Provide autonomy and participation.
	Focus on job enrichment.
	Emphasize teamwork.
	Ensure egalitarianism and upward influence.

tion no one cherishes. There is a collective commitment to the index. If it falls below the corporate goal, the company's top three hundred managers lose their bonuses (Waterman, 1994).

Invest in People

An effective human resource philosophy provides overall guidance and direction. Principles come alive through activities and practices that make the commitment to investing in people a reality: hiring the right people and rewarding them.

Hiring Right and Rewarding Well

Strong companies are clear about the kinds of people they want and hire only those who fit. Nordstrom, an American retail chain, wants "customer service heroes" who will do whatever it takes to make a customer happy (Collins and Porras, 1994). Southwest Airlines looks for attitude and interpersonal skills, with particular emphasis on a sense of humor (Farkas and De Backer, 1996; Labich, 1994; Levering and Moskowitz, 1993). Microsoft's formidably intelligent CEO, Bill Gates, insists on "intelligence or smartness over anything else, even, in many cases, experience" (Stross, 1996, p. 162). A study of highly successful midsized companies in Germany (Simon, 1996) found that a carefully selected, highly motivated workforce was a key strength. Companies in Simon's sample had very little employee turnover—except among new hires: "Many new employees leave, or are terminated, shortly after joining the work force, both sides having learned that a worker does not fit into the firm's culture and cannot stand its pace" (p. 199).

To get people they want, selective companies offer attractive pay and benefits. Osterman (1995) found, for example, that firms with "high-commitment" human resource practices were more likely to offer work and family benefits such as day care and flexible hours. Such firms also build loyalty by providing opportunities for growth and development, including education and cross-training. Reichheld (1993, 1996) notes the linkage between employee loyalty and customer loyalty: "Employees who deal directly with customers day after day have a powerful effect on customer loyalty. It is with employees that the customer builds a bond of trust and expectations, and when those people leave, the bond is broken" (1993, p. 68). More generally, Lawler (1996) argues that employees' pay should reflect the value they add. Overpaying employees who add little value is a recipe for failure, but skilled, motivated, and involved employees can justify high pay by the contribution they make.

Providing Security

Job security in the 1990s seems an anachronism, a relic of the slow-moving, paternalistic days of lifelong employment. With job security depending on getting results in a highly competitive economy, how can any company make long-term commitments to its workforce? It is not easy and often impossible. Some companies that offered long-term employee security finally abandoned their commitment in the face of severe economic reversals (Delta Airlines and IBM are notable in recent years). Yet others have continued as conspicuous exemplars by making job security a cornerstone of their human resource philosophy. One of the most visible is Lincoln Electric, the world's largest manufacturer of arc welding equipment. Since 1914, Lincoln has honored a policy that no employee with more than three years of service would be laid off. In the 1980s, the company experienced a 40 percent year-to-year drop in demand for its products. Instead of laying people off, production workers were converted to salespeople. They canvassed businesses rarely reached by the company's regular distribution channels. "Not only did these people sell arc welding equipment in new places to new users, but since much of the profit of this equipment comes from the sale of replacement parts, Lincoln subsequently enjoyed greater market penetration and greater sales as a consequence" (Pfeffer, 1994, p. 47). Facing similar circumstances, Japan's Mazda had the same experience: "At the end of the year, when awards were presented to the best salespeople, the company discovered that the top ten were all former factory workers. They could explain the product effectively, and when business picked up, the fact that factory workers had experience talking to customers yielded useful ideas about product characteristics" (Pfeffer, 1994, p. 47).

Promoting from Within

Promoting from within offers several advantages: (1) it encourages both organization and employees to invest time and resources in upgrading skills, (2) it provides a powerful performance incentive, (3) it increases trust and loyalty, (4) it capitalizes on the knowledge and skills of veteran employees, and (5) it reduces serious errors by newcomers unfamiliar with history and proven ways. Collins and Porras (1994), for example, found that highly successful corporations almost never hired a chief executive from the outside. Less effective companies did so regularly.

Training and Education

As products, markets, and organizations become more complicated, the value of knowledgeable employees increases. Knowledge and skill deficits hurt organizations in many ways: shoddy quality, poor service, higher costs, and costly mistakes. Pfeffer (1994), for example, reports that a very high proportion of accidents in the petrochemical industry in the 1990s have involved contract employees.

Yet organizations often fail to invest in their human capital. Training costs are immediate and easy to measure; benefits are more elusive and longer term. Training temporary or contract workers carries added disincentives. Still, some companies report sizable returns on investments in training. Motorola found a gain of $29 for every dollar invested in sales training (Waterman, 1994).

Sophisticated organizations also recognize that learning must occur on the job as well as in classrooms. Carnaud in France, the world's third largest packaging company, puts great emphasis on creating a learning organization: "Learning in an organization takes place when three elements are in place: good mentors who teach others, a management system that lets people try new things as much as possible, and a very good exchange with the environment" (Aubrey and Tilliette, 1990, pp. 144–145). Carnaud's chief executive, Jean-Marie Descarpentries, felt that the biggest flaw in managers was being less aggressive and systematic about learning than they needed to be.

Sharing the Wealth

Many employees feel little responsibility for an organization's success. They expect any gains in efficiency and profitability to benefit only executives and shareholders. Organizations have devised a variety of ways to link employee rewards more directly to corporate productivity, including gain sharing, profit sharing, and employee stock ownership. Scanlon plans, first introduced in the 1930s, gave workers an incentive to reduce costs and improve efficiency by offering a share of any gains. Profit-sharing plans gave employees a bonus commensurate with the overall profitability of the firm or of their local unit. A review of research in the area found that both gain-sharing and profit-sharing plans generally had a positive impact on organizational performance and profitability. Kanter (1989) suggests that gain-sharing plans spread slowly because they require significant organizational changes: cross-unit teams, suggestion systems, and, particularly, much more open and complete communication of financial information to employees.

Some of the same barriers have slowed the progress of employee stock ownership plans (ESOPs). "Evidence shows that, to be effective, ownership has to be combined with ground-floor efforts to involve employees in decisions through schemes such as work teams and quality-improvement groups. Many companies have been doing this, of course, including plenty without ESOPs. But employee-owners often begin to expect rights that other groups of shareholders have: a voice in broad corporate decisions, board seats, and voting rights. And that's where the trouble can start, since few executives seem comfortable with this level of power-sharing" (Bernstein, 1996, p. 101).

Though some ESOPs have struggled, particularly when the company encounters business reverses, others have thrived. After United Airlines's employees took 15 percent pay cuts in exchange for 55 percent of the company and three of its twelve board seats in 1994, the company's stock more than doubled in the next two years. United made impressive gains in profits, productivity, and market share following the employee buyout (Chandler, 1996).

Bonus and profit-sharing plans spread rapidly in the 1980s. Top managers were much more likely than other employees to be the beneficiaries, but many highly successful firms spread the plans more widely. The plans could make awards based on overall corporate performance, subunit performance, or some mixture of the two. They can also be targeted to specific priorities, such as innovation and developing new businesses. In the 1980s, for example, one company developed an approach to new business units that gave people a choice of three different compensation schemes with different risk-to-reward ratios: the most conservative was just to draw a salary, and the riskiest let participants invest part of their salary in the venture, thereby increasing the potential reward. As word got out, ideas for new ventures began to flow in to the managers in charge of the program. They've been funding about one of every 250 ideas (Kanter, 1989). Some skeptics note a significant downside risk to profit-sharing plans: they may work well so long as there are rewards but may breed disappointment and anger if the company experiences a financial downturn. Should employees share losses as well as gains?

Empowerment and Redesign of Work

A solid human resource philosophy and a significant investment in people are necessary but not sufficient conditions for fully engaging employees. The work itself still needs to provide opportunities for autonomy, influence, and intrinsic rewards.

Autonomy and Participation

McGregor, Argyris, and other human resource scholars argue that traditional management patterns force employees to be dependent on superiors and give them little control over their work. Adults are often treated like children. A popular human resource remedy is *participation*—giving workers more opportunity to influence decisions about their work and working conditions. The results can be remarkable.

A classic illustration comes from a group of manual workers— all women—who painted dolls in a toy factory (Whyte, 1955). In a reengineered process, each woman took a toy from a tray, painted it, and put it on a passing hook. The women received an hourly rate, a group bonus, and a learning bonus. Although management expected little difficulty with the new system, production was disappointing and morale even poorer. Workers complained that the room was too hot and the hooks moved too fast.

Reluctantly, the foreman followed a consultant's advice to meet face to face with the employees. After hearing the women's complaints, the foreman agreed to bring in fans. Though he and the industrial engineer who designed the original manufacturing process expected no benefit, the fans led to a significant improvement in morale. Discussions continued, and after several meetings, the employees came up with a radical suggestion—let them control the belt's speed. The engineer argued vehemently against this suggestion. He had already carefully calculated the optimal speed. The foreman was also skeptical but, against the engineer's protests, agreed to give the women's suggestion a try. The employees developed a complicated production schedule—start slow at the beginning of the day, increase the speed once they had warmed up, slow it down before lunch, and so on.

Results of this inadvertent experiment in participation were stunning. Morale skyrocketed. Production increased far beyond the engineer's most optimistic calculations. The women's bonuses escalated so much that they were earning more than many workers with significantly higher levels of skill and experience. The experiment ended unhappily. The women's production and high pay became disruptive. Workers in the rest of the plant protested. To restore harmony, management reverted to the engineer's earlier recommendation: a fixed speed for the belt. Production plunged, morale plummeted, and most of the women quit.

Worldwide, examples of successful participative management experiments have multiplied. A Venezuelan example is illustrative. Historically, the nation's health care was provided by a two-tier system: small, high-quality, private health care for the affluent, a large, public system for everyone else. The public system, operated by the national ministry of health, was in a state of continual crisis. It suffered from overcentralization, chronic deficits, poor hygiene, decaying facilities, and theft of everything from cotton balls to X-ray machines (Palumbo, 1991).

A small group of health care providers founded Ascardio to provide cardiac care in one part of rural Venezuela (Palumbo, 1991; Malavé, 1995). Participative management helped Ascardio become an extraordinary success with remarkably high standards of patient care: "The Ascardio style requires, beyond mastery of a technical specialty, the willingness to get involved in an environment of team decision making instead of working in isolation. This is particularly evident in the General Assembly, which brings together doctors, technical personnel, workers, board members, and community representatives (none of whom are physicians). In its monthly meetings, the Assembly discusses everything from the poor performance of a doctor to the repercussions of giving salary increases decreed by the President of Venezuela" (Malavé, 1995, p. 16).

Research on participation shows it to be one of few ways to increase morale and productivity simultaneously (Blumberg, 1968; Katzell and Yankelovich, 1975; Levine and Tyson, 1990). But even when it works, participation often creates the need for systemic changes resisted by other parts of the organization. Moreover, participative management is often more rhetoric than reality (Argyris and Schön, 1974; Bolman, 1975). Efforts at fostering participation have failed for two main reasons: (1) the difficulties of designing workable participative systems, and (2) managers' ambivalence—they espouse participation but fear that subordinates will abuse it. As a result, managers mandate participation in a controlling, top-down fashion, a contradiction that virtually guarantees failure.

Job Enrichment and Cross-Utilization

In his pioneering research, Frederick Herzberg (1966) asked employees to talk about their best and worst work experiences. "Good feelings" stories featured achievement, recognition, responsibility, advancement, and learning. Herzberg called these *motivators*. "Bad feelings" stories centered around company policy and administration, supervision, and working conditions. Herzberg gave them the label *hygiene factors*. Motivators deal mostly with the work itself; hygiene factors cluster around the work context. Attempts to motivate workers with better pay and fringe benefits, improved working conditions, communications programs, or human relations training missed the point, said Herzberg. He called such efforts "KITA motivators"—the belief a kick in the tail is the best way to get things done. Herzberg saw job enrichment as central to motivation. He distinguished enrichment from simply adding more dull tasks to a tedious job. Enrichment meant giving workers more freedom and authority, more feedback, and greater challenges while making them more accountable and letting them use more skills.

Hackman and his colleagues (Hackman and Oldham, 1980) extended Herzberg's ideas by identifying three critical factors in job redesign: "Individuals need (1) to see their work as meaningful and worthwhile, more likely when jobs produce a visible and useful 'whole,' (2) to use discretion and judgment so they can feel personally accountable for results, and (3) to receive feedback about their efforts so they can improve" (Hackman, Oldham, Janson, and Purdy, 1987, p. 320).

Experiments with job redesign have grown significantly over the last several decades. Many efforts have been successful, some resoundingly so (Kopelman, 1985; Lawler, 1986; Pfeffer, 1994). Typically, job enrichment has a stronger impact on quality than on productivity—probably there is more satisfaction in doing work well than in simply doing more work (Lawler, 1986). Most workers prefer redesigned jobs, though some still like the old ways better. Hackman emphasized that employees with "high growth needs" would welcome job enrichment, while others with "low growth needs" would not.

Recent years have witnessed a gradual reduction in dull, routine, and unchallenging jobs. Such work is either redesigned or turned over to machines and computers. But significant obstacles block the progress of job enlargement, and monotonous jobs will not disappear soon. There are several barriers, including lingering assumptions from the structural frame that jobs should be organized around technical imperatives and that repetition makes people more efficient. Another barrier is the durability of the belief that workers produce more in a Theory X environment. A third barrier is economic. Many jobs cannot be altered significantly without major investments in redesigning physical plant and machinery.

A fourth barrier was illustrated in the doll manufacturing experiment. When it works, job enrichment leads to pressures for more basic systemwide changes. Workers on enriched jobs often develop higher opinions of themselves. They may come to demand more from the organization—sometimes increased benefits, sometimes new career opportunities and training for new tasks (Lawler, 1986).

Teaming

One systemic limit to job enrichment is that individuals typically contribute only a small part of a product or service. No one would seriously propose designing automobile plants as collections of self-contained boutiques in which a single worker builds an entire vehicle. Meaningful work redesign becomes possible only when responsibility is given to autonomous or self-managing work groups. Early research on autonomous teams flourished in Scandinavia under the guidance of Einar Thorsrud (1977, 1984; Lawler, 1986). Now more and more firms around the world (including Cummins Engine, Procter & Gamble, and Saturn in the United States; software powerhouse SAP in Germany; and Matsushita and Toyota in Japan) are experimenting with autonomous teams. Some experiments have been conducted in existing manufacturing plants, others in facilities redesigned from the outset to accommodate work teams.

The central idea is assigning to groups of people responsibility for a meaningful whole—a product, subassembly, or complete service—with ample autonomy and resources and collective accountability for results. Teams meet regularly to discuss and decide work assignments, scheduling, and current production. Supervision typically rests with a team leader, either appointed or left to emerge from the group. Levels of discretion vary. At one extreme, a team may have authority to hire, fire, determine pay rates, specify work methods, and manage inventory. Decisions are made with the assistance of a computerized system providing up-to-date information on the team's results. In other cases, the team's scope of decision making is more narrow—typically focusing on issues of production, quality, and work methods.

The team concept rarely works unless accompanied by ample training. Workers need to learn group skills and a broader range of technical skills so that each person understands and can perform someone else's job. "Pay for skills" often gives teams an incentive to keep expanding the range of competencies:

> At Topeka's General Foods pet food plant . . . new employees are paid a starting rate, and then advance one pay grade for each job they learn. All jobs earn equal amounts of additional pay, and they can be learned in any sequence. . . . All in all, pay for skills is a clever approach. It stresses individual responsibility but does not have the drawbacks of other pay-for-performance systems that pit team member against team member in contention for the highest ratings. Because there is no limit to the number of people who can reach the highest pay levels, there is little formal inducement to maintain a monopoly of skills or withhold training from newcomers in order to preserve a superior position [Kanter, 1989, pp. 248–249].

Democracy and Egalitarianism

Participative management is often viewed as a matter of style and climate rather than as a way to share authority. Managers—whether participative or not—still make the decisions. Broader, more egalitarian sharing of power is resisted around the world. Managers have particularly resisted organizational democracy—the idea of building worker participation into the formal structure and thus protecting it from managerial discretion. Most U.S. firms report one or another form of employee involvement, but many are approaches (like suggestion boxes or quality circles) that "do not fundamentally change the level of decision-making authority extended to the lowest levels of the organization" (Ledford, 1993, p. 148). Pfeffer (1994) and Ledford (1993) both observe that techniques for workforce involvement are less visible in American companies than evidence of their effectiveness would warrant. A number of

European nations have attempted to make workplaces democratic. Both Sweden and Norway legally mandated worker participation in decision making in the 1970s. In 1977, Norway passed a law against alienating and dehumanizing jobs and requiring quality-of-work-life (QWL) councils in Norwegian firms (Elden, 1983, 1986). Major Scandinavian corporations pioneered efforts to democratize and improve the quality of work life. In Kalmar, Sweden, Volvo built one of the world's first plants designed to accommodate self-managing work groups.

The Brazilian manufacturer Semco provides a dramatic illustration of organizational democracy in action (Semler, 1993). Workers hire new employees, evaluate their bosses, and vote on all major decisions. In one instance, employees outvoted CEO Ricardo Semler to prevent him from acquiring a company he wanted to buy. Conversely, the workforce also voted to buy an abandoned factory Semler didn't want. The workers proceeded to make the new plant a remarkable success. Semco's experiments produced dramatic gains in productivity, and the company was repeatedly rated the best place to work in Brazil.

Industrial democracy has been viewed in two ways: as an enormously powerful timely idea or as an unrealistic, overrated fad. The truth is somewhere in between. Like almost any significant organizational change, organizational democracy produces an initial decline in effectiveness. But long-term results show either a gain in productivity or maintenance of the status quo. Workers almost always prefer more power to less, and democratization is hard to reverse. When workers gain influence, they often want more. But despite the evidence, many managers and union leaders continue to oppose the idea.

Managers resist democracy for fear of losing prerogatives they currently enjoy and believe essential to success. Union leaders sometimes see democracy as a management ploy to get workers to accept gimmicks instead of gains in wages and benefits. Union leaders also fear that organizational democracy might lead to closer worker-management collaboration, thus undermining the union. But a number of pioneering union leaders, including Irving Bluestone of the UAW, have pushed for greater union-management collaboration. An increasing number of unions in the United States and elsewhere have become strongly supportive of QWL efforts.

Organizations that stop short of formal democracy can still practice "symbolic egalitarianism" (Pfeffer, 1994, p. 48). Traditional organizations made it easy to judge an individual's place in the pecking order from such cues as office size and access to perks like limousines and corporate jets. Companies that invest in people, by contrast, often reinforce participation and job redesign by replacing symbols of hierarchy with those of cooperation and equality. At the American automaker Saturn, conference tables are round rather than square. There is no "head of the table," and leadership rotates according to the topic at hand.

Putting It All Together: TQM and NUMMI

When the human resource management strategies described in this chapter are implemented in a halfhearted, piecemeal fashion, they lead to predictable failure. Success requires a comprehensive strategy and long-term commitment that many organizations espouse but few deliver. One example of a comprehensive strategy that combines structural and human resource elements is total quality management (TQM), which swept across corporate America in the 1980s. Quality gurus such as W. Edwards Deming (1986), Joseph Juran (1989), Philip Crosby (1989), and Kaoru Ishikawa (1985) differed on specifics, but all emphasized workforce involvement, participation, and teaming as essential components of a serious quality effort. Hackman and Wageman (1995) analyzed the theory and practice of the quality movement and concluded that it represented a coherent and distinctive philosophy, consistent on the whole with existing research on effective human resource management.

Hackman and Wageman (1995) summarized four core assumptions in TQM: (1) high quality is actually cheaper than low quality, (2) people want to do good work, (3) quality problems are cross-functional, and (4) top management is ultimately responsible for quality. In practice, many organizations diluted the philosophy by implementing only certain parts, usually those that were easiest and least disruptive to the status quo. It is no surprise that a majority of quality programs have failed to achieve their objectives (Gertz and Baptista, 1995; Port, 1992), even though companies like Ford, Motorola, and Xerox have obtained extraordinary results (Engardio and DeGeorge, 1994; Greising, 1994; Waterman, 1994).

The power of an integrated approach to TQM is illustrated in the case of New United Motors Manufacturing, Inc. (NUMMI), the General Motors–Toyota joint venture. In 1985, NUMMI reopened an old GM plant in Fremont, California, and began to build cars. It drew its workforce from five thousand employees laid off by GM the previous year. These workers had a reputation at GM for militancy, poor attendance, alcohol and drug abuse, and even fistfights on the assembly line (Holusha, 1989; Lawrence and Weckler, 1990; Lee, 1988). Two years later, absenteeism had declined from 20 percent under GM to 2 percent under NUMMI, and the plant was producing cars of higher quality at a lower labor cost than any other GM plant. NUMMI's Chevrolets ranked second among all cars sold in the United States in initial owner satisfaction; no other GM car was even in the top fifteen.

What accounted for this manufacturing miracle? The answer, in a word, was Toyota, GM's partner in the joint venture. GM provided the plant, the workers, and an American nameplate, but both car and production processes had been designed in Japan. Toyota managed the plant, and production was split fifty-fifty between Chevrolets and Toyotas. NUMMI's success was built on a comprehensive human resource philosophy. There was symbolic egalitarianism: workers and executives wore the same uniforms, parked in the same lots, and ate in the same cafeteria. Grouped in small, self-managing teams, employees participated in designing their own jobs and rotated through different jobs. NUMMI's motto was "There are no managers, no supervisors, only team members."

Lee (1988) used images of dance and poetry to capture NUMMI's production process:

> Every motion should be flowing and natural, like a ballet. If a worker has to bend awkwardly to do his job, then the symmetry of his motion is disturbed, and he will tire. One should never have to fight the car to build it, the NUMMI trainer explains. If you must hold nine bolts in one hand and fumble with an air wrench in the other, that is clumsy and wasteful. One understands that the sin of awkwardness, of assembly in fits of effort, is as much an esthetic fault as it is a flaw in the quest for efficiency. The entire system is pure oriental poetry that emphasizes the beauty of the process of life, the grace of 10,000 stalks of rice bending in unison in the winds [pp. 234–235].

Both union and management stressed collaboration. If a worker took a complaint to the union, the union representative was likely to be accompanied by a member of the company's human relations staff. The three would try to work the problem out on the spot. If workers fell behind, they could pull a cord to stop the line, and help would arrive quickly. NUMMI's president, Kan Higashi, saw the cord as a sign of trust between management and labor: "We had heavy arguments about installing the cord here. We wondered if workers would pull it just to get a rest. That has not happened." When car sales slumped in 1988, NUMMI laid off no one. Workers were sent at full pay to training sessions on problem solving and interpersonal relations. One worker commented, "With GM, if the line slowed down, some of us would have been on the street" (Holusha, 1989).

Even union leaders liked NUMMI. Bruce Lee, a UAW official, said that the team system liberated workers by giving them more control over their jobs and that it is "increasing the plant's productivity and competitiveness while making jobs easier" (Holusha, 1989). UAW president Owen Bieber said when he toured the plant, "I was most struck that there is hardly any management here at all" (Lee, 1988, pp. 232–233).

NUMMI was not a trouble-free paradise. A dissident union group complained that the brisk pace of work amounted to "management by stress" and the plant's policy on absenteeism was inhumane. A worker absent on more than three different occasions within a three-month period was charged with an "offense." Four offenses in a year meant dismissal. But even dissidents conceded that the basic concept was better than in the past. Most workers were happy simply for the chance to make automobiles. As one worker said, "We got a second chance here, and we are trying to take advantage of it. Many people don't get a second chance" (Holusha, 1989).

GM was sufficiently impressed to try to transfer NUMMI techniques to other plants. Sometimes it worked—innovations such as self-managing teams doing their own quality audits led to a 21 percent reduction in costs and a substantial increase in quality at GM's Lansing plant (Hampton and Norman, 1987). But the transplants often failed to root because bits of the NUMMI philosophy were implemented piecemeal, with predictably marginal results. "Team decision making" became a fad at GM but often backfired because managers dictated to the teams (Lee, 1988). Higashi told a *Wall Street*

Journal reporter at one point that he was "afraid that the GM upper management does not understand the basic concept" (Schlesinger, 1987, p. 30).

As the NUMMI case illustrates, successful human resource applications are neither as idyllic as idealists might hope nor as soft as old-line managers often fear. The NUMMI experiment combined creative human resource management with demanding work standards to produce an automobile highly competitive in terms of both cost and quality. Such combinations have become more and more common in recent decades.

Training and Organization Development

NUMMI is only one demonstration of the power of a systematic investment in human resources. But other organizations moving in this direction must rise to the challenge of building skills and attitudes necessary to make programs successful. As early as the 1950s, U.S. corporations began to recognize that "human relations" skills were a critical component of effective management. Managers were sent off to lectures on how to listen and communicate better. Many skeptics lamented, "They're sending me to charm school." Even when such programs produced initial enthusiasm, they lacked long-term impact. The lack of transfer led to an observation that seems obvious in retrospect: If people cannot learn to play tennis or a violin by listening to a lecture, why should they be able to develop human relations skills that way?

This line of questioning led to the development of experiential approaches: learning by doing. One provocative and influential example was "sensitivity training" in "T-groups." The T-group was a serendipitous discovery by social psychologists in the late 1940s. During a conference on race relations, participants met in groups. Researchers were stationed in each group to take notes. In the evening, researchers reported their observations to program staff. When participants heard about the sessions, they asked to be included. They were fascinated to hear things about themselves and their behavior they had never learned before.

Researchers soon recognized that they had discovered something important and began a more systematic program of "human relations laboratories." Trainers and participants joined in small groups, working together and learning from work at the same time. Several features of what came to be known as the T-group made it a powerful, even startling experience. Trainers refused to fill the customary leadership role. Groups began in a social vacuum, with little in the way of rules or content. The task was to learn by examining "here and now" events, a definition initially puzzling for most participants. A group had to establish its own agenda, goals, and procedures. It was at first enormously frustrating and unsettling but often led to achievement and satisfaction when groups created viable ways of working together. It came as a surprise to many participants that such loose structure and unorthodox leadership could work so well.

A second source of the T-group's power was interpersonal feedback. Most participants had never before experienced such direct, honest feedback. Levels of communication in T-groups provided a mirror that often left members saying, "I never knew that's how people see me."

As word spread, T-groups replaced lectures as a way to develop human relations skills. And because many proponents were trained as social scientists, T-groups also generated numerous studies of their impact. Through a haze of charges and countercharges from true believers and zealous critics, evidence accumulated around two basic conclusions: T-groups had an effect on people's feelings about themselves, their self-perceptions, and sometimes on their behavior, but individual effects rarely led to widespread organizational change (Gibb, 1975; Campbell and Dunnette, 1968).

Evidence of limited systemic impact stimulated T-group trainers to experiment with new approaches. Though some writers (among them Heffron, 1989) still view organization development (OD) and sensitivity training as synonymous, the two human resource strategies have become quite distinct. OD practitioners borrowed basic elements of laboratory training (experiential learning, small groups, and interpersonal feedback) and adapted these to a variety of contexts. "Conflict laboratories" were designed for situations involving friction among different groups and organizational units. "Team-building" programs were created to help groups work better. "Future Search" (Weisbord and Janoff, 1995), "Open Space" (Owen, 1993, 1995), and other large group designs (Bunker and Alban, 1996) were created to bring together large numbers of people from a variety of constituencies to work cooperatively in moving an organization or a community forward on a set of key issues or challenges. A famous example of a large group intervention is the "Work-Out" conferences initiated by Jack Welch, CEO of General Electric. Frustrated by the slow pace of change in his organization, Welch convened a series of town hall meetings, typically with one hundred to two hundred employees, to identify and resolve issues "that participants thought were dumb, a waste of time, or needed to be changed" (Bunker and Alban, 1996, p. 170). The conferences were generally viewed as highly successful, and Work-Outs spread throughout the company (Bunker and Alban, 1996).

Survey Feedback

As laboratory training was getting its start in the late 1940s, a group of researchers at the University of Michigan began to develop surveys to measure human resource patterns. They focused on motivation, communication, leadership styles, and organizational climate. Rensis Likert helped found the Survey Research Center at Michigan. His 1961 book, *New Patterns of Management,* became a classic in the human resource tradition. Likert used survey data to show that "employee-centered" supervisors, who focused more on people and relationships, typically managed higher-producing units than "job-centered" supervisors, who made decisions themselves and dictated to subordinates.

Survey research paved the way for survey feedback as an approach to organizational improvement. The process begins with questionnaires aimed at human resource issues. The results are tabulated and then shown to managers. The results might show, for example, that information within a unit flows well and members of the group are highly motivated. At the same time, decisions might be seen as made in the wrong place and on the basis of inaccurate information. Often with the help of a consultant, group members would discuss the results and explore ways to improve their effectiveness.

Evolution of OD

T-groups and survey research gave birth to the field of organization development. Both parents were heavily steeped in human resource assumptions. Their lineage stood apart from the other tradition at the time, the more rational structural perspective. But most structural theorists were more interested in studying organizations than in trying to improve them. Since its early beginnings, OD has continued to evolve as a discipline. Mirvis (1988, 1990) describes 1960s OD as a process-oriented philosophy built around values of human expression. The 1970s saw OD shift to more emphasis on technique, developing a broader base of interventions for a wider range of organizational problems. In the 1980s, Mirvis observed another shift—from a facilitative, person-centered approach to a more directive, organization-centered one. OD came to be viewed as a strategy for helping organizations achieve and maintain stability in the face of changing and turbulent environments. "In OD of the 1960s, it was assumed that by developing people we could create healthier and more effective organizations. Today, many [theorists] advocate that we must develop organizations to create healthier and more effective people" (Mirvis, 1988, pp. 17–18).

All the while, OD consultation has grown in popularity. In 1965, few managers had heard of OD. By the 1990s, there were few who had not. Most major organizations (particularly in the United States) have experimented with OD in some form. General Motors, the United States Postal Service, IBM, the Internal Revenue Service, Texas Instruments, and the U.S. Navy have all employed their own brand of OD to improve performance.

Fullan, Miles, and Taylor (1981) argued that the label "OD" should be applied only to efforts that are "*simultaneously* . . . planned [and] long-range; involve a change agent or agents; focus on organizational processes, tasks, and structures; address the development of individuals as well as the organization; and use behavioral science techniques to generate valid data for both individual and organizational decisions" (p. 6). On the basis of their review, Fullan and colleagues concluded that the success rate of OD projects was about 50 percent, primarily because so many were "ineptly conducted."

Summary

Human resource assumptions emphasize the fit between individual and organization. When the fit is good, both benefit: individuals find satisfaction and meaning in work; the organization makes effective use of individual talent and energy. Poor fit underutilizes human energy and talent, frustrates individuals, and encourages people to withdraw, resist, or rebel. In the end, everyone pays. As such costs have become more apparent, progressive organizations have developed a variety of "high-involvement" strategies for improving human resource management. One set of approaches strengthens the bond between individual and organization by paying well, providing job security, promoting from within, training the workforce, and sharing the fruits of organizational success. Another set empowers workers and gives work more significance through participation, job enrichment, teaming, democracy, and egalitarianism. No single strategy is likely to be effective by itself. Success typically requires a comprehensive strategy undergirded by a long-term human resource management philosophy.

Chapter Eight

Interpersonal and Group Dynamics

Anne Barreta was excited but scared when she became the first woman and the first Hispanic American ever promoted to district marketing manager at the Hillcrest Corporation. She knew that she could do the job, but she would be watched carefully. Her boss, Steve Carter, the regional marketing manager, was very supportive. Other people were less enthusiastic—like the coworker who smiled as he patted her on the shoulder and said, "Congratulations! I just wish *I* was an affirmative action candidate."

Anne was responsible for one of two districts in the same city. Her counterpart in the other district, Harry Reynolds, was twenty-five years older and had been with Hillcrest twenty years longer. Some people said that the term *good old boy* could have been invented to describe Harry. Usually genial, his temper flared quickly when someone got in his way. Anne tried to maintain a positive and professional relationship, but Harry often seemed condescending and arrogant.

Things came to a head one afternoon as Anne, Harry, and their immediate subordinates were discussing marketing plans. Anne and Harry were disagreeing politely. Mark, one of Anne's subordinates, tried to support her views, but Harry kept cutting him off. Anne saw Mark's frustration building, but she was nevertheless surprised when he angrily told Harry, "If you'd ever listen to anyone besides yourself, and think a little before you open your mouth, we'd make a lot more progress." With barely controlled fury, Harry declared that "this meeting is adjourned" and stormed out.

A day later, Harry phoned to demand that Anne fire Mark. Anne tried to reason with him, but Harry was adamant. Worried about the fallout, Anne talked to Steve, their joint boss. He agreed that firing Mark was too drastic but suggested a reprimand. Anne agreed and informed Harry. He again became angry and shouted, "If you want to get along in this company, you'd better fire that guy!" Anne calmly replied that Mark reported to her. Harry's final words were, "You'll regret this!"

Three months later, Steve called Anne to a private meeting. "I just learned," he said, "that someone's been spreading a rumor that I promoted you because we're involved in a sexual relationship."

Anne was stunned by a jumble of feelings—confusion, rage, surprise, shame. She groped for words, but none came.

"It's crazy, I know," Steve continued. "But the company hired a private detective to check it out. Of course, they didn't find anything. So they're dropping it. But some of the damage is already done. I can't prove it, but I'm pretty sure who's behind it."

"Harry?" Anne asked.

"Who else?"

The human resource frame focuses on the relationship between individuals and organizations, but people at work relate mostly to other people. Managers spend most of their time in conversations and meetings, in groups and committees, over coffee or over lunch, on the phone, or, in recent years, on the net[1] (Kotter, 1982; Mintzberg, 1973).

Psychological theory and folk wisdom agree that social needs and interpersonal styles are substantially influenced by experiences early in life. Those patterns do not change quickly or easily in response to organizational requirements. Thompson (1967) and others have argued that the socializing institutions of a bureaucratic society shape individuals to make them better suited to the workplace. Schools, for example, train students to be punctual, complete assignments, and follow rules. But schools are not always fully successful. The human inputs of organizations are shaped initially by a decentralized cottage industry known as the family. Families seldom produce raw materials exactly to specifications.

To be human is to be an imperfect cog in the bureaucratic machinery. People conduct interpersonal relationships to fit their individual styles and preferences, often disregarding what the organization wants. They may work, but never *only* on assigned tasks. They also attend to personal and social needs that often conflict with formal rules and requirements. As Anne Barreta's case illustrates, gender and sexual dynamics are among the enduring human issues managers and theorists often try to ignore (Burrell and Hearn, 1989).

Individual differences and interpersonal dynamics regularly spawn organizational muddles. Projects falter because no one likes the manager's style. Departments mire in protracted warfare because of friction between their respective heads. Committees get little done because of tensions everyone sees but no one mentions. School principals spend an inordinate amount of time dealing with a handful of abrasive or ineffectual teachers responsible for most discipline problems and parental complaints.

Interpersonal Dynamics

In organizations, as elsewhere in life, many of the greatest joys and most intense sorrows occur in relationships with other people. Three recurrent questions regularly haunt managers:

- What is really happening in this relationship?
- Why do other people behave as they do?
- What can I do about it?

All were questions for Anne Barreta. What was happening between her and Harry Reynolds? Did Harry really start the vicious rumor? If so, why? How should she deal with someone as difficult and devious as he seemed? Could she talk to him? What options did she have?

Some observers assume the obvious: Harry resented a young, minority woman who had become his peer. He became even more bitter when she rejected his demand to fire Mark. Harry sought revenge through a sneak attack. The case resembles many others in which men dominate or victimize women (Collinson and Collinson, 1989). What should Anne, or women in similar circumstances, do? Confront the larger issues? That might change norms in the long run, but women who initiate confrontations are often branded as "troublemakers" (Collinson and Collinson, 1989). Should Anne try to get Harry before he gets her? If she does, she might kindle a war no one wins.

Human resource theorists acknowledge political dynamics but suggest that constructive responses are possible. Argyris (1962) emphasizes the importance of "interpersonal competence" as a basic managerial skill. He showed that managers' effectiveness was often impaired because they were overcontrolling, excessively competitive, uncomfortable with feelings, closed to others' ideas, and blind to their own impact.

Argyris and Schön (1974, 1996) carry the issue of interpersonal effectiveness a step further. They argue that individuals' behavior is controlled by personal theories for action: assumptions that inform and guide their behavior. These authors distinguish two kinds of theories. *Espoused theories* are the accounts that individuals provide whenever they try to describe, explain, or predict their behavior. *Theories-in-use* guide what people actually do. A theory-in-use is an implicit program or set of rules that specifies how to behave.

Argyris and Schön found significant discrepancies between espoused theories and theories-in-use. Managers' talk is often unconnected to their actions. They typically see themselves as rational, open, concerned for others, and democratic, not realizing that their actions are competitive, controlling, and defensive. Such blindness is pervasive because most managers employ a self-protective model of interpersonal behavior, particularly in dealing with issues that are embarrassing or threatening. Argyris and Schön refer to this theory-in-use as Model I (see Table 8.1).

Lurking in Model I is the core assumption that organizations are competitive, dangerous places where you have to look out for yourself or someone else will do you in. That assumption leads individuals to follow a predictable set of steps in their attempts to influence others that we can see in the relationship between Harry and Anne.

1. *Assume that the problem is caused by the other person(s).* Harry seemed to think that his problems were caused by Mark and Anne—Mark was insulting, and Anne protected him. Anne, for her part, blamed Harry for being biased, unreasonable, and devious. This assumption is at the core of Model I. So long as problems result from someone else's screwup, you never have to learn or change.

Table 8.1. Model I Theory-in-Use.

Core Values (Governing Variables)	Action Strategies	Consequences for the Behavioral World	Consequences for Learning
Define and achieve your goals.	Design and manage the environment unilaterally.	You will be seen as defensive, inconsistent, fearful, selfish.	You seal yourself off (so you won't know about the negative consequences of your actions).
Maximize winning, minimize losing.	Own and control whatever is relevant to your interests.	You create defensiveness in interpersonal relationships.	You get caught up in single-loop learning (you don't question your core values and assumptions).
Minimize generating or expressing negative feelings.	Unilaterally protect yourself (from criticism, discomfort, vulnerability, and so on).	You reinforce defensive norms (mistrust, risk avoidance, conformity, rivalry, and so on).	You test your assumptions and beliefs privately, not publicly.
Be rational.	Unilaterally protect others from being upset or hurt (censor bad news, hold private meetings, and so on).	Key issues become undiscussable.	You engage in unconscious collusion to protect yourself and others from learning.

Source: Adapted from Argyris and Schön (1996), p. 93.

2. *Develop a private, unilateral diagnosis and solution.* Harry developed his own diagnosis and solution—Anne should fire Mark. When she declined, he apparently developed another, more private strategy: undermine Anne without her knowledge.

3. *Since the other person is the cause of the problem, get that person to change, using one or more of three basic strategies: facts, logic, and rational persuasion (argue the merits of your point of view); indirect influence (ease in, ask leading questions, manipulate the other person); direct critique (tell the other person directly what he or she is doing wrong and how he or she should change).* Harry started with logic, moved quickly to direct critique, and, if Steve's diagnosis is correct, finally resorted to subterfuge and sabotage.

4. *If the other person resists or becomes defensive, it confirms that the other person caused the problem.* Anne's refusal to fire Mark may have confirmed Harry's perception of her as an ineffective troublemaker.

5. *Respond to resistance through some combination of intensifying pressure and protecting or rejecting the other person.* When Anne resisted, Harry intensified the pressure. Anne tried to soothe him without firing Mark. Harry apparently concluded that she was impossible to deal with and that the best solution was to sabotage her.

6. *If your efforts are unsuccessful or less successful than hoped, it is the other person's fault. You need feel no personal responsibility.* Harry did not succeed in getting rid of Mark or Anne. He stained Anne's reputation but damaged his own in the process. Everyone was hurt. But Harry probably never realized the error of his ways. The incident may have confirmed to Harry's colleagues that he was too temperamental and defensive and not fully trustworthy. Such perceptions will probably block Harry's promotion to a more senior position. But who would want to say all that to someone as defensive and cranky as Harry?

The result is wasted energy, strained relationships, and deterioration in decision-making processes—all predictable consequences of Model I. What else can be done about situations like Anne's? Argyris and Schön (1996) propose Model II as an alternative:

1. *Emphasize common goals and mutual influence.* Even in a situation as difficult as the Anne Barreta case, shared goals are possible. Anne and Harry both want to be effective. Neither benefits from mutual destruction. At times, each needs help and might learn from and profit from the other. To emphasize common goals, Anne might ask Harry, "What kind of relationship do we want? Do we want an ongoing battle? Wouldn't we both be better off if we worked together?"

2. *Communicate openly, and publicly test assumptions and beliefs.*
Model II suggests that Anne talk directly to Harry and test her assumptions. She *believed* Harry deliberately started the rumor, but she was not *certain.* She suspected that Harry would lie if she confronted him, another untested assumption. Anne might say, for example, "Harry, someone started a rumor about me and Steve. What do you know about that story and how it got started?" Though many managers see directness as startling and dangerous, Model II argues that Anne has little to lose and much to gain. Even if she does not get the truth, she lets Harry know she is aware of his game and is not afraid to confront him.

3. *Combine advocacy with inquiry.* Advocacy includes statements that communicate what an individual thinks, knows, wants, or feels. Inquiry seeks to learn what others think, know, want, or feel. Figure 8.1 provides a simple model of the relationship between advocacy and inquiry.

Model II emphasizes the integration of advocacy and inquiry. It asks managers to express openly what they think and feel and actively to seek understanding of others' thoughts and feelings. Harry's demand that Anne fire Mark combined *high* advocacy with *low* inquiry. He told her what he wanted while showing no interest in her point of view. Such behavior tends to be perceived as assertive at best, dominating or arrogant at worst. Anne's response was low in both advocacy and inquiry. In her discomfort, she tried to get out of the meeting without making any concessions. Harry might have seen her as apathetic, unresponsive, or weak.

Model II counsels Anne to combine advocacy and inquiry in an open dialogue. She would tell Harry what she thinks and feels

Figure 8.1. Advocacy and Inquiry.

		Inquiry	
		Low	High
Advocacy	High	Assertive	Integrative
	Low	Passive	Accommodative

while testing her assumptions and trying to learn from him. This is difficult to learn and practice. Openness carries risks, and it is hard to be effective when you are ambivalent, uncomfortable, or frightened. It gets easier as you become more confident that you can cope with other people's responses. Anne's ability to confront Harry depends a lot on her confidence in herself and her interpersonal skills. Beliefs can be self-fulfilling. If you tell yourself that it's too dangerous to be open and that you do not know how to deal with difficult people, you will usually be right.

When managers feel vulnerable, they revert to self-protection. They skirt issues or attack others and escalate games of camouflage and deception (Argyris and Schön, 1978). Feeling inadequate, they camouflage their inadequacy. To avoid detection, they pile subterfuge on top of camouflage. This generates even more uncertainty and ambiguity and makes it difficult or impossible to detect errors. As a result, organizations often persist in following a course everyone privately thinks is a path to disaster. No one wants to be the one to speak the truth. Who wants to be the messenger bearing bad news?

The result is often catastrophe. In a number of well-documented aviation accidents, the copilot believed that the captain was making a serious mistake yet chose not to say so directly. Instead, he used vague questions to nudge the captain gently. In each case, the captain missed the message. Perhaps the copilots feared upsetting their commander. Perhaps they were not sure the captain was wrong. In any event, the errors were fatal. More direct communication could not have made things any worse and might have saved airplane, passengers, and crew.

Many change efforts fail not because managers' intentions are incorrect or insincere but because managers lack interpersonal skills and understandings. Popular organizational remedies such as quality improvement, process reengineering, and self-managing teams often mire in bogs of interpersonal misunderstanding and miscommunication. Not long ago, a manufacturing organization proudly announced its "Put Quality First" program. A young manager was assigned to chair a "quality team" in the plant where she worked. But whenever the plant manager dropped in on a team meeting, he would dismiss every suggestion for change as "impractical" or "unworkable." The team manager's enthusiasm quickly faded. In the plant manager's espoused theory, he was demonstrating accessibility and "management by walking around." The team and its manager perceived his theory-in-use as intrusive and dictatorial.

Management Styles

Model I focuses on characteristics held in common by many managers and organizations. But there is the additional question of differences among individuals in personality and style. A line of research spanning seven decades has tried to determine the most effective kinds of behavior and style in task settings. In a classic experiment (Lewin, Lippitt, and White, 1939), researchers compared autocratic, democratic, and laissez-faire leadership in a study of boys' clubs. They found that leadership style had a powerful impact on both productivity and morale. Under autocratic leadership, the boys were productive but joyless and experienced high levels of dependence and frustration. Laissez-faire leadership led to aimlessness and confusion. The boys strongly preferred democratic leadership, which produced a more positive group climate.

A number of subsequent researchers have examined leadership in work settings (much of that work is reviewed in Stogdill, 1974, and Bass, 1981, 1990). Fleishman and Harris (1962) conducted a series of studies focusing on two dimensions of leadership: consideration (how well a leader showed concern for and sensitivity to people) and initiating structure (to what degree a leader actively structured subordinates' activities). Their research, and many subsequent studies using their leadership variables, produced a complex pattern of findings. High consideration for employees is generally associated with lower turnover, fewer grievances, and less absenteeism. Overall, more effective supervisors tended to be high on both consideration and structure. Similar results were produced by Likert (1961), who presented evidence that "employee-centered" managers were more effective in the long run than "task-centered" managers.

Countless theories, books, workshops, and tests have been devoted to helping managers identify their own and others' personal or interpersonal styles. Are leaders introverts or extroverts? Are they friendly helpers, tough battlers, or objective thinkers? Do managers care more about control, inclusion, or affection? Do they behave more like parents or like children? Are they superstars concerned for both people and production, "country club" managers who care only about people, or hard-driving taskmasters who ignore human needs and feelings (Blake and Mouton, 1969)? In the 1980s, the forty-year-old Myers-Briggs Inventory (Myers, 1980) became an enormously popular tool for examining management styles. Built on principles from Jungian psychology, the inventory assesses four dimensions: introversion versus extroversion, sensing versus intuition, thinking versus feeling, and perceiving versus judging. Based on scores on those dimensions, it categorizes individuals into one of sixteen "types." Are you, for example, an ISTJ (serious, quiet, thorough, practical, and dependable) or an ENFP (warmly enthusiastic, high-spirited, ingenious, and imaginative) or perhaps an ENTJ (hearty, frank, decisive, and inclined to take leadership)?

Despite the risk of turning managers into amateur psychologists, it often helps to have a shared language and concepts to make sense of the elusive, complex world of individual styles. When managers are blind to their own style, they usually need help from others to learn about it. Their friends and colleagues may be more helpful if they have some way to talk about the issues.

Groups in Organizations

Anne Barreta's case shows how demanding even a two-person relationship can be. Managers face even more difficult challenges because they spend much of their time in groups. Groups take many forms: standing committees, task forces, project teams, boards of trustees, faculty committees, advisory groups, and cliques, to name a few. Whatever the labels, groups constantly challenge and frustrate everyone. Cynics offer a range of jaundiced perspectives on committees as "a cul-de-sac down which ideas are lured and then quietly strangled" or "a group of the unwilling, chosen by the unfit, to do the unnecessary." Many observers believe that groups are almost invariably inefficient, confused, and frustrating.

But even people who hate groups can often recall at least one peak experience. Groups have both assets and liabilities (Collins and Guetzkow, 1964; McGrath, 1984; Hackman, 1989). Groups have more knowledge, diversity of perspective, time, and energy than individuals working alone. Groups often improve communication and increase acceptance of decisions. On the downside, groups may overrespond to social pressure or individual domination, bog down in inefficiency, or let personal agendas smother collective purposes (Maier, 1967).

Groups can be wonderful or terrible, productive or stagnant, imprisoning or freeing, conformist or creative. At best, they are places of loyalty, mutual commitment, excitement, and motivation. Many group problems result from interpersonal dynamics, problems that can be reduced if identified and effectively managed. Paradise or inferno, groups are indispensable in modern organizations and are becoming even more so. They solve problems, make decisions, coordinate work, promote information sharing, build participation and commitment, and negotiate disputes (Handy, 1993). As modern organizations rely less on hierarchical coordination, groups have become even more important in such forms as self-managing teams, quality circles, and, increasingly, virtual groups whose members are linked by information technology.

Groups operate on two different levels: an overt, conscious level focused on task and a more implicit level of *process,* emphasizing group maintenance and interpersonal dynamics (Bion, 1961; Leavitt, 1978; Maier, 1967; Schein, 1969; Bales, 1970). Many people see only confusion in group processes. The informed eye sees much more. Groups, like modern art, are complex and subtle. A few basic dimensions can provide a map for bringing clarity and order out of apparent chaos and confusion. Our map emphasizes four central issues: informal roles, informal norms, interpersonal conflict, and leadership and decision making.

Informal Roles

Traditionally, the structural frame emphasized formal roles, often defined by a title and a job description. In small groups, roles are often much more informal and implicit, with both task and personal dimensions. Every work group needs a structure of *task roles* so that members understand who is going to do what. Different group members bring different interests (some love research but hate writing), different skills (some may communicate better in writing than face to face), and different degrees of enthusiasm (some may be highly committed to the project, while others drag their feet). Groups do better when they recognize and respond to individual differences.

It is costly, for example, to assign the task of writing a final report to a poor writer or to put your most insecure member on stage in front of a demanding group of senior executives.

Beyond informal task roles, every group also evolves *personal roles*. Anyone entering a group hopes to find a comfortable and satisfying role. Imagine a three-person task force. One member, Karen, is happy only when she feels influential and visible. Bob prefers to be quiet and inconspicuous. Teresa finds it hard to participate until she feels liked and valued. In the early going, members send implicit signals about roles they prefer, usually without realizing they are doing it. In the first meeting, Karen jumps in, takes the initiative, and pushes hard for her ideas. Teresa smiles, compliments other people, asks questions, and says she hopes everyone will get along. Bob watches, speaking only when asked a direct question.

If the three individuals' preferred roles dovetail, things may go well. Karen is happy to have Bob as a listener, and Bob is pleased that Karen lets him be inconspicuous. Teresa will be content if she feels that Karen and Bob like her. But suppose that Tony, who likes to be in charge, joins the group. Karen and Tony may collide—both want the same role. The prognosis looks bleaker. Now suppose that one more member, Susan, signs on. Susan's mission in life is to help other people get along. If Susan can help Karen feel visible, Teresa feel loved, and Tony feel powerful while Bob is left alone, everyone may be happy—and the group should be productive.

In small groups, as in large organizations, the fit between the individual and the larger system is a central human resource concern. A group's role system is critical. The right set of task roles helps get the work done and makes optimal use of each member's resources. But without a corresponding set of informal roles, individuals will feel frustrated and dissatisfied. They likely become unproductive or disruptive.

Some groups are blessed with a rich set of resources and highly compatible individuals, but most groups are not that lucky. They have limited quantities of talent, skill, and motivation. They have areas of both compatibility and potential conflict. Many groups never recognize issues that need attention or avoid talking about them even if they do see them. Avoidance often backfires. Neglected issues come back to haunt them, particularly under pressure. It usually works better to deal with issues early on. A consulting firm produced a dramatic improvement in effectiveness and morale by conducting a team-building process whenever a group formed to work on a new project. Extra time for group process at the beginning more than paid for itself farther down the road. Members discussed the roles they preferred, how they wanted the group to operate, and the resources each individual brought to the group. In the project group discussed earlier, if Karen and Tony recognize both like to be in charge, they can discuss how to deal with the potential conflict before it becomes debilitating.

Informal Group Norms

Every group develops informal rules to live by—norms that govern how the group will function and how the members will conduct themselves. We once observed two families in adjacent sites in the same campground. At first glance, both were alike: two adults, two small children, and California license plates. Further observation made it clear that each family had very different norms. Family A practiced a strong form of "do your own thing." Everyone did what he or she wanted, and no one paid much attention to anyone else. Their two-year-old wandered around the campground until he fell down a fifteen-foot embankment. He lay there wailing while a professor of leadership pondered the risks and rewards of intervening in someone else's family. Finally, the professor rescued and returned the child to his parents, who seemed oblivious to their son's mishap.

Family B, in contrast, was a model of interdependence and efficiency, operating like a well-oiled machine. Everything was done collectively; each member had a role. A drill sergeant would have admired the speed and precision with which they packed up for departure. Even their three-year-old approached her tasks with purpose and enthusiasm. Every group, including the family, evolves a set of informal rules for "how we do things around here." Eventually, such rules are taken for granted. They come to be accepted as unalterable social realities. The parents in Family A envied Family B. They were plainly puzzled as they asked, "How did they ever get those kids under control? *Our* kids would never tolerate that!"

With norms, as with roles, early intervention helps. Do we want to be task-oriented, no-nonsense, and get on with the job? Or would we prefer to be more relaxed, playful, and responsive to one another? Do we expect full attendance at every meeting, or should we be more flexible? Must people be unerringly punctual, or would that cramp our style? Do we prize boisterous debate or courtesy and restraint? Groups develop norms to answer such questions.

Interpersonal Conflict in Groups

Personal conflicts spawn many of the worst horror stories about group life. Interpersonal strife can block progress and waste time. It can make things unpleasant at best, painful at worst. Some groups are blessed with little conflict, but most encounter predictable differences in goals, perceptions, preferences, and beliefs. The larger and more diverse the group, the greater the likelihood of conflict.

How can groups cope with interpersonal conflict? Model I managers typically rely on two strategies: "pour oil on troubled waters" and "might makes right." As a result, things get worse instead of better. The oil-on-troubled-waters strategy views conflict as something to avoid at all costs: minimize it, deny its existence, smooth it over, bury it, circumvent it. Suppose, for example, that Tony says that the group needs a leader and Karen replies that a leader would selfishly dominate the group. Teresa, dreading conflict, might rush to say, "I think we're all basically saying the same thing" or "We can talk about leadership later; right now, why don't we find out a little more about each other?"

Smoothing tactics may work if the issue is temporary or peripheral. In such cases, conflict may disappear of its own accord—much to everyone's relief. But conflicts early in a group's life have a remarkable tendency to come back again and again. If smoothing tactics fail and conflict continues, another option is "might makes right." If Tony senses conflict between him and Karen, he will employ Model I thinking: Since we disagree, and my view is right, she is the problem. And since she is the problem, the only way to get anything done is for her to change. Tony may try any of several strategies to change Karen. He may try to persuade her of the validity of his position. He may try to get others in the group to side with him and put pressure on Karen. He may subtly, or not so subtly, criticize or attack her. If Karen thinks she is right and Tony is the problem, the two are headed for collision. The result may be very painful for everyone.

If Model I is a costly approach to conflict, what else might a group do? The following guidelines may prove helpful:

1. *Develop skills.* More and more organizations are recognizing that group effectiveness depends heavily on members' ability to understand what is happening and contribute effectively. Such skills as listening, communicating, managing conflict, and building consensus are critical building blocks in high-performing groups.

2. *Agree on the basics.* Too often, groups plunge ahead without taking the time to agree on goals and procedures. Down the road, they continually stumble over unresolved issues. Shared understanding and commitment around the basics provides a powerful glue to hold things together in the face of inevitable stresses and strains of group life.

3. *Search for interests in common.* How does a group reach agreement if it begins divided? It helps to keep asking, "What do we have in common? If we disagree on the issue at hand, can we put it in a larger framework where we can agree?" If Tony and Karen clash on the need for a leader, can they find other areas of agreement? Perhaps both want to do the task well. Recognizing commonalities makes it easier to discuss differences. It also helps to remember that some common interests are rooted in complementary differences (Lax and Sebenius, 1986). Karen's desire to be visible is compatible with Bob's preference to be in the background. Conversely, similarities (as when Karen and Tony both want to lead) are often the source of conflict.

4. *Experiment.* If Tony is sure the group needs a leader and Karen is equally convinced it does not, the group could bog down in endless debate. Susan, the group's social specialist, might propose an experiment: since Karen sees it one way and Tony sees it another, how could we gather more information to help the group decide? Try one meeting with a leader and one without to see what happens.

Experiments can be a powerful response to conflict. They provide a way to move beyond stalemates without forcing either party to lose face or admit defeat. Parties may agree on a test when they cannot agree on anything else. Equally important, they may learn something that moves the conversation to a new, more productive point.

5. *Doubt your infallibility.* This was the advice that Benjamin Franklin offered his fellow delegates to the United States consti-

tutional convention in 1787: "Having lived long, I have experienced many instances of being obliged by better information, or fuller consideration, to change opinions even on important subjects, which I once thought right, but found to be otherwise. It is therefore that the older I grow, the more apt I am to doubt my own judgment, and to pay more respect to the judgment of others" (Rossiter, 1966).

Groups provide diverse resources, ideas, and perspectives. A group that sees diversity as an asset and a source of learning has a good chance for a productive discussion of differences. In the heat of the moment, though, a five-person group easily can turn into five teachers in search of a learner. At such times, it helps if at least one person asks, "Are we all sure we're infallible? Are we really hearing one another?"

6. *Treat differences as a group responsibility.* If Tony and Karen are on a collision course, it is tempting for others to stand aside. But everyone is aboard the same social vehicle. All will suffer if it careens off the road. The debate between Karen and Tony reflects personal feelings and preferences but deals with an issue of importance to the entire group. Leadership is an issue for everyone, not just Karen and Tony.

Leadership and Decision Making.

A final problem that every group must resolve is the question of navigation: "How will we steer the ship, particularly in stormy weather?" Groups often get lost. Meetings are punctuated with statements like "I'm not sure where we're going" or "We've been talking for an hour without getting anywhere" or "Does anyone know what we're talking about?"

The task of leadership is to help groups develop a shared sense of direction and commitment. Otherwise, a group becomes rudderless or moves in directions that no one supports. Though leadership is essential, it need not come from only one person. A single leader focuses responsibility and clarifies accountability. But the same individual may not be equally effective in different situations. Groups often do better with a shared and fluid approach, regularly asking, "Who can best lead in *this* situation?" As mentioned earlier, Katzenbach and Smith (1993) found that a key characteristic of high-performance teams was mutual accountability, which was fostered when leaders shared in the work and team members shared in the leadership.

Leadership, whether shared or individual, plays a critical role in group effectiveness and individual satisfaction. Maier (1967) found that leaders who either overcontrol or understructure tend to produce frustration and ineffectiveness. Good leaders are sensitive to both task and process. They enlist others actively in managing both. Effective leaders help group members communicate and work together, while less effective leaders try to dominate and get their own ideas accepted.

Summary

Employees are hired to do a job but always bring social and personal needs with them to the workplace. Moreover, they spend much of their time in organizations interacting with others, one on one and in groups. Both individual satisfaction and organizational effectiveness depend heavily on the quality of interpersonal interactions.

Argyris and Schön argue that interpersonal dynamics in organizations are often counterproductive. People employ theories-in-use (behavioral programs) that emphasize self-protection and the control of others. Argyris and Schön developed an alternative model of effectiveness built on values of mutuality and learning.

Small groups are often condemned for wasting time while producing little, but groups *can* be both satisfying and efficient. In any event, organizations cannot function without them. Managers need to understand that groups always operate at two levels: task and process. Both levels need to be managed if groups are to be effective. Among the significant process issues that groups need to manage are informal roles, group norms, interpersonal conflict, and leadership.

Note
1. *The net* refers here to the growing importance of electronic networks—including the Internet and intranets—and associated media, such as e-mail and groupware.

Part Four

The Political Frame

Chapter Nine

Power, Conflict, and Coalitions

Sunrise, January 28, 1986. Clear but very cold in Cape Canaveral. More like New Hampshire, where Christa McAuliffe was a high school teacher, than Florida. Curtains of ice greeted ground crews as they inspected Flight 51-L, the space shuttle *Challenger*. The temperature had plunged overnight to a record low of 24 degrees Fahrenheit (−4 degrees Celsius). The ice team removed as much as they could. Temperatures gradually warmed, but it was still brisk at 8:30 A.M. *Challenger*'s crew of seven astronauts noted the ice around them as they climbed into the shuttle. As McAuliffe, the first teacher to venture into space, entered the ship, a technician offered her an apple. She held it and beamed, then asked the technician to save it for her until she returned. At 11:38 A.M., *Challenger* lifted off. A minute later, there was a massive explosion in the booster rockets. Millions watched their television screens in horror as the shuttle and its crew were destroyed.

On the eve of the launch, an emergency teleconference had been called between the National Aeronautics and Space Administration (NASA) and the Morton Thiokol Corporation, the contractor that provided solid rocket motors for the shuttle. At the teleconference, a group of Thiokol engineers had pleaded with their superiors and NASA to delay the launch. They feared that the cold temperatures would cause a failure in synthetic rubber O-rings that sealed joints in the rocket motor. If the rings failed, the motor could blow up. The engineers recommended strongly that NASA wait for warmer weather. But Thiokol and NASA both faced strong pressures to get the shuttle in the air:

> Thiokol had gained the lucrative sole source contract for the solid rocket boosters thirteen years earlier, during a bitterly disputed award process characterized by some veteran observers as a low point in squalid political

intrigue. At the time of the award to then relatively small Thiokol Chemical Company in Brigham City, Utah, both the newly appointed chairman of the Senate Aeronautics and Space Science Committee, Democratic Senator Frank Moss, and the new NASA administrator, Dr. James Fletcher, were insiders in the tightly knit Utah political hierarchy. By summer 1985, however, Thiokol's monopoly position was under attack, and the corporation's executives were afraid to risk their billion-dollar contract by halting shuttle flight operations long enough to correct flaws in the booster joint design [McConnell, 1987, p. 7].

Meanwhile, managers at NASA were experiencing pressures of their own. As part of their effort to build congressional support for the space program, NASA had promised that the shuttle would eventually pay for itself in cargo fees, like a boxcar in space. The projections of profitability were based on a very ambitious plan: twelve flights in 1984, fourteen in 1985, and seventeen in 1986. NASA had fallen well behind schedule—only five launches in 1984 and eight in 1985. The promise of "routine access to space" and flights that would pay for themselves looked more and more dubious. With every flight costing the taxpayers about $100 million, NASA needed a lot of money from Congress, but the prospects were getting bleaker. NASA's credibility was eroding while the U.S. budget deficit was soaring.

That was the context in which Thiokol's engineers recommended canceling the next day's launch. The response from NASA officials was swift and pointed. One NASA manager said he was "appalled" at the recommendation, and another said, "My God, Thiokol, when do you want me to launch? Next April?" (McConnell, 1987, p. 196). Thiokol asked for time to caucus. Thiokol's senior managers huddled and decided, against the advice of their engineers, to recommend the launch. NASA accepted the recommendation and launched Flight 51-L the next morning. The O-rings failed almost immediately, and the flight was doomed [Jensen, 1995; McConnell, 1987; Marx, Stubbart, Traub, and Cavanaugh, 1987; Bell and Esch, 1987; Vaughn, 1990, 1995].

It is disturbing to see political forces corrupting decision making, particularly for highly technical issues with human lives at stake. It is tempting to blame individual selfishness, myopia, and stupidity. But such explanations provide little help in understanding or avoiding tragedies like *Challenger*. Key decision makers were experienced, highly trained, and intelligent. If we tried to get better people, where would we find them? Even if we found them, how could we ensure that they, too, would not become ensnared by the politics of work?

Although the space shuttle program suffered both structural and human resource problems, neither perspective addresses the central issues in the *Challenger* disaster. The structural frame's orderly, rational optic and the humane, collaborative images of the human resource frame miss the dynamics of power and politics so visible in the *Challenger* incident.

From a structural perspective, organizations are guided by goals and policies set at the top. In the *Challenger* case we find a welter of dispersed and conflicting goals. Some were set at the top (in the White House and in Congress), others were established by NASA administrators, and many were shaped by no one in particular—they gradually emerged like weeds from a political swamp.

The human resource frame emphasizes malfunctions arising from person-organization misalignment or from flawed handling of interpersonal and group dynamics. Though Model I pathologies (see Chapter Eight) were rampant in the NASA-Thiokol teleconference, the human resource frame glosses over the political forces that set the stage for conflict and power plays.

The political frame views organizations as alive and screaming political arenas that host a complex web of individual and group interests. Five propositions summarize the perspective:

1. Organizations are *coalitions* of various individuals and interest groups.
2. There are *enduring differences* among coalition members in values, beliefs, information, interests, and perceptions of reality.
3. Most important decisions involve the allocation of *scarce resources*—who gets what.
4. Scarce resources and enduring differences give *conflict* a central role in organizational dynamics and make *power* the most important resource.
5. Goals and decisions emerge from *bargaining, negotiation,* and *jockeying for position* among different stakeholders.

All five propositions came to the fore in the *Challenger* incident. NASA did not run the space shuttle program in isolation. NASA was part of a complex coalition that included contractors, Congress, the White House, the military, the media—and even the American public. Consider, for example, why Christa McAuliffe was aboard. Her fellow crew members had little need of her expertise as a social science teacher. But the American public had become bored with white male test pilot astronauts. Human interest was good for NASA and Congress—it built public support for the program. It was also good for the media because it made for more interesting stories. Three years earlier, Dr. Sally Ride had generated excitement as the first female astronaut. Now the idea of putting an ordinary citizen in space—a teacher, no less—caught the imagination of the American people. Symbolically, Christa McAuliffe represented every American. When she flew, her fellow citizens flew with her.

The president, the press, the public, Congress, the contractors, and NASA were all part of the coalition, but there were *enduring differences* among them. NASA's hunger for funding competed with the public's interest in lower taxes. Astronauts' concerns about safety were at odds with pressures on NASA and its contractors to maintain an ambitious flight schedule.

The political frame asserts that in the face of enduring differences and scarce resources, conflict is inevitable and power is a key resource. Scarce resources force trade-offs. Enduring differences ensure that parties will disagree on both what and how to decide. Thus on the eve of the *Challenger* launch, key parties argued about how to balance technical and political concerns. How much risk was it worth to get the shuttle in the air?

The assumptions of the political frame define sources of political dynamics in organizations. A coalition forms because of interdependence among its members; they need one another, even though their interests may be only partly in synchrony. The assumption of enduring difference implies that political activity will be more visible and dominant under conditions of diversity than under conditions of homogeneity. Agreement and harmony are much easier to achieve when everyone shares similar values, beliefs, and culture.

The concept of scarce resources suggests that politics will be more salient and intense in difficult times. Some veteran teachers and administrators in America's public schools still remember the 1960s as a golden age. School systems grew rapidly and were blessed with abundant resources. School administrators spent time deciding which buildings to erect and which programs to initiate. The human resource frame became the dominant model for school management—until the 1970s, when the bottom fell out. Taxpayer protests and declining enrollments forced school districts to close schools and lay off teachers. Conflict mushroomed, and many school administrators succumbed to political forces that they could neither understand nor control.

Another key political issue is *power*—its distribution and exercise. Power in organizations is basically the capacity to get things to happen. Pfeffer (1992, p. 30) defines power as "the potential ability to influence behavior, to change the course of events, to overcome resistance, and to get people to do things they would not otherwise do." Russ (1994, p. 38) puts it more strongly as the ability to "make one's will prevail and to attain one's goal." From the view of the political frame, power is a "daily mechanism of our social existence" (Crozier and Friedberg, 1977, p. 32).

The final proposition of the political frame emphasizes that organizational goals are set not by fiat at the top but through an ongoing process of negotiation and interaction among the key players. The aftermath of the crackdown in Beijing's Tiananmen Square is one of many examples. Shortly after the incident, Chinese Communist leaders announced a major purge to rid the party of disloyal "capitalist roaders." Yet a year later, almost no one had been purged. Even prominent opponents of the crackdown had not yet been expelled, though some found that the processing of their application for membership renewal was taking longer than usual. Meanwhile, many provincial governors became openly disdainful of the central government, often ignoring directives from Beijing (Kristof, 1989). Leadership at the center used control of the media to mount a steady barrage of propaganda, but a cynical Chinese public paid little attention. Fierce internal bargaining and continuing divisions severely limited the ability of the party hierarchy to translate its intentions into effective action.

The propositions of the political frame do not attribute politics to individual selfishness, myopia, or incompetence. Interdependence, difference, scarcity, and power relations will inevitably produce political activity, regardless of the players. It is naive and romantic to hope that politics can be eliminated in organizations. Managers can, however, learn to understand and manage political processes.

Organizations as Coalitions

Traditional views—both academic and commonsense—assume that organizations have, or ought to have, clear and consistent goals. Generally, goals are presumed to be established by the persons with authority. In businesses, owners or top managers set a goal of maximizing profits. Goals in government agencies are presumably set by the legislature and executive to whom the agency is accountable. The political frame insists that organizations are coalitions. Individuals and groups have different objectives and resources, and each attempts to bargain with other players to influence goals and decisions. Cyert and March (1963, p. 30) articulate the difference between structural and political views of goals:

> To what extent is it arbitrary, in conventional accounting, that we call wage payments "costs" and dividend payments "profit" rather than the other way around? Why is it that in our quasi-genetic moments we are inclined to say that in the beginning there was a manager, and he recruited workers and capital? . . . The emphasis on the asymmetry has seriously confused the understanding of organizational goals. The confusion arises because ultimately it makes only slightly more sense to say that the goal of a business enterprise is to maximize profit than to say that its goal is to maximize the salary of Sam Smith, assistant to the janitor.

Cyert and March are saying something like this: Smith, the assistant janitor; Jones, the foreman; and Miller, the company president, are members of a grand coalition, Miller Enterprises. All make demands on resources, and each bargains to get as much as possible. Miller has more authority than Smith or Jones but no divine or inalienable right to determine goals. Miller's influence depends on how much power she mobilizes in comparison with that of Smith, Jones, and other members of the coalition.

If political pressures on goals are visible in the private sector, they are blatant in the public arena. As we saw in the *Challenger* incident, public agencies operate amid a complex welter of constituencies, each making demands and trying to get its way. The result is a confusing multiplicity of goals, many in conflict. In the early 1990s, for example, the French national airline, Air France, found itself in a tightening vise. Its survival in an era of deregulation depended on cutting its bloated costs, but powerful unions fought tooth and nail to protect workers' pay and jobs. Was Air France's goal to serve its passengers, protect its workers, or relieve the suffering of French taxpayers? From a political perspective, it was all of the above and more.

Power and Decision Making

In analyzing power, structural theorists emphasize authority: the legitimate prerogative to make decisions binding on others. Managers make rational decisions (optimal and consistent with purpose), monitor actions to assure that decisions are implemented, and evaluate how well subordinates carry out directives. Human resource theorists place little emphasis on power, though they often promote the idea of *empowerment* (Bennis and Nanus, 1985; Block, 1987). Unlike structuralists, they emphasize limits of authority. As an asymmetric source of influence, authority often stands in the way of integrating organizational and individual needs. When A can influence B, but not vice versa, there is a good chance that the relationship will be more satisfying for A than for B. Human resource theorists tend to focus on influence that enhances mutuality and collaboration. The implicit hope is that participation, openness, and collaboration make power a nonissue.

The political frame views authority as only one among many forms of power. It recognizes the importance of human (and group) needs but emphasizes that scarce resources and incompatible preferences cause needs to collide. Consider a case of policy conflict. A group of graduate students in an academic department wants the university to become more democratic and responsive, while faculty members insist on tightening controls and standards. The human resource theorist is likely to ask: What are the needs and perspectives of each group? How can the two engage in a productive dialogue to learn from one another, explore differences, and find a mutually satisfactory solution? The human resource view assumes that incompatible preferences can be resolved in a win-win outcome.

The structural perspective implies that some solutions are "better" than others—based on sound analysis or because they produce better outcomes. Parties can presumably recognize better solutions through a rational examination of alternatives.

Political theorists are more likely to view divergent interests as enduring facts of life and are less optimistic about distinguishing among "better" and "worse" solutions. The question becomes, how does each group articulate preferences and mobilize power to get what it wants? Power, in this view, is not necessarily bad. "We have to stop describing power always in negative terms: it excludes, it represses. In fact, power produces; it produces reality" (Foucault, 1975, p. 12).

Gamson's analysis of political processes focuses on two major players in social systems: authorities and partisans. Authorities are entitled to make decisions binding on partisans. Gamson (1968) describes the relationship between authorities and partisans in this way: "Authorities are the recipients or targets of influence, and the agents or initiators of social control. Potential partisans have the opposite roles—as agents or initiators of influence, and targets or recipients of social control" (p. 76).

In families, parents function as authorities and children as partisans. Parents make binding decisions about bedtime, television viewing, or which child uses a particular toy. Parents initiate social control, and children are the recipients of parental decisions. Children in turn try to influence the decision makers. They argue for a later bedtime or point out the injustice of giving one child something another wants. They try to split authorities by lobbying one parent after the other has refused. They may form coalitions (with siblings, grandparents, and so on) in an attempt to strengthen their bargaining position.

Social control is essential to those in formal positions because their authority depends on it. Officeholders retain authority only if the system remains viable. If partisan conflict becomes too powerful for the authorities to control, their positions are undermined. The process can be very swift, as events in Eastern Europe in 1989 illustrated. Established regimes had lost much of their legitimacy years earlier but held on through coercion and control of access to decision making. Senior government officials had reason to hold on: their power and privilege were tied to maintaining the "leading role" of the Communist party. As massive demonstrations erupted, authorities faced an unnerving choice: activate the police and army in hopes of preserving power or watch their power evaporate. Authorities in China and Romania chose the first course. That path led to bloodshed in both cases, but only the Chinese were able to quash the opposition. Elsewhere in Eastern Europe, authorities' attempts to quell dissent were futile, and their power evaporated as swiftly as water in a desert.

The period of evaporation is heady but dangerous. The question is whether new authority can reconstitute itself quickly enough to avoid chaos. Authorities and partisans both have reason to fear a specter such as Lebanon in the 1980s or Bosnia and Liberia in the 1990s—perpetual turmoil with no authority able to bring partisan conflict under control. Russia has teetered on the edge of chaos for much of the past decade. Still, when partisans are convinced that the existing authority is too evil or too incompetent to continue, they will take that risk and try to wrest power away— unless they regard the authorities as too formidable to confront. Conversely, when partisans trust authority, they will leave it alone and support it if it is attacked (Gamson, 1968; Baldridge, 1971).

Even though partisans lack authority, they may have other sources of power. A number of social scientists (French and Raven, 1959; Baldridge, 1971; Kanter, 1977; Pfeffer, 1992; Russ, 1994) have tried to identify the various wellsprings of power. Their answers include the following:

1. *Position power (authority).* Positions confer certain levels of formal authority—professors assign grades, and judges decide disputes. Positions also place incumbents in more or less powerful locations in communications and power networks. It helps to be in the right unit as well as the right job: a lofty title in a backwater department may not mean much, but junior members of a powerful unit may have substantial clout (Pfeffer, 1992).

2. *Information and expertise.* Power flows to those who have information and know-how to solve important problems. It flows to marketing experts in consumer products industries, to the faculty in elite universities, and to superstar conductors of symphony orchestras.

3. *Control of rewards.* The ability to deliver jobs, money, political support, or other rewards brings power. France and Italy were

among many countries rocked in the early 1990s by scandals involving political bosses who kept themselves in power through control of patronage, public services, and other payoffs.

4. *Coercive power.* Coercive power rests on the ability to constrain, block, interfere, or punish. A union's ability to walk out, students' ability to sit in, and an army's ability to clamp down all exemplify coercive power.

5. *Alliances and networks.* Getting things done in organizations involves working through a complex network of individuals and groups. Friends and allies make that a lot easier. Kotter (1982) found that a key difference between more and less successful senior managers was attentiveness to building and cultivating links with friends and allies. Managers who spent too little time building their networks had much more difficulty getting things done.

6. *Access and control of agendas.* A by-product of networks and alliances is access to decision arenas. Organizations and political systems typically give some groups more access than others. When decisions are made, the interests of those with "a seat at the table" are well represented, while the concerns of absentees are often distorted or ignored (Lukes, 1974; Brown, 1986).

7. *Framing: control of meaning and symbols.* "Establishing the framework within which issues will be viewed and decided is often tantamount to determining the result" (Pfeffer, 1992, p. 203). Elites and opinion leaders often have substantial ability to define and even impose the meanings and myths that define identity, beliefs, and values. Viewed positively, this provides meaning and hope. Viewed cynically, elites can convince others to accept and support things not in their best interests (Brown, 1986). This can be a very subtle and unobtrusive form of power: when the powerless accept the myths promulgated by the powerful, overt conflict and power struggles may disappear (Brown, 1986; Frost, 1985; Gaventa, 1980).

8. *Personal power.* Individuals with charisma, energy and stamina, political skills, verbal facility, or the capacity to articulate visions are imbued with power independent of other sources.

The availability of multiple sources of power constrains authorities' capacity to make binding decisions. Relying solely on position power tends to undermine their ability to influence: they generate resistance and are outflanked, outmaneuvered, or overrun by those more versatile in exercising power. Kotter (1985) argues that managerial jobs come with a built-in "power gap" in that power conferred by position is rarely enough to get the job done. Expertise, rewards, coercion, allies, access, framing, and personal power help close the gap.

A decision maker's power also depends on constituents' leverage and satisfaction. An organization that sets new profit records every year is rarely besieged by complaints and demands for change. As many company presidents have learned, however, the first bad quarter triggers a stream of calls and letters from board members, stockholders, and financial analysts. After a series of management and marketing snafus, Apple Computer's board of directors chose to remove Steven Jobs as chief executive, even though he was one of the founders and the largest single stockholder of the highly successful company. In 1996, with Apple's future looking dim, Jobs is back to encouraging innovation. One college president remarked ruefully that his primary job seemed to be to provide "sex for the students, parking for the faculty, and football for the alumni." The remark was half facetious, but it reflects an important reality: the president's power lies particularly in *zones of indifference*—areas that few people care much about. The zone of indifference can expand or contract markedly, depending on how the organization is doing in the eyes of its major constituents.

Alderfer (1979) and Brown (1983) distinguish between overbounded and underbounded systems. In overbounded systems, power is highly concentrated, and everything is tightly regulated. In underbounded systems, power is diffuse, and the system is very loosely controlled. Overbounded systems regulate politics tightly. Underbounded systems are an open invitation to conflict and power games.

When power is concentrated at the top of a highly regulated system, political activity is often forced underground. Before the emergence of Mikhail Gorbachev and *glasnost* ("openness") in the 1980s, it was common for westerners to view the Soviets as a vast, undifferentiated mass of like-minded people, brainwashed by decades of government propaganda. The truth was otherwise, but even so-called experts on Soviet affairs missed its significance (Alterman, 1989). Ethnic, political, philosophical, and religious differences simmered quietly beneath the surface so long as the Kremlin was able to maintain a tightly regulated society. *Glasnost* took the lid off, leading to an outpouring of debate and dissent that rapidly caused the collapse of the old order in the Soviet Union and throughout Eastern Europe. Almost overnight, much of Eastern Europe went from overbounded to underbounded, and the region has struggled since to bring order out of the ensuing chaos.

Conflict in Organizations

The structural perspective emphasizes social control and norms of rationality. Conflict is viewed as a problem that interferes with the accomplishment of purposes. Hierarchical conflict raises the possibility that lower levels will ignore or subvert management directives. Conflict among major partisan groups can undermine effectiveness and the ability of leadership to function. Such dangers are precisely why the structural perspective champions a chain of command. A basic function of authority is to resolve conflict. If two individuals or departments cannot reach agreement, a higher level adjudicates the dispute and makes a final decision consistent with plans and goals.

From a political perspective, conflict is not necessarily a problem or a sign that something is amiss. Organizational resources are notoriously in short supply: there is not enough to give everyone everything they want. There are too many lower-level jobs and too few at the top. If one group controls the policy process, others may be frozen out. Individuals compete for jobs, titles, and prestige. Departments compete for resources and power. Interest groups vie for policy concessions. Conflict is natural and inevitable.

The focus of the political frame is not on *resolution* of conflict (as is often the case in both the structural and human resource frames) but on *strategy* and *tactics*. If conflict will not go away, the question becomes how to make the best of it. Conflict has benefits as well as costs: "a tranquil, harmonious organization may very well be an apathetic, uncreative, stagnant, inflexible, and unresponsive organization. Conflict challenges the status quo [and] stimulates interest and curiosity. It is the root of personal and social change, creativity, and innovation. Conflict encourages new ideas and approaches to problems, stimulating innovation" (Heffron, 1989, p. 185). Thus an organization can experience either too much or too little conflict (Brown, 1983; Heffron, 1989; Jehn, 1995). Intervention may be needed to increase or decrease conflict, depending on the situation. Even more important than the amount of conflict is how it is managed. Poor conflict management regularly produces the kinds of infighting and destructive power struggle we saw in the *Challenger* case. But well-handled conflict can stimulate the creativity and innovation that make an organization a livelier, more adaptive, and more effective place (Kotter, 1985).

Conflict is particularly likely to occur at boundaries, or interfaces, between groups and units. *Horizontal conflict* occurs in interfaces between departments or divisions. *Vertical conflict* occurs between levels. *Cultural conflict* occurs between groups with different values, traditions, beliefs, and lifestyles. Cultural conflicts in the larger society are often imported into the workplace. Tensions form around gender, racial, and other differences. But organizations also create their own cultural conflicts. The culture of management is different from that of blue-collar workers. Workers who move up the ladder sometimes struggle with cultural adjustments required by their new role.

Moral Mazes: The Politics of Getting Ahead

> Not long after the big purge at Covenant Corporation, when 600 people were fired, the CEO spent $1 million for a Family Day to bring everyone together. The massive party was attended by over 14,000 people and featured clowns, sports idols, and booths complete with beanbag and ring tosses, foot and bus races, computer games, dice rolls, and, perhaps appropriately, mazes. In his letter to his Fellow Employees following the event, the CEO said, "I think Family Day made a very strong statement about the 'family' of employees at Corporate Headquarters. And that is that we can accomplish whatever we set out to do if we work together; if we share the effort, we will share the rewards" [Jackall, 1988, p. 37].

Jackall adds that "wise and ambitious managers resist the lulling platitudes of unity, though they invoke them with fervor, and look for the inevitable clash of interests beneath the bouncy, cheerful surface of corporate life" (p. 37). Beneath that surface is a world of circles and alliances, dominance and submission, conflict and self-interest, and, in Jackall's phrase, "moral mazes." Moving up the ladder inevitably involves competition for the scarce resource of status. The preferred myth is that free and fair competition ensures that better performers will win, at least in the long run.

But assessing performance in managerial jobs is fraught with ambiguity. There are multiple criteria, some of which can be assessed only through subjective judgment (particularly by bosses and other superiors). It is often hard to separate individual performance from the group's or a host of external factors. Did Thiokol engineers who fought to stop the launch of *Challenger* deserve high grades for persistence and integrity or low grades because they failed to convince senior managers? When some of those same engineers went public with their criticisms, were they demonstrating courage or disloyalty? Whistleblowers are regularly lauded by the press yet punished or banished by their employers.

Managers frequently learn that getting ahead is a matter of personal "credibility," which comes from doing what is socially and politically correct. Definitions of political correctness reflect tacit forms of power deeply embedded in organizational patterns and structure (Frost, 1986). Because getting ahead and making it to the top dominate the attention of many managers (Dalton, 1959; Jackall, 1988; Ritti and Funkhouser, 1982), both organizations and individuals need to develop constructive and positive ways to master the political game. The question is not whether organizations will have politics but rather what kind of politics they will have. Will political contests be energizing or debilitating, hostile or constructive, devastating or creative? Jackall's view is bleak:

> Bureaucracy breaks apart the ownership of property from its control, social independence from occupation, substance from appearances, action from responsibility, obligation from guilt, language from meaning, and notions of truth from reality. Most important, and at the bottom of all these fractures, it breaks apart the traditional connection between the meaning of work and salvation. In the bureaucratic world, one's success, one's sign of election, no longer depends on an inscrutable God, but on the capriciousness of one's superiors and the market; and one achieves economic salvation to the extent that one pleases and submits to new gods, that is, one's bosses and the exigencies of an impersonal market [Jackall, 1988, pp. 191–192].

This is not a pretty picture, but it is often accurate. Productive politics is possible but not easy. In the next chapter, we explore some of the possibilities for the manager as constructive politician.

Summary

The traditional view of organizations is that they are created and controlled by legitimate authorities who set goals, design structure, hire and manage employees, and seek to ensure that the organization pursues the right objectives. The political frame offers a different perspective. Authorities have position power, but they must vie with many other contenders for other forms of organizational clout. Contenders bring different beliefs, values, and interests. They seek access to various forms of power and compete for their share of scarce resources in a limited organizational pie.

From a political perspective, organizational goals, structure, and policies emerge from an ongoing process of bargaining and negotiation among major interest groups. Sometimes legitimate authorities are the dominant members of the organizational coalition: this is likely to be the case in a small, entrepreneurial organization where the chief executive is also the owner. But large corporations are often controlled by senior management rather than by stockholders or the board of directors. Government agencies may be controlled more by the permanent civil servants than by the political leaders at the top. The dominant group in a school district may be the teachers' union rather than the school board or the superintendent. In all such cases, naive rationalists will feel that the wrong people are setting the organizational agenda. But the political view suggests that the exercise of power is a natural part of an ongoing contest. Those who get and use power best will be the winners.

There is no guarantee that those who gain power will use it wisely or justly. But it is *not* inevitable that power and politics are demeaning and destructive. Constructive politics is a possibility—indeed, a necessary possibility if we are to create institutions and societies that are both just and efficient.

Chapter Ten

The Manager as Politician

Bill Gates was standing on the right corner in the early 1980s when IBM's fledgling personal computer business came along looking for an operating system. Gates didn't have one, but his partner, Paul Allen, knew someone who did. Gates paid $75,000 for QDOS (Quick and Dirty Operating System) in what has been characterized as the deal—or steal—of the century. Gates changed the name to DOS and resold it to IBM, shrewdly retaining the right to license it to anyone else. DOS became the operating system for most of the world's personal computers, and Gates was on the road to becoming one of the world's richest men (Manes and Andrews, 1994; Zachary, 1994). Windows, a graphic interface that rode atop DOS, fueled another great leap forward for Gates's Microsoft empire. But by 1988, Gates had a problem. He and everyone else knew that DOS was obsolete, woefully deficient for existing personal computers and even more inadequate for those to come. Millions of PC users were stuck in a seemingly endless high-tech version of *Waiting for Godot*.

The solution was supposed to be OS/2, an operating system jointly developed by Microsoft and IBM. It was a tense partnership. IBMers saw "Microsofties" as undisciplined adolescents. Microsoft folks moaned that "Big Blue" was a hopelessly bureaucratic producer of "poor code, poor design, poor process and other overhead" (Manes and Andrews, 1994, p. 425). Increasingly pessimistic about OS/2, Gates decided to bet on another option—a portable operating system that became known as Windows NT. Needing someone to head the effort, Gates recruited the brilliant but crotchety Dave Cutler away from Digital Equipment Corporation. Cutler

176

had led the development of the VMS operating system that helped DEC dominate the minicomputer industry for many years. Zachary (1993) described Cutler as a rough-cut combination of Captain Bligh and Captain Ahab. Gates agreed that Cutler was known "more for his code than his charm" (Zachary, 1993, p. A1).

Things started well, but Cutler insisted on keeping his team small and wanted no responsibility for anything beyond the "kernel" of the operating system. He figured that someone else could worry about such things as the user interface. Gates began to see a potential disaster in the making, but giving orders to the temperamental Cutler was as promising as ordering Picasso to paint differently. So Gates brought in the calm, understated Paul Maritz. Born in South Africa, Maritz had studied mathematics and economics at Cape Town before deciding that software was his destiny. After five years with Intel, Maritz had joined Microsoft in 1986 and was now in charge of the OS/2 effort. When he was assigned informal oversight of Windows NT as well, no one told Cutler, who adamantly refused to work for Maritz. Twelve years junior to Cutler, Maritz got a frosty welcome:

> As he began meeting regularly with Cutler on NT matters, Maritz often found himself the victim of slights. Once Maritz innocently suggested to Cutler that "We should—" Cutler interrupted, "We! Who's we? You mean you and the mouse in your pocket?"
>
> Maritz brushed off such retorts, even finding humor in Cutler's apparently inexhaustible supply of epithets. He refused to allow Cutler to draw him into a brawl. Instead, he hoped Cutler would "volunteer" for greater responsibility as the shortcomings of the status quo became more apparent [Zachary, 1994, p. 76].

Maritz enticed Cutler with tempting challenges. In early 1990, he asked Cutler if it were possible to put together a demonstration of NT for the industry's biggest convention, COMDEX, in November. Cutler took the bait. Maritz knew better than Cutler that the task would expose NT's weaknesses (Zachary, 1994). Eventually, Maritz was given formal authority over all of Microsoft's operating systems, but he continued his patient, persistent approach. When Gates seethed that NT was too late, too big, and too slow, Maritz scrambled to "filter that stuff from Dave" (p. 208). It eventually paid off. "The promotion gave Maritz formal and actual authority over Cutler and the entire NT project. Still, he avoided confrontations, preferring to wait until Cutler came to see the benefits of Maritz's views. Increasingly Cutler and his inner circle viewed Maritz as a powerhouse and not an empty suit. 'He's critical to the project,' said [one of Cutler's most loyal lieutenants]. He got into it a little bit at a time. Slowly he blended his way in until it was obvious who was running the show. Him" (p. 204).

The *Challenger* case (see Chapter Nine) taught a chilling lesson about how political pressures distort momentous decisions. Many managers believe that the antidote to such catastrophes is to free management from politics. But this is unrealistic so long as the political frame's basic conditions apply. Enduring differences lead to multiple interpretations of what is important and even what is true. Scarce resources require tough decisions about who gets what. Interdependence means that people cannot ignore one another: they need each other's assistance, support, and resources. Under such conditions, efforts to eliminate politics drive the differences under the rug or into the closet, where they fester into even more counterproductive and less manageable issues. We need to develop a more positive image of politics and of the manager as constructive politician. Paul Maritz provides a contemporary example.

Kotter (1985) contends that too many managers are either naive or cynical. Naive managers view the world through rose-colored glasses, insisting that just about everyone is good, kind, and trustworthy. Their cynical counterparts believe the opposite: everyone is selfish, everything is political, and "get them before they get you" is the best tactic. Neither stance is effective: "Organizational excellence . . . demands a sophisticated type of social skill: a leadership skill that can mobilize people and accomplish important objectives despite dozens of obstacles; a skill that can pull people together for meaningful purposes despite the thousands of forces that push us apart; a skill that can keep our corporations and public institutions from descending into a mediocrity characterized by bureaucratic infighting, parochial politics, and vicious power struggles" (p. 11).

Organizations need "benevolent politicians" who steer a course between naiveté and cynicism: "Beyond the yellow brick road of naiveté and the mugger's lane of cynicism, there is a narrow path, poorly lighted, hard to find, and even harder to stay on once found.

People who have the skill and the perseverance to take that path serve us in countless ways. We need more of these people. Many more" (Kotter, 1985, p. xi).

Skills of the Manager as Politician

What political skills does a manager need? In a world of chronic scarcity, diversity, and conflict, astute managers need to develop a direction, build a base of support, and learn how to manage relations with both allies and opponents. This requires at least four key political skills: agenda setting (Kanter, 1983; Kotter, 1988; Pfeffer, 1992; Smith, 1988); mapping the political terrain (Pfeffer, 1992; Pichault, 1993); networking and forming coalitions (Kanter, 1983; Kotter, 1982, 1985, 1988; Pfeffer, 1992; Smith, 1988); and bargaining and negotiating (Bellow and Moulton, 1978; Fisher and Ury, 1981; Lax and Sebenius, 1986).

Agenda Setting

Structurally, an agenda outlines a goal and a schedule of activities. Politically, agendas are statements of interests and direction. In reflecting on his experience as a university president, Bennis (1989) arrived at a deceptively simple observation: "It struck me that I was most effective when I knew what I wanted" (p. 20). Kanter's study of internal entrepreneurs in American corporations (1983), Kotter's analysis of effective corporate leaders (1988), and Smith's examination of effective U.S. presidents (1988) reached similar conclusions: the first step in effective leadership is setting an agenda. Effective leaders create an "agenda for change" with two major elements: a *vision* balancing the long-term interests of parties involved and a *strategy for achieving the vision*, recognizing the full range of competing internal and external forces (Kotter, 1988). The agenda must provide direction while addressing concerns of major stakeholders. Kanter (1983) and Pfeffer (1992) underscore the close relationship between gathering information and setting an agenda. Pfeffer's list of key political attributes includes "sensitivity"—knowing how others think and what they care about so that you can fashion an agenda that responds to their concerns. "Many people think of politicians as arm-twisters, and that is, in part, true. But in order to be a successful arm-twister, one needs to know which arm to twist, and how" (Pfeffer, 1992, p. 172).

Kanter (1983) adds: "While gathering information, entrepreneurs can also be 'planting seeds'—leaving the kernel of an idea behind and letting it germinate and blossom so that it begins to float around the system from many sources other than the innovator" (p. 218). This was exactly Paul Maritz's approach to Dave Cutler. Ignoring Cutler's barbs and insults, Maritz focused on getting information, building relationships, and formulating an agenda. He quickly concluded that the project was in disarray and that Cutler had to take on more responsibility. But Maritz's strategy was exquisitely attuned to his quarry: "Maritz protected Cutler from undue criticism and resisted the urge to reform him. [He] kept the peace by exacting from Cutler no ritual expressions of obedience" (Zachary, 1994, pp. 281–282).

A vision without a strategy remains an illusion. A strategy has to recognize major forces working for and against the agenda. Smith (1988, p. 333) makes this point about the American presidency:

> In the grand scheme of American government, the paramount task and power of the president is to articulate the national purpose: to fix the nation's agenda. Of all the big games at the summit of American politics, the agenda game must be won first. The effectiveness of the presidency and the capacity of any president to lead depends on focusing the nation's political attention and its energies on two or three top priorities. From the standpoint of history, the flow of events seems to have immutable logic, but political reality is inherently chaotic: it contains no automatic agenda. Order must be imposed.

Agendas are almost never automatic. The bigger the job, the more difficult it is to wade through issues clamoring for attention to find order amid chaos. Contrary to Woody Allen's dictum, success requires a good deal more than just showing up. High office, even if the incumbent has great personal popularity, is no guarantee of success. Ronald Reagan was remarkably successful in his first year as president because he followed a classic strategy for winning the agenda game: "First impressions are critical. In the agenda game, a swift beginning is crucial for a new president to establish himself as leader—to show the nation that he will make a difference in people's lives. The first one hundred days are the vital test; in those weeks, the political community and the public measure a new president—to see whether he is active, dominant, sure, purposeful" (Smith, 1988, p. 334).

Reagan began with a vision but no strategy. He was not gifted as a manager or a strategist, even though he had an extraordinary ability to portray complex issues in broad, symbolic brushstrokes. Reagan's staff painstakingly studied the first hundred days of four predecessors. They concluded that it was essential to move with speed and focus. Pushing competing issues aside, they focused on two: cutting taxes and reducing the federal budget. They also discovered a secret weapon in David Stockman, the only person in the Reagan White House who really understood the federal budget process. Stockman later admitted that he was astounded by the "low level of fiscal literacy" of Reagan and his key advisers (Smith, 1988, p. 354). According to Smith, "Stockman got a jump on everyone else for two reasons: he had an agenda and a legislative blueprint already prepared, and he understood the real levers of power. Two terms as a Michigan congressman plus a network of key Republican and Democratic connections had taught Stockman how to play the power game" (p. 351). Reagan and his advisers had the vision. Stockman provided strategic direction.

Mapping the Political Terrain

It makes little sense to plunge into a minefield without knowing where the explosives are buried, yet managers unwittingly do it all the time—they launch new initiatives with little or no effort to map the political field. Pichault (1993) suggests four steps for developing a political map:

1. Determine the channels of informal communication
2. Identify the principal agents of political influence
3. Analyze the possibilities for both internal and external mobilization
4. Anticipate the strategies that others are likely to employ

Pichault gives an example of planned change in a large government agency in Belgium. The agency wanted to replace its antiquated, manual records system with a fully automated, paperless computer network. But proponents of the new system had virtually no understanding of how the existing system actually worked, nor of the interests and power held by key middle managers and front-line bureaucrats. It seemed obvious to the "techies" that better access to data would dramatically improve efficiency. In reality, front-line bureaucrats made almost no use of the data. They applied standard procedures in 90 percent of the cases they encountered and asked their boss what to do about the rest. They talked to bosses partly to get the "right" answer but, even more important, to cover themselves politically. Even if the new technology were installed, it was likely that the front-line bureaucrats would ignore it or work around it. After a consultant clarified the political map, a new battle erupted between unrepentant techies who still insisted their vision was correct and other senior managers who argued for a less ambitious, more grounded solution. The two sides ultimately compromised.

A simple way to develop a political map for a given situation is to create a two-dimensional diagram that maps players (who is in the game), power (how much clout each player is likely to exercise), and interests (what does each player want). Figures 10.1 and 10.2 provide two hypothetical versions of the political map for the Belgian bureaucracy. Figure 10.1 shows the map as the proponents of the new technology (the "techies") might have seen it. In their map, there is little serious opposition to the new system, and the change advocates hold all the high cards. The map suggests a quick and easy win. Figure 10.2, the "real" map (as it might be seen by an objective analyst), shows a very different picture. The opposition is more intense and more powerful. This map forecasts a stormy change process with protracted conflict. Though less comforting, the second map has an important message to the politically wise: success will require substantial effort to realign the existing field of political forces. The next two sections describe strategies for doing that.

Networking and Building Coalitions

The *Challenger* disaster occurred despite recognition of the O-ring problem by engineers at both Morton Thiokol and NASA. For a long time, they tried to call it to their superiors' attention, mostly

Figure 10.1.   The Map the "Techies" See.

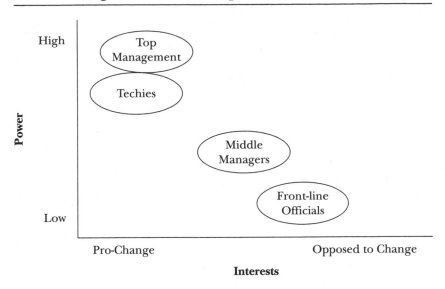

Figure 10.2.   The Real Political Map.

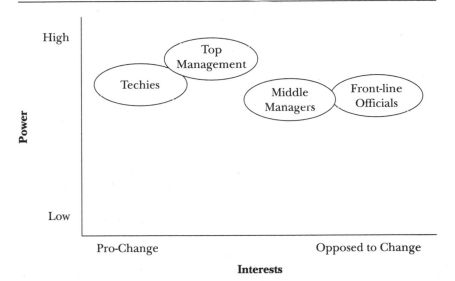

through memos. Six months before the accident, Roger Boisjoly, an engineer at Morton Thiokol, wrote: "The result [of an O-ring failure] would be a catastrophe of the highest order—loss of human life" (Bell and Esch, 1987, p. 45). Two months later, another Thiokol engineer wrote a memo that opened, "HELP! The seal task force is constantly being delayed by every possible means" (p. 45). The memo detailed resistance from other departments in Thiokol. A memo to the boss is sometimes effective, but it is just as often a sign of political innocence. Kotter (1985) suggests four basic steps for political influence:

1. Identify relevant relationships (figure out who needs to be led).
2. Assess who might resist, why, and how strongly (figure out where the leadership challenges will be).
3. Develop, wherever possible, relationships with potential opponents to facilitate communication, education, or negotiation.
4. When step three fails, carefully select and implement either more subtle or more forceful methods.

The political frame emphasizes that no strategy will work without a power base. Managers need cooperation from others, often large numbers of people. Moving up the ladder confers authority but also brings increasing dependence. A manager's success depends on the cooperation of many others (Kotter, 1985, 1988). Rarely will people provide their best efforts and fullest cooperation because they have been told to do so. They need to perceive the people in authority as credible, competent, and pursuing sensible directions.

The first task in building networks and coalitions is to figure out whose help you need. The second is to develop relationships with these people so that they will be there when you need them. Middle managers seeking to promote change typically begin by getting their boss to agree (Kanter, 1983). They then move to "preselling" or "making cheerleaders": "Peers, managers of related functions, stakeholders in the issue, potential collaborators, and sometimes even customers would be approached individually, in one-on-one meetings that gave people a chance to influence the project and the innovator the maximum opportunity to sell it. Seeing them alone and on their territory was important: the rule was to act as if each person were *the* most important one for the project's success" (p. 223).

Once you have cheerleaders, you can move to "horse trading"—promising rewards in exchange for resources and support. This builds a resource base that helps in "securing blessings"—getting necessary approvals and mandates from higher management (Kanter, 1983). Kanter found that the usual route to success at that stage is to identify critical senior managers and to develop a polished, formal presentation to get their support. The best presentations respond to both substantive and political concerns because senior managers typically care about two questions: Is it a good idea? And how will my constituents react to it? Once innovators had the blessing of higher management, they could go back to their boss to formalize the coalition and make specific plans for pursuing the project (Kanter, 1983).

The basic point is simple: as a manager, you need friends and allies to get things done. To get their support, you need to cultivate relationships. Hard-core rationalists and incurable romantics sometimes react with horror to such a scenario. Why should you have to play political games to get something accepted if it's the right thing to do? One of the great works in French drama, Molière's play *The Misanthrope,* tells the story of a protagonist whose rigid rejection of all things political is destructive for him and everyone around him. The point that Molière made three centuries ago still has merit: it is hard to dislike politics without also disliking people. Like it or not, political dynamics are inevitable under conditions most managers face every day: ambiguity, diversity, and scarcity.

Mistakes can be very costly. Smith (1988) reports a case in point. Thomas Wyman, board chairman of the CBS television network, went to Washington in 1983 to lobby U.S. Attorney General Edwin Meese. A White House emergency forced Meese to miss the meeting, and Wyman was sent to the office of Craig Fuller, one of Meese's top advisers:

> "I know something about this issue," Fuller suggested, "Perhaps you'd like to discuss it with me."
>
> Wyman waved him off, unaware of Fuller's actual role, and evidently regarding him as a mere staff man.

"No, I'd rather wait and talk to Meese," Wyman said.

For nearly an hour, Wyman sat leafing through magazines in Fuller's office, making no effort to talk to Fuller, who kept working at his desk just a few feet away.

Finally, Meese burst into Fuller's office, full of apologies that he simply wouldn't have time for substantive talk. "Did you talk to Fuller?" he asked.

Wyman shook his head.

"You should have talked to Fuller," Meese said. "He's very important on this issue. He knows it better than any of the rest of us. He's writing a memo for the president on the pros and cons. You could have given him your side of the argument" [Smith, 1988, pp. xviii–xix].

Wyman missed an important opportunity because he failed to test his assumptions about who actually had power.

Bargaining and Negotiation

Bargaining is often associated with commercial, legal, and labor relations settings. From a political perspective, bargaining is central to all decision making. The horse trading Kanter describes as part of coalition building is just one of many examples. Negotiation is needed whenever two or more parties with some interests in common and others in conflict need to reach agreement. Labor and management may agree that a firm should make money and provide good jobs for its employees but disagree on how to balance pay and profitability. Engineers and top managers at Morton Thiokol had a common interest in the success of the shuttle program. They differed sharply on how to balance technical and political trade-offs.

A fundamental dilemma in negotiations is choosing between "creating value" and "claiming value":

Value creators tend to believe that, above all, successful negotiators must be inventive and cooperative enough to devise an agreement that yields considerable gain to each party, relative to no-agreement possibilities. Some speak about the need for replacing the win-lose image of negotiation with win-win negotiation. In addition to information sharing and honest communication, the drive to create value can require ingenuity and may benefit from a variety of techniques and attitudes. The parties can treat the negotiation as solving a joint problem; they can organize brainstorming sessions to invent creative solutions to their problems. . . .

Value claimers, on the other hand, tend to see this drive for joint gain as naive and weak-minded. For them, negotiation is hard, tough bargaining. The object of negotiation is to convince the other guy that he wants what you have to offer much more than you want what he has; moreover, you have all the time in the world, while he is up against pressing deadlines. To "win" at negotiating—and thus make the other fellow "lose"—one must start high, concede slowly, exaggerate the value of concessions, minimize the benefits of the other's concessions, conceal information, argue forcibly on behalf of principles that imply favorable settlements, make commitments to accept only highly favorable agreements, and be willing to out wait the other fellow [Lax and Sebenius, 1986, pp. 30–32].

One of the best-known win-win approaches to negotiation was developed by Fisher and Ury (1981) in *Getting to Yes*. They argue that people too often engage in "positional bargaining": stake out positions and then reluctantly make concessions to reach agreement. Fisher and Ury contend that positional bargaining is inefficient and misses opportunities to create an agreement beneficial to both parties. They propose an alternative: "principled bargaining," built around four strategies. The first is to "separate the people from the problem." The stress and tension of negotiations easily escalate into anger and personal attacks. The result is that negotiators sometimes want to defeat or hurt the other person at almost any cost. Because every negotiation involves both substance and relationships, the wise negotiator will "deal with the people as human beings and with the problem on its merits."

The second rule of thumb is to "focus on interests, not positions." If you get locked into a position, you might overlook other ways to achieve goals. An example is the 1978 Camp David treaty resolving issues between Israel and Egypt. The sides were at an impasse over where to draw the boundary line between the two countries. Israel wanted to keep part of the Sinai, while Egypt wanted all of it back. Resolution became possible only when they looked at each other's underlying interests. Israel was concerned about security: no Egyptian tanks on the border. Egypt was concerned about sovereignty: the

Sinai had been part of Egypt from the time of the Pharaohs. The parties agreed on a plan that gave all of the Sinai back to Egypt while demilitarizing large parts of it (Fisher and Ury, 1981). That solution led to a durable peace agreement.

Fisher and Ury's third recommendation is to invent options for mutual gain—to look for new possibilities that bring advantages to both sides. Parties often consider only the first few alternatives that come to mind. Efforts to generate more options increase the chances of better decisions. Paul Maritz recognized this in his dealings with the prickly Dave Cutler. Instead of barreling ahead and giving Cutler orders, he asked innocently, "Could you do a demo at November COMDEX?" It was a new option that created gains for both parties.

Fisher and Ury's fourth strategy is to "insist on objective criteria"—standards of fairness for both substance and procedures. When a school board and a teachers' union are at loggerheads over the size of the teachers' pay increase, they can look for objective criteria—such as the rate of inflation or terms of settlement in other districts. A classic example of fair procedure finds two sisters deadlocked over how to divide a pie between them. The solution they agreed to was that one would cut the pie into two pieces and the other would choose the piece that she wanted.

Fisher and Ury devote most of their attention to creating value—finding better solutions for both parties. They downplay the question of claiming value—how negotiators can maximize individual gains. In many ways, win-win bargaining is more consistent with a human resource or structural view than a political one. By contrast, tactics for value claiming better represent the political frame. A classic example is Schelling's essay (1960), which focuses on the problem of how to make credible threats.

Suppose that I want to buy your house and am willing to pay $150,000. How could I convince you that I am willing to pay only $125,000? Contrary to a common assumption, I am not always better off if I am stronger and have more resources. If you believe that I am very wealthy, you might take my threat less seriously than if I can get you to believe that it is barely possible for me to scrape up $125,000. Common sense also suggests that I should be better off if I have considerable freedom of action. Yet I may get a better price if I can convince you that my hands are tied—for example, I am negotiating for a very stubborn buyer who will not go above $125,000, even if the house is worth more. Such examples suggest that the ideal situation for bargainers is to have substantial resources and freedom while convincing the other side of the opposite. Value claiming gives us the following picture of the bargaining process:

1. Bargaining is a mixed-motive game. Both parties want an agreement but have different interests and preferences.
2. Bargaining is a process of interdependent decisions. What each party does affects the other. Each player wants, as much as possible, to be able to predict what the other will do while limiting the other's ability to do likewise.
3. The more player A can control player B's level of uncertainty, the more powerful A is.
4. Bargaining involves the judicious use of *threats* rather than sanctions. Players may threaten to use force, go on strike, or break off negotiations. In most cases, they much prefer not to bear the costs of carrying out the threats.
5. Making threats credible is crucial. A threat is effective only if your opponent believes it. Noncredible threats weaken your bargaining position and confuse the process.
6. Calculation of the appropriate level of threat is also critical. If I "underthreaten," I may weaken my own position. If I "overthreaten," you may not believe me, may break off the negotiations, or may escalate your own threats.

Creating value and claiming value are both intrinsic to the bargaining process. How does a manager decide how to balance the two? At least two questions are important: How much opportunity is there for a win-win solution? And will I have to work with these people again? If an agreement can make everyone better off, it makes sense to emphasize creating value. If you expect to work with the same people in the future, it is risky to use value-claiming tactics that leave anger and mistrust in their wake. Managers who get a reputation for being manipulative and self-interested have a hard time building networks and coalitions they need for future success.

Axelrod (1980) found that a strategy of conditional openness worked best when negotiators needed to work together over time. This strategy starts with open and collaborative behavior and maintains the approach if the other responds in kind. If the other party becomes adversarial, however, the negotiator responds in kind and remains adversarial until the opponent makes a collaborative move. It is, in effect, a friendly and forgiving version of tit for tat—do unto others as they do unto you. Axelrod's research revealed that this conditional openness strategy worked better than even the most fiendishly diabolical adversarial strategies.

A final question in balancing collaborative and adversarial tactics is what is *ethical?* Bargainers often deliberately misrepresent their positions—even though lying is almost universally condemned as unethical (Bok, 1978). This leads to a profoundly difficult question for the manager as politician: What actions are ethical and just?

Morality and Politics

Block (1987), Burns (1978), and Lax and Sebenius (1986) all explore ethical issues in bargaining and organizational politics. Block's view rests on the assumption that individuals empower themselves through understanding: "The process of organizational politics as we know it works against people taking responsibility. We empower ourselves by discovering a positive way of being political. The line between positive and negative politics is a tightrope we have to walk" (Block, 1987, p. xiii).

Block argues that bureaucratic cycles often leave individuals feeling vulnerable, powerless, and helpless. When we give too much power to the organization and to others, we fear that power will be used against us. Consequently, we develop manipulative strategies to protect ourselves. To escape the dilemma, managers need to support organizational structures, policies, and procedures that promote empowerment. They must also make personal choices to empower themselves.

Block urges managers to begin by building an "image of greatness"—a vision of what their department can contribute that is meaningful and worthwhile. Then they need to build support for their vision by negotiating agreement and trust. Block suggests dealing differently with friends and opponents. Adversaries, he says, are simultaneously the most difficult and most interesting people to deal with. He argues that it is usually ineffective to pressure them and that a more effective strategy is to "let go of them." He offers four steps for letting go: (1) tell them your vision, (2) state your best understanding of their position, (3) identify your own contribution to the problem, and (4) tell them what you plan to do without making demands on them.

Such a strategy might work for conflict originating in misunderstanding or an unduly narrow understanding of one's self-interest. In situations of scarce resources and durable differences, bringing politics into the open may backfire, making conflict more obvious and overt but no more resolvable. Block argues that "war games in organizations lose their power when brought into the light of day" (1987, p. 148), but the political frame questions that assumption.

Burns's conception of positive politics (1978) draws on examples as diverse and complex as Franklin Roosevelt and Adolph Hitler, Gandhi and Mao, Woodrow Wilson and Joan of Arc. He sees both conflict and power as central to leadership. Searching for firm moral footing in a world of cultural and ethical diversity, Burns turned to the motivation theory of Maslow (1954) and the ethical theory of Kohlberg (1973). From Maslow he borrowed the idea of the hierarchy of motives. Moral leaders, he argued, appeal to higher levels on the needs hierarchy.

From Kohlberg he adopted the idea of stages of moral reasoning. At the lowest "preconventional" level, moral judgments are based primarily on perceived consequences: an action is right if you are rewarded and wrong if you are punished. In the intermediate "conventional" level, the emphasis is on conforming to authority and established rules. At the highest "postconventional" level, ethical judgments rest on general principles: the greatest good for the greatest number, or universal and comprehensive moral principles.

Maslow and Kohlberg provided a foundation on which Burns (1978) constructed a positive view of politics:

> If leaders are to be effective in helping to mobilize and elevate
> their constituencies, leaders must be whole persons, persons with
> full functioning capacities for thinking and feeling. The problem
> for them as educators, as leaders, is not to promote narrow, egocen-
> tric self-actualization, but to extend awareness of human needs and
> the means of gratifying them, to improve the larger social situation
> for which educators or leaders have responsibility and over which
> they have power. What does all this mean for the teaching of lead-
> ership as opposed to manipulation? "Teachers"—in whatever
> guise—treat students neither coercively nor instrumentally but as

joint seekers of truth and of mutual actualization. They help students define moral values not by imposing their own moralities on
them but by positing situations that pose moral choices and then
encouraging conflict and debate. They seek to help students rise to
higher stages of moral reasoning and hence to higher levels of
principled judgment [pp. 448–449].

Thus in Burns's view, positive politics evolve when individuals choose
actions that appeal to higher motives and higher stages of moral
judgment.

Lax and Sebenius (1986), regarding ethical issues as inescap-
able, provide a set of questions to help managers decide what is
ethical:

1. Are you following rules that are understood and accepted? (In
   poker, for example, everyone understands that bluffing is part
   of the game.)
2. Are you comfortable discussing and defending your action?
   (Would you want your colleagues and friends to be aware of it?
   Your spouse, children, or parents? Would you be comfortable
   if it were on the front page of a major newspaper?)
3. Would you want someone to do it to you? To a member of your
   family?
4. What if everyone acted that way? Would the resulting society
   be desirable? (If you were designing an organization, would
   you want people to act that way? Would you teach your children to do it?)
5. Are there alternatives that rest on firmer ethical ground?

Although these questions do not provide a comprehensive ethical framework, they embody three important principles of moral
judgment:

1. *Mutuality*—are all parties to a relationship operating under the
   same understanding about the rules of the game?
2. *Generality*—does a specific action follow a principle of moral
   conduct applicable to all comparable situations?
3. *Caring*—does this action show care for the legitimate interests
   of others?

Such questions raise issues that should be part of an ongoing dialogue about the moral dimension of management and leadership. Porter (1989) notes the dearth of such conversations: "In a seminar with seventeen executives from nine corporations, we learned how the privatization of moral discourse in our society has created a deep sense of moral loneliness and moral illiteracy; how the absence of a common language prevents people from talking about and reading the moral issues they face. We learned how the isolation of individuals—the taboo against talking about spiritual matters in the public sphere—robs people of courage, of the strength of heart to do what deep down they believe to be right" (p. 2).

If we choose to banish moral discourse and leave managers to face ethical issues alone, we invite dreary and brutish political dynamics. In a pluralistic secular world, organizations cannot impose a narrow ethical framework on employees. But as we will argue in Chapter Nineteen, they can and should take a moral stance. They can make their values clear, hold employees accountable, and validate the need for dialogue about ethical choices. Positive politics absent an ethical framework and a moral dialogue is as likely as successful farming without sunlight or water.

Summary

The question is not whether organizations will have politics but rather what kind of politics they will have. The dynamics of politics can be sordid and destructive. But politics can also be the vehicle for achieving noble purposes. Organizational change and effectiveness depend on managers' political skills. Constructive politicians recognize and understand political realities. They know how to fashion agendas, create networks of support, and negotiate effectively with both allies and adversaries. In the process, they encounter a practical and ethical dilemma—when to adopt open, collaborative strategies and when to choose tougher, more adversarial approaches. They will need to consider the potential for collaboration, the importance of long-term relationships, and, most important, their own values and ethical principles.

Chapter Eleven

Organizations as Political Arenas and Political Agents

It's not easy to make the cover of *Time* magazine as a poster boy for corporate greed and insensitivity, but Ross Johnson managed. In *Barbarians at the Gate,* Bryan Burrough and John Helyar (1990) explain how. Johnson began his career plodding through a series of middle-management jobs for General Electric in Canada. At age thirty-two, he was earning a modest $14,000 a year and teaching at night to bring in extra cash. Frustrated, he left GE to seek his fortune elsewhere. His charm, humor, and charisma moved him ahead. Several jobs later, the mid-1970s found him in New York heading international operations for a consumer products firm, Standard Brands. Johnson's lavish spending (on limousines and sumptuous entertainment) put him on a collision course with his boss, Henry Weigl. Weigl, a tightfisted autocrat, was proud of twenty consecutive years of profit growth during his tenure as Standard Brands's president. Fed up with Johnson's extravagance, Weigl went after him. Johnson's political acumen averted a personal disaster. "Johnson prepared for war. A headhunter who gathered employee intelligence for Weigl became a double agent, also reporting to Johnson. A gathering of conspirators descended upon Johnson's home over several weekends. Together they assembled a report that would show how Weigl's tightfisted ways were slowly strangling Standard Brands" (Burrough and Helyar, 1990, p. 19).

Knowing that Weigl was heading for a confrontation, Johnson networked with friends on the board of directors. He got unexpected help from a tragedy: two weeks before the board meeting, a popular executive died. Many blamed his death on overexposure to Weigl's caustic and autocratic management style. At the board meeting, Weigl reviewed a long list of Johnson's expense account abuses. Johnson admitted minor excesses and said he would resign. The board caucused, kicked Weigl upstairs, and put Johnson in charge of the company. Johnson accepted on one condition: Weigl had to move out of the headquarters building.

Johnson fired many of Standard Brands's senior executives, promoted his friends to high office, and embarked on a spectacular period of lavish spending: corporate jets, country club memberships, corporate apartments, and generous contracts to star athletes. After four years of unspectacular business results, an unexpected call came from Bob Schaeberle, chairman of the food giant Nabisco. Schaeberle wanted to talk merger. Within two weeks, the deal was done: a $1.9 billion stock swap—a very big deal for 1981.

Everyone knew who would be in charge: Nabisco was by far the stronger player. But people underestimated Ross Johnson. Schaeberle became chairman and chief executive of the merged company, Johnson president and chief operating officer:

> On paper, Schaeberle remained the top executive of Nabisco Brands, but Johnson found it easy to get his way. Their offices were adjacent, and Johnson wasted no time ingratiating himself with his boss. He deferred to Schaeberle in every regard, obsequiously addressing him in meetings as "Mr. Chairman." Johnson donated $250,000 to Pace University to endow a Robert M. Schaeberle Chair in accounting. Surprised by the announcement at a Pace dinner, an honored but stunned Schaeberle said, "Who's going to pay for this?" The company was, of course.
>
> Slowly but surely, Johnson closed his grip around Schaeberle's company. One by one, veteran Nabisco executives began to vanish, replaced by Johnson men. . . . Within three years, twenty-one of the company's top twenty-four officers were Standard Brands men. The Nabisco officers had been killed so softly that Schaeberle never realized what happened. At meetings, he would say, "It's nice to see all these young people around the table" [Burrough and Helyar, 1990, pp. 33–35].

Johnson also impressed Schaeberle with his ability to sell some of Nabisco's weaker units for top dollar. He used his charm, telling potential buyers they could run the business much better than

Nabisco had. He won a cookie war: under attack in Kansas City by Frito-Lay and Procter & Gamble, Johnson threw money at the problem, virtually giving Nabisco's cookies away. After a few years, Schaeberle made Johnson chief executive, and Johnson named the company's new research unit after Schaeberle. Once in charge, Johnson often seemed more interested in hobnobbing with celebrities than in actually running the company. But then, in 1985, he got another phone call. Tylee Wilson, chief executive of R. J. Reynolds, the huge tobacco company based in Winston-Salem, North Carolina, wanted to talk merger. Wilson needed a partner to help Reynolds move away from its heavy dependence on the profitable but controversial cigarette business. Johnson held out for a lot more than Wilson wanted to give, but the deal was soon done: Reynolds paid $4.9 billion for Nabisco.

More than one of Wilson's friends warned him about Johnson. Wilson discounted the risk: it was Reynolds's deal, and consequently, Reynolds would be in charge. But Wilson had alienated part of his board—he lacked Johnson's awesome skills at ingratiation. Things came to a head when the board learned that Wilson had authorized a huge effort to develop a smokeless cigarette without board approval. As that tempest weakened Wilson, Johnson relied again on the strategy that had worked for him at Standard Brands: he told several friends on the board that he would be leaving because there was only room for one CEO. A few weeks later, Wilson was startled to learn that a majority of his board wanted him out. He resigned, taking a multimillion-dollar settlement with him.

Johnson was now atop a business throwing off more than a billion dollars a year—more money than even he could spend. He tried: a new headquarters building in Atlanta; a fleet of corporate jets soon known as the RJR Air Force; lavish fees to directors, senior executives, and star athletes (top of the line: golfer Jack Nicklaus at $1 million a year). Johnson was having the time of his life—until RJR Nabisco's stock lost a third of its value in the market crash of October 1987. Convinced that the stock was unfairly tainted by its tobacco business, Johnson wanted it back up. He settled on a craze of the time: a leveraged buyout (LBO). The basic idea of an LBO is to find an undervalued company, buy up the shares with someone else's money, fix it up or break it up, and sell it at a profit. It's a high-stakes, high-risk venture. The leverage from borrowed money can mean prodigious profits—or crushing losses. The interest burden can be staggering. Once you announce an LBO, your company is in play. It's open season for anyone to try to top your bid. Anyone in this case meant Henry Kravis: "Practically unknown five years before, Kravis and his secretive firm, KKR, had ridden Wall Street's leveraged buyout wave to prominence in the mid-eighties. If it were ranked as an industrial company, the businesses KKR controlled, from Duracell batteries to Safeway supermarkets, would place it among the top ten U.S. corporations. Now, with $45 billion in buying power, Kravis was the unquestioned king of Wall Street acquisitors, his war chest greater than the gross national products of Pakistan or Greece, his clout rivaling that of any in financial history" (Burrough and Helyar, 1990, p. 130).

If anyone could compete with management's bid for RJR Nabisco, it was Kravis. Before announcing the LBO, Johnson had declined several overtures from Kravis to meet and talk. Johnson didn't want to tip his hand, but he expected Kravis to stay out anyway. The deal was too big: $17 billion, maybe more—three times bigger than any LBO in history. And Kravis mostly did friendly deals on management's side. Johnson did not realize that he had annoyed a very dangerous adversary. "I can't believe this," Kravis fumed after he first got word of the deal. "We gave them the idea. He wouldn't even meet with us" (Burrough and Helyar, 1990, p. 191).

What followed was one of the biggest six-week poker games in business history. Huge coalitions formed. Ross Johnson engaged the merger department at Shearson Lehman Hutton to lead his charge. Shearson, the brokerage unit of American Express, brought the money and the LBO expertise that Johnson needed. Johnson brought top management and the board. But being on the same team is no guarantee of having the same interests. Johnson insisted on the fattest management package in LBO history. Shearson reluctantly went along because Johnson was their ticket into the deal. Eventually, when the agreement hit the *New York Times*, it drove a huge wedge between Johnson and his board—they'd never seen it.

Millions of dollars in fees gushed into the hands of bankers, lawyers, and brokers. Just about every big player on Wall Street got some piece of the action. It had everything but sex: confusion, conflict, reams of computer printouts, sleepless nights, threats and bluffs, brilliant stratagems, childish mistakes. Ego, image, and personal antipathy regularly threw the process off track. It finally culminated in a frantic, last-minute bidding war. When the dust cleared, Henry Kravis and the KKR group won by a nose. RJR Nabisco was theirs for a cool $25 billion. It was a Pyrrhic victory. RJR Nabisco never performed as well as hoped, and KKR spent several years getting out from under the unprofitable deal.

The RJR Nabisco story illustrates two sides of organizational politics: organizations are both arenas and agents. As arenas, they provide a setting for the ongoing interplay of interests and agendas among different individuals and groups. As agents, they are tools, often very powerful tools, for achieving the purposes of those who master them. Ross Johnson was a consummate practitioner of internal politics, with no qualms about treating a corporation as a personal plaything. He won every battle—until he found himself in the role of a novice playing against the grandmasters of the LBO game.

In the political view, there is no such thing as permanent improvement: "happily ever after" exists only in fairy tales. In the real world, today's winners may quickly become tomorrow's losers. The political perspective views change and stability paradoxically, asserting that organizations constantly change and never change. There is continual jockeying for position, and yesterday's elites may be tomorrow's also-rans. Yet as in football and chess, players come and go, but the game continues.

Organizations as Arenas

As arenas, organizations house contests. Arenas help determine what game will be played, who will be on the field, and what interests will be pursued. From this perspective, every organizational process is political. Consider design, the process of shaping and structuring organizations. Most theories of design, built on structural premises, assume that the best design is the one that will contribute the most to efficient attainment of the organization's goals and strategy. Pfeffer (1978) offered an explicitly political conception as an alternative: "Since organizations are coalitions, and the different participants have varying interests and preferences, the critical question becomes not how organizations should be designed to maximize effectiveness, but rather, whose preferences and interests are to be served by the organization. . . . What is effective for students may be ineffective for administrators. What is effectiveness as defined by consumers may be ineffectiveness as defined by stockholders. The assessment of organizations is dependent upon one's preferences and one's perspective" (p. 223).

Even though different groups in an organization have conflicting preferences, they also have a shared interest in avoiding continuously destructive conflict. So they agree on ways to divide power and resources, and those settlements are reflected in the design of the organization. Structures are "the resolution, at a given time, of the contending claims for control, subject to the constraint that the structures permit the organization to survive" (Pfeffer, 1978, p. 224).

An example is Ross Johnson's controversial decision to move RJR's headquarters from Winston-Salem, where it had been for a century, to Atlanta. Reynolds was the commercial heart of Winston-Salem. It engendered fierce pride and loyalty among much of the citizenry, many of whom were substantial stockholders. But Johnson and his key lieutenants felt that the small city in the heart of tobacco country was boring and provincial. The move to Atlanta had scant business justification, was unpopular among the RJR board, and made Johnson the most hated man in Winston-Salem. But Johnson headed the dominant coalition. He got what he wanted.

Pfeffer uses participative management to make the case that human resource initiatives may mask political agendas. The human resource frame views participation as a way to build motivation and commitment. Pfeffer analyzes it as co-optation—a process of giving people something to induce them to ally themselves with organizational needs and purposes. If women in a university are vocal in demanding equality, the administration might create a "committee on the status of women," provide a secretary and a research assistant, and schedule occasional meetings with top administrators. By putting the most vocal women on the committee, the administration hopes that they will expend their energies mostly in the internal process of the committee rather than in changing the university. If the strategy works, the administration defuses potential problems while holding up the committee as public evidence of the university's commitment to equality and fairness. Similarly, when lower-level employees demand more influence, management can create self-managing teams while still controlling the information and the alternatives available to the groups.

Gamson's distinction between authorities and partisans (1968) implies two major sources of political initiatives: bottom-up initiatives, relying on mobilization of interest groups to assert their agendas, and top-down initiatives, relying on authorities' capacity to influence subordinates. We discuss examples of both to illustrate some of the basic processes of political action.

Bottom-Up Political Action

The rise of trade unions and the emergence of the civil rights movement in the United States exemplify the process of bottom-up change in organizations and societies. In both cases, the precondition for change was a significant disruption in previous patterns. Trade unions developed in the context of the industrial revolution, rapid urbanization, and the decline of the family farm. The civil rights movement arose after a period of massive occupational and geographic shifts for black citizens. In each case, changing conditions unfroze old patterns and intensified dissatisfaction for one group within a larger system. Both movements reflected the classic pattern of revolutions: a period of rising expectations followed by widespread disappointment.

In each case, the initial stimulus was grassroots mobilizing and organizing—the formation of trade unions or of civil rights organizations. Elites bitterly contested the legitimacy of such grassroots activities and used coercive tactics to block them. At various times, employers used everything from lawsuits to violence in the battle against unionization. The civil rights movement, particularly in its early stages, was subject to violent repression by whites. In the face of intense opposition, newly organized groups engaged the policy process and fought to have their rights embodied in law. Either movement might have failed had it been weaker or its opposition stronger. Both suffered profound setbacks but mobilized enough power to survive and grow. Compared to many efforts at bottom-up change, they were relatively successful. Although there is no accurate census of the success of grassroots change efforts, many—

perhaps most—such efforts fail. Even the most successful may yield only modest reforms. Union busting is still practiced in the United States and elsewhere, and union power itself diminished considerably in the 1980s in the face of global competition and the decline in blue-collar work. The difficulties of bottom-up political action lead many people to believe that you have to begin at the top to get anything done. Yet research on top-down efforts catalogues many failures, as we discuss in the next section.

Political Barriers to Control from the Top

Deal and Nutt (1980) conducted a revealing secondary analysis of local school districts that received U.S. Department of Education funding to develop experimental programs for comprehensive changes in education. A typical scenario for these projects included the following steps:

1. The central administration learned of the opportunity to obtain federal funding.
2. A small group of administrators met to develop a proposal for improving some aspect of the educational program. (The process was usually rushed. Few people were involved because there was so little time to meet the proposal deadline.)
3. When funding was approved, the administration announced with pride and enthusiasm that the district's success in a national competition would bring it substantial money to support an exciting new project to improve instruction.
4. Teachers were stunned to learn that the administration had committed to new teaching methods without faculty input. The administration was startled and perplexed when teachers greeted the news with resistance, criticism, and anger.
5. The administration, caught in the middle between teachers and the funding agency, interpreted teacher resistance as a sign of defensiveness and unwillingness to change.
6. The new program became a political football, producing more disharmony, mistrust, and conflict than tangible improvement in education.

The programs studied by Deal and Nutt represented examples of top-down change efforts under comparatively favorable circumstances. The districts were not in crisis. The change efforts were well funded and blessed by the federal government. Yet across the board, the new initiatives set off heated political battles. In many cases, the local administration found itself outgunned. In one district, the teachers mobilized such intense community opposition to the project that the superintendent of schools was forced out of office. Only one superintendent survived in office over the program's five-year funding cycle.

In most instances, the administrators never anticipated major political battles. Their proposal called for programs they thought would be progressive, effective, and good for everyone. They had overlooked the risks in proposing changes that someone else is expected to carry out. As a result, they got conflict instead of the huzzahs they were expecting.

Similar patterns appear repeatedly in attempts to achieve top-down change. Countless improvement efforts mounted by chief executives, frustrated managers, hopeful study teams, and high-status management consultants end in failure. The usual mistake is the implicit assumption that the right idea (as perceived by the idea's champions) and legitimate authority are enough to ensure success. This assumption neglects the agendas and power of the "lower-archy"—the partisans and groups in middle- and lower-level positions who devise a host of creative and maddening ways to resist, divert, undermine, ignore, or overthrow change efforts.

Organizations as Political Agents

Organizations are arenas for internal politics. They are also political agents in larger arenas or "ecosystems" (Moore, 1993). Just as frogs, flies, and lily pads coevolve in a swamp, organizations develop in tandem in the context of shared environments. Moore (1993) illustrates with two ecosystems in the personal computer business, one pioneered by Apple Computer and the other by IBM. Apple's ecosystem dominated the personal computer business before IBM's entry, but IBM's ecosystem rapidly came to dominate the worldwide PC industry—IBM had enormous business clout, and the open architecture of its PC induced new players to flock into its arena.

Some of these players competed head-on (for example, Compaq and IBM in hardware, Microsoft and Lotus in software). Others were related much like bees and flowers—each performed an indispensable service for the other. One symbiotic pairing was particularly fateful. As Microsoft gained control of the operating system and Intel of the microprocessor in the IBM ecosystem, the two increasingly became mutually indispensable. More sophisticated software needed faster microprocessors, and vice versa, so the two had every reason to cheer each other on. Two companies that began as servants to IBM eventually took over what had become the "Wintel" ecosystem.

The same factors that generate internal politics also create political dynamics in relationships within and between ecosystems. Organizations have their own interests and compete with others for scarce resources. The RJR Nabisco bidding war created a fluid, temporary ecosystem that illustrates many of the complexities. Dozens of individuals, groups, and organizations were involved. RJR Nabisco itself, the big prize in the contest, was largely a bystander, its board on the sidelines for most of the game. Ross Johnson and his Shearson allies represented their own interests more than the corporation's. The financial stakes were enormous, yet the game was often driven more by issues of power, reputation, and personal animosity. Everyone wanted the prize, but you could win by losing and lose by winning.

Organizational ecosystems come in many forms and sizes. Some are small and local, like the ecosystem of laundries in Dallas or Milan. Others are very large and complex, like the global automobile industry. We will examine several significant types of ecosystem to illustrate the dynamics involved.

Business Ecosystems

General Motors, the company that Billy Durant founded in 1906 and Alfred Sloan rebuilt in the 1920s, became the world's largest industrial corporation. It pioneered in the ecosystem of the auto industry and became the dominant player for more than half a century. Its resources and its power were and still are immense—in 1995, GM earned almost $7 billion on sales of $169 billion. But GM's niche crumbled in the 1970s and 1980s with the arrival of powerful foreign competitors. The environmental shifts revealed all too clearly that GM had become a lumbering, slow-to-adapt beast. Despite all its power, the company struggled to convince consumers to keep buying its cars. In 1992, GM reported a loss of $23.5 billion, "the largest ocean of red ink that has ever engulfed a *Fortune 500* company" (Loomis, 1993, p. 41). GM's size and financial strength were an enormous cushion—a lesser beast might not have survived its marketing and management problems. But history shows that even great companies falter.

General Electric thrived during the 1980s—unlike many of its peers. Its success then and earlier stemmed from adroit adaptation to a changing environment. In the first two decades after World War II, the engineers who ran GE's functional structure created an extremely efficient system for producing whatever *they* thought consumers needed. Almost a stereotype of old-fashioned hierarchy, it would have been a disaster in the late-twentieth-century world of frenetic global competition. But it was hugely successful in an era when much of the world's industrial capacity outside the United States had been devastated and huge pent-up consumer demand chased after just about anything GE could manufacture. By 1981, when Jack Welch became CEO, GE had evolved considerably from its postwar engineering mentality. Welch concluded nonetheless that only dramatic change could save the company from a downhill slide. He set to work to build a culture that emphasized quality, entrepreneurship, and candor. He made a key decision to compete only in ecosystems where GE could be a dominant player. He insisted that every GE business be number one or two in its industry. If not, said Welch, "we'll fix it, sell it, or close it" (Morris, 1995, p. 90). He radically revised GE's business mix, selling off about a third of the businesses he inherited and moving resources into more promising opportunities. In four years, GE reduced its payroll from more than 400,000 to about 330,000. Welch's "destaffing" initiatives earned him the nickname "Neutron Jack," after the bomb that wipes out people but leaves buildings intact (Bartlett and Elderkin, 1991). Welch was certainly not infallible: some of his investments soured, and GE was troubled by periodic ethics scandals (Paré, 1994). But earnings growth made GE a very profitable company. Between 1982 and 1992, market value increased from $21.6 billion to $73.9 billion. In 1982, IBM had more than twice the market value of GE; ten years later, their positions were reversed (Loomis, 1993, p. 37).

Public Policy Ecosystems

In the public sector, policy arenas form around virtually every government activity. Air carriers, airplane manufacturers, travelers, legislators, and regulators are all active participants in the commercial aviation ecosystem. In the United States, the Federal Aviation Administration was a troubled central player in the 1980s and 1990s. Charged with the often divergent goals of defending safety, promoting the economic health of the industry, and keeping its own costs down, it came under heavy fire from virtually every direction. Lax oversight permitted marginal carriers to shortcut safety but continue flying. Bureaucratic and political squabbles delayed for years the replacement of a desperately antiquated computer system for air traffic control.

Education provides another illustration of a complex policy ecosystem. In the late 1980s, for example, it was widely thought that American public schools could be improved by giving parents and students more choice about which schools children would attend. Proponents of choice plans argued that parents would choose the school that fit their children's needs best and competition would have an invigorating effect on schools. But school boards and school administrators almost universally resisted the idea. Coalitions formed on both sides of the issue and lobbied at both the state and national levels.

Business and Government Ecosystems

Government and business inevitably evolve in tandem, spawning in the process a multitude of intersecting ecosystems. Perrow (1986) discusses one example: pharmaceutical companies, physicians, and government. A major threat to the companies' profit margins is generic drugs—drugs that sell at prices much lower than their brand-name equivalents. In the United States, the industry trade association—an interorganizational coalition—successfully lobbied many state legislatures to prohibit the sale of such drugs, ostensibly to protect consumers. The industry also persuaded the American Medical Association (AMA) to change policy to permit drugs to be advertised by brand name in its journals. Consumers normally buy whatever the doctor prescribes, and the drug companies wanted doctors to think in brand names rather than chemical names. As a result of the policy shift, the AMA's advertising income tripled in seven years, and the manufacturers strengthened the position of their brands (Perrow, 1986). More recently, the ecosystem shifted again with the rapid rise of a newly powerful player: managed health care providers. HMOs used their increasing leverage to push physicians to prescribe less expensive generic drugs whenever possible. Several states now actually require pharmacists to offer the generic equivalent when a brand name is prescribed in an effort to save consumers money.

Drug companies are by no means unique in their attention to politics. In Chapter Seven, we described the highly sophisticated approach to human resource management developed at Federal Express. FedEx was equally agile in managing its political environment and was described as "one of the most formidable and successful corporate lobbies in the capital" (Lewis, 1996, p. 17). Its CEO, Fred Smith, "spends considerable time in Washington, where he is regarded as Federal Express's chief advocate. It was Mr. Smith who hit a lobbying home run in 1977 when he persuaded Congress to allow the fledgling company to use full-sized jetliners to carry its cargo, rather than the small planes to which it had been restricted. . . . That was the watershed event that allowed the company to grow to its present dominating position with almost $10.3 billion in business" (p. 30).

FedEx's political action committee ranked among the nation's top ten, making generous donations to hundreds of candidates for Congress. Its board was adorned with popular former congressional leaders from both major political parties. Its corporate jets regularly ferried officeholders to events around the country. All this generosity paid off. In October 1996, when FedEx wanted two words inserted into a 1923 law regulating railway express companies, the Senate stayed in session a couple of extra days to get it done, even with elections only a month away. A first-term senator commented, "I was stunned by the breadth and depth of their clout up here" (Lewis, 1996, p. 17).

A similar coevolution of business and politics occurs around the world:

No one would dispute that business and politics are closely intertwined in Japan. As one leading financial journalist puts it, "If you don't use politicians, you can't expand business these days in

Japan—that's basic." Businessmen provide politicians with funds, politicians provide businessmen with information. If you wish to develop a department store, a hotel or a ski resort, you need licenses and permissions and the cooperation of leading political figures in the area. And it is always useful to hear that a certain area is slated for development, preferably several years before development starts, when land prices are still low [Downer, 1994, p. 299].

Society as Ecosystem

At a still larger scale, we find society: the massive ecosystem in which business, government, and the public are all embedded and co-evolve. A critical question in this arena is the power relationship between organizations and society. All organizations have power. Large organizations have a lot of it. "Of the 100 largest economies in the world, 51 are corporations, and only 49 are countries. Wal-Mart is bigger than Israel, Poland or Greece. Mitsubishi is bigger than Indonesia. General Motors is bigger than Denmark. . . . If governments can't set the rules, who will? The corporations? But they're the players. Who's the referee" (Longworth, 1996, p. 4)?

A number of organizational scholars (including Korten, 1995; Perrow, 1986; and Stern and Barley, 1996) emphasize that whoever controls a multibillion-dollar tool wields enormous power. Korten's view is particularly dark:

An active propaganda machinery controlled by the world's largest corporations constantly reassures us that consumerism is the path to happiness, government restraint of market excess is the cause of our distress, and economic globalization is both a historical inevitability and a boon to the human species. In fact, these are all myths propagated to justify profligate greed and mask the extent to which the global transformation of human institutions is a consequence of the sophisticated, well-funded, and intentional interventions of a small elite whose money enables them to live in a world of illusion apart from the rest of humanity. These forces have transformed once beneficial corporations and financial institutions into instruments of a market tyranny that is extending its reach across the planet like a cancer, colonizing ever more of the planet's living spaces, destroying livelihoods, displacing people, rendering democratic institutions impotent, and feeding on life in an insatiable quest for money [Korten, 1995, p. 12].

Do sophisticated consumer marketing firms create and control consumer tastes, or do they simply react to needs created by larger social forces? Critics like Korten are convinced that the advantage lies with the corporations, but other observers see it the other way around:

> The marketing concept of management is based on the premise that over the longer term all businesses are born and survive or die because people (the market) either want them or don't want them. In short, the market creates, shapes, and defines the character of the demand for all classes of products and services. Almost needless to say, many managers tend to think that they can design goods and services and then create a demand for them. The marketing concept denies this proposition. Instead, the marketing concept emphasizes that the creative aspect of marketing is the discovery, definition, and fulfillment of what people want or need or which solves their life-style problems [Marshall, 1984, p. 1].

Proponents of this view note that even the most successful marketers have had their share of Edsels—products released with great fanfare and huge marketing budgets that fluttered briefly and then sank like stones.

Are large multinational corporations so powerful that they have become a law unto themselves, or are they strongly shaped by the need to respond to the governments, people, and cultures in the countries where they operate? An ecological view suggests that the answer is some of both. Ecosystems and competitors within them continually rise and fall. Power relations are never static, and even the most powerful have no guarantee of immortality. Of the top twenty-five U.S. companies at the beginning of the twentieth century, all but one had dropped off the list or vanished altogether as the century came to a close. The lone survivor? General Electric.

Over much of the century, power in major corporations tended to become more concentrated in the hands of management. So long as the companies performed well, stakeholders had enough confidence in management not to raise serious questions. The myth of accountability—that managers are accountable to both the shareholders and the market—was accepted at face value. When the U.S. economy faltered in the 1970s, things changed dramatically. *Business Week* said in the late 1980s: "The tight hold professional managers have on the corporation is slipping. Investors are no longer passive. Outside directors are asserting themselves. Other stakeholders—from employees to communities—want a voice. The balance of power is beginning to shift. By any measure, the current crop of corporate managers has reigned over an era of unprecedented American economic decline. For at least a decade, America's standard of living has been eroding, its share of the world market shrinking, and its products retreating in the face of foreign competition. So it's no accident that the dominance of management is being challenged today" (Nussbaum and Dobrzynski, 1987, pp. 102–103).

After sleeping through Roger Smith's tenure in the 1980s, GM's board of directors woke up in 1992 and took a step unprecedented in GM's history: they forced out Smith's handpicked successor, Robert Stempel. GM, IBM, Sears, and other corporate behemoths that stumbled through the turbulent 1980s were seen, at least for a time, as dinosaurs, too large and lumbering to survive in a new era (Loomis, 1993). Big institutional investors (who hold a third or more of all corporate shares in the United States), corporate raiders, concerned politicians, aggressive unions, environmental activists, consumer groups, and many others all began to take more active roles as power became more fluid and diffuse in an increasingly complex corporate environment (Kanter, 1983; Useem, 1996).

The 1990s brought a reprieve for embattled managers. Just as worries about the decline and fall of the U.S. economy reached a crescendo, productivity and profits soared. Shareholder returns and CEO salaries reached unprecedented heights, while the incomes of the poor and the middle class stagnated. Once again a chorus of critics attacked the concentration of power and wealth in the hands of a small elite. The battle over corporate power will continue on a global scale. Large multinational companies have enormous power but must also cope with the demands of other powerful players, including governments, labor unions, investors, and consumers. Useem (1996) argues that much of the turbulence in corporate America—shake-ups, breakups, downsizings, and the like—results from the pressures of institutional investors. Big pension and mutual funds with millions or billions to invest often use "voice" (that is, influence and pressure) because they cannot easily exit—it is easy to sell one hundred shares of General Electric but much harder to sell one hundred thousand. The consequence, says Useem, is an increasingly stressful, tense relationship between management and investors. Before announcing his buyout plan, Ross Johnson—a powerful manager—declined to meet with Henry Kravis—a very big investor. Johnson ultimately lost his company as a result. Such a lesson is hard for managers to ignore.

Barber (1995) sees a tension between tribalism and global capitalism dominating the world scene for the foreseeable future, with potentially devastating consequences:

> Jihad and McWorld operate with equal strength in opposite directions, the one driven by parochial hatreds, the other by universalizing markets, the one re-creating ancient subnational and ethnic borders from within, the other making national borders porous from without. Yet Jihad and McWorld have this in common: they both make war on the sovereign nation-state and thus undermine the nation-state's democratic institutions. Their common thread is indifference to civil liberty. Jihad forges communities of blood rooted in exclusion and hatred, communities that slight democracy in favor of tyrannical paternalism or consensual tribalism. McWorld forges global markets rooted in consumption and profit, leaving to an untrustworthy, if not altogether fictitious, invisible hand issues of public interests and common good that once might have been nurtured by democratic citizenries and their watchful governments. . . . Unless we can offer an alternative to the struggle between Jihad and McWorld, the epoch on whose threshold we stand—postcommunist, postindustrial, postnational, yet sectarian, fearful, and bigoted—is likely also to be terminally postdemocratic [Barber, 1995, pp. 6–8].

As the world becomes a global village, this is the biggest political contest of all.

Summary

Organizations are both arenas for internal politics and political agents with their own agendas, resources, and strategies. As arenas, they house contests and provide a setting for the ongoing interplay of interests and agendas among different individuals and groups. The nature of an arena and the rules it creates help determine what game will be played, who will be on the field, and what interests will be pursued. From this perspective, every significant organizational process is inherently political.

As agents, organizations are tools, often very powerful tools, for achieving the purposes of whoever controls them. They exist, compete, and coevolve in business or political ecosystems—clusters of organizations in a shared environment, each pursuing its own interests and seeking a viable niche. As in nature, relationships within and between ecosystems are sometimes fiercely competitive, sometimes collaborative and interdependent.

A particularly urgent and controversial question is the relative power of organizations and society. Giant multinational corporations have achieved scale and resources unprecedented in human history. Some critics foresee them increasingly dominating and distorting politics and society. More optimistic observers argue that organizations are inherently dependent on a changing and turbulent environment and in the long run retain their clout only by successful adaptation to larger social forces.

Part Five

The Symbolic Frame

Chapter Twelve

Organizational Culture and Symbols

To awestruck sightseers in the land of the business hierarchy, the architectural grandeur is overpowering and impressive. Stately edifices dominate landscaped vistas of suburbia and mighty skyscrapers silhouette the profiles of major cities. Flowering gardens, soaring plazas, ample parking, vaulted lobbies, air conditioning, musical elevators, carpeted lounges, spacious dining rooms, and hundreds upon hundreds of linear offices bathed relentlessly in fluorescent brilliance dutifully impress gaping tourists.

But all this structural munificence does not divert the expert gamester who looks beyond the steel and concrete public visor of the corporate persona to identify the heraldic markings painted on the battle armor. Like the shields carried by knights of legend, the modern corporate building reeks with symbolism. Far from being a mere architectural wonder, every pane of glass, slab of marble, and foot of carpet performs a dual function in identifying the tournament site. The buildings are impersonal monuments to the power and wealth contained therein. Space itself, in both the exterior and interior layout, is weighted with abstract significance. Just as a heraldic seal reveals a great deal about the one using it, so spatial divisions reveal important information about the modern-day knights [Harragan, 1977, pp. 211–212].

The corporate temples that Harragan artfully describes exemplify only one of many ways in which symbols permeate every fiber of organizations. From the beginning of time, humans have wrestled with the meaning of life. Without faith, people falter and perish. In our highly complex world, persistent questions trouble us at every turn. The symbolic frame seeks to interpret and illuminate basic issues of meaning and belief that make symbols so powerful. It depicts a world far different from traditional canons of rationality, certainty, and linearity.

Meaning, belief, and faith are central to a symbolic perspective. Humans have forever found life bewildering. Events often cannot be explained: loved ones die before their time; evil is sometimes better rewarded than virtue. Circumstances cannot always be controlled: tornadoes wipe out communities; fires destroy churches and factories; recessions put venerable firms out of business. Contradictions seek reconciliation: good people do bad and bad people do good. Dilemmas and paradoxes abound: How can we keep peace without huge arsenals? How can we protect lives and property without impinging on someone else? More prosaically, how can we help people learn from evaluations they find threatening?

The symbolic frame forms a conceptual umbrella for ideas from a variety of disciplines, including organization theory and sociology (Selznick, 1957; Blumer, 1969; Clark, 1975; Corwin, 1976; March and Olsen, 1976; Meyer and Rowan, 1978; Weick, 1976; Davis and others, 1976) and political science (Dittmer, 1977; Edelman, 1971). Freud and Jung relied heavily on symbolic concepts in attempting to understand the human psyche. Anthropologists have traditionally focused on symbols and their place in the culture and lives of humans (Ortner, 1973). The symbolic frame distills these diverse ideas into several core assumptions:

1. What is most important about any event is not what happened but what it means.
2. Activity and meaning are loosely coupled: events have multiple meanings because people interpret experience differently.
3. Most of life is ambiguous or uncertain—what happened, why it happened, or what will happen next are all puzzles.
4. High levels of ambiguity and uncertainty undercut rational analysis, problem solving, and decision making.
5. In the face of uncertainty and ambiguity, people create symbols to resolve confusion, increase predictability, provide direction, and anchor hope and faith.
6. Many events and processes are more important for what is expressed than what is produced. They form a cultural tapestry

of secular myths, rituals, ceremonies, and stories that help people find meaning, purpose, and passion.

The symbolic frame sees life as more *fluid* than linear. Organizations function like complex, constantly changing, organic pinball machines. Decisions, actors, plans, and issues continuously carom through an elastic, ever-changing labyrinth of cushions, barriers, and traps. Managers who turn to Peter Drucker's *Effective Executive* for guidance might do better to study Lewis Carroll's *Through the Looking Glass*. In recent years, the importance of symbols in corporate life has become more widely appreciated. Books like Kotter and Heskett's *Corporate Culture and Performance* (1992) and Collins and Porras's *Built to Last* (1994) offer impressive longitudinal evidence linking symbols to the financial bottom line.

Symbols embody and express an organization's culture—the interwoven pattern of beliefs, values, practices, and artifacts that define for members who they are and how they are to do things. Culture is both a product and a process. As a product, it embodies accumulated wisdom from those who came before us. As a process, it is continually renewed and re-created as newcomers learn the old ways and eventually become teachers themselves.

A case in point is Goren Carstedt's arrival to head Volvo France in the 1980s. It was a big challenge. Volvo had hoped to double sales to twenty thousand cars a year in France. Instead, sales were declining while other imported cars were increasing their market share. Even more troubling was the net of excuses offered to rationalize the dismal performance: "The products were said to be too old, too heavy, too stodgy, too expensive, and all had stiff rear axles, which were not *pointé* (hip) in France. Too much performance had been sacrificed to safety. Deliveries were slow, and promised new models were late. Carstedt was told time and time again that 'this is France.' It was a Latin nation, passionate and hot-blooded, whereas Volvo was a cerebral car, something melancholy Scandinavians thought about on long winter evenings" (Hampden-Turner, 1992, pp. 156–157).

Rejecting excuses, Carstedt was determined to put a more positive spin on a dreary situation. His actions illustrate the possibilities for a leader who understands the power of symbols and culture. He began by listening: he convened nine regional meetings with

Volvo's 150 French dealers. Seated around tables, he asked for their ideas: "I want to know what you think should be done and what Volvo can do to help you sell more cars. Tell me what we are doing wrong, what you want from us, and I'll see that it is done if I possibly can" (Hampden-Turner, 1992, p. 158). His approach was a dramatic departure from anything the dealers had seen before. His straightforward, open style soon earned him the nickname *le vol du nord* (the northern wind).

Carstedt's next steps relied heavily on values, ritual, ceremony, and humor to show that he was listening and willing to make real changes. He drew a cartoon that turned the traditional chain of command upside down. As Carstedt describes it, "The customer was king. The dealers were his courtiers, and it was our job—mine, Volvo France's and HQ's—to make sure the dealers had what they needed" (Hampden-Turner, 1992, p. 159).

He invited the dealers and their spouses to a conference center near Paris. The meeting opened with a humorous film, *Où est Volvo?* ("Where's Volvo?") French citizens were shown answering questions about Volvo and its dealers. Shrugs and gestures of indifference told the story: *"Je ne sais pas."* Next, Volvo's new models were shown via telecast from a beautifully appointed showroom somewhere in France. When asked to reveal the location, Carstedt raised the curtain behind him. There it was, a showroom assembled on the spot to show the dealers what a little ingenuity could do.

Next, Carstedt took the dealers on an excursion in Sweden. He wanted them to experience the culture behind the car: "Eighty percent of our marketing efforts are internal to help dealers assume the Volvo identity and take pride in the quality of the vehicles and see their own service is an inseparable part of this" (Hampden-Turner, 1992, p. 161). The group flew by chartered plane to Gothenburg, where they toured the factory and met with top managers. Later, said Carstedt, "we gave out prizes to our best dealers in front of our president and senior managers" (p. 162). The following day, the group traveled by train through the countryside. They met Volvo workers, toured old Stockholm, and were feted at a Viking party, complete with Swedish musicians and folksingers in traditional costume, where "they drank Schnapps, wore helmets, ate with their fingers, and threw the debris over their shoulders" (p. 162).

Carstedt closed with a speech—in French:

"For two years now, I've been trying to explain to you that there is something special about Volvo: our philosophy and values are important to our success. And to understand Volvo, it helps to understand something about Sweden. So we've invited you on a trip to see our lakes, forests, trees and houses for yourselves. Now we're here, in the heart of Sweden, in the room where Nobel dinners are served before the prizes are given, and you have the Nobel menus before you to remind you that this is the place that gives hospitality to the greatest achievements and the finest quality of which you are all a part" [Hampden-Turner, 1992, p. 162].

Back in France, Carstedt declared war on memos of excuse and defense. To convey the difference between where they had been and where they needed to go, he created two visual images: the first a square made of four fingers each pointing out what was wrong with someone else. The second depicted four hands in a supportive grasp. A graphic advertisement emphasized safety by showing a little girl strapped snugly in the rear seat of a Volvo. The caption read, "You need to protect the future, especially when the future is behind you." Volvo was cited that year for the best automotive advertising in France. The work paid off. In the next four years, Volvo's sales and market share doubled.

Organizational Symbols

Carstedt's strategy at Volvo is only one example of using symbols to find meaning in chaos, clarity in confusion, and predictability in mystery. *Myths* and other narrative forms such as *fairy tales* and *stories* provide explanations, reconcile contradictions, and resolve dilemmas (Cohen, 1969). Symbolic activities—such as *rituals* and *ceremonies*—provide direction in uncharted and seemingly unchartable terrain (Ortner, 1973). *Metaphor, humor, and play* loosen things up and take participants to a deeper level. Modern reincarnations of such symbolic figures as heroes, heroines, shamans, priests, and storytellers offer interpretations of what life in organizations really means. An organization's character is revealed and communicated most clearly through its symbols. McDonald's franchises are united as much by golden arches, core values, and the legend of Ray Kroc as by sophisticated control systems. Harvard professors, remarkably free of structural limits, are tightly constrained by rituals of teaching, values of scholarship, and the myths and mystique of Harvard.

Myths

Myths, operating at deep reaches of consciousness, provide the story behind the story (Campbell, 1988). They explain. They express. They maintain solidarity and cohesion. They legitimize. They communicate unconscious wishes and conflicts. They mediate contradictions. They provide narrative to anchor the present in the past (Cohen, 1969).

Myths have two facets. The negative side is they can blind us to new information and learning opportunities. The myth that "authority must always equal responsibility," still widely believed, is misleading and unrealistic. There are many other myths that managers live by: organizations are rational, change is planned, managers are in control, experts are objective, there is always one best way. We have all embraced one or more of these enduring fictions. We may still cling to them despite continuing evidence to the contrary. If we give up our cherished myths, we risk being overwhelmed. Myths keep us sane—but also dampen curiosity, refract images, and misdirect attention.

Manning (1979) describes the functions of myth in police work:

> The police myth sits apart from the actors in a drama of crime, gives them names and faces, and makes them subject to predictable scenarios with beginnings, middles, and ends. . . . Myths of police action concentrate public attention upon their force and conserving potential, even in times of rapid change. . . . Police myths freeze the organization in time and space, giving it a verified authority over the thing it opposes, and establish it in a timeless Manichean *pas de deux* between the two poles of social life. Law enforcement is no longer seen as mere work, involving decision, discretion, boredom and unpleasantries; it becomes a sort of creed [pp. 325–327].

All organizations rely on myths or sagas of varying strength and intensity (Clark, 1975). One of the distinctive characteristics of elite institutions—such as Harvard, the U.S. Marines, or McKinsey & Company—is the presence of strong myths and sagas, widely shared and regularly invoked. Myths support claims of distinctiveness, transforming a place of work into a revered institution and an all-encompassing way of life.

A shared myth fosters internal cohesion and a sense of direction while helping maintain confidence and the support of external constituencies. At the same time, myths are stubbornly persistent, potentially blocking adaptation to changing conditions. Consider the 1982 experience of the U.S. telephone giant AT&T. For a century, it pursued a goal of "universal service" in a noncompetitive environment. Forced by judicial order to divest the local operating companies, the firm struggled to compete aggressively in a deregulated environment. But in changing, it risked losing what had once made it successful.

Stories and Fairy Tales

Fairy tales are more than entertainment and moral instruction for small children. They comfort, reassure, and offer direction and hope. They externalize inner conflicts and tensions (Bettelheim, 1977). Stories are sometimes dismissed as the last resort of people with nothing of substance—like a professor accused of telling "war stories," providing entertainment rather than truth or wisdom. Yet stories also convey information, morals, values, and myths vividly and convincingly (Mitroff and Kilmann, 1975). They perpetuate values and keep the historical exploits of heroes and heroines alive.

Marriott Hotels founder J. W. Marriott Sr. died years ago, but his presence is still felt. Stories of his unwavering commitment to customer service are told and retold. His aphorism "Take good care of your employees and they'll take good care of your customers" is still vital to Marriott's philosophy. According to legend, Marriott Sr. visited every new hotel general manager and took the manager for a walk around the property. He would point out every broken branch, sidewalk pebble, and obscure cobweb. By tour's end, the new manager left with a long to-do list. More important, the manager took away an indelible lesson in what really mattered at Marriott.

Not all stories center on founders or chief executives. Ritz-Carlton is famous for the unique, upscale treatment it offers guests around the world. "My pleasure" is employees' universal response to requests, no matter how demanding or trivial. One hurried guest jumped into a taxi to the airport but left his briefcase on the sidewalk. The doorman retrieved the briefcase, abandoned his post, sped to the airport, and delivered the briefcase to the panicked guest. Instead of being fired, the doorman became a permanent part of the legends and lore—a living example of the company's commitment to going the extra mile (Deal and Jenkins, 1994).

Stories are a key medium for communicating corporate myths. They establish and perpetuate tradition. They are recalled and embellished in formal meetings and informal coffee breaks. They convey the value and identity of the organization to insiders and outsiders, thereby building confidence and support. One school administrator responded to criticisms of a new reading program by recounting stories of several children whose ability to read had increased dramatically. The stories spread through the community, and test scores became almost irrelevant because the stories built so much confidence and support. Stories can communicate the success of a good program—or obscure the failure of a bad one. If reading scores go down, a few dramatic success stories might prevent a close look at the program's actual effectiveness. Like myths, stories and fairy tales are double-edged swords.

Ritual

Around the world, at home and at work, ritual gives structure and meaning to daily life. "We find these magical moments every day—drinking our morning coffee, reading the daily paper, eating lunch with a friend, drinking a glass of wine while admiring the sunset, or saying, 'Good night, sleep tight . . .' at bedtime. The holy in the daily; the sacred in the single act of living" (Fulghum, 1995, p. 3).

> For sunrise and sundown, for moon and rain, for stars.
> A time for the first breath—'ah'—and the last breath—'oh'
> But in the meantime, there is the infinite moment—
> A time to do the dishes.
> And a time to walk the dog [p. 254].

Humans create both personal and communal rituals. Those that work and carry meaning become the dance of life. "Rituals anchor us to a center while freeing us to move on and confront the ever-lasting unpredictability of life. The paradox of ritual patterns and sacred habits is that they simultaneously serve as a solid footing and springboard, providing a stable dynamic in our lives" (Fulghum, 1995, p. 261). The power of ritual is palpable if one experiences the emptiness of losing it. When the Roman Catholic Church changed its liturgy from Latin to the vernacular, many Catholics felt a profound loss of conviction and faith in the Mass.

Historically, cultures have relied on ritual and ceremony to create order, clarity, and predictability—particularly around issues or dilemmas too complex, mysterious, or random to be controlled otherwise. Rain dances, harvest celebrations, and annual meetings invoke supernatural assistance in the critical but unpredictable processes of raising crops or building market share. Conventions provide yearly opportunities to renew old ties and revive deep collective commitments. "Convention centers are the basilicas of secular religion" (Fulghum, 1995, p. 96).

Initiation rituals induct newcomers into communal membership. "Greenhorns" encounter powerful symbolic issues from the moment they join a group or organization:

> The first problem faced by the new member is that of gaining entry into the men's hut—of gaining access to the basic organizational secrets. A key episode here is the rite of passage. This is more or less an affirmation to the individual of the fact that he has been accepted into the men's hut. And, as in the tribe, simply attaining puberty is not sufficient. There must be an accompanying trial and appropriate ritual to mark the event. The so-called primitives had the good sense to make these trials meaningful and direct. Upon attaining puberty you killed a lion and were circumcised. After a little dancing and whatnot, you were admitted as a junior member and learned some secrets. The hut is a symbol of, and a medium for maintaining, the *status quo* and the good of the order [Ritti and Funkhouser, 1982, p. 3].

Modern amenities such as central heating, flush toilets, and Novocain insulate us from the discomforts and uncertainties of earlier eras. It is tempting to believe that we are equally far beyond the primitive drives, sexism, and superstition that gave rise to institutions such as the men's hut. But consider the experience of a new member of the United States Senate.

Paul Tsongas attended his first meeting of the Senate Energy Committee in January 1979. . . . At the time, Tsongas had just finished a well-publicized race against Senator Edward Brooke, his name having thus appeared almost daily in the Washington newspapers for weeks. Taking his seat quietly at the far end of the table as befits a freshman, he listened intently as Chairman Henry Jackson welcomed everyone back for the new Congress and greeted the new members, including Senator "Ton'gas." Repeatedly stumbling over the name, Jackson drew ripples of laughter from the audience of lobbyists, staff, and press while Tsongas squirmed in the mandatory silence of freshmen [Weatherford, 1985, pp. 32–33].

Henry "Scoop" Jackson was no juvenile prankster; he was a savvy, powerful, and widely respected veteran of the Senate. He was simply welcoming Tsongas to the men's hut in a ritual that employed a verbal surrogate for ritual circumcision. Nor are women spared Senate initiation rituals:

One of the early female victims was a representative who was a serious feminist. Soon after arriving in Congress, she broke propriety by audaciously proposing an amendment to a military bill of Edward Hebert, Chief of the Defense Clan. When the amendment received only a single vote, she supposedly snapped at the aged committee chairman: "I know the only reason my amendment failed is that I've got a vagina." To which Herbert retorted, "If you'd been using your vagina instead of your mouth, maybe you'd have gotten a few more votes" [Weatherford, 1985, p. 35].

That last exchange seems particularly harsh and offensive, but its multiple meanings and various interpretations take us right to the heart of the symbolic frame. A kinder and gentler anecdote would lose some of the power of this extraordinary demonstration of how much can happen in a two-sentence, multilayered transaction.

If we take the words literally, the parties are saying:

Newcomer: Because of my physical characteristics as a woman, you are unwilling to accept me as a full member.

Old-Timer: If you would use your physical characteristics and offer your sexual favors to us, we *might* accept you.

That is an archetypal exchange in the relations between men and women. Symbolically, it is attempted rape, deeply offensive to anyone committed to gender equality. It is emotionally explosive because of so much human experience in which men communicate to women that their highest role is to be sexual servants. It creates a very difficult dilemma for the newcomer: "How do I respond to this attack? If I let him know how hurt and infuriated I am, that confirms the power of his comment. If I ignore it, then I let him get away with a blatantly sexist comment. If I fight back, the deck is stacked against me."

One possibility is to reverse the attack. If, for example, she were to respond, "Are you suggesting that the way for women to get votes in Congress is to sleep with other members?" she is likely to turn the tables and create a dilemma for the old-timer. He has, indeed, suggested exactly that, but he cannot admit it. His words would haunt him during his next reelection campaign.

If we frame the transaction as an initiation ritual, we focus on the clash between a new arrival and an established veteran. Here the exchange is very similar to what Senator Tsongas experienced:

Newcomer: I thought my performance deserved a better outcome.
Old-Timer: Kid, that's because you're wet behind the ears. You don't know the ropes and don't know your place. We know how to deal with uppity rookies around here. You had better pay a lot more attention to your elders.

Decoded this way, the exchange is a universal feature of initiation rituals, independent of time, place, or gender: the old-timer is reminding the rookies about how things work and who's in charge.

This interpretation adds to our understanding of the emotional power, but there is still more going on. The exchange can also be interpreted as two-level negotiation about the newcomer's role:

Newcomer: I expect that, as a woman, I will receive the same rights and privileges as a man. Now that I'm here I expect full membership.
Old-Timer: *We'll* decide on your rights, and you won't get *any* unless you shape up. There's a *price* for membership, and in your case it's a high one.

The old-timer is communicating another universal and fundamentally important message: we are willing to accept you as one of us *if* you are willing to pay the price. A family, group, organization, or society with cohesion and a sense of itself rarely offers free admission to outsiders. The price is usually higher for people who are different and who question or threaten existing values, norms, and patterns. Representatives of groups that have been excluded because of their gender, race, ethnicity, or religion cannot become full-fledged members of a group or organization unless they are initiated into the inner sanctum. The initiation may be bitterly painful and may raise poignant questions for the newcomer: "What price am I willing to pay to join this group? Where is the line between legitimate adjustment to a new culture and sacrificing my own values or identity? Why should I have to tolerate values or practices that I see as wrong or unjust?" Yet only a weak culture will accept newcomers with no initiation. The stronger a culture, the stronger the message to newcomers that "you are different and not yet one of us." The initiation reinforces the existing culture at the same time that it tests the newcomer's ability to become a member. The sophisticated newcomer will attend carefully to those cultural signals. The better a newcomer understands a new culture, the better the chances of passing the initiation without paying an unacceptable price.

The exchange can also be seen as a classic negotiation about the newcomer's agenda for reforming the organization:

Newcomer: I know this place is hostile to women, and I expect that to change.

Old-Timer: If you want hostility, I'll show you hostility. Let me remind you that we're in charge here, and we like this place the way it is.

Newcomers are expected to bring new ideas and perspectives. It is their *destiny* to be agents of evolution and reform. Old-timers act as a force for stability and the wisdom of the past. They are supposed to pass along old values and practices. If newcomers fully succumb to the press of historical tradition, an organization risks stultification and decay. Conversely, if old-timers fail to induct new arrivals properly, an organization risks chaos and disarray.

Ceremony

The distinction between ritual and ceremony is subtle. Ceremonies are grander, more elaborate, less frequent occasions. Rituals are simpler day-to-day patterns. A manager might marry only once but insist on a newspaper, croissant, and coffee at the same hour each morning. Ritual and ceremony are both illustrated in an account from Japan:

> It has been the same every night since the death in 1964 of Yasujiro Tsutsumi, the legendary patriarch of the huge Seibu real-estate and transportation group. Two employees stand an overnight vigil at his tomb. There are always plenty of volunteers from a business that owns about one-sixth of the real estate in Japan, along with a large collection of hotels, resorts and railways. On New Year's, the weather is often bitter, but at dawn the vigil expands to include five or six hundred top executives—directors, vice presidents, presidents—arrayed by company and rank, the most senior in front. A limousine delivers Yasujiro's third son, Yoshiaki Tsutsumi, the head of the family business and Japan's richest man. A great brass bell booms out six times as Yoshiaki approaches his father's tomb. He claps his hands twice, bows deeply, and says, "Happy New Year, Father, Happy New Year." Then he turns to deliver a brief-but-stern sermon to the assembled congregation. The basic themes change little from year to year: last year was tough, this year will be even tougher, and you'll be washing dishes in one of the hotels if your performance is bad. Finally, he toasts his father with warm sake and departs [Downer, 1994].

Ceremonies punctuate our lives at special moments. Baptisms, bar mitzvahs, graduations, weddings, and anniversaries offer meaning and spiritual connection at important transitions. Ceremonies serve four major roles: they socialize, stabilize, reassure, and convey messages to external constituencies. Several thousand people gather at the annual seminar of the Mary Kay Cosmetics company. They come to hear personal messages from Mary Kay, to applaud the achievements of star salespeople, to hear success stories from people who replaced soap operas with sales calls, and to celebrate. The ceremony brings new members into the fold and helps maintain uniformity among members of the Mary Kay family long after the seminar ends. It creates a distinctive pageant and makes the Mary Kay culture accessible to outsiders, particularly to consumers. Failure recedes and obstacles disappear as the "you can do it" spirit of the company manifests itself in the symbol of the bumblebee— a creature that, according to aerodynamics experts, should not be able to fly. Apparently unaware of its limitations, it flies anyway.

In the U.S. Congress, ceremony is almost always the order of the day:

> Ceremony operates best in a symbolically rich setting that calls for special seating arrangements, particular forms of dress, and various ritual accoutrements such as crosses, thrones, flags, and masks. The full panoply of these objects marches around the congressional chamber in the process of legislation, but it is in the particular use of ritual language that the real nature of congressional ceremony emerges. Because of the sanctity of words, special speech forms are often used . . . to separate normal human interaction from interaction with particularly powerful beings such as gods or potentates. . . . Taboos on the use of personal names and certain pronouns reach an inordinate level in the American Congress, where neither the word *I* nor *you* is proper. Nor can the legislators address one another directly by name, as in "Edward Kennedy," "Ted," or even the more formal "Senator Kennedy." A simple phrase such as "I would like to ask you" becomes "Mr. President, the Senator from Texas would like to ask the Senator from California" [Weatherford, 1985, pp. 189–190].

Ceremony is also evident in other matters of national importance. In the United States, political conventions select candidates, even though there is rarely much suspense about the outcome, carefully scripted for television. For several months, competing candidates trade clichés and exchange epithets. The same pageantry unfolds each election year. Rhetoric and spontaneous demonstrations are staged in advance. Campaigning is notoriously repetitious and superficial, and voting often seems disconnected from the main drama. The process of electing a president is still a momentous ceremony. It provides a sense of social involvement. It is an outlet for expression of discontent and enthusiasm. It stages live drama for citizens to witness and debate. It gives millions of people a sense of participation in an exciting adventure. It lets candidates reassure the public that there are answers to our most important questions and solutions to our biggest problems. It draws attention to common social ties and to the importance of accepting whichever candidate eventually wins (Edelman, 1977).

Ritual and ceremony are equally significant in business. Rituals communicate meaning from one individual to another and from an organization to its environment. Some organizational events, like retirement dinners and welcoming speeches for new employees, are clearly ceremonial. But many significant rituals are misapprehended solely as rational and instrumental activities.

Expressive events provide order and meaning and bind an organization or a society together. When properly conducted and attuned to valued myths, rituals fire the imagination and deepen faith; otherwise, they become cold, empty forms that people resent and avoid. Rituals and ceremonies can release creativity and transform meanings. They can also cement the status quo and block adaptation and learning. As with other symbols, they cut both ways.

Metaphor, Humor, and Play

Metaphors, humor, and play illustrate the important "as if" quality of symbols. They are indirect ways to grapple with issues that are too complex, mysterious, or threatening to approach head-on. Metaphors make the strange familiar and the familiar strange. They help us capture subtle themes that normal language can overlook. Consider the following metaphors from managers asked to produce a metaphor for their agency as it is and as they hope it might become:

Is	*Might Become*
A maze	A well-oiled wheel
Wet noodle	Oak tree
Aggregation of tribes with competing agendas	Symphony orchestra
Three-ring circus	Championship team
A puzzle no one can put together	A smooth-running machine
Twilight zone	Utopia
Herd of horses	Tribe

Is	*Might Become*
Herd of cattle on the rampage	Fleet of ships heading for the same port
Oldsmobile '98 with four-barrel, eight-cylinder engine with a full tank of gas, in need of a tuneup, heading up a hill	Honda Civic that doesn't use much gas, constantly kept in tune, with manual transmission capable of adjusting to any terrain

Metaphors compress complicated issues into understandable images, affecting our attitudes, evaluations, and actions. A university head who views the institution as a factory will establish different policies from one who conceives of it as a craft guild or a shopping center. Consultants who see themselves as physicians are likely to differ from those who see themselves as salespeople or rain dancers.

Fine (1996) suggests that metaphors are also central to the process of defining and justifying one's work identity. He found that restaurant cooks use four different metaphors to describe who they are and what they do. They describe themselves as professionals (like lawyers and doctors), artists (like painters and architects), businesspeople (like executives and entrepreneurs), and workers (like manual laborers). Each image gives rise to a different "occupational rhetoric," and cooks draw on all of them for different times and situations.

Humor serves important "as if" functions. Hansot (1979) argues that it is less important to ask why people use humor in organizations than to ask why they are so serious. She contends that humor plays a number of important functions. Humor integrates, expresses skepticism, contributes to flexibility and adaptiveness, and signals status. Though a classic device for distancing, humor can also socialize, include, and convey membership. It can establish solidarity and facilitate face-saving. Above all, it is a way to illuminate and break frames, indicating that any single definition of a situation is arbitrary.

In most work settings, play and humor are sharply distinguished from work. Play is what people do when they are not working. Images of play in the conversation of managers typically connote aggression, competition, and struggle ("We've got to beat them at their own game"; "We dropped the ball on that one"; "The ball is in his court now") rather than relaxation and fun. If play is viewed as a state of mind (Bateson, 1972; Goffman, 1974), any activity can be playful. Play permits relaxing the rules to explore alternatives. It encourages experimentation, flexibility, and adaptiveness. March (1976) suggests five guidelines for play in organizations:

1. Treat goals as hypotheses.
2. Treat intuition as real.
3. Treat hypocrisy as transition.
4. Treat memory as an enemy.
5. Treat experience as a theory.

Organizations as Cultures

Culture: What is it, and what is its role in organizations? Both questions are hotly contested. Some people argue that organizations *have* cultures; others insist that organizations *are* cultures. Schein (1992, p. 12) offers a more formal definition: "a pattern of shared basic assumptions that a group learned as it solved its problems of external adaptation and integration, that has worked well enough to be considered valid and therefore to be taught to new members as the correct way to perceive, think, and feel in relation to those problems." Deal and Kennedy (1982, p. 4) define culture more succinctly as "the way we do things around here."

There is controversy about the relationship between culture and leadership. Do leaders shape culture, or are they shaped by it? Is symbolic leadership more often empowering or manipulative? Do organizations with strong cultures outperform those relying on policies and rules? Does success breed a cohesive culture or the other way around?

Over time, every organization develops distinctive beliefs and patterns. Many of these are unconscious or taken for granted, reflected in myths, fairy tales, stories, rituals, ceremonies, and other symbolic forms. Managers who understand the power of symbols are much better equipped to understand and influence their organizations. From a symbolic perspective, meaning is the basic human need. Managers who understand symbolic forms and activities and encourage their use help shape an effective organization—so long as the organizational culture is aligned with the challenges of the marketplace.

Nordstrom department stores exemplify the power of culture at work. Customers rave about its no-hassle, no-questions-asked commitment to high-quality service: "not service the way it used to be, but service that never was" (Spector and McCarthy, 1995, p. 1). Founder John Nordstrom was a Swedish immigrant who settled in Seattle after an odyssey across America and a brief stint in Alaska looking for gold. He and Carl Wallin, a shoemaker, opened a shoe store. Nordstrom's sons Elmer, Everett, and Lloyd joined the business. Collectively, they anchored the firm in an enduring philosophical principle: the customer is always right. The following generation of Nordstroms expanded the business while maintaining a tight connection with its historical roots.

The company relies on experienced, acculturated "Nordies" to induct new employees into customer service the Nordstrom way. Newcomers always begin in sales, learning traditions from the ground up. "When we are at our best, our frontline people are lieutenants because they control the business. Our competition has foot soldiers on the front line and lieutenants in the back" (Spector and McCarthy, 1995, p. 106).

Nordstrom's unique commitment to customer service is heralded in true tales of heroes and heroines going out of their way:

- One customer fell in love with a particular pair of pleated burgundy slacks that were on sale at Nordstrom's downtown Seattle store. Unfortunately, the store was out of her size. The sales associate got some cash from her department managers, marched across the street, bought the slacks at full price from a competitor, brought them back, and sold them to the customer at Nordstrom's reduced price (Spector and McCarthy, 1995, p. 26).
- When a customer inadvertently left her airline ticket on a Nordstrom's counter, the sales associate tried to solve the problem with a call to the airline. When that didn't work, she used the Ritz-Carlton doorman strategy: hop a cab, head for the airport, and make a personal delivery to the customer (Spector and McCarthy, 1995, p. 125).

- A Nordie cheerfully issued a refund on a set of automobile tires, even though Nordstrom had never sold tires. In 1975, Nordstrom had bought three stores from Northern Commercial Company in Alaska. The customer had bought the tires from Northern Commercial—so Nordstrom took them back (Spector and McCarthy, 1995, p. 27).

Nordstrom's commitment to customer service is regularly reinforced in storewide rituals. Newcomers to Nordstrom encounter the company's values in the initial employee orientation. They are given a five-inch by eight-inch card labeled the "Nordstrom Employee Handbook," which reads:

WELCOME TO NORDSTROM

We're glad to have you with our company. Our number one goal is to provide outstanding customer service.

Set both your personal and professional goals high. We have great confidence in your ability to achieve them.

Nordstrom Rules:

Rule #1: Use your good judgment in all situations.

There will be no additional rules [Spector and McCarthy, 1995, pp. 15–16].

At staff meetings, Nordstrom sales associates compare and discuss sales techniques and role-play customer encounters. Periodic ceremonies reinforce the company's cherished values. From the company's early years, the Nordstrom family sponsored summer picnics and Christmas dance parties. More recently, numerous events provide occasions to celebrate customer service: "We do crazy stuff. . . . Monthly store pow-wows serve as a kind of revival meeting, where customer letters of appreciation are read and positive achievements are recognized, while co-workers whoop and cheer for one another. . . . Letters of complaint about Nordstrom customer service are also read over the intercom (omitting the names of offending salespeople)" (Spector and McCarthy, 1995, pp. 120, 129).

At one spirited sales meeting, the regional manager asked all present to call out their sales targets for the year, which he posted on a large chart. Then the regional manager uncovered his own target for each individual. Anyone whose target was below the regional manager's was roundly booed. Anyone whose individual goals were higher than the regional manager's was rewarded with enthusiastic cheers (Spector and McCarthy, 1995).

The delicate balance of competition, cooperation, and customer service has served Nordstrom well. In a sermon titled "The Gospel According to Nordstrom," one California minister "praised the retailer for carrying out the call of the gospel in ways more consistent and caring than we sometimes do in the church" (Spector and McCarthy, 1995, p. 21).

Summary

In contrast to traditional views emphasizing rationality and objectivity, the symbolic frame highlights the tribal aspect of contemporary organizations. It centers on complexity and ambiguity in organizational phenomena and the extent to which symbols mediate the meaning of organizational events and activities. Myths and stories provide drama, cohesiveness, clarity, and direction in the presence of confusion and mystery. Rituals and ceremonies provide ways to take action in the face of confusion, unpredictability, and threat. Metaphors, humor, and play provide ways for individuals and organizations to escape from the tyranny of facts and logic, to view organizations and their own participation in them *as if* they were new and different from what they seem, and to find creative alternatives to old choices. In *The Feast of Fools,* Cox (1969, p. 13) summarizes the importance of symbolism in modern life: "Our links to yesterday and tomorrow depend also on the aesthetic, emotional, and symbolic aspects of human life—on saga, play, and celebration. Without festival and fantasy, man would not really be a historical being at all."

Chapter Thirteen

Organization as Theater

Theater as an activity, as a staging of reality, depends on the
ability of the audience to frame what they experience as theater.
It depends precisely on the audience recognizing, being aware,
that they are an audience; they are witnesses to, not participants
in, a performance. It depends further on a distinction between
actors and the parts they play—characters may die on stage, but
actors will live to take a bow. Finally, theater depends on a recognition that performances play with reality in such a way as to turn
the taken-for-granted into a plausible appearance [Mangham and
Overington, 1987, p. 49].

Organizations were once viewed as closed systems that protected the technical core from external pressures. Functional demands shaped social architecture. The environment served as a
source of raw materials and a market for finished products. The
name of the game was efficiency, internal control of the means of
production. External fluctuations and production uncertainties
were buffered by rational devices such as forecasting, stockpiling,
leveling the peaks and valleys of supply and demand, and growth
(so as to get more leverage over the environment).

Institutional theorists offer a less rational image. Organizations,
particularly those with vague goals and weak technologies, can
never seal themselves off from external events and pressures. Their
environment is never passive or neutral. They are constantly buffeted by larger social, political, and economic trends. The name of
the game is maintaining legitimacy and support in the eyes of multiple constituencies. Organizations must therefore reflect contemporary beliefs and expectations. Widely held myths shape social

architecture. Correct appearance, rather than efficient production, is the prevailing measure of effectiveness. "In technical organizations, the development of a rational plan is a prelude to the reconstruction and reintegration of a pattern of production activities. In institutionalized organizations, the creation of a rational plan constitutes an alternative to changes in the actual provision of services. In the latter case, the plans are regarded as ends in themselves— as evidence that we are a humane and scientific people who have brought yet another problem under rational control" (Meyer and Rowan, 1983a, p. 126).

Highly technical organizations concentrate attention on the means of production. Organizations with higher levels of uncertainty turn their backs on technical processes and stage dramatic performances for internal and external audiences (Meyer and Rowan, 1983a). Decision making is more ritual than rational (March and Olsen, 1976). Evaluations serve purposes other than assessing performance (Dornbusch and Scott, 1975). Events affect leadership more than leaders influence events (Edelman, 1977). Structure, decoupled from actual work, serves as a theatrical, ceremonial portrayal of prevailing social myths (Meyer and Rowan, 1983b).

The story of the U.S. Navy's Polaris missile system provides a fascinating example of an organization's dramaturgical performance, playing to both internal and external audiences. The Polaris project was heralded in its time as an exemplar of effective, efficient government-sponsored activity. One of its distinctive attributes was modern management techniques such as PERT charts and the Program Planning and Budgeting System (PPBS). The techniques were embodied in several structural forms: specialist roles, technical divisions, management meetings, and the Special Projects Office. In the wake of Polaris's success—it was produced on time and under budget—analysts concluded that the project's modern management approach must have been a major causal factor. The admiral in charge received a plaque recognizing his role in bringing modern management techniques to the U.S. Navy. A visiting team of British experts recommended PERT to the British Admiralty.

A later study by Sapolsky (1972) revealed a less linear explanation for Polaris's stellar performance. Specialists' activities were loosely coupled to other aspects of the project. The technical division produced plans and charts that were mostly ignored. Management meetings served as public arenas in which to chide poor performers and as revival meetings to reinforce the project's religious fervor. The Special Projects Office served as an official briefing area. Visiting dignitaries were regaled with impressive diagrams and charts unrelated to the project's actual progress. The team from the British Navy apparently surmised all this on its visit and still recommended a similar approach to their admiralty (Sapolsky, 1972).

Instead of serving their supposed purposes, structural forms contributed to a myth that garnered strong external support and kept critics at bay. The myth provided breathing space for the work to go forward and kept spirits and self-confidence high. Polaris demonstrated the power of theater to engage the attention and appreciation of both internal and external audiences. "An alchemous combination of whirling computers, bright-colored charts, and fast-talking public relations officers gave the Special Projects Office a truly effective management system. It mattered not whether the parts of the system functioned, or even existed. It mattered only that certain people, for a certain period of time, believed that they did" (Sapolsky, 1972, p. 129).

Activities without results? The very thought casts doubt on a substantial proportion of organized endeavor. Might such heresy lead to wholesale cynicism—undermining faith and morale for anyone struggling to make a difference? The symbolic frame offers a more hopeful interpretation. Institutionalized structures, activities, and events are expressive components of organizational theater. They provide ongoing drama that entertains, creates meaning, and portrays the organization to itself. Geertz observed of Balinese pageants, "The carefully crafted and scripted, assiduously enacted ritualism of court culture was . . . 'not merely the drapery of political order but its substance'" (Mangham and Overington, 1987, p. 39).

As Polaris demonstrates, good drama signals to the outside world that all is well: decisions and plans, new units in response to emerging problems, sophisticated evaluation and control systems to ensure accountability. All this creates an image of a well-managed organization worthy of confidence and support. Getting the drama right is particularly critical in sectors where outputs are ambiguous and success is hard to measure. But good theater also plays a role in highly technical organizations. Fluctuations in stock prices of American businesses are a case in point. When external constituencies question the worth of existing practices, organizations promise improvement and stage a familiar drama called *Change*. If consumers complain about quality, businesses create a "total quality program" and promise tighter quality standards. Crises stimulate a call for new leaders, who in turn promise major reform.

The symbolic frame views instrumental structures and processes as secular theater—dramas that express our fears, joys, and expectations. Drama arouses emotions and kindles our spirit. It reduces uncertainty and soothes bewilderment. It provides a shared basis for understanding the present and a vision of a more promising future.

Structure as Theater

The structural frame portrays a workplace as a network of interdependent roles and units coordinated through a variety of horizontal and vertical linkages. Structural patterns align with purpose and are determined by goals, technologies, and environment (Woodward, 1970; Perrow, 1979; Lawrence and Lorsch, 1967). A symbolic view approaches structure as stage design: an arrangement of space, lighting, props, and costumes that make the drama vivid and credible to its audience.

One dramaturgical role of structure is to reflect and convey prevailing social values and myths. In many schools, churches, personnel departments, and mental health firms, goals are multiple and elusive, technology is underdeveloped, linkages between means and ends are poorly understood, and effectiveness is difficult to determine. Legitimacy requires an appearance that conforms to how society *thinks* organizations should look. Settings and costumes should be appropriate: churches should have a building, religious artifacts, and a properly attired member of the clergy; clinics should have examination rooms, uniformed nurses, and licensed physicians with diplomas on their walls.

Meyer and Rowan (1978) depict the structure of public schools as largely symbolic. A school will have difficulty sustaining public support unless it offers fashionable answers to three questions: Does it offer appropriate topics (for example, third-grade mathematics, world history)? Are topics taught to age-graded students by certified teachers? Does it look like a school (with classrooms, a gymnasium, a library, and a flag near the front door)? An institution of higher education is judged by age, the size and beauty of the campus, the size of its library collection, its faculty-student ratio, and the number of professors who received doctorates from prestigious institutions. Kamens (1977) suggests that the major function of colleges and universities is to redefine novice students as graduates who possess special qualities or skills. The transformation's value must be negotiated with important constituencies. This is done through constant references to the quality and rigor of educational programs and is validated by the structural characteristics or appearance of the institution.

The correct structural configuration, in Kamens's view, depends on whether an institution is elite or nonelite and whether it allocates students to a specific corporate group in the society. Each type of institution espouses a different myth and dramatizes different aspects of structure. The main considerations are casting the right actors, writing a suitable script, and setting the appropriate stage. Elite schools, for example, dramatize selectivity, develop an attractive residential campus, advertise a favorable ratio of faculty to students, and develop a core curriculum that restrains specialization.

If an institution or its environment changes, theatrical adaptations are needed. New audiences require revisions in actors, scripts, or settings. Since legitimacy and worth are anchored primarily in alignment of structural characteristics to prevailing myths, organizations alter appearances to mirror changes in social expectations. Until the 1930s, America's elite Ivy League colleges were essentially finishing schools for the aristocracy. Admission depended on wealth and breeding more than talent. When the Great Depression cast the rich as predators and villains, the old way became indefensible. The colleges revised admission policy to admit the academically talented regardless of economic background (Delbanco, 1996).

Formal structures are built largely from "blocks" of contemporary myth. Legitimate organizations project a "modern" appearance, constructed of contemporary issues and dilemmas. When Total Quality Management, or reengineering, becomes the badge of honor for progressive companies, programs and consultants spread like fire in a parched forest. As laws mandate education for children with special needs, schools hire specialists who perform highly visible functions that classroom teachers rarely see or understand. In response to criticisms of antiquated management methods, universities adopt sophisticated control systems producing elaborate printouts with little effect on operations. Legislatures pass laws on occupational safety, and factories create safety units to post signs no one reads. New structures reflect legal and social expectations and represent a bid for acceptance and support from the attending audience. An organization without an affirmative action program is suspiciously out of step with prevailing concerns for diversity and equity. Nonconformity invites questions, criticism, and inspection. It is much easier to appoint an affirmative action officer than to change hiring practices deeply embedded in both individual beliefs and organizational culture. Since the presence of the affirmative action officer is much more visible than new hiring priorities, the addition of a new role may successfully signal to those outside an organization that change has occurred, even if only as a formality. In the mid-nineties, affirmative action was challenged in several states. If its popularity wanes, revisions in the institutional facade may be in order.

Government agencies encapsulate existing ambivalence or conflicts (Edelman, 1977). In the United States, conflict between shippers and railroads led to the founding of the Interstate Commerce Commission. Conflict between labor and management produced the National Labor Relations Board. Conflict between consumers and producers resulted in the Food and Drug Administration. Concern over pollution gave rise to the Environmental Protection Agency. In reality, these agencies serve mostly political and symbolic functions. "Congress passes on to these agencies a type of symbolic control; they represent our belief in the virtues of planning and the value of an integrated program of action. But the agencies are given no formal authority over the organizations whose services they are to control and few funds to use as incentives to stimulate the cooperation of these existing organizations" (Scott, 1983, p. 126).

Politically, regulatory agencies are often "captured" by the entities they are supposed to regulate. Major drug companies are far more effective than the public in lobbying and influencing decisions about drug safety. The Federal Aviation Agency came under fire for its perceived "coziness" with airline companies following the 1996 crash of a ValuJet plane. In practice, agencies legitimize elite values, reassure the public that they are zealously protecting its interests, and struggle for funding from the legislature. They reduce tension and uncertainty and increase the public's sense of confidence and security. Only in a crisis is their actual performance called into question (Edelman, 1977).

Organizational Process as Theater

Administrative processes coordinate work through such devices as formal meetings, evaluation systems, accounting systems, management information systems, and labor negotiations. Technical processes produce goods and services. Factory workers assemble parts into products. Professors give lectures to impart knowledge and wisdom. Physicians diagnose illnesses and prescribe medical treatment. Social workers write case reports to identify and remedy social ills.

People at work spend much of their time engaged in such processes. To justify their labor, they need to believe that their activity produces intended outcomes. But even the best intentions do not always lead to desired results. Meetings may make no decisions and solve no problems, though they often lead to more meetings. Planning often produces documents no one uses. Even without results, activities play a vital role in theatrical performance. They serve as scripts and stage markings that provide opportunities for self-expression, forums for airing grievances, and arenas for negotiating new understandings and meanings.

Meetings

March and Olsen (1976) were ahead of the times in their depiction of meetings as "garbage cans." Organizations are notorious as settings for managers looking for ways to expend time and energy, problems in search of solutions, and people with solutions looking for problems. Meetings attract all three: people, problems, and solutions. Outcomes depend on a complicated and often serendipitous interplay among inputs that happen to arrive: Who came to the meeting? What problems, concerns, or needs did they bring? What solutions or suggestions were available? Garbage cans are particularly likely for emotionally powerful, symbolically visible, technically fuzzy issues. A conversation on mission is likely to attract a larger, more diverse set of people, problems, and solutions than one on cost accounting. Reorganization (Olsen, 1976b), choosing a new chief administrator (Olsen, 1976a), and conflicts over desegregation (Weiner, 1976) are well-documented occasions for dramatic performances. Meetings may not always produce rational discourse, sound plans, or radical improvements. But they serve as symbolic arenas that help prevent individual and organizational disintegration. They are expressive occasions. Some players become clearer about their role in the collective drama and get a chance to practice and polish their lines. Others revel in the chance to find some excitement at work. Audiences take comfort that issues are getting attention and that better times may lie ahead.

Planning

An organization without a plan is thought to be reactive, short-sighted, and rudderless. Planning is a ceremony any reputable organization must conduct periodically to maintain legitimacy. A plan is a badge of honor that organizations wear conspicuously and with pride. A strategic plan carries even higher status. Mintzberg's insightful book *The Rise and Fall of Strategic Planning* (1994) presents an impressive array of survey and anecdotal evidence questioning how well strategic planning really works. He shows that the presumed linear progression from analysis to objectives to action to results is more fanciful than factual. Many executives clearly recognize the shortcomings yet continue to champion strategic planning: "Recently I asked three corporate executives what decisions they had made in the last year that they would not have made were it not for their corporate plans. All had difficulty identifying one such decision. Since each of their plans [was] marked 'secret' or 'confidential,' I asked them how their competitors might benefit from the possession of their plans. Each answered with embarrassment that their competitors would not benefit. Yet these executives were strong advocates of corporate planning" (Russell Ackoff, quoted in Mintzberg, 1994, p. 98).

If an activity persists without accomplishing what it is supposed to, it may play a vital role in the organizational drama. J. B. Quinn notes, "A good deal of the corporate planning I have observed is like a ritual rain dance; it has no effect on the weather that follows, but those who engage in it think it does. Moreover, it seems to me that much of the advice and instruction related to corporate planning is directed at improving the dancing, not the weather" (quoted in Mintzberg, 1994, p. 139).

Cohen and March's list of four symbolic roles for plans in universities (1974) is relevant for other organizations as well:

1. *Plans are symbols.* Academic organizations provide few "real" pieces of objective evidence to evaluate performance. They have nothing comparable to profit or sales figures. How are we doing? No one really knows. Planning is a signal that all is well or improvement is just around the corner. A failing institution can announce that it has a plan to revitalize itself. An institution without a nuclear reactor or an economics department can announce a plan to get one. Its stock may then soar.

2. *Plans become games.* Especially where goals and technology are unclear, planning becomes a test of will. If a department wants a new program badly, it must justify the expenditure by substantial effort, writing it into a plan. If an administrator wishes to avoid saying yes with no real basis for saying no, asking a department to submit a plan tests its commitment. Benefits come more from the process than the result.

3. *Plans become excuses for interaction.* Developing a plan forces discussion and may increase interest in and commitment to new priorities in departments and schools. Occasionally, interaction yields positive results. But rarely does it yield an accurate forecast. Discussions of the future modify views of what should be done differently today. Conclusions about what will happen next year are notoriously susceptible to alteration as people, politics, policies, or preferences change.

4. *Plans become advertisements.* What is frequently called a plan is more like an investment brochure. It is an attempt to persuade private and public donors of an institution's attractiveness. Plans are typically adorned with glossy photographs of beautiful people in pristine settings, ex cathedra pronouncements of excellence, and a noticeable absence of specific information.

Cohen and March (1974) asked college presidents their views of the linkage between plans and decisions. Responses fell into four main categories. There is little to suggest that the results would be any different a quarter century later:

"Yes, we have a plan. It is used in capital project and physical location decisions."

"Yes, we have a plan. Here it is. It was made during the administration of our last president. We are working on a new one."

"No, we do not have a plan. We should. We're working on one."

"I think there's a plan around here someplace. Miss Jones, do we
have a copy of our comprehensive, ten-year plan" [p. 113]?

A study of a large-scale planning project in a suburban school
district (Edelfson, Johnson, and Stromquist, 1977) provides another
illustration of the symbolic importance of planning. Project Redesign was a five-year planning effort, supported by federal funds, that
involved a significant proportion of the district's professionals and
citizens in creating ways for the school district to meet the challenges of the next decade.

The plan produced no major decisions or changes. But it did
give participants the chance to participate and interact, which they
liked. It provided a forum for a variety of problems, solutions, and
conflicts that might have been more troublesome had they sur-
faced in some other arena. It enabled the district to present itself
as a model district. It renewed faith in the virtues of participation,
the merits of grassroots democracy, the value of good ideas, and
the efficacy of modern planning techniques.

Evaluation

Assessing the performance or productivity of individuals, departments, or programs is a major undertaking. Evaluations consume
substantial time, effort, and money, leading to lengthy reports presented with considerable ceremony. Universities convene visiting
committees to evaluate schools or departments. Governments mandate evaluations of their programs. Social service agencies commission studies or audits when important problems or issues arise.
Yet rarely are insights or recommendations heeded. Results typically
disappear into the recesses of people's minds or the far reaches of
administrators' file cabinets.

From a different perspective, evaluation is necessary to ensure
a responsible, serious, and well-managed image. Its widespread use
persists largely for symbolic reasons. Evaluations produce magic
numbers to help us believe that things are working. They show that
an organization takes goals seriously, cares about its performance,
and wants to improve. The evaluation process gives participants
opportunities to share opinions and have them recognized publicly.

Evaluation results help people relabel old practices, escape the normal routine, and build new beliefs (Rallis, 1980). Even if rarely used for decision making, evaluations serve as weapons in political battles or as justifications for decisions already made (Weiss, 1980).

In public organizations, Floden and Weiner (1978, p. 17) argue, "Evaluation is a ritual whose function is to calm the anxieties of the citizenry and to perpetuate an image of government rationality, efficiency, and accountability. The very act of requiring and commissioning evaluations may create the impression that government is seriously committed to the pursuit of publicly espoused goals, such as increasing student achievement or reducing malnutrition. Evaluations lend credence to this image even when programs are created to appease interest groups."

The evaluation process often takes the form of high drama. Prestigious evaluators are hired, and the process receives considerable publicity. Participants wear more formal "costumes" than usual. New roles are enacted: evaluators ask penetrating questions, and respondents give answers that portray the world as it is supposed to be. The results are often presented dramatically, especially when they are favorable. Negative results, in contrast, are often couched in vacuous language with high-sounding recommendations that no one is likely to take very seriously. Attempts to solve the problems disappear after the ceremony is over.

Occasionally, an evaluator blows the whistle by producing a highly critical report. The drama then becomes a tragedy that is often injurious to both parties. In the United States, a widely publicized report on public education (the Coleman Report) advanced the thesis that "schools don't make a difference." The report and the subsequent debate undermined public confidence in the schools at the same time as it raised questions about the cohesion and maturity of the social sciences.

Collective Bargaining

Labor and management meet and confer to reshape divisive standoffs into workable agreements. The process typically pits two reasonable sets of interests against each other: unions want better working conditions and benefits for members; management tries to keep costs down and maximize profits for shareholders. Negotiating teams come together on a public stage and follow a well-known script: "Negotiators have to act like opponents, representatives and experts, showing that they are aligned with team-mates and constituents, willing to push hard to achieve constituent goals, and constantly in control. . . . On the public stage, anger and opposition dominate; rituals of opposition, representation and control produce a drama of conflict. At the same time, there are mechanisms for private understanding between opposing lead bargainers, such as signaling and sidebar discussions" (Friedman, 1994, pp. 86–87).

On the surface, the negotiation process appears to be a political contest where power determines the distribution of scarce resources (see Chapter Eleven). On a deeper plane, negotiation provides a carefully crafted ritual that delivers the performance audiences demand. Departures from the script carry high risk: "A young executive took the helm of a firm with the intention of eliminating bickering and conflict between management and labor. He commissioned a study of the company's wage structure and went to the bargaining table to present his offer. He informed the union representatives what he had done, and offered them more than they had expected to get. The astonished union leaders berated the executive for undermining the process of collective bargaining and asked for another five cents an hour beyond his offer" (Blum, 1961, pp. 63–64).

Similar problems have been documented by Friedman in his studies of mutual gains bargaining (which emphasizes cooperation and win-win outcomes rather than conflict). A disillusioned participant in a mutual gains process that failed lamented: "It hurt us. We got real chummy. Everyone talked. Then, in the final hours, it was the same old shit. Maybe we should have been pounding on the table" (Friedman, 1994, p. 216).

In theater, actors who deviate from the script disrupt everyone else's ability to deliver their lines. The bargaining drama is designed to convince each side the outcomes were the result of a heroic battle. If well performed, the drama conveys the message that two opponents fought hard and persistently for what they believed was right (Blum, 1961; Friedman, 1994). It obscures the widespread reality that actors almost always know in advance exactly how the play will end.

Power

Power is usually viewed as a tangible attribute that individuals or systems possess—as something that can be seized, exercised, or redistributed. But power is inherently ambiguous. It is not always easy to determine what power is, who has it, or how to get it. Sometimes it is even harder to know when power is being used. You are powerful if others think you are. Power is often attributed to particular individuals or groups to account for observed outcomes. If the unemployment rate improves, political incumbents take credit. If a firm's results improve, we give credit to the chief executive. If a program is started when things are getting better anyway, it inherits success.

Power is attributed to certain behaviors. People who talk a lot, belong to committees, and seem close to the action are typically perceived as powerful. Yet there may be little real relationship between observed behavior and ability to get what one wants. The relationship may even be negative—the frustrated may talk a lot, and the disgruntled may resort to political intrigue or posturing without discernible impact (Enderud, 1976).

Myths of leadership attribute causality to individuals in high places. Whether things are going well or badly, we like to hold someone responsible. Cohen and March (1974) have this to say about college presidents:

> Presidents negotiate with their audiences on the interpretations of
> their power. As a result, during recent years of campus troubles,
> many college presidents sought to emphasize the limitations of
> presidential control. During the more glorious days of conspicuous
> success, they solicited a recognition of their responsibility for
> events. This is likely to lead to popular impressions of strong presi-
> dents during good times and weak presidents during bad times.
> Persons who are primarily exposed to the symbolic presidency (for
> example, outsiders) will tend to exaggerate the power of the presi-
> dency. Those people who have tried to accomplish something in
> the institution with presidential support (for example, educational
> reforms) will tend to underestimate presidential power or presiden-
> tial will [pp. 198–199].

As Edelman (1977, p. 73) puts it: "Leaders lead, followers follow, and organizations prosper. While this logic is pervasive, it can be misleading. Marching one step ahead of a crowd moving in a chosen direction may define realistically the connection between leadership and followership. Successful leadership is having followers who believe in the leader. By believing, people are encouraged to link positive events with leadership behaviors. George Gallup once remarked, 'People tend to judge a man by his goals, by what he is trying to do, and not necessarily by what he accomplishes or how well he succeeds.'"

Leaders are typically judged by their style and their coping skills. Dramatic performances emphasizing traits popularly associated with leadership—such as forcefulness, responsibility, courage, and decency—contribute to a leader's image. Though reassuring, the assumption that leaders make a real difference is often misleading. Cohen and March (1974) compare the college president to the driver of a skidding automobile: "The marginal judgments he makes, his skill, and his luck will probably make some difference to the life prospects of his riders. As a result, his responsibilities are heavy. But whether he is convicted of manslaughter or receives a medal for heroism is largely outside his control" (p. 203). As with other processes, leaders' power is less a matter of action than one of appearance. When leaders do make a difference, it is by enriching and updating the drama—constructing new myths that alter beliefs and generate faith.

Summary

From a symbolic perspective, organizations are judged primarily by appearance. An appropriate structure provides a ceremonial stage, projecting to audiences the dramatic performance that is expected. The drama provides reassurance, fosters belief in the organization's purposes, and cultivates faith. Structures that do little to coordinate activity serve an important symbolic role. They provide internal glue, helping participants cope, find meaning, and play their role without reading the wrong lines, upstaging the lead actors, or confusing tragedy with comedy. Externally, they provide a basis for confidence and hope.

The symbolic frame introduces and elaborates concepts rarely applied to organizations in the past. These concepts sharply redefine organizational dynamics and have significant implications for managing and changing organizations. Historically, theories of management and organization have focused on instrumental issues. We see problems, try to develop and implement solutions, and then ask, "What did we accomplish?" Often, the answer is nothing or not much. We find ourselves repeating the old saw that the more things change, the more they remain the same. Such a message is disheartening and disillusioning. It produces a sense of helplessness and a belief that things will never get much better.

The symbolic frame sounds a more hopeful note. For a variety of reasons, we have decided to reframe our organization. We may be restless, frustrated, or searching to renew our faith. We therefore mount a new play called *Change*. At the end of the pageant, we can ask three questions:

1. What was expressed?
2. What was attracted?
3. What was legitimized?

The answers are often enormously uplifting. The drama allows us to resolve contradictions and envision a solution to our problems. Old conflicts, new blood, borrowed expertise, and vital issues are attracted into the arena of change, where they combine and begin to produce new myths and beliefs. Change becomes exciting, uplifting, and vital. The message is heartening and spiritually invigorating. There is always hope. The world is always different. Each day is potentially more exciting and full of meaning than the next. If not, change the symbols, revise the drama, develop new myths— or dance.

Chapter Fourteen

Organizational Culture in Action

How does the symbolic frame apply to small groups? What general principles do managers need to observe in building or shaping team cultures? Prescriptions and theories that abound in the management literature often miss deeper secrets of how groups and teams reach the special state of grace and peak performance. Former Visa CEO Dee Hock captured the heart of the issue: "In the field of group endeavor, you will see incredible events in which the group performs far beyond the sum of its individual talents. It happens in the symphony, in the ballet, in the theater, in sports, and equally in business. It is easy to recognize and impossible to define. It is a mystique. It cannot be achieved without immense effort, training, and cooperation, but effort, training, and cooperation alone rarely create it" (quoted in Schlesinger, Eccles, and Gabarro, 1983, p. 173)

Is peak performance simply a great mystery—beautiful when it happens but no more predictable or controllable than the next earthquake in California? In this chapter, we analyze a well-documented case of a team that *did* achieve a state of transcendence. The story takes us directly into the symbolic roots of flow, spirit, and magic. Tracy Kidder, in *The Soul of a New Machine* (1981), provides a dazzling account of a small group of Data General engineers who created a new computer in record time in the 1970s. Despite scant resources and limited support, the Eagle Group outperformed all other Data General divisions to produce a new, state-of-the-art machine.

Sources of the Eagle Group's Success

Why did this group succeed? So many groups of engineers—or educators, physicians, executives, or graduate students—start out with high hopes but eventually fail. Were the individuals on the Eagle project extraordinarily talented? Not really. Each was highly skilled, but there were equally talented engineers working on other Data General projects. Were team members always treated with dignity and respect? Quite the contrary. As one engineer noted, "No one ever pats anyone on the back" (Kidder, 1981, p. 179). Instead, the group experienced what they called mushroom management: "Put 'em in the dark, feed 'em shit, and watch 'em grow" (p. 109). For over a year, group members jeopardized their health, their families, and their careers: "I'm flat out by definition. I'm a mess, It's terrible. . . . It's a lot of fun" (p. 119).

Were financial rewards a motivating factor? Group members said explicitly that they did not work for money. Nor were they motivated by fame. Their heroic efforts were rewarded neither by formal appreciation nor by official applause. The group quietly dissolved shortly after completing the new computer, and most members of the team moved unrecognized to other parts of Data General—or to other companies.

Perhaps the group's structure accounted for its success. Were its members pursuing well-defined and laudable goals? The group leader, Tom West, offered the precept that "not everything worth doing is worth doing well." Pushed to translate his maxim, he elaborated, "If you can do a quick-and-dirty job and it works, do it" (p. 119). Did the group have an especially clear and well-coordinated set of roles and relationships? According to Kidder, it kept no meaningful charts, graphs, or organization tables. One of the group's engineers put it bluntly: "The whole management structure—anyone in Harvard Business School would have barfed" (p. 116).

Can the political frame unravel the secret of the group's phenomenal performance? Perhaps its members were motivated more by power than by money: "There's a big high in here somewhere for me that I don't fully understand. . . . Some of it's a raw power trip. . . . The reason I work is because I win" (p. 179). They were encouraged to circumvent the formal structure to advance the group's interests: "If you can't get what you need from some manager at your level in another department, go to his boss—that's the way to get things done" (pp. 109–191). Group members were also unusually direct and confrontational: "Feeling sorely provoked, [David] Peck one day said to this engineer, 'You're an asshole.' Ordered by his boss to apologize, Peck went to the man he had insulted, looking sheepish, and said, 'I'm sorry you're an asshole'" (p. 224).

The group was highly competitive with others in the company: "There's a thing you learn at Data General, if you work here for any period of time . . . that nothing ever happens unless you push it" (p. 111). They also competed with one another. Their "tube wars" provide a typical example. Carl Alsing, the head of a subgroup known as the Microkids, came back from lunch one day to find that all of his files had been turned into empty shells: the names were there, but the contents had vanished. It took him an hour to find the real files hidden elsewhere. Alsing counterattacked by creating an encrypted file and tantalizing the team, "There's erotic writing in there and if you can find it, you can read it'" (p. 107).

Here we begin to encounter the secrets of the group's success. The tube wars—and other exchanges among group members— were more than power struggles. They were a form of play that released tensions, created bonds, and contributed to group spirit. A shared and cohesive culture, rather than a clear, well-defined structure, was the real invisible force that gave the team its drive.

Leading Principles

From the Eagle Group's experience we can distill several important tenets of the symbolic frame that apply to any group.

1. How Someone Becomes a Group Member Is Important

Joining a team involves more than a rational decision. It is a mutual choice marked by some special form of ritual. In the Eagle Group, the process of becoming a member was called signing up. When interviewing recruits, Alsing conveyed the message that they were volunteering to climb Mount Everest without a rope and probably lacked the right stuff to keep up with the other climbers in the party. When the new recruits protested that they wanted to climb Mount Everest anyway, Alsing told them they would have to wait to find out if they were good enough. After it was all done and the selections had been made, Alsing summed it up this way: "It was kind of like recruiting for a suicide mission. You're gonna die, but you're gonna die in glory" (Kidder, 1981, p. 66).

Through the signing-up ritual, an engineer became part of a special effort and agreed to forsake family, friends, and health to accomplish the impossible. It was a sacred declaration: "I want to do this job and I'll give it my heart and soul" (Kidder, 1981, p. 63).

2. Diversity Provides a Team's Competitive Advantage

Though nearly all the group's members were engineers, each had unique skills and style. Tom West, the group's leader, was by reputation a highly talented technical debugger. He was also aloof and unapproachable, the "Prince of Darkness." Steve Wallach, the group's computer architect, was a highly creative maverick. According to Kidder (1981, p. 75), before accepting West's invitation to join the group, he went to Edson de Castro, the president of Data General, to find out precisely what he'd be working on.

"Okay," Wallach said, "what the fuck do you want?"

"I want a thirty-two-bit Eclipse," de Castro told him.

"If we can do this, you won't cancel it on us?" Wallach asked. "You'll leave us alone?"

"That's what I want, a thirty-two," de Castro assured him, "a thirty-two-bit Eclipse and no mode bit."

Wallach signed up. His love of literature, stories, and verse provided a literary substructure for the technical architecture of the new machine. Alsing, the group's microcode expert, was as warm and approachable as Tom West was cold and remote. He headed the Microkids, the group of young engineers who programmed the new machine. Ed Rasala, Alsing's counterpart, headed the Hardy Boys, the group's hardware design team. In contrast to Alsing's creative fecundity, Rasala was a solid, hyperactive, risk-taking, and detail-oriented mechanic: "I may not be the smartest designer in the world, a CPU giant, but I'm dumb enough to stick with it to the end" (Kidder, 1981, p. 142).

Diversity among the group's top engineers was institutionalized in specialized functions. One engineer, for example, was viewed as a creative genius who liked inventing an esoteric idea and then trying to get it to work. Another was a craftsman who enjoyed fixing things, working tirelessly until the last bug had been tracked down and eliminated. West buffered the team from upper management interference and served as a group "devil." Wallach created the original design. Alsing and the Microkids created "a synaptic language that would fuse the physical machine with the programs that would tell it what to do" (Kidder, 1981, p. 60). Rasala and the Hardy Boys built the physical circuitry. Understandably, there was tension among these diverse individuals and groups. Harnessing the resulting energy galvanized the different parts into a working team.

3. Example, Not Command, Holds a Team Together

Wallach's design provided modest coordination for Eagle's autonomous individuals and groups. The group had some rules but paid little attention to them. De Castro, the CEO, was viewed as a distant god. He was never there physically, but his presence was always felt. West, the group's official leader, rarely interfered with the actual work, nor was he particularly visible in the laboratory. One Sunday morning in January, however, when the team was supposed to be resting, a Hardy Boy happened to come by the lab and found West sitting in front of one of the prototypes. The next Sunday, West wasn't in the lab, and after that they rarely saw him there. For a long time he did not even hint that he might again put his own hands inside the machine.

West contributed primarily by causing problems for the engineers to solve and making mundane events and issues appear to be special. He created almost endless series of "brushfires" so that he could inspire his staff to put them out. He had a genius for finding drama and romance in the group's everyday routine. Other members of the group's formal leadership followed de Castro and West in creating ambiguity, encouraging inventiveness, and leading by example. Heroes of the moment provided inspiration and direction. Subtle and implicit signals rather than concrete and explicit guidelines or decisions held the group together and directed it toward a common goal.

4. A Specialized Language Fosters Cohesion and Commitment

Every group develops words, phrases, and metaphors unique to its circumstances. A specialized language both reflects and shapes a group's culture. Common language allows team members to communicate easily, with minimal misunderstandings. To the members of the Eagle Group, for example, a *kludge* was a poor, inelegant solution—such as a machine with loose wires held together with adhesive tape. A *canard* was anything false. *Fundamentals* were the source of enlightening thinking. The word *realistically* typically prefaced flights of fantasy. "Give me a *core dump*" meant tell me your thoughts. A *stack overflow* meant that an engineer's memory compartments were too full; a *one-stack-deep mind* indicated shallow thinking. "Eagle" provided a label for the project, while "Hardy Boys" and "Microkids" gave identity to the major subgroups. The two prototype computers were named Woodstock and Trixie.

A shared language binds a group together and is a visible sign of membership. It also sets a group apart from outsiders and reinforces the group's unique values and beliefs. Asked about the Eagle Group's headquarters, Tom West observed, "It's basically a cattle yard. What goes on here is not part of the real world." Asked for an explanation, West remarked, "Mm-hmm. The language is different" (Kidder, 1981, p. 50).

5. Stories Carry History and Values and Reinforce Group Identity

In high-performing organizations and groups, stories keep traditions alive and provide examples to guide everyday behavior. The group's lore extended and reinforced the subtle and powerful influence of Eagle's leaders—some of them distant and remote. Tom West's reputation as a "troublemaker" and an "excitement junkie" was conveyed through stories about the computer wars of the mid-1970s. Alsing said of West that he was always prepared and never raised his voice. Still, he conveyed intensity and the conviction that he knew the way out of whatever storm was currently battering the group. West also had the skills of a good politician. He knew how to develop agendas, build alliances, and negotiate with potential supporters or opponents. When he had a particular objective in mind, he would first go upstairs to get senior executives signed on. Then he went around to people one at a time, telling them that the bosses liked the idea and asking them to come on board. "They say, 'Ah, it sounds like you're just gonna put a bag on the side of the Eclipse,' and Tom'll give 'em his little grin and say,

'It's more than that, we're really gonna build this fucker and it's gonna be fast as greased lightning.' He tells them, 'We're gonna do it by April'" (Kidder, p. 44).

Stories of persistence, irreverence, and creativity encouraged others to go beyond themselves, adding new exploits and tales to the Eagle Group's lore. For example, as the group neared completion, a debugging problem threatened the entire project. Jim Veres, one of the engineers, worked day and night to find the error. Ken Holberger, one of the Hardy Boys, drove to work early one morning, pondering all the problems of the project and wondering if it would ever be finished. He was awakened from his reverie by an unexpected scene as he entered the lab. "A great heap of paper lies on the floor, a continuous sheet of computer paper streaming out of the carriage at [the] system console. Stretched out, the sheet would run across the room and back again several times. You could fit a fairly detailed description of American history . . . on it. Veres sits in the midst of this chaos, the picture of the scholar. He's examined it all. He turns to Holberger. 'I found it,' he says" (Kidder, 1981, p. 207).

6. Humor and Play Reduce Tension and Encourage Creativity

Groups often focus single-mindedly on the task at hand, shunning anything not directly work-related. Seriousness replaces godliness as a cardinal virtue. Effective teams balance seriousness with play and humor. Surgical teams, cockpit crews, and many other groups have learned that joking and playful banter are an essential source of invention and team spirit. Humor releases tension and helps resolve issues that arise from day-to-day routines as well as from sudden emergencies.

Play among the members of the Eagle project was an essential part of the group process. When Alsing wanted the Microkids to learn how to manipulate the computer known as Trixie, he made up a game. As the Microkids came on board, he told each of them to figure how to write a program in Trixie's assembly language. The program had to fetch and print out the contents of a certain file stored inside the computer. The Microkids went to work, learned their way around the machine, and felt great satisfaction—until

Alsing's perverse sense of humor tripped them up at the end of the hunt. When they finally found the elusive file, they were greeted with the message "Access Denied." Through such play, the Microkids learned to use the computer, coalesced into a team, and learned to negotiate their new technical environment. They also learned that their playful leader cared about creativity.

Humor provided a continuous thread as the team struggled to accomplish its formidable task. The humor often stretched the boundaries of good taste, but that, too, was part of the group's identity:

> [Alsing] drew his chair up to his terminal and typed a few letters— a short code that put him in touch with Trixie, which was the machine reserved for the use of his microcoding team. "We've anthropomorphized Trixie to a ridiculous extent," he said.
>
> He typed, WHO.
>
> On the dark-blue screen of the cathode-ray tube, with alacrity, an answer appeared: CARL.
>
> WHERE, typed Alsing.
>
> IN THE ROAD, WHERE ELSE! Trixie replied.
>
> HOW.
>
> ERROR, read the message on the screen.
>
> "Oh, yeah, I forgot," said Alsing, and he typed, PLEASE HOW.
>
> THAT'S FOR US TO KNOW AND YOU TO FIND OUT.
>
> Alsing seemed satisfied with that, and he typed, WHEN.
>
> RIGHT FUCKING NOW, wrote the machine.
>
> WHY, wrote Alsing.
>
> BECAUSE WE LIKE TO CARL [Kidder, 1981, pp. 90–91].

Throughout the year and a half it took to build their new machine, the engineers of the Eagle project relied on play and humor as a source of relaxation, stimulation, enlightenment, and spiritual renewal.

7. Ritual and Ceremony Lift Spirits and Reinforce Values

Ritual and ceremony are expressive occasions. As parentheses in an ordinary workday, they enclose and define special forms of behavior. What occurs on the surface is not nearly so important as the deeper meanings that are communicated beneath visible behavior. Despite stereotypes of narrowly task-focused engineers with little time for anything nonrational, the Eagle Group was very aware of the importance of symbolic activity, and the leadership encouraged ritual and ceremony from the beginning.

Ed Rasala, head of the Hardy Boys, for example, established a rule requiring that changes in the boards of the prototype be updated each morning. This activity allowed efforts to be coordinated in a formal way. More important, the daily updating provided an occasion for informal communication, bantering, and gaining a sense of the whole. The engineers disliked the daily procedure, so Rasala changed it to once a week—on Saturday. He made it a point always to be there himself for the updating.

Eagle's leaders met regularly, but their meetings focused more on symbolic issues than on substance. "'We could be in a lot of trouble here,' West might say, referring to some current problem. And Wallach or Rasala or Alsing would reply, 'You mean *you* could be in a lot of trouble, right, Tom?' It was Friday, they were going home soon, and relaxing, they could half forget that they would be coming back to work tomorrow" (Kidder, 1981, p. 132). Friday afternoon is a traditional time to wind down and relax. Honoring such a tradition was all the more important for a group whose members often worked all week and then all weekend. West made himself available to anyone who wanted to chat. Near the end of the day, before hurrying home, West would lean back in his chair with his office door open and entertain any visitor.

In addition to recurring rituals, the Eagle Group convened periodic ceremonies to raise their spirits and reinforce their sense of shared mission. Toward the end of the project, Alsing instigated a ceremony to provide a burst of renewed energy for the final push. The festivities called attention to the values of creativity, hard work, and teamwork. A favorite pretext for parties was presentation of the Honorary Microcoder Awards that Alsing and the Microcoder Team instituted. Not to be outdone, the Hardy Boys cooked up the

PAL Awards, the first of which was presented after work at a local establishment called the Cain Ridge Saloon. The citation read as follows (Kidder, 1981, p. 250):

Honorary PAL Award
In recognition of unsolicited contributions
to the advancement of Eclipse hardware
above and beyond the normal call of duty,
we hereby convey unto you our thanks and congratulations
on achieving this "high" honor.

The same values and spirit were reinforced again and again in a continued cycle of celebratory events. "Chuck Holland [Alsing's main submanager] handed out his own special awards to each member of the Microteam, the Under Extraordinary Pressure Awards. They looked like diplomas. There was one for Neal Firth, 'who gave us a computer before the hardware guys did,' and one to Betty Shanahan, 'for putting up with a bunch of creepy guys.' Having dispensed the Honorary Microcoder Awards to almost every possible candidate, the Microteam instituted the All-Nighter Award. The first of these went to Jim Guyer, the citation ingeniously inserted under the clear plastic coating of an insulated coffee cup" (Kidder, 1981, p. 250).

8. Informal Cultural Players Make Contributions Disproportionate to their Formal Roles

Alsing was the main organizer and instigator of parties. He was also the Eagle Group's conscience and nearly everyone's confidant.

> For a time, when he was still in college, Alsing had wanted to become a psychologist. He adopted that sort of role now. Although he kept track of his team's technical progress, he acted most visibly as the social director of the Microteam, and often of the entire Eclipse Group. Fairly early in the project, Chuck Holland had complained, "Alsing's hard to be a manager for, because he goes around you a lot and tells your people to do something else." But Holland also conceded, "The good thing about him is that you can go and talk to him. He's more of a regular guy than most managers" [Kidder, 1981, p. 105].

Every group or organization has a "priest" or "priestess" who ministers to spiritual needs. Informally, these people hear confessions, give blessings, maintain traditions, encourage ceremonies, and intercede in matters of gravest importance. Alsing did all these things and, like the tribal priest, was a counterpart and interpreter of the intentions of the chief:

> West warned him several times, "If you get too close to the people who work for you, Alsing, you're gonna get burned." But West didn't interfere, and he soon stopped issuing warnings.
>
> One evening, while alone with West in West's office, Alsing said: "Tom, the kids think you're an ogre. You don't even say hello to them."
>
> West smiled and replied. "You're doing fine, Alsing" [Kidder, 1981, pp. 109–110].

Rosemarie Seale's duties also expanded well beyond those of a typical secretary. If Alsing was the priest, she was the mother superior. She did all the usual secretarial chores—answering the phones, preparing documents, and preparing budgets. But she found particular joy in solving the minor crises that arose almost daily and serving as a kind of den mother for the members of the Eagle team. When new members came on, it was Rosemarie Seale who worried about finding them a desk and some pencils. When paychecks went astray, she would track them down and get them to their intended recipient. She liked the job, she said, because she felt that she was doing something important.

In any group, a network of informal players deals with human issues outside formal channels. On the Eagle project, their efforts were encouraged, appreciated, and rewarded outside the formal chain of command; they helped keep the project on track.

9. Soul Is the Secret of Success

The symbolic side of the Eagle Group was the real secret of its success. Its soul, or culture, created a new machine: "Ninety-eight percent of the thrill comes from knowing that the thing you designed works, and works almost the way you expected it would. If that happens, part of *you* is in that machine" (Kidder, 1981, p. 273). All members of the Eagle Group put something of themselves into the new computer. Individual efforts went well beyond the job and were supported by a way of life that encouraged each person to commit to doing something of significance. This commitment was elicited through the ritual of signing up and then maintained and accentuated by shared diversity, exceptional leaders, common language, stories, rituals, ceremonies, play, and humor. In the best sense of the word, the Eagle Group was a team, and the efforts of the individual members were knitted together by a cohesive culture. Symbolic elements were at the heart of the group's success.

The experience of the Eagle Group is not unusual. After extensive research on high-performing groups, Vaill (1982) concluded that spirit was at the core of every such group he studied. Members of such groups consistently "felt the spirit," a feeling essential to the meaning and value of their work. More and more teams and organizations now realize that culture, soul, and spirit are the wellsprings of high performance. The U.S. Air Force, in the aftermath of the Vietnam War, embarked on a vigorous effort to reaffirm traditions and rebuild its culture. "Cohesion is a principle of war" was added to the list of core values. Project Warrior brought heroes— living and dead—forward as visible examples of the "right stuff." Rituals were revitalized and reinforced. For example, the air force instituted a "reblueing" ceremony to encourage recommitment to its tradition and values.

Countless other organizations have taken similar steps. Facing intense foreign competition and a severe profit squeeze, the Ford Motor Company set out in the 1980s to build a culture committed to the principle that "quality is job one." Mitsubishi Corporation, with over twenty-five thousand products, ranging from "noodles to space satellites" (Lifson and Takagi, 1981, p. 11), used an elaborate entrance ceremony for newly hired employees as part of its effort to reinforce a corporate culture that stressed professionalism, cooperation, and entrepreneurship. Jan Carlzon revitalized the culture of the Scandinavian Air System around the precepts that every encounter between a customer and an SAS employee was a "moment of truth" and that SAS "flies people, not planes" (Carlzon, 1987, p. 27)

Summary

Symbolic perspectives question traditional views that building a team mainly means finding the right people and designing an appropriate structure. The essence of high performance is spirit. If we were to banish play, ritual, ceremony, and myth, we would destroy teamwork, not enhance it. There are many signs that late-twentieth-century organizations are at a critical juncture because of a crisis of meaning and faith. Managers wonder how to build team spirit when turnover is high, resources are tight, and people worry about losing their jobs. Such questions are important, but by themselves, they limit managerial imagination and divert attention from deeper issues of faith and purpose. Managers are inescapably accountable for budgets and bottom lines. They have to respond to individual needs, legal requirements, and economic pressures. But they can serve a deeper and more durable function when they recognize that team building at its heart is a spiritual undertaking. It is both a search for the spirit within and the creation of a community of believers united by shared faith and shared culture. Peak performance emerges as a team discovers its soul.

Part Six

Improving Leadership Practice

Chapter Fifteen

Integrating Frames for Effective Practice

Earlier chapters probed each frame's relevance for diagnosis and action. This chapter considers them in combination. How do you choose a frame? How do you integrate multiple frames in the same situation. We begin by revisiting the turbulent world of managers. We then explore what happens when people employ different frames. We offer questions and guidelines to stimulate thinking about which frames are likely to apply in different situations. Finally, we examine literature on effective managers and organizations to see which frames dominate current management theory.

Life as Managers Know It

Prevailing mythology depicts managers as rational men and women who plan, organize, coordinate, and control activities of subordinates. Periodicals, books, and business schools portray an image of modern managers: unruffled, well organized, with clean desks, power suits, and sophisticated information systems. Such "super-managers" develop and implement farsighted strategies, producing predictable and effective results. What a reassuring picture of clarity and order this is! Unfortunately, it's wrong.

A different picture emerges if you take some time to watch managers at work (Carlson, 1951; Mintzberg, 1973; Kotter, 1982). It's a hectic life, shifting rapidly from one situation to another, each with a different blend of challenges. In months of observing senior managers, Kotter (1982) rarely saw them *making* a decision. Decisions *emerged* from a fluid, swirling vortex of conversations,

265

meetings, and memos. Sophisticated information systems ensure an overload of detail about what happened last month or last year. Yet they fail to answer a far more important question: What will happen tomorrow? In deciding what to do next, managers operate mostly on the basis of intuition—hunches and judgment derived from prior experience. Too busy to spend time thinking or reading, they get most of their information verbally—in meetings or over the phone. They are hassled priests, modern muddlers, and corporate wheeler-dealers.

How does one reconcile the actual work of managers with the heroic imagery? "Whenever I report this frenetic pattern to groups of executives, regardless of hierarchical level or nationality, they always respond with a mix of discomfiture and recognition. Reluctantly, and somewhat sheepishly, they will admit that the description fits, but they don't like to be told about it. If they were really good managers, they seem to feel, they would be in control, their desks would be clean, and their shops would run as smoothly as a Mercedes engine" (Leavitt, 1996, p. 294). Led to believe that they should be rational and on top of it all, managers become confused and bewildered. They are supposed to plan and organize, yet they find themselves muddling and playing catch-up. They want to solve problems and make decisions. But problems are ill defined and options murky. Control is an illusion and rationality an afterthought.

Across the Frames: Organizations as Multiple Realities

Organizational life is always full of simultaneous events that can be interpreted in a variety of ways. Table 15.1 examines familiar processes through four lenses. As the table shows, any event can be framed in many ways and serve multiple purposes. Planning produces specific objectives. But it also creates arenas for airing conflict and becomes a sacred occasion to renegotiate symbolic meanings.

Multiple realities produce confusion and conflict when individuals view the same event through different lenses. Consider a meeting called by a hospital administrator to make an important decision. The chief technician viewed the meeting as a chance to express feelings and build relationships. The director of nursing hoped to use it to gain power vis-à-vis physicians. The medical director saw it as an occasion for reaffirming the hospital's distinctive

Table 15.1. Four Interpretations of Organizational Processes.

Process	Structural Frame	Human Resource Frame	Political Frame	Symbolic Frame
Strategic planning	Strategies to set objectives and coordinate resources	Gatherings to promote participation	Arenas to air conflicts and realign power	Ritual to signal responsibility, produce symbols, negotiate meanings
Decision making	Rational sequence to produce right decision	Open process to produce commitment	Opportunity to gain or exercise power	Ritual to confirm values and provide opportunities for bonding
Reorganizing	Realign roles and responsibilities to fit tasks and environment	Maintain balance between human needs and formal roles	Redistribute power and form new coalitions	Maintain image of accountability and responsiveness; negotiate new social order
Evaluating	Way to distribute rewards or penalties and control performance	Process for helping individuals grow and improve	Opportunity to exercise power	Occasion to play roles in shared ritual
Approaching conflict	Maintain organizational goals by having authorities resolve conflict	Develop relationships by having individuals confront conflict	Develop power by bargaining, forcing, or manipulating others to win	Develop shared values and use conflict to negotiate meaning

Table 15.1. Four Interpretations of Organizational Processes (*Continued*).

Process	Structural Frame	Human Resource Frame	Political Frame	Symbolic Frame
Goal setting	Keep organization headed in right direction	Keep people involved and communication open	Provide opportunity for individuals and groups to make interests known	Develop symbols and shared values
Communication	Transmit facts and information	Exchange information, needs, and feelings	Influence or manipulate others	Tell stories
Meetings	Formal occasions for making decisions	Informal occasions for involvement, sharing feelings	Competitive occasions to win points	Sacred occasions to celebrate and transform the culture
Motivation	Economic incentives	Growth and self-actualization	Coercion, manipulation, and seduction	Symbols and celebrations

approach to medical care. The meeting became a cacophonous jumble—like a group of musicians each playing from a different score.

The confusion that results when everyone sees the world through a different lens is illustrated in the following case:

Doctor Fights Order to Quit Maine Island

Dr. Gregory O'Keefe found himself the focus of a fierce battle between 1,200 year-round residents of Vinalhaven, Maine (an island fishing community), and the National Health Service Corps (NHSC), which pays his salary and is insisting he take a promotion to an administrator's desk in Rockville, Md.

O'Keefe doesn't want to go, and his patients don't want him to either. The islanders are so upset that, much to the surprise of NHSC officials, they have enlisted the aid of Sen. William Cohen (R-Maine) and U.S. Health and Human Services Secretary Margaret Heckler to keep him here.

It's certainly not the prestige or glamour of the job that is holding O'Keefe, who drives the town's only ambulance and, as often as twice a week, takes critically ill patients to mainland hospitals via an emergency ferry run or a Coast Guard cutter, private plane, or even a lobster boat.

Apparently unyielding in their insistence that O'Keefe accept the promotion or resign, NHSC officials seemed startled last week by the spate of protests from angry islanders, which prompted nationwide media attention and inquiries from the Maine Congressional delegation. NHSC says it probably would not replace O'Keefe on the island, which, in the agency's view, is now able to support a private medical practice.

Cohen described himself as "frustrated by the lack of responsiveness of lower-level bureaucrats." But to the NHSC, O'Keefe is a foot soldier in a military organization of more than 1,600 physicians assigned to isolated, medically needy communities. And he's had the audacity to question the orders of a superior officer.

"It's like a soldier who wanted to stay at Ft. Myers and jumped on TV and called the Defense Secretary a rat for wanting him to move," Shirley Barth, press officer for the federal Public Health Service, said in a telephone interview Thursday [Goodman, 1983, p. 1].

The NHSC officials had trouble seeing beyond the structural frame—they had a task to do and a strategy for achieving it; O'Keefe's opposition was illegitimate. O'Keefe saw it in human resource terms—he felt that the work he was doing was meaningful and satisfying and the islanders needed him. For Senator Cohen, it was a political issue—could minor bureaucrats be allowed to hurt his constituents through mindless abuse of power? For the hardy residents of Vinalhaven, O'Keefe was a heroic figure of mythic proportions—"If he gets one night's sleep out of twenty, he's lucky, but he's always up there smiling and working." The islanders were full of stories about O'Keefe's humility, skill, humanness, dedication, wit, confidence, and caring.

With everyone peering through different frames, confusion and conflict were predictable. The inability of NHSC officials to understand and acknowledge the existence of other perceptions illustrates the costs of clinging to a single view of a situation. Whenever someone's actions seem to make no sense, it is worth asking if you and they are seeing different realities. It helps to understand their perspective, even if it seems inappropriate. Their frame—not yours—determines how they will act.

Matching Frames to Situations

For different times and situations, one perspective may be more helpful than others. At a strategic crossroads, a rational process focused on gathering and analyzing information may be exactly what is needed. At other times, developing commitment or building a power base may be more critical. In times of great stress, such as AT&T experienced after divesting its regional operating companies, decision processes may become a form of ritual that provides comfort and support. Choosing a frame, or understanding others' perspectives, involves a combination of analysis, intuition, and artistry. Table 15.2 provides questions to facilitate analysis and stimulate intuition. It suggests conditions under which each frame is likely to be most effective.

Are commitment and motivation essential to success? The human resource and symbolic frames need to be considered whenever issues of individual commitment, energy, and skill are keys to effective implementation. A new curriculum in a school district will fail

Table 15.2.   Choosing a Frame.

Question	Frame If Answer Is Yes	Frame If Answer Is No
Are individual commitment and motivation essential to success?	Human resource, symbolic	Structural, political
Is the technical quality of the decision important?	Structural	Human resource, political, symbolic
Are there high levels of ambiguity and uncertainty?	Political, symbolic	Structural, human resource
Are conflict and scarce resources significant?	Political, symbolic	Structural, human resource
Are you working from the bottom up?	Political	Structural, human resource, symbolic

without teacher support. Support might be strengthened by human resource approaches like participation and self-managing teams or through symbolic approaches linking the innovation to values and symbols teachers cherish.

Is the technical quality important? When a good decision needs to be technically correct, the structural frame's emphasis on rationality and logical procedure is essential. But if a decision must be acceptable to major constituents, human resource, political, or symbolic issues will be more significant. In the R. J. Reynolds leveraged buyout story (Chapter Eleven), none of the bidders wanted to win the battle but lose the war by paying more than RJR's real value. Massive effort went into data collection and analysis to determine how much the company was worth. Could the technical quality of a decision ever be *unimportant*? Yes, particularly for decisions allocating scarce resources. A college found itself embroiled in a three-month battle over the choice of a commencement speaker. The faculty pushed for a great scholar, the students for a movie star. The president was more than willing to invite anyone acceptable to both groups—she could find no technical criteria to prove that one choice was better than the other.

Sophisticated magnetic resonance imaging (MRI) technology has demonstrated its diagnostic superiority, but it comes at a significant price. Hospitals and HMOs have struggled to make decisions acceptable to physicians, patients, and shareholders.

Are ambiguity and uncertainty high? When goals are clear, technology is well understood, and behavior is reasonably predictable, the structural and human resource frames are likely to apply. As ambiguity increases, the political and symbolic frames become more relevant. The political frame expects people to be rational in pursuing self-interests, but contests among individuals and interest groups often become confused and chaotic. The symbolic frame sees symbols as a way of finding order, meaning, and "truth" in situations too complex, uncertain, or mysterious for rational or political analysis. In the R. J. Reynolds case, the most critical ambiguity was what other bidders were doing and what it meant. Everyone scouted the competition intensely and tried to interpret even the weakest signals. At a key point in the endgame, Henry Kravis started to drop hints that he might drop out. To make the hints credible, he went off for a long weekend in Colorado just before final bids were due. The opposition picked up the signals and started telling one another, "Henry's not bidding." It was, according to one member of the Shearson team, "our fatal error."

Are conflict and scarce resources significant? The human resource frame fits best in situations that favor collaboration—such as profitable, growing firms, or highly unified schools. But when conflict is high and resources are scarce, dynamics of conflict, power, and self-interest regularly come to the fore. In situations like the Reynolds bidding war, sophisticated political strategies are vital to success. In other cases, skilled leaders may find an overarching symbol that helps would-be adversaries transcend their differences and work together. In the early 1980s, Yale University was paralyzed by a clerical and technical workers' strike. No one, including Yale's president, A. Bartlett Giamatti, knew how to settle the strike. Then Phil Donahue invited the Yale community to appear on his television show. Union members energetically presented their side, and Giamatti appeared for the administration. The audience was active and vocal but polarized. Near the program's end, Giamatti told a story about his father, an Italian immigrant, who was admitted to the neighborhood university, which happened to be Yale. His father couldn't pay the tuition, but Yale had a core value of "admission by ability, support by need." The story and the invocation of a shared value helped bridge the chasm dividing the parties.

The structural frame fits situations in the middle. Structure imposes limits on available options, which in turn implies conditions of moderate scarcity. Extreme scarcity fosters conflict that quickly exceeds the capacity of existing authority systems. Because symbols play a part in every culture and every social class—from the very poor to the very wealthy—the symbolic frame may be appropriate across a wide range of situations.

Are you working from the bottom up? Restructuring is an option primarily for those in positions of authority. Human resource approaches to organizational improvement—such as training, job enrichment, and participation—need support from the top to be successful. The political frame, in contrast, fits well for making change from the bottom up. Because partisans—bottom-up change agents—rarely have much formal clout, they must find other bases of power.

The questions in Table 15.2 are no substitute for judgment and intuition in deciding how to frame or respond to a situation. But they can guide and augment the process. Consider once again the Helen Demarco case (Chapter Two). Demarco's boss, Paul Osborne, had a plan for major change. Demarco thought the plan was a mistake but did not feel she could directly oppose her boss. What should she do? The issue of commitment and motivation was important, both in terms of her lack of commitment to Osborne's plan and her concern about finding a solution he would accept. The table suggests that the human resource frame was worth considering, though Demarco never did. The technical quality of the plan was critical in Demarco's judgment, but she was convinced that Osborne was immune to technical arguments.

Ambiguity played a significant role in the case. Even if technical issues were reasonably clear, the key issue of how to influence Osborne was shrouded in ambiguity. Implicitly, Demarco acknowledged the importance of the symbolic frame in using a form of theater (the research that wasn't research, the technical report that was window-dressing) as her key strategy. Above all, Table 15.2 suggests that Demarco's situation aligns with the political frame: resources were scarce, conflict was high, and she was trying to influence from the bottom up. The logic ran toward politics and symbols. Demarco went with the flow.

The questions in Table 15.2 cannot be followed mechanically to arrive at a correct response for every situation. In some cases, the analysis might lead you to a familiar frame. If the old frame shows signs of inadequacy, it may still be appropriate to reframe. You may discover an exciting and creative new lens for deciphering the situation. Then you will face another problem: how to communicate your discovery to others who still see a different reality.

Effective Managers and Organizations

Does the ability to use multiple frames actually help managers decipher events and determine how to respond? If so, how are the frames combined and integrated in everyday situations? We will examine several strands of research. First we look at two influential reports on organizational excellence, *In Search of Excellence* (Peters and Waterman, 1982) and *Built to Last* (Collins and Porras, 1994). Then we review two important studies of effective senior managers, *The General Managers* (Kotter, 1982) and *Managing Public Policy* (Lynn, 1987). Finally, we look at recent research on managers' frame orientations.

Peters and Waterman's spectacular 1982 best-seller explored the question "What do high-performing corporations have in common?" They studied more than sixty large companies in six major industries: high technology (Digital Equipment and IBM, for example), consumer products (Kodak, Procter & Gamble), manufacturing (3M, Caterpillar), service (McDonald's, Delta Airlines), project management (Boeing, Bechtel), and natural resources (Exxon, Du Pont). The companies were chosen on the basis of both objective performance indicators (such as long-term growth and profitability) and the judgments of knowledgeable observers.

Collins and Porras (1994) attempted a similar study of what they termed "visionary" companies but tried to address two methodological limitations in Peters and Waterman's study. Collins and Porras included a comparison group (missing in Peters and Waterman) by matching each of their excellent companies with another firm in the same industry founded at about the same time. Their pairings included Citibank with Chase Manhattan, General Electric with Westinghouse, Sony with Kenwood, Hewlett-Packard with Texas

Table 15.3.   Characteristics of "Excellent" or "Visionary" Companies.

Frame	Peters and Waterman (1982)	Collins and Porras (1994)
Structural	Autonomy and entrepreneurship; bias for action; simple form, lean staff	Clock-building, not time-telling; try a lot, keep what works
Human resource	Close to the customer; productivity through people	Home-grown management
Political	[None]	[None]
Symbolic	Hands on, value-driven; simultaneous loose/tight properties; stick to the knitting	Big, hairy, audacious goals; cultlike cultures; good enough never is; preserve the core, stimulate progress; more than profits

Note: None of the characteristics in either study fit into the political frame.

Instruments, and Merck with Pfizer. Collins and Porras emphasized long-term results by restricting their study to companies at least fifty years old with evidence of consistent success over many decades.

Both studies identified eight critical characteristics of excellent companies, similar in some respects and distinct in others, as Table 15.3 shows.

Both studies concluded that excellent companies have relatively loose structures that reward innovation and entrepreneurship but are tightly controlled by culture and values. Peters and Waterman's "bias for action" and Collins and Porras's "try a lot, keep what works" both point to risk and experiment as a way to learn and avoid bogging down in analysis paralysis. Both studies emphasize a clear core identity that helps firms stay on track and "stick to the knitting." Peters and Waterman's list has more emphasis on structural and human resource dimensions, while Collins and Porras's more recent study puts a stronger emphasis on symbolic and cultural variables.

As Table 15.3 shows, both studies produced three-frame models. None of the characteristics of excellence are political. Do effective organizations eliminate politics? Or did the authors miss something? By definition, their samples focused on companies with strong records of sustained growth and profitability. With relatively abundant resources, political dynamics are less likely to be prominent because slack resources can be used to buy off conflicting interests. Recall, too, that strong cultures tend to increase homogeneity and reduce pluralism. Unifying cultures reduce conflicts and political strife—or make them easier to manage.

Even in successful companies, it is likely that power and conflict are more important than these reports suggest. Ask a few managers, "What makes your organization successful?" They will rarely talk about coalitions, conflict, or jockeying for position. Even if they exist, politics are typically kept in the closet—secrets known to every insider but rarely on public display. If we change our focus from effective organizations to effective managers, we find a different picture.

Effective Senior Managers

Kotter (1982) conducted an intensive study of fifteen corporate "general managers" (GMs). His sample included "individuals who hold positions with some multifunctional responsibility for a business" (p. 2); each managed an organization with at least several hundred employees. Lynn (1987) analyzed five subcabinet-level executives in the U.S. federal government: political appointees with responsibility for a major federal agency. Table 15.4 shows the characteristics that Kotter and Lynn emphasize as key to the effectiveness of senior managers.

Kotter and Lynn both described jobs of enormous complexity and uncertainty, coupled with substantial dependence on networks of people whose support and energy were essential for the executives to do their job. Both focused on three basic challenges: setting an agenda, building a network, and using the network to get things done. Lynn would presumably agree with Kotter's observation, "As a result of these demands, the typical GM faced significant obstacles in both figuring out what to do and in getting things done" (1982, p. 122).

Kotter and Lynn both emphasized the importance of the political dimension in senior managers' jobs. Lynn described the need for a significant dose of political skill and sophistication: "building legislative support, negotiating, and identifying changing positions

Table 15.4.   Challenges in Senior Executives' Jobs.

Frame	Kotter (1982)	Lynn (1987)
Structural	Keep on top of large, complex set of activities; set goals and policies under conditions of uncertainty	Attain intellectual grasp of policy issues
Human resource	Motivate, coordinate, and control large, diverse group of subordinates	Use their personalities to best advantage
Political	Achieve "delicate balance" in allocating scarce resources; get support from bosses; get support from corporate staff and other constituents	Exploit all opportunities to achieve strategic gains
Symbolic	Develop credible strategic premises; identify and focus on core activities that give meaning to employees	

and interests" (1987, p. 248). Kotter's model includes elements of all four frames; Lynn's includes all but the symbolic.

Comparing all four studies reveals both similarities and differences. All give roughly similar emphasis to structural and human resource considerations. But political issues are invisible in the organizational excellence studies, whereas they are central in both studies of senior executives. Politics was as important for Kotter's corporate executives as for Lynn's political appointees. Conversely, symbols and culture were more prominent in the studies of organizational excellence. For one reason or another, the different studies tended to neglect one frame or another. In assessing any framework for improving organizations, ask if anything is left out. The frame you don't see could be the one that bites you.

Managers' Frame Preferences

In recent years, a new line of research on managers' cognitive styles has provided additional data on how frame preferences influence leadership effectiveness. Bolman and Deal (1991, 1992a, 1992b) studied populations of managers and administrators in both business and education. They found that the ability to use multiple frames was a consistent correlate of effectiveness. Effectiveness as a *manager* was particularly associated with the structural frame, whereas the symbolic and political frames tended to be the primary determinants of effectiveness as a *leader.*

Bensimon (1989, 1990) studied college presidents and found that multiframe presidents were viewed as more effective than single-frame presidents. In her sample, more than a third of the presidents used only one frame, and only a quarter relied on more than two. Single-frame presidents tended to be less experienced and relied mainly on structural or human resource perspectives. Presidents who relied solely on the structural frame were particularly likely to be seen as ineffective leaders. Heimovics, Herman, and Jurkiewicz Coughlin (1993) found the same thing for chief executives in the nonprofit sector, and Wimpelberg (1987) found similar results in a study of eighteen school principals. His study paired nine effective and less effective schools. Principals of ineffective schools relied almost entirely on the structural frame, whereas principals in effective schools used multiple frames. When asked about hiring teachers, principals in less effective schools talked about standard procedures (how vacancies are posted, how the central office sends candidates for interviews), while more effective principals talked about "playing the system" to get the teachers they needed.

Bensimon found that presidents thought they used more frames than their colleagues saw them use. They were particularly likely to overrrate themselves on the human resource and symbolic frames, a finding also reported by Bolman and Deal (1991). Only half of the presidents who saw themselves as symbolic leaders were perceived that way by others on their campus.

Despite the low image of organizational politics in the minds of most managers, the political frame appears to be the primary determinant of success in certain jobs. Heimovics, Herman, and Jurkiewicz Coughlin (1993, 1995) found that to be true for the chief executives of nonprofit organizations, and Doktor (1993) found the same thing for the directors of family service organizations in Kentucky.

Summary

The image of firm control and crisp rationality often attributed to managers has little relevance to the messy world of complexity, conflict, and uncertainty that they inhabit. They need multiple frames to survive. They need to understand that any event or process can serve multiple purposes and that different participants are often operating in different frames. They need a diagnostic map that helps them assess which frames are likely to be salient and helpful in any given situation. Among the key variables are motivation, technical constraints, uncertainty, scarcity, conflict, and whether an individual is operating from the top down or from the bottom up.

Several lines of recent research find that effective leaders and effective organizations rely on multiple frames. Studies of effective corporations, of individuals in senior management roles, and of public administrators all point to the need for multiple perspectives in developing a holistic picture of complex systems.

Chapter Sixteen

Reframing in Action

Opportunities and Perils

The essence of reframing is examining the same situation from multiple vantage points to develop a holistic picture. Effective leaders change lenses when things don't make sense or aren't working. Reframing offers the promise of powerful new options but carries the risk that not every new strategy will be successful. Each of the frames offers distinctive advantages, but each also has blind spots and shortcomings.

The *structural frame* risks ignoring everything that falls outside the rational jurisdiction of procedures, policies, and organization charts. Structural thinking can overestimate the power of authority and underestimate the authority of power. Paradoxically, overreliance on structural assumptions and a narrow emphasis on rationality too often lead to an irrational neglect of human, political, and cultural variables that are crucial to organizational effectiveness.

Adherents of the *human resource frame* sometimes cling to a romanticized view of human nature in which everyone always hungers for growth and collaboration. Human resource enthusiasts can be too optimistic about integrating individual and organizational needs while neglecting the power of structure and the stubborn realities of conflict and scarcity.

The *political frame* captures dynamics that other frames miss but has its own limits. A fixation on politics easily becomes a cynical self-fulfilling prophecy that reinforces conflict and mistrust while sacrificing opportunities for rational discourse, collaboration, and

280

hope. *Political* is too often understood to mean amoral, scheming, and unconcerned about the common good.

The *symbolic frame* offers powerful insights into fundamental issues of meaning and belief—ideas that can bond people into a cohesive group pursing a shared mission. But its concepts are also vague and elusive—effectiveness depends greatly on the artistry of the user. Symbols are sometimes mere fluff or camouflage, the tools of scoundrels who seek to manipulate the unsuspecting, or awkward attempts that embarrass more than energize.

In this chapter, we seek to illuminate both the pluses and the minuses. We will show how the frames can be used as scripts, or scenarios, to guide action in challenging circumstances. In the process, we emphasize reframing as a tool for coping with some of the challenges of being different.

Meryl Streep, like other great actors, shows an extraordinary capacity to lose herself in screen roles. She *becomes* the character she plays, whether an Australian mother accused of killing her child or a Polish mother interned in a Nazi concentration camp. She changes with the script: who she is, how she appears, what she does. The same sort of transformation occurs in everyday life. Everyone changes roles when situations demand different performances.

Few of us have the dramatic skill and versatility of Meryl Streep, but we *can* alter what we do by following different scripts or scenarios. We have been learning how to do this since birth. Both men and women typically employ different scenarios for encounters with members of their own sex and members of the opposite sex. Students who are guarded and formal when talking to professors become energized and intimate when talking to peers. Managers who are polite and deferent with their bosses may be gruff and autocratic with subordinates before coming home at night to romp playfully with the kids. The tender-hearted neighbor becomes a ruthless competitor when his company's market share is threatened. Consciously or not, we all read situations to figure out the underlying script and then respond in character.

Different frames generate different ways to respond to situations—by rescripting or generating new scenarios. Managers can enhance their flexibility and freedom by devising alternative scenarios for themselves. To illustrate that process, we will visit the frames to generate eight different leadership approaches for Cindy

Marshall, a manager whose first day in a new job was far more challenging than she expected.

Cindy Marshall

Put yourself in the shoes of Cindy Marshall, headed to the office for your first day in a new job. Your company has transferred you to its Kansas City office to become a department manager. You have worked for the company since you left college. But this is a big promotion, with a substantial increase in pay and responsibility. You know you face a major challenge. You have inherited a department with a reputation for slow, substandard customer service. Senior management credits much of the problem to your predecessor, Bill Howard. He is seen as authoritarian and weak in customer orientation. Howard is being transferred to another job, but the company asked him to stay on for a week to help you get oriented. You know he hired most of your new staff. Many may still feel loyal to him.

When you arrive, you get a frosty hello from Susan Bond, your new secretary. As you walk into your new office, you see Bill Howard behind the desk in a conversation with three other staff members. You say hello, and Howard responds by saying, "Didn't the secretary tell you that we're in a meeting right now? If you'll wait outside, I'll be able to see you in about an hour."

As Cindy Marshall, how would you respond?

This is a classic example of a manager's nightmare: a totally unexpected and almost unmanageable situation. You feel the glare of the spotlight, and you know the audience is waiting eagerly for your response. If you feel threatened or attacked—as many of us would—you'll be emotionally pulled toward fight or flight. Fighting back and escalating the conflict are likely to be damaging for both parties. Backing away or fleeing could suggest that you are too emotional or not tough enough. The frames suggest another set of possibilities. Take advantage of different lenses. What's really going on here? What choices do you have? What does the script demand? How might you rewrite the script to create a more effective scenario? Reframing is a powerful tool for generating possibilities other than fight or flight in a tough situation.

As Cindy Marshall, your first decision is whether to respond to Howard on the spot or buy time. If you're at a loss for what to say or think you might make things worse instead of better, take time to "go to the balcony"—try to get above the confusion on the main floor long enough to get a better perspective and develop a workable strategy. Even better, though, would be to find an effective response on the spot.

Each of the frames generates different possibilities, and those differences can be translated into alternative scenarios. They can also be misapplied or misused. Success depends on the skill and artistry of the person seeking a suitable scenario. To illustrate this, we will generate scenarios for both effective and ineffective responses that Cindy could make using each of four frames.

Structural Frame

Exhibit 16.1. A Structural Scenario.

A structural scenario casts managers and leaders in fundamental roles of clarifying goals, attending to the relationship between structure and environment, and developing a structure that is clear to everyone and appropriate to what needs to be done. Without a workable structure, people become unsure about what they are supposed to be doing. The result is confusion, frustration, and conflict. In an effective organization, individuals are relatively clear about their responsibilities and their contribution to the mission. Policies, linkages, and lines of authority are straightforward and widely accepted. When you have the right structure, one that people understand, organizations can achieve goals and individuals can see their role in the big picture.

The main job of a leader is to focus on task, facts, and logic, rather than personality and emotions. Most "people problems" stem from structural flaws and not personal limitations or liabilities. Structural leaders are not rigidly authoritarian and do not necessarily solve every problem by issuing orders (though that is sometimes appropriate). Instead, they try to design and implement a process or structure appropriate to the circumstances.

Think about possible structural responses that Cindy Marshall might make to Bill Howard's opening salvo. Here's one example:

Howard: Didn't the secretary tell you that we're in a meeting right now? If you'll wait outside, I'll be able to see you in about an hour.

Marshall: My appointment as manager of this office began at nine this morning. This is now my office, and you're sitting behind my desk. Either you relinquish the desk immediately, or I will call headquarters and report you for insubordination.

Howard: I was asked to stay on the job for one more week to try to help you learn the ropes. Frankly, I doubt that you're ready for this job, but if you don't want my help, perhaps I should leave right away.

Marshall: I repeat, I am now in charge of this office. Let me also remind you that headquarters assigned you to stay this week to assist me. I expect you to carry out that assignment. If you don't, I will submit a letter for your file detailing your lack of cooperation. Now, *(firmly)* I want my desk.

Howard: Well, we were working on important office business, but since the princess here is more interested in giving orders than in getting work done, let's move our meeting down to your office, Joe.

In this exchange, Cindy places heavy emphasis on her authority and the formal chain of command. By invoking her superiors and her legitimate authority, she got Howard to back down. But she now risks long-term tensions with her new subordinates. She may be seen as defensive and insecure. She also risks reinforcing a stereotype of women managers as "critical, bossy, and overcontrolling" (Kanter, 1977, p. 189).

There are other structural options. Here's another example of how Marshall might respond to Howard, still in the structural frame:

Howard: Didn't the secretary tell you that we're in a meeting right now? If you'll wait outside, I'll be able to see you in about an hour.

Marshall: She didn't mention it, and I don't want to interrupt important work, but we also need to set some priorities and work out an agenda for the day anyway. Bill, have you developed a plan for how you and I can get to work on the transition?

Howard: I thought we'd meet later on, after I get through some pressing business.

Marshall: The pressing business is just the kind of thing I need to learn about as the new manager here. What issues are you discussing?

Howard: How to keep the office functioning when the new manager is not ready for the job.

Marshall: Well, I have a lot to learn about this office, but I feel I'm ready. With your help, I think we can have a smooth and productive transition. How about if you continue your meeting and I just sit in as an observer? Then, Bill, you and I could meet to work out a plan for how we'll handle the transition. After that, I'd like to schedule a meeting with each manager to get an individual progress report. I'd like to hear from each of you about your major customer service objectives and how you would assess your progress against objectives. Now, what were you talking about before I got here?

This time Marshall is clear and firm in establishing her authority without appearing harsh or dictatorial. She underscores the importance of setting priorities. She asks if Howard has a plan for making the transition productive. She emphasizes shared goals and defines a temporary role for herself as an observer. She focuses steadfastly on the task and not on Howard's provocations. In keeping the exchange on a rational level and outlining a transition plan, she avoids escalating or submerging the conflict. She also communicates to her new staff that she has done her homework, is organized, and knows what she wants to do. When she says she would like to hear from each of them about their objectives and progress, she communicates an expectation that they should follow her example.

Human Resource Frame

Exhibit 16.2. A Human Resource Scenario.

Human resource leaders believe that people are the heart of any organization. When people feel the organization is responsive to their needs and supportive of their goals, you can count on their commitment and loyalty. Administrators who are authoritarian or insensitive, who don't communicate effectively, or who don't care about their people can never be effective leaders. The human resource leader works on behalf of both the organization and its people, seeking to serve the best interests of both.

The job of the leader is support and empowerment. Support takes a variety of forms: letting people know that you are concerned about them, listening to find out about their aspirations and goals, and communicating personal warmth and openness. You empower people through participation and openness and by making sure that they have the autonomy and the resources that they need to do their jobs well.

Some people go a little too far in trying to be responsive:

Howard: Didn't the secretary tell you that we're in a meeting right now? If you'll wait outside, I'll be able to see you in about an hour.

Marshall: Oh, gosh, no, she didn't. I just feel terrible about interrupting your meeting. I hope I didn't offend anyone because to me, it's really important to establish good working relationships right from the outset. While I'm waiting, is there anything I can do to help? Would anyone like a cup of coffee?

Howard: No. We'll let you know when we're finished.

Marshall: Oh . . . well, have a good meeting, and I'll see you in an hour.

In the effort to be friendly and accommodating, Marshall acted more like a waitress than a manager. She defused the conflict, but her staff is likely see their new boss as weak.

She could instead capitalize on an interest in people. Consider the following:

Howard: Didn't the secretary tell you that we're in a meeting right now? If you'll wait outside, I'll be able to see you in about an hour.

Marshall: I'm sorry if I'm interrupting, but I'm eager to get started, and I'll need all your help. *(She walks around, introduces herself, and shakes hand with each member of her*

staff. Howard scowls silently.) Bill, could we take a few
minutes to talk about how we can work together on
the transition, now that I'm coming in to manage the
department?

Howard: You're not the manager yet. I was asked to stay on for a
week to get you started—though, frankly, I doubt that
you're ready for this job.

Marshall: I understand your concern, Bill, because I know how
committed you are to the success of the department.
If I were you, I might be worried about whether I was
turning my baby over to someone who wouldn't be
able to take care of it. But I wouldn't be here if I didn't
feel ready. I want to benefit as much as I can from your
experience. Is it urgent to get on with what you were
talking about, or could we take some time first to talk
about how we can start working together?

Howard: We have some things we need to finish.

Marshall: Well, as a manager, I always prefer to trust the judgment of the people who are closest to the action. I'll
just sit in as an observer while you finish up, and then
we can talk about how we move forward from there.

Here Marshall is unfazed and relentlessly cheerful; she avoids
a battle and acknowledges Howard's position. When Howard says
she is not ready for the job, she resists the temptation to debate or
return his salvo. Instead, she acknowledges his concern but calmly
communicates her confidence and her focus on moving ahead. She
demonstrates an important skill of human resource leaders: the
ability to combine advocacy with inquiry. She listens carefully to
Howard but gently stands her ground. She asks for his help while
expressing confidence that she can do the job. When Howard says
that they have things to finish, she responds with the agility of a
martial artist, using Howard's energy to her own advantage. She
expresses part of her philosophy—she prefers to trust her staff's
judgment—and positions herself as an observer, thus gaining an
opportunity to learn more about her staff and the issues they are
addressing. By reframing the situation, she is off to a much better
start with Howard and is able to signal to others the kind of people-
oriented leader she intends to be.

Political Frame

Exhibit 16.3. A Political Scenario.

Political leaders believe that managers have to recognize political reality and know how to deal with it. Inside and outside any organization, there are always a variety of interest groups, each with its own agenda. There are never enough resources to give all parties what they want, so there will always be conflict.

The job of the leader is to recognize the major constituencies, develop ties to their leadership, and manage conflict as productively as possible. Above all, you need to build a power base and use power carefully. You can't give every group everything it wants. You can try to create arenas where groups can negotiate their differences and come up with reasonable compromises. You also have to work hard at articulating what everyone in your organization has in common. Tell the people in your organization that they cannot afford to waste their energies fighting each other when there are plenty of enemies outside that they can all fight together. Groups that don't get their act together internally tend to get trounced by outsiders who have their own agendas.

Some managers translate the political approach to mean management by intimidation and manipulation. It sometimes works, but the risks are high. Here's an example:

Howard: Didn't the secretary tell you that we're in a meeting right now? If you'll wait outside, I'll be able to see you in about an hour.

Marshall: In your next job, maybe you should train your secretary better. Anyway, I can't waste time sitting around in the hallways. Everyone in this room knows why I'm here. You've got a choice, Bill. You can cooperate with me, or you can lose any credibility you still have in this company.

Howard: If I didn't have more experience than you do, I wouldn't be so quick to throw my weight around. But if you think you know it all already, I guess you won't need any help from me.

Marshall: What I know is that this department has gone downhill under your leadership, and it's my job to turn it around. You can go home right now, if you want—

you know where the door is. But if you're smart, you'll stay and help. The vice president wants my report on the transition. You'll be a lot better off if I can tell him you've been cooperative.

Moviegoers cheer when the villains get their comeuppance. It can be satisfying to give the verbal equivalent of a kick in the groin to someone who seems to deserve it. In this exchange, Marshall established that she is tough, even dangerous. But such coercive tactics can be expensive in the long run. She is likely to win this battle because her hand is stronger. But she may lose the war. She increases Howard's antagonism, and her attack on Howard may offend and frighten her new staff. Even if they dislike Howard, they might see Marshall as arrogant and callous. She may have done political damage that will be difficult to reverse.

Sophisticated political leaders prefer to avoid head-on demonstrations of power, looking for ways to appeal to the self-interests of potential adversaries:

Howard: Didn't the secretary tell you that we're in a meeting right now? If you'll wait outside, I'll be able to see you in about an hour.

Marshall: *(pleasantly)* Bill, how about we skip the games and go to work. I want this department to be a winner, and I hope that's what all of us want. I also would like to manage the transition in a way that's good for your career, Bill, and for the careers of everyone in the room.

Howard: If I need help from you on my career, I'll ask.

Marshall: OK, but the vice president has asked me to let him know about the cooperation I get here. I'd like to be able to say that everyone has been helping me as much as possible. I hope that's what you'd like, too.

Howard: I've known the vice president a lot longer than you have. I can talk to him myself.

Marshall: I know, Bill, he's told me that. In fact, I saw him a few minutes ago. What do you say you and I walk over and see him right now?

Howard: Uh . . . no, not right now.

Marshall: Well, then, let's get on with it. Do you want to finish what you were discussing, or is this a good time for us to develop some agreement on how we're going to work together?

In this politically based response, Marshall was both direct and diplomatic. She used a light touch in dismissing Howard's opening salvo ("How about we skip the games . . ."). She spoke directly to Bill's interest in his career and her subordinates' interest in theirs. She deftly deflated Howard's posturing by asking if he wanted to go with her to talk to the vice president. Clearly, she was confident of her political position and knew that there was little strength behind Howard's bluster.

Note that in both political scenarios, Marshall drew on her power resources, but in the first Marshall used those resources to humiliate Howard. In the second, Marshall's approach was subtler. She conserved her political capital and took charge while leaving him with as much pride as possible. It was closer to a win-win than a win-lose outcome.

Symbolic Frame

Exhibit 16.4. A Symbolic Scenario.

Symbolic leaders believe that the most important part of a leader's job is inspiration—giving people something that they can believe in. People become excited and committed to an organization that is special, a place with a unique identity, a place where people feel that what they do is really important. Effective symbolic believers are passionate about making their organization the best of its kind and communicate that passion to others. They use dramatic, visible symbols to get people excited and to give them a sense of the organization's mission. They are visible and energetic. They create slogans, tell stories, hold rallies, give awards, appear where they are least expected, and manage by wandering around.

Symbolic leaders are sensitive to an organization's history and culture. They seek to use the best in an organization's traditions and values as a base for building a culture that provides cohesiveness and meaning. They articulate a vision that communicates the organization's unique capabilities and mission.

At first glance, Cindy Marshall's encounter with Bill Howard might seem a poor candidate for a symbolic approach. An ineffective effort could produce embarrassing results, making the would-be symbolic leader look foolish:

Howard: Didn't the secretary tell you that we're in a meeting right now? If you'll wait outside, I'll be able to see you in about an hour.

Marshall: It's great to see that you're all hard at work. It's proof that we all share a commitment to excellence in customer service. In fact, I've already made up buttons for all the staff. Here, I have one for each of you. They read, "The customer is always first." They look great, and they communicate the spirit that we all want in the department. Go on with your meeting. I can use the hour to talk to some of the staff about their visions for the department. *(She walks out of the office.)*

Howard: *(to remaining staff)* Did you believe that? I told you they hired a real space cadet to replace me. Maybe you didn't believe me, but you just saw it with your own eyes.

Marshall's symbolic direction might have been on the right track, but symbols work only when they are attuned to people and place. As a newcomer to the department culture, Marshall needed to pay close attention to her audience. Meaningless symbols antagonize, and empty symbolic events backfire.

Conversely, more skilled symbolic leaders understand that situations of challenge and stress can serve as powerful opportunities to articulate values and build a sense of mission. Cindy Marshall demonstrates how in a well-formed symbolic approach to Bill Howard's gruffness:

Howard: Didn't the secretary tell you that we're in a meeting right now? If you'll wait outside, I'll be able to see you in about an hour.

Marshall: *(smiling)* Maybe this is just the traditional initiation ritual in this department, Bill, but let me ask a question.

If one of our customers came through the door right now, would you ask her to wait outside for an hour?

Howard: If she just came barging in like you did, sure.

Marshall: Are you working on something that's more important than responding to our customers?

Howard: They're not *your* customers. You've only been here five minutes.

Marshall: True, but I've been with this company long enough to know the importance of putting customers first.

Howard: Look, you don't know the first thing about how this department functions. Before you go off on some customer crusade, you ought to learn a little about how we do things.

Marshall: There's a lot I can learn from all of you, and I'm eager to get started. For example, I'm very interested in your ideas on how we can make this a department where as soon as a person walks in, he or she gets the sense that this is a place where people care, they're responsive, they want to be helpful. I'd like that to be true for anyone who comes in—a staff member, a customer, or just someone who got lost and came into the wrong office. That's not the message I got from my initiation a couple of minutes ago, but I'm sure we can think of lots of ways to change that. How does that fit with your image of what the department should be like?

Notice how Marshall reframed the conversation. Instead of engaging in a personal confrontation with Howard, she focused on the department's core values. She brought her "customer first" commitment with her, but she avoided positioning that value as something imposed from outside. Instead, she grounded it in an experience everyone in the room had just shared: the way she was greeted when she entered. Like many successful symbolic leaders, she was attuned to the cues about values and culture that are continually expressed in everyday life. She communicated her philosophy, but she also asked questions to draw out Howard and her new staff members. If she can use the organization's history to her advantage in rekindling a commitment to customer service, she is off to a good start.

Summary

Until the frames and reframing are automatic for you, it will take more than the few seconds available to Cindy Marshall to generate an effective response in every frame. In practicing any new skill—playing tennis, flying an airplane, or handling a tough leadership challenge—the process is often slow and painstaking at first. But as your skill level improves, it gets easier, faster, and more fluid.

Cindy Marshall's initial encounter with Bill Howard is not atypical. It exemplifies the kinds of challenges and tests that she is likely to confront as she moves forward in her career. The scenarios presented in this chapter provide a glimmer of what she can expect, depending on the approach that she chooses. Managers regularly feel powerless and trapped when they use only one or two frames for all situations. This is particularly true for women and members of other excluded groups who experience "the dogged frustration of people living daily in a system not made for them and with no plans soon to adjust for them or their differences" (Gallos and Ramsey, 1996, p. 216). Since they are less likely to get a second or third chance when they fail, judicious reframing is vital in enabling them to transform managerial traps into leadership opportunities.

Structural and human resource approaches may be all you need to build a successful career in middle management, but they will not equip you to rise to top management or to break through the glass ceiling if you face one. The ability to reframe and use multiple lenses will help you go farther while feeling less strain and confusion along the way.

Though progressive organizations have made heroic strides in building a fairer opportunity structure (Levering and Moskowitz, 1993; Morrison, 1992), the path to success is still fraught with obstacles placed in the way of women and minorities. But the more people who break through the glass ceiling, the quicker those barriers will disappear. The glass ceiling feels every bit as foreboding and impenetrable as the Berlin Wall did until it was suddenly dismantled. Learning to reframe can speed the day when we will suddenly notice that the ceiling is no longer there.

Chapter Seventeen

Reframing Leadership

Leadership is universally offered as a panacea for almost any social problem. Around the world, middle managers say their enterprises would thrive if only senior management provided "real leadership." A widely accepted canon holds that leadership is a very good thing that we need more of—at least, more of the right kind. "For many—perhaps for most—Americans, leadership is a word that has risen above normal workaday usage as a conveyer of meaning and has become a kind of incantation. We feel that if we repeat it often enough with sufficient ardor, we shall ease our sense of having lost our way, our sense of things unaccomplished, of duties unfulfilled" (Gardner, 1986, p. 1). Yet there is much confusion and disagreement about what leadership really means.

Sennett (1980, p. 197) writes, "Authority is not a thing; it is a search for solidity and security in the strength of others which will seem to be like a thing." The same is true of leadership. It is not a tangible thing. It exists only in relationships and in the imagination and perception of the engaged parties. Most images of leadership suggest that leaders get things done and get people to do things: leaders are powerful. Yet many examples of the exercise of power fall outside our images of leadership: armed robbers, extortionists, bullies, traffic cops. Implicitly, we expect leaders to persuade or inspire rather than to coerce or give orders. We also expect leaders to produce cooperative efforts and to pursue goals that transcend their own narrow self-interest.

Leadership is also distinct from authority, though authorities may be leaders. Weber (1947) linked authority to legitimacy. People voluntarily obey authority so long as they believe it is legitimate.

Authority and leadership are both built on legitimacy and voluntary obedience. When leaders lose legitimacy, they lose the capacity to lead. Obedience to leaders is primarily voluntary rather than forced. But many examples of obeying authority fall outside the domain of leadership. As Gardner (1989, p. 7) put it, "The meter maid has authority, but not necessarily leadership."

Heifetz (1994) argues that authority is often an impediment to leadership: "Authority constrains leadership because in times of distress, people expect too much. They form inappropriate dependencies that isolate their authorities behind a mask of knowing. [The leadership role] is played badly if authorities reinforce dependency and delude themselves into thinking that they have the answers when they do not. Feeling pressured to know, they will surely come up with an answer, even if poorly tested, misleading, and wrong" (p. 180).

Leadership is also different from management, though the two are typically confused. One may be a leader without being a manager, and many managers could not "lead a squad of seven-year-olds to the ice-cream counter" (Gardner, 1989, p. 2). Bennis and Nanus (1985) offer the distinction that "managers do things right, and leaders do the right thing" (p. 21). Kotter (1988) views management as primarily being about structural nuts and bolts: planning, organizing, and controlling. He views leadership as a change-oriented process of visioning, networking, and building relationships. Gardner (1989) argues against contrasting leadership and management too sharply because leaders may "end up looking like a cross between Napoleon and the Pied Piper, and managers like unimaginative clods" (p. 3). He suggests several dimensions for distinguishing leadership from management. Leaders think longer-term, look outside as well as inside, and influence constituents beyond their immediate formal jurisdictions. They emphasize vision and renewal and have the political skills to cope with the challenging requirements of multiple constituencies.

It is hard to imagine an outstanding manager who is not also a leader. But it is misleading and elitist to imagine that leadership is provided *only* by people in high positions. Such a view causes us to ask too much of too few. Popular images of John Wayne, Bruce Lee, and Sylvester Stallone provide a distorted and romanticized view of how leaders function. We need *more* leaders as well as *better* leadership.

Leadership Context

Traditional notions of the solitary, heroic leader have led us to focus too much on the actors and too little on the stage they play their parts on. Leaders make things happen, but things also make leaders happen. Context influences both what leaders must do and what they can do. No single formula is possible or advisable for the great range of situations that potential leaders encounter.

Heroic images of leadership convey the notion of a one-way process: leaders lead and followers follow. This view blinds us to the reality of a relationship between leaders and their followers. Leaders are not independent actors. They both shape and are shaped by their constituents (Gardner, 1989; Simmel, 1950). Leaders often promote a new idea or initiative only *after* large numbers of their constituents already favor it (Cleveland, 1985). Leadership is not simply a matter of what a leader does but also of what occurs in a relationship. Leaders' actions generate responses from others that in turn affect the leaders' capacity for taking further initiatives (Murphy, 1985). As Briand (1993, p. 39) puts it, "A 'leader' who makes a decision and then attempts to 'sell' it to the public is not a wise leader and will likely not prove an effective one. The point is not that those who are already leaders should do less, but that everyone else can and should do more. Everyone must accept responsibility for the people's well-being, and everyone has a role to play in sustaining it."

It is common to equate leadership with position, but this relegates all those in the "lowerarchy" to the passive role of follower. It also reinforces the widespread tendency of senior executives to take on more responsibility than they can adequately discharge (Oshry, 1995). Administrators are leaders only to the extent that others grant them cooperation and follow their lead. Conversely, one can be a leader without a position of formal authority. Good organizations encourage leadership from many quarters (Kanter, 1983; Barnes and Kriger, 1986).

Leadership is thus a subtle process of mutual influence fusing thought, feeling, and action to produce cooperative effort in the service of purposes and values of *both* the leader and the led. Single-frame managers are unlikely to understand and attend to the intricacies of a holistic process.

What Do We Know About Good Leadership?

Perhaps the two most widely accepted propositions about leadership are that all good leaders must have the "right stuff"—qualities like vision, strength, and commitment that are essential to leadership—and that good leadership is situational—what works in one setting will not work in another. A proposition from the "effective schools" literature illustrates the "right stuff" perspective: a good school will be headed by a strong and visionary instructional leader. An example of the situational view is this widely held assumption: "It takes a different kind of person to lead when you're growing and adding staff than when you're cutting budgets and laying people off."

Despite the apparent tension between the one-best-way and contingency views of leadership, both capture part of the truth. Several studies have found similar characteristics among unusually effective leaders across a variety of sectors and situations. Another body of research has identified situational variables that critically influence the kind of leadership that works best under different conditions.

One Best Way

Recent years have spawned a series of studies of "good leadership" in organizations (Bennis and Nanus, 1985; Clifford and Cavanagh, 1985; Collins and Porras, 1994; Conger, 1989; Farkas and De Backer, 1996; Kotter, 1982, 1988; Kouzes and Posner, 1987; Levinson and Rosenthal, 1984; Maccoby, 1981; Peters and Austin, 1985; Vaill, 1982). Most have been qualitative studies of leaders, mostly corporate executives. Methodology has varied from casual impressions to systematic interviews and observation.

No characteristic is universal in these reports, though vision comes closest. Effective leaders help establish a vision, set standards for performance, and create focus and direction for collective efforts. A related characteristic explicit in some reports (Clifford and Cavanagh, 1985; Kouzes and Posner, 1987; Peters and Austin, 1985) and implicit in most others is the ability to communicate a vision effectively, often through the use of symbols. Another characteristic mentioned in many studies is commitment or passion (Clifford and Cavanagh, 1985; Vaill, 1982; Peters and Austin, 1985). Good leaders care deeply about whatever their organization or group does. They believe that nothing in life is more important than doing that work well. A third frequently mentioned characteristic is the ability to inspire trust and build relationships (Kotter, 1988; Maccoby, 1981; Bennis and Nanus, 1985). Kouzes and Posner (1987) found that honesty came first on a list of traits that managers said they most admired in a leader.

Beyond vision, the ability to communicate the vision with passion, and the capacity to inspire trust, consensus breaks down. The studies cited so far, along with extensive reviews of the leadership literature (Bass, 1981, 1990; Hollander, 1978; Gardner, 1987), provide a long list of attributes associated with effective leadership: risk taking, flexibility, self-confidence, interpersonal skills, managing by walking around, task competence, intelligence, decisiveness, understanding of followers, and courage, to name a few. The oldest reliable finding about effective leaders—they are smarter and work harder than other people—continues to find research support (O'Reilly and Chatman, 1994), but those characteristics are found in people who are better at almost anything.

Blake and Mouton's "managerial grid" (1969, 1985) is a classic and still popular example of a one-best-way approach. Diffused through scores of books, articles, and training programs, the grid postulates two fundamental dimensions of leader effectiveness: concern for task and concern for people. The model assumes that all approaches to leadership can be arrayed on a two-dimensional grid like the one in Figure 17.1. Theoretically, the grid contains eighty-one cells, though Blake and Mouton emphasize only five of those possibilities:

1,1: The manager who has little concern for task or people and is simply going through the motions

1,9: The friendly manager who is concerned about people but has little concern for task

9,1: The hard-driving taskmaster

5,5: The compromising manager who tries to balance task and people

9,9: The ideal manager who integrates task and people and produces outstanding performance

Figure 17.1. Managerial Grid Model.

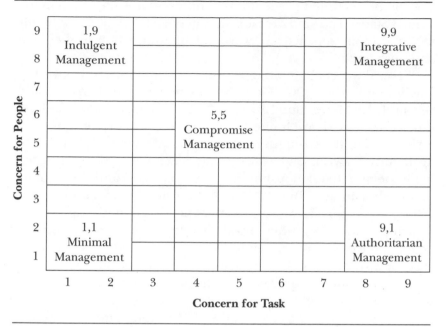

Source: Adapted from Blake and Mouton (1985).

Blake and Mouton have vigorously defended their conviction that a 9,9 style is a leadership approach for all situations and all seasons (Blake and Mouton, 1982), but this claim has been heavily criticized. The grid approach focuses almost exclusively on issues of task and human resources. It gives little attention to constituents other than direct subordinates and assumes that a leader need simply integrate concern for task with concern for people to be effective in any situation. If structure has become unwieldy, political conflicts have become debilitating, or the organization's culture is empty and threadbare, the grid model has little to say.

Contingency Theories

The dearth of attributes consistently associated with effective leadership reinforces the argument that leadership varies with the situation. Leadership is different for first-level supervisors than for chief executives. It is different in the public and private sectors. The job of a college president is very different in China than in the United States. The kind of leadership needed for skilled and highly motivated followers may not work for followers who are alienated and unskilled.

Several writers have offered situational theories of leadership (including Fiedler, 1967; Fiedler and Chemers, 1974; Vroom and Yetton, 1973; Hersey and Blanchard, 1977; Hersey, 1984; and Reddin, 1970), but all are limited in their conceptualization of leadership and in the strength of the empirical support. Most fail to distinguish between leadership and management, typically restricting leadership to relationships between managers and their immediate subordinates. Burns (1978), Gardner (1986), and Kotter (1985) argue persuasively that leaders need skill in managing relationships with all significant stakeholders, including superiors, peers, and external constituents. Contingency theories are a major area for further research. Almost everyone believes that widely varying circumstances require different forms of leadership, but research is still sparse.

Even so, approaches such as the Hersey and Blanchard (1977) situational leadership model have become widely popular as a training approach. The model uses two dimensions of leadership similar to those in the Managerial Grid: task and people. Hersey (1984, p. 31) defines task behavior as "the extent to which the leader engages in spelling out the duties and responsibilities of an individual or group." Relationship behavior is "the extent to which the leader engages in two-way or multi-way communication." It includes "listening, encouraging, facilitating, providing clarification, and giving socioemotional support" (p. 32). Hersey combines task and people into the two-by-two chart in Figure 17.2, which shows four possible "leadership styles": telling, selling, participating, and delegating.

When should a manager use each style? The model says it depends on subordinates' "maturity" (Hersey and Blanchard, 1977) or "readiness level" (Hersey, 1984). Hersey defines readiness in terms of subordinate attitudes (how *willing* they are to do a good job) and skills (how *able* they are to do the job well). The model distinguishes four levels of subordinate readiness and argues that different styles are appropriate for different situations.

Figure 17.2.   Situational Leadership Model.

Task

	Low	High
High (Relationship)	**Leadership Through Participation** Use when followers are *able* but *unwilling* or *insecure*.	**Leadership Through Selling** Use when followers are *unable* but *willing* or *motivated*.
Low (Relationship)	**Leadership Through Delegation** Use when followers are *able* but *willing* or *motivated*.	**Leadership Through Telling** Use when followers are *unable* but *unwilling* or *insecure*.

Source: Adapted from Hersey (1984).

For subordinates at the lowest level (unable and unwilling to do a good job), the model counsels managers to "tell": such people need direction from their boss. At the next level up (willing but unable), subordinates want to do the job but lack skills. The model tells leaders to "sell" in such situations: explain their decisions and provide subordinates with an opportunity for clarification. At the next level, when subordinates are able but unwilling, the leader should use "participating" to increase motivation: share ideas and have a participative discussion. At the highest level, with subordinates who are both able and willing, the leader should simply delegate: the subordinates will do fine without leader input.

Though at first glance the model may seem plausible, research casts doubts on its validity (Hambleton and Gumpert, 1982; Graeff, 1983; Blank, Weitzel, and Green, 1990). If, for example, managers give unwilling and unable subordinates high direction and low support, what would cause their motivation to improve? The manager of a design team in a computer company told us with regret, "I treated my group with a 'telling' management style and found that in fact they became both less able and less willing." Like Blake and Mouton, Hersey and Blanchard focus mostly on the relationship between managers and immediate subordinates and say little about issues of structure, politics, or symbols.

Leadership Models as Secular Faiths

Dealing with people is a perennially perplexing aspect of managing. Managers are always looking for ideas to make the job easier. Too often the search for simplicity overlooks important realities. Even so, managers may conclude that any model is better than no model in the face of confusion and mystery. True believers may defend their commitments with fervor, as the following case illustrates.

> A major corporation was developing a new management training program for a group of some two thousand technical managers. A task force with representatives from two divisions in the company came together to decide what should be taught. The representatives from Division A had participated in Managerial Grid seminars. They knew in their hearts that the grid was the one best way and that it should be the foundation of the seminar. The managers in Division B had attended situational leadership seminars, and their faith in the situational model was equally unshakable.
>
> Initially, the two sides engaged in polite talk and rational argument. When that failed, the conversation gradually became more heated. Eventually, the group found itself hopelessly deadlocked. An outside consultant came in to mediate the dispute. He listened while the representatives from each division reviewed the conversation. The consultant then said to the group, "I'm impressed by the passion on both sides. I'm curious about one thing. If you all believe so deeply in these models and if it makes a difference which model someone learns, why can't I see any difference in the behavior of the two groups?" Stunned silence fell over the room. Finally one member said, "You know, I think he's right. We don't use the damn models, we just preach them." That was the end of the impasse.

Reframing Leadership

Reframing offers a way to get beyond narrow and oversimplified views of leadership. Each of the frames offers a distinctive image

Table 17.1. Reframing Leadership.

	Effective Leadership		Ineffective Leadership	
Frame	Leader	Leadership Process	Leader	Leadership Process
Structural	Analyst, architect	Analysis, design	Petty tyrant	Management by detail and fiat
Human resource	Catalyst, servant	Support, empower-ment	Weakling, pushover	Abdication
Political	Advocate, negotiator	Advocacy, coalition building	Con artist, thug	Manipulation, fraud
Symbolic	Prophet, poet	Inspiration, framing experience	Fanatic, fool	Mirage, smoke and mirrors

of the leadership process. Depending on leader and circumstance, each can lead to compelling and constructive leadership, but none is right for all times and seasons. In this chapter, we discuss the four images of leadership summarized in Table 17.1. For each, we examine skills and processes and provide rules of thumb for successful leadership practice.

Architects or Tyrants? Structural Leadership

Structural leadership often evokes images of petty tyrants and rigid bureaucrats who never met a rule they didn't like. The Cindy Marshall case (Chapter Sixteen) showed how easily a structural image of leadership can lead to petty authoritarianism. In contrast to other frames, little literature exists on structural leadership. Many structural theorists have argued that leadership is neither important nor basic (Hall, 1987). But the effects of structural leadership can be powerful and enduring, if more subtle and less obviously heroic, than other forms. Collins and Porras (1994) found that the founders of many highly successful companies—such as Hewlett-Packard and Sony—had neither a clear vision for their organization nor even a particular product in mind. They were "clockbuilders"—social architects who focused on designing and building an effective organization. One of the greatest architects was Alfred P. Sloan Jr.

Sloan, who became president of General Motors in 1923, was a dominant force in the company until his 1956 retirement. The structure and strategy he established made GM the world's largest corporation. He has been described as "the George Washington of the GM culture" (Lee, 1988, p. 42), even though his "genius was not in inspirational leadership, but in organizational structures" (p. 43).

At the turn of the twentieth century, there were some thirty manufacturers of automobiles in the United States. In 1899, they produced a grand total of about six hundred cars. Most of these small carmakers stumbled shortly out of the starting gate, leaving two late entries, the Ford Motor Company (founded by Henry Ford in 1903) and GM (founded by William Durant in 1908) as front-runners in the race to dominate the American automobile industry. Henry Ford's single-minded determination to build an affordable car had Ford in a commanding lead when Sloan took over General Motors.

Under GM's founder, Billy Durant, the company's divisions operated as independent fiefdoms. Uncontrolled costs and a business slump in 1920 created a financial crisis—Chevrolet lost $5 million in 1921, and only Du Pont money and Buick's profitability kept GM afloat (Sloan, 1965). In Sloan's first year, matters got worse. GM's market share dropped from 20 percent to 17 percent, while Ford's increased to 55 percent. But things were about to change. Henry Ford had a disdain for organization and clung to his original vision of a single, low-priced, mass-market car. The Model T was cheap and reliable, and Ford stayed with the same design for almost twenty years. That worked fine in the early years when customers would buy anything with four wheels and a motor. Whereas Ford saw no great need for creature comforts in the Model T, Sloan surmised that consumers would pay more for amenities like windows to keep out rain and snow. His strategy worked, and Chevrolet soon began to gnaw off large chunks of Ford's market. By 1928, Model T sales had dropped so precipitously that Henry Ford was forced to close his River Rouge plant for a year to retool. General Motors took the lead in the great auto race for the first time in twenty years. In the next seventy years, no one ever sold more cars than General Motors.

Durant had built GM by buying everything in sight, thus forming a loose combination of previously independent firms. "GM did not have adequate knowledge or control of the individual operating divisions. It was management by crony, with the divisions operating on a horse-trading basis. The main thing to note here is that no one had the needed information or the needed control over the divisions. The divisions continued to spend lavishly, and their requests for additional funds were met" (Sloan, 1965, pp. 27–28).

Sloan recognized that GM needed a better structural form. The primary option at the time was a centralized, functional organization, but Sloan felt that such a structure would not work for GM. Instead, he created one of the world's first decentralized organizations. His strategy was simple: centralize planning and resource allocation; decentralize operating decisions. Under Sloan's model, divisions focused on making and selling cars, while top management focused on long-range strategy and the allocation of resources. The central staff made sure that top management had the information and control systems it needed to make strategic decisions.

The structure worked. By the late 1920s, Sloan headed a more versatile organization with a broader product line than Ford. With Henry Ford still dominating his highly centralized company, Ford was poorly positioned to compete with GM's multiple divisions, each producing different cars at different prices. GM pioneered a structural form that eventually set the standard for others: "Although they developed many variations and although in very recent years they have been occasionally mixed into a matrix form, only two basic organizational structures have been used for the management of large industrial enterprises. One is the centralized, functional departmentalized type perfected by General Electric and Du Pont before World War I. The other is the multidivisional, decentralized structure initially developed at General Motors and also at Du Pont in the 1920s" (Chandler, 1977, p. 463).

In the 1980s, GM found itself with another structural leader at the helm, Roger Smith. But the results were less satisfying. Like Sloan, Smith ascended to the top job at a difficult time. In 1980, his first year as GM's chief executive, all American automakers lost money. It was GM's first loss since 1921. Recognizing that the company had serious competitive problems, Smith relied on structure and technology to make it "the world's first 21st century corporation"

(Lee, 1988, p. 16). He restructured vehicle operations and spent billions of dollars in a quest for paperless offices and robotized assembly plants. The changes were dramatic, but the results were not:

> [Smith's] tenure has been a tragic era in General Motors history. No GM chairman has disrupted as many lives without commensurate rewards, has spent as much money without returns, or has alienated so many along the way. An endless string of public relations and internal relations insensitivities has confused his organization and complicated the attainment of its goals. Few employees believe that [Smith] is in the least concerned with their well-being, and even fewer below executive row anticipate any measure of respect, or reward, for their contributions. No GM chief executive's motives have ever been as universally questioned or his decisions as thoroughly mistrusted [Lee, 1988, pp. 286–287].

Why did Sloan succeed but Smith have trouble? They were about equally uncharismatic. Sloan was a somber, quiet engineer who habitually looked as if he were sucking a lemon. Smith's leadership aura was not helped by his blotchy complexion and squeaky voice. Neither had great sensitivity to human resource or symbolic issues. Why was Sloan's structural contribution so durable and Smith's so problematic? The answer comes down to how well each implemented the right structural form. Structural leaders succeed not because of inspiration but because they have the right design for the times and are able to get their structural changes implemented. Effective structural leaders share several characteristics.

1. *Structural leaders do their homework.* Sloan was a brilliant engineer who had grown up in the auto industry. Before coming to GM, he was chief executive of an auto accessories company where he had implemented a divisional structure. When GM bought his firm in 1916, Sloan became a vice president and board member. Working under Durant, he devoted much of his energy to studying GM's structural problems. He pioneered the development of sophisticated internal information systems and better market research. He was an early convert to group decision making and created a committee structure to make major decisions. Roger Smith had spent his entire career with General Motors, but most of his

jobs were in finance. Much of his vision for General Motors involved changes in production technology, an area where he had little experience or expertise.

2. *Structural leaders rethink the relationship of structure, strategy, and environment.* Sloan's new structure was intimately tied to a strategy for reaching the automotive market. He foresaw a growing market, improvements in automobiles, and more discriminating consumers. In the face of Henry Ford's stubborn attachment to the Model T, Sloan introduced the "price pyramid" (a different car for every pocketbook) and the annual model change. Automotive technology in the 1920s was evolving almost as fast as electronics in the 1990s, and the annual model change soon became the industry norm.

For a variety of reasons, GM in the 1960s began to move away from Sloan's concepts. Fearing a government effort to break up the corporation, GM reduced the independence of the car divisions and centralized design and engineering. Increasingly, divisions became marketing groups required to build and sell cars the corporation designed for them. In the early 1980s, "look-alike cars" became the standard across divisions. Many consumers became confused and angry when they found it hard to see the subtle differences between a Chevrolet and a Cadillac.

Smith's vision focused more on costs and technology than on marketing. As he saw it, GM's primary competitive problem was high costs driven by high wages. He gave little support to efforts already under way at GM to improve working conditions on the shop floor. He saw technology, not human resource management, as the wave of the future. Ironically, his two best investments— NUMMI and Saturn—succeeded precisely because of innovative approaches to managing people. "With only a fraction of the money invested in GM's heavily robotized plants, [the NUMMI plant at] Fremont is more efficient and produces better-quality cars than any plant in the GM system" (Hampton and Norman, 1987, p. 102).

3. *Structural leaders focus on implementation.* Structural leaders often miscalculate the difficulty of putting their design in place. They underestimate resistance, skimp on training, neglect the process of building a political base, and misread cultural cues. As a result, they are often thwarted by neglected human resource, political, and symbolic barriers. Sloan was no human resource specialist,

but he intuitively saw the need to get understanding and acceptance of major decisions. He did that by continually asking for advice and by establishing committees and task forces to address major issues.

4. *Effective structural leaders experiment, evaluate, and adapt.* Sloan tinkered constantly with GM's structure and strategy and encouraged others to do likewise. The Great Depression produced a drop of 72 percent in sales at GM between 1929 and 1932, but the company adapted very adroitly to hard times. It increased its market share and made money every year. Sloan briefly centralized operations to survive the Great Depression but decentralized again once business began to recover. In the 1980s, Smith spent billions on his campaign to modernize the corporation and cut costs, yet GM lost market share every year and continued to be the industry's highest-cost producer. "Much of the advanced technology that GM acquired at such high cost hindered rather than improved productivity. Runaway robots started welding doors shut at the new Detroit-Hamtramck Cadillac plant. Luckily for Ford and Chrysler, poverty prevented them from indulging in the same orgy of spending on robots" ("On a Clear Day. . . ," 1989, p. 77).

Catalysts or Wimps? Human Resource Leadership

The tiny trickle of writing about structural leadership is swamped by a torrent of human resource literature (among the best: Argyris, 1962; Bennis and Nanus, 1985; Blanchard and Johnson, 1982; Bradford and Cohen, 1984; Fiedler, 1967, 1974; Hersey, 1984; Hollander, 1978; House, 1971; Levinson, 1968; Likert, 1961, 1967; Vroom and Yetton, 1973; and Waterman, 1994). Human resource theorists typically advocate openness, mutuality, listening, coaching, participation, and empowerment. They view the leader as a facilitator and catalyst who motivates and empowers subordinates. The leader's power comes from talent, sensitivity, and service rather than position or force. Greenleaf (1973) argues that followers "will freely respond only to individuals who are chosen as leaders because they are proven and trusted as servants" (p. 4). He adds, "The servant-leader makes sure that other people's highest priority needs are being served. The best test [of leadership] is: do those served grow as persons; do they, *while being served,* become healthier, wiser, freer, more autonomous, more likely themselves to become servants?" (p. 7).

Will managers who adhere to such images be respected leaders who make a difference? Or will they be seen as naive and weak, carried along on the current of other people's energy? The Cindy Marshall case (Chapter Sixteen) illustrated both sides. In one human resource encounter, Marshall seemed more a flunky than a leader. In the other, she combined some of the virtues of both servant and catalyst. The leadership tightrope is real, and some managers hide behind participation and sensitivity as excuses not to walk it. There are also many human resource leaders whose skill and artistry produce extraordinary results. They apply leadership principles such as the following:

1. *Human resource leaders believe in people and communicate their belief.* Human resource leaders are passionate about "productivity through people" (Peters and Waterman, 1982). They demonstrate this faith in their words and actions and often build it into a core philosophy or credo. Fred Smith, founder and CEO of Federal Express, sees "putting people first" as the cornerstone of his company's success: "We discovered a long time ago that customer satisfaction really begins with employee satisfaction. That belief is incorporated in our corporate philosophy statement: People—Service—Profit" (Waterman, 1994, p. 89).

William Hewlett, cofounder of the electronics giant Hewlett-Packard Corporation, put it this way.

> The dignity and worth of the individual is a very important part of the HP Way. With this in mind, many years ago we did away with time clocks, and more recently we introduced the flexible work hours program. This is meant to be an expression of trust and confidence in people, as well as providing them with an opportunity to adjust their work schedules to their personal lives. Many new HP people as well as visitors often note and comment to us about another HP way—that is, our informality and our being on a first-name basis. I could cite other examples, but the problem is that none by [itself] really catches the essence of what the HP Way is all about. You can't describe it in numbers and statistics. In the last analysis, it is a spirit, a point of view. There is a feeling that everyone is part of a team, and that team is HP. It is an idea that is based on the individual [Peters and Waterman, 1982, p. 244].

2. *Human resource leaders are visible and accessible.* Peters and Waterman (1982) popularized the notion of "management by wandering around"—the idea that managers need to get out of their offices and spend time with workers and customers. Patricia Carrigan, the first woman ever to be a plant manager at General Motors, modeled this technique in the course of turning around two different GM plants, each with a long history of union-management conflict (Kouzes and Posner, 1987). In both situations, she began by going onto the plant floor to introduce herself to workers and ask how they thought the plant could be improved. One worker commented that before Carrigan came, "I didn't know who the plant manager was. I wouldn't have recognized him if I saw him." When she left her first assignment after three years, the local union gave her a plaque. It concluded, "Be it resolved that Pat M. Carrigan, through the exhibiting of these qualities as a people person, has played a vital role in the creation of a new way of life at the Lakewood plant. Therefore, be it resolved that the members of Local 34 will always warmly remember Pat M. Carrigan as one of us" (Kouzes and Posner, 1987, p. 36).

3. *Effective human resource leaders empower others.* Human resource leaders often like to refer to their employees as "partners," "owners," or "associates." They make it clear that employees have a stake in the organization's success and a right to be involved in making decisions. Nordstrom has its "rule number one": "Use your good judgment in all situations; there will be no other rules" (Collins and Porras, 1994, p. 117). In the 1980s, Jan Carlzon, CEO of Scandinavian Air Systems (SAS), built a turnaround effort around making the airline "the best airline in the world for business travelers" (Carlzon, 1987, p. 46). To find out what the business traveler wanted, he turned to SAS's front-line service employees to collect their ideas and suggestions. Focus groups generated hundreds of ideas and emphasized the importance of front-line autonomy to decide on the spot what passengers needed. Carlzon concluded that SAS's image to its customers was built out of a series of "moments of truth"—fifteen-second encounters between employees and customers. "If we are truly dedicated toward orienting our company to each customer's individual needs, we cannot rely on rule books and instruction from distant corporate offices. We have to place responsibility for ideas, decisions, and actions with the people who are SAS during those 15 seconds. If they

have to go up the organizational chain of command for a decision on an individual problem, then those 15 golden seconds will elapse without a response and we will have lost an opportunity to earn a loyal customer" (p. 66). The French packaging giant Carnaud enjoyed enormous growth and success after Jean-Marie Descarpentries became its chief executive in 1982. Descarpentries said his approach to management was simple: "You catalyze toward the future, you trust people, and they discover things you never would have thought of" (Aubrey and Tilliette, 1990, p. 142).

Advocates or Hustlers? Political Leadership

Lee Iacocca's career at Ford Motor Company was a meteoric rise through a series of sales and marketing triumphs to become the company's president. Then, on July 1, 1978, his boss, Henry Ford II, fired him, reportedly with the simple explanation, "Let's just say I don't like you" (O'Toole, 1984, p. 231). Iacocca's unemployment was brief. Chrysler Corporation, desperate for new leadership, believed that Iacocca was the answer.

Even though Iacocca had done his homework before accepting Chrysler's offer, he encountered problems worse than he anticipated. Chrysler was losing money so fast that bankruptcy seemed almost inevitable. The only way out was to persuade the U.S. government to guarantee massive loans. It was a tough sell—much of Congress, the media, and the American public were against the idea. Iacocca had to convince all of them that government intervention was in their interest as well as Chrysler's. He pulled it off with a remarkable combination of personal artistry and adroit political maneuvering. He successfully employed a set of rules for political leaders.

1. *Political leaders clarify what they want and what they can get.* Political leaders are realists above all. They avoid letting what they want cloud their judgment about what is possible. Chrysler's problem was survival. Iacocca translated that into the realistic goal of getting enough help to make it through a couple of difficult years without going under. Iacocca was careful to ask not for money but for loan guarantees. He insisted that government guarantees would cost the taxpayers nothing because Chrysler would pay the money back.

2. *Political leaders assess the distribution of power and interests.* They map the political terrain by thinking carefully about the players, their interests, and their power. They ask: Whose support do I need? How do I go about getting it? Who are my opponents? How much power do they have? What can I do to reduce or overcome their opposition? Is this battle winnable? Iacocca needed the support of Chrysler's employees and unions, but he knew that they had little choice. The key players were Congress and the public. Congress would vote for the guarantees only if Iacocca's proposal had sufficient popular support.

3. *Political leaders build linkages to key stakeholders.* They focus their attention on building relationships and networks. They recognize the value of personal contact and face-to-face conversations. Iacocca worked hard to build linkages with Congress, the media, and the public. He spent hours meeting with members of Congress and testifying before congressional committees. After he met with thirty-one Italian-American members of Congress, all but one voted for the loan guarantees. Said Iacocca, "Some were Republicans, some were Democrats, but in this case they voted the straight Italian ticket. We were desperate, and we had to play every angle. It was democracy in action" (Iacocca and Novak, 1984, p. 221).

Iacocca gave interviews to anyone in the media who would listen. He personally signed Chrysler's advertisements in newspapers and magazines and appeared on television to make Chrysler's case. Over time, he became one of America's best-known and most respected chief executives.

4. *Political leaders persuade first, negotiate second, and use coercion only if necessary.* Wise political leaders recognize that power is essential to their effectiveness; they also know to use it judiciously. William P. Kelly, an experienced public administrator, put it well: "Power is like the old Esso ad—a tiger in your tank. But you can't let the tiger out, you just let people hear him roar. You use power terribly sparingly because it has a short half-life. You let people know you have it and hope that you don't have to use it" (Ridout and Fenn, 1974, p. 10).

The sophisticated political leader knows that influence begins with an understanding of others' concerns and interests. What is important to them? How can I help them get what they want? Iacocca knew that he had to address the widespread belief that federal guarantees would throw millions of taxpayers' dollars down a rat hole. He used advertising to respond directly to public concerns. Does Chrysler have a future? Yes, he said, we've been here fifty-four years, and we'll be here another fifty-four years. Would the loan guarantees be a dangerous precedent? No, the government already had $400 billion in other loan guarantees on the books, and in any event, Chrysler was going to pay its loans back. "You can count on it!" he said over and over. Iacocca also spoke directly to congressional concerns. Chrysler prepared computer printouts showing how many jobs would be lost in every district if Chrysler were to go under.

Iacocca got his loan guarantees. Eight years later, in 1987, Chrysler reported earnings of more than $1 billion, ranking it eleventh among all U.S. corporations. The company survived and paid back the loans early.

Prophets or Zealots? Symbolic Leadership

The symbolic frame provides a fourth turn of the leadership kaleidoscope. This frame sees organizations as both theaters and temples. In the theater, every actor plays certain roles and tries to communicate the right impressions to the right audiences. As temple, organizations are communities of faith, bonded by shared beliefs, traditions, myths, rituals, and ceremonies.

Symbolically, leaders *interpret and reinterpret experience*. What are the real lessons of history? What is really happening in the world? What will the future bring? What mission is worthy of our loyalty and investment? Data and analysis provide few adequate answers to such questions. Symbolic leaders interpret experience so as to provide meaning and purpose through phrases of beauty and passion. Franklin D. Roosevelt reassured a nation in the midst of its deepest economic depression that "the only thing we have to fear is fear itself." At almost the same time, Adolph Hitler assured Germans that their severe economic and social problems were the result of betrayal by Jews and communists. Germans, he said, were a superior people who could still fulfill their nation's destiny of world mastery. Though many saw the destructive paranoia in Hitler's message, millions of fearful citizens were swept up in Hitler's bold vision of German ascendancy.

Burns (1978) was mindful of leaders such as Franklin Roosevelt, Mohandas Gandhi, and Martin Luther King Jr. when he drew a distinction between "transforming" and "transactional" leaders.

According to Burns, transactional leaders "approach their followers with an eye to trading one thing for another: jobs for votes, sub-
sidies for campaign contributions" (p. 4). Transforming leaders are
rarer. As Burns describes them, they evoke their constituents' better nature and move them toward higher and more universal needs
and purposes. They are visionary leaders, and visionary leadership
is inherently symbolic. Symbolic leaders follow a consistent set of
practices and rules.

1. *They use symbols to capture attention.* When Diana Lam became
principal of the Mackey Middle School in Boston in 1985, she faced
a substantial challenge. Mackey had the usual problems of urban
schools: decaying physical plant, poor discipline, racial tension, disgruntled teachers, and limited resources (Kaufer and Leader, 1987a).
In such a situation, symbolic leaders will do something visible and
dramatic to signal that change is coming. During the summer before
assuming her duties, Lam wrote a personal letter to every teacher
requesting an individual meeting. She met teachers wherever they
wanted, in one case driving two hours. She asked teachers how they
felt about the school and what changes they wanted. She recruited
members of her family as a crew to repaint the school's front door
and some of the most decrepit classrooms. "When school opened,
students and staff members immediately saw that things were going
to be different, if only symbolically. Perhaps even more important,
staff members received a subtle challenge to make a contribution
themselves" (Kaufer and Leader, 1987b, p. 3).

When Lee Iacocca first became president of Chrysler, one of
his first steps was to announce that he was reducing his salary from
$360,000 to $1 a year. "I did it for good, cold pragmatic reasons. I
wanted our employees and our suppliers to be thinking: 'I can follow a guy who sets that kind of example,'" Iacocca explained in his
autobiography (Iacocca and Novak, 1984, pp. 229–230).

2. *Symbolic leaders frame experience.* In a world of uncertainty and
ambiguity, a key function of symbolic leadership is to provide plausible interpretations of experience. Jan Carlzon mobilized front-line
staff at SAS around the idea that each short encounter with a customer was a "moment of truth" (Carlzon, 1987). When Martin Luther
King Jr. spoke at the March on Washington in 1963 and gave his extraordinary "I Have a Dream" speech, his opening line was, "I am
happy to join with you today in what will go down in history as the

greatest demonstration for freedom in the history of our nation."
He could have interpreted the event in a number of other ways: "We
are here because progress has been slow, but we are not ready to
quit yet"; "We are here because nothing else has worked"; "We are
here because it's summer and it's a good day to be outside." Each
of those versions is about as accurate as the next, but accuracy is not
the real issue. King's assertion was bold and inspiring; it told members of the audience that they were making history by their presence at a momentous event.

3. *Symbolic leaders discover and communicate a vision.* One of the
most powerful ways in which leaders can interpret experience is by
distilling and disseminating a vision—a persuasive and hopeful
image of the future. A vision needs to address both the challenges
of the present and the hopes and values of followers. Vision is particularly important in times of crisis and uncertainty. When people
are in pain, when they are confused and uncertain, or when they feel
despair and hopelessness, they desperately seek meaning and hope.

Where does such vision come from? One view is that leaders
create a vision and then persuade others to accept it (Bass, 1985;
Bennis and Nanus, 1985). An alternative view is that leaders discover and articulate a vision that is already there, even if in an
inchoate and unexpressed form (Cleveland, 1985). Kouzes and
Posner (1987) put it well: "Corporate leaders know very well that
what seeds the vision are those imperfectly formed images in the
marketing department about what the customers really wanted and
those inarticulate mumblings from the manufacturing folks about
the poor product quality, not crystal ball gazing in upper levels of
the corporate stratosphere. The best leaders are the best followers.
They pay attention to those weak signals and quickly respond to
changes in the corporate course" (p. 114).

Early in his career, Jan Carlzon had learned this lesson the hard
way when he and a group of young executives designed a set of tour
packages offering Swedish senior citizens just what Carlzon thought
they wanted—safe, risk-free travel to familiar places. The product
bombed because the seniors really wanted variety and adventure.
For Carlzon it was a memorable lesson: listen to your customers and
to the front-line staff who know them (Carlzon, 1987).

Leadership is a two-way street. No amount of charisma or rhe-
torical skill can sell a vision that reflects only the leader's values
and needs—Carlzon's team had spent a fortune on beautiful color

brochures to promote the doomed tour packages. Effective symbolic leadership is possible only for leaders who understand the deepest values and most pressing concerns of their constituents. But leaders still play a critical role. They can bring a unique, personal blend of poetry, passion, conviction, and courage to the articulation of a vision. They can play a key role in distilling and shaping the vision to be pursued. Most important, they can choose which stories to tell as a means of communicating the vision.

4. *Symbolic leaders tell stories.* Often symbolic leaders embody their vision in a story—a story about "us" and about "our" past, present, and future. "Us" could be the Sorbonne, the Chrysler Corporation, the people of Thailand, or any other audience a leader hopes to reach. The past is usually a golden one, a time of noble purposes, of great deeds, of heroes and heroines. The present is a time of trouble, challenge, or crisis: a critical moment when we have to make fateful choices. The future is the dream: a vision of hope and greatness, often linked directly to greatness in the past.

That is just the kind of story that helped Ronald Reagan, a master storyteller, become president of the United States. Reagan's golden past was the frontier, a place of rugged, sturdy, self-reliant men and women who built a great nation and took care of themselves and their neighbors without the intervention of a monstrous national government. It was an America of small towns and volunteer fire departments. America had fallen into crisis, said Reagan, because "the liberals" had created a federal government that was levying oppressive taxes and eroding freedom through regulation and bureaucracy. Reagan offered a vision: a return to American greatness by "getting government off the backs of the American people" and restoring traditional American values of freedom and self-reliance.

The success of such stories is only partly related to their historical validity or empirical support. The central question is whether they are credible and persuasive to their audiences. A story, even a flawed story, will work if it taps persuasively into the experience, values, and aspirations of listeners. Good stories are truer than true: this reflects both the power and the danger of symbolic leadership. In the hands of a Gandhi or a King, the constructive power of stories is immense. Told by a Hitler, their destructive power is almost incalculable. In the wake of World War I and the Great Depression, Germany in the 1930s was hungry for hope. Other stories might have caught the imagination of the German people, but Hitler's passion and single-mindedness brought his story to center stage and carried Europe to a catastrophe of war and holocaust.

Summary

Though leadership is widely accepted as a cure for organizational ills, it is also widely misunderstood. Many views of leadership fail to recognize its relational and contextual nature and its distinction from power and position. Inadequate ideas about leadership often produce oversimplified advice to managers. We need to reframe leadership to move beyond the impasses created by oversimplified models.

Each of the frames highlights significant possibilities for leadership, but each is incomplete in capturing a holistic picture. Early in the twentieth century, implicit models of managerial leadership were narrowly rational. In the 1960s and 1970s, human resource leadership became fashionable. In recent years, symbolic leadership has moved to center stage, and the literature abounds with advice on how to become a visionary leader capable of transforming cultural patterns. Organizations need vision, but it is not their only need and not always their most important one. Ideally, managers combine multiple frames into a comprehensive approach to leadership. Still, it is unrealistic to expect everyone to be a leader for all times and seasons. Wise leaders understand their own strengths, work to expand them, and build teams that can provide leadership in all four modes—structural, political, human resource, and symbolic.

Chapter Eighteen

Reframing Change

Training, Realigning, Negotiating, Grieving

DDB Bank is one of the largest banks in Southeast Asia, with over sixty branches, more than thirteen thousand employees, and a network of correspondent banks throughout the world. The bank has been uniformly profitable since its founding more than fifty years ago. Its loan portfolio is sound. Shareholders, capital markets, and government regulators universally give the bank high marks.

When Thomas Lo became general manager of DDB's main branch, he was one of few who was not satisfied with the bank's performance. In fourteen years with Citibank in various parts of the world, he had learned to think strategically and to feel at home in a dynamic, fast-moving organization. For years—generations even—DDB's strategy had been very conservative. Its branches created a large deposit base. Particularly in rural areas, depositors stayed with DDB so long as they felt their money was safe and readily accessible. A low-cost deposit base enabled DDB to make loans at reasonable but profitable rates of interest—key to the bank's solidity. It had stable, long-term relationships with both borrowers and depositors. To make decisions, managers could usually rely on clearly spelled out policies and procedures.

Staff and personnel policies also reflected DDB's reliance on stability and systems. Jobs and grades were sharply defined, with a clear career path from entry-level positions up to branch manager. Two main requirements governed upward movement: completing the minimum time in grade and following established rules and procedures to the letter. Meeting these criteria assured a stable and predictable career.

The decision to hire Lo was controversial. The management team was split. A faction led by executive vice president William Tun, head of all domestic branches, embraced the principle "if it's not broken, don't try to fix it." This group favored leaving well enough alone. An opposing group argued that the bank had to anticipate potential changes on the horizon. This group was led by Philip Neo, executive vice president in charge of corporate banking.

The second group emphasized that the industry was becoming much more competitive as government regulation relaxed. This faction felt that the bank's traditional deposit base could no longer be taken for granted. To stay competitive, these managers said, DDB had to focus on superior customer service and innovative strategies to defend and extend the deposit base. Lo was recruited to make the main branch a role model for other DDB branches.

Lo "hit the ground running." Within three months, a five-year plan was produced, and implementation got under way. Branch managers received targets for loans, deposits, and profitability. The last got highest priority. Information systems were revamped so that targets could be monitored continuously. The main branch was reorganized. New positions, for a marketing manager and a planning manager, were added. Though Lo advertised internally so as to appear to follow existing policies, his real intention was to hire outsiders to inject new blood into the main branch.

Lo also pressed for other changes. He argued for a new performance appraisal system to identify strong performers and move them rapidly upward. He wanted more flexible salary scales: less emphasis on time in grade and more room for merit increases. He encouraged the human resources department to develop new career paths for moving people between branches and for lateral transfers between branches and the head office. Though most of the staff had degrees in accounting or economics, Lo wanted a new breed of dynamic individuals— even if their studies were unrelated to banking.

Six months later, Lo concluded that his innovations were having almost no effect on day-to-day activities. The problem was not open resistance but covert foot-dragging. Some managers claimed that they were working to implement the changes but offered many explanations of why they were behind schedule. Others nodded their head in public agreement but privately carried on doing things the old ways. Lo began seriously considering leaving DDB to join a smaller, more dynamic investment banking firm.

Lo's story is all too familiar: hopeful beginnings, a turbulent middle, and a discouraging ending. Alert readers might note that

Lo's story has much in common with the Helen Demarco case in Chapter Two. Lo's subordinates may have felt much like Demarco: they were not resisting change but protecting the organization from bad ideas. Similarly, Paul Osborne and Thomas Lo had much in common: both brought in new, fresh ideas to revitalize stodgy organizations in general, and both felt frustrated at the difficulty of moving change through their own. Such stories illustrate an ironclad law: changes rationally conceived traditionally fail. Like Lo, change agents misread or overlook unanticipated consequences of their actions. They march blindly down their chosen paths despite signs that they are headed in the wrong direction. Over scores of change efforts, we continually see managers whose strategies are limited because they are wedded to one or two frames. Some try to produce major change by redesigning formal structures, only to find people unable or unwilling to carry out new responsibilities. Others import new people or retrain old ones, only to find new blood and new ideas rejected or assimilated, often disappearing without a trace.

Machiavelli observed many years ago in *The Prince* ([1514] 1961, p. 27): "It must be realized that there is nothing more difficult to plan, more uncertain of success, or more dangerous to manage than the establishment of a new order of [things]; for he who introduces [change] makes enemies of all those who derived advantage from the old order and finds but lukewarm defenders among those who stand to gain from the new one."

Restructuring, recruiting, and retraining can be powerful levers for change. But they must be done in concert. Retraining people without revising roles or revamping roles without retraining people never works. Managers who anticipate that new roles require new skills and vice versa have much greater likelihood of success. But change also alters power relationships and undermines existing agreements and pacts. Even more profoundly, it intrudes on deeply rooted symbolic agreements and ritual behavior. Below the surface, the organization's social tapestry begins to unravel, threatening both time-honored traditions and prevailing cultural values and practices.

Each frame suggests a different view of major issues in change, as summarized in Table 18.1. The human resource frame focuses on needs and skills, the structural frame on alignment and clarity, the political frame on conflict and arenas, and the symbolic frame

Table 18.1. Reframing Organizational Change.

Frame	Barriers to Change	Essential Strategies
Human resource	Anxiety, uncertainty, feelings of incompetence, neediness	Training to develop new skills, participation and involvement, psychological support
Structural	Loss of clarity and stability, confusion, chaos	Communicating, realigning and renegotiating formal patterns and policies
Political	Disempowerment, conflict between winners and losers	Creating arenas where issues can be renegotiated and new coalitions formed
Symbolic	Loss of meaning and purpose, clinging to the past	Creating transition rituals: mourning the past, celebrating the future

on loss and transition. Each frame highlights a different set of barriers and strategies change processes must overcome.

Change and Training

It sounds simplistic to point out that investments in change call for collateral investments in training. Yet countless reform initiatives falter and fail because managers neglect to spend time and money on developing necessary knowledge and skills. In too many organizations, human resources departments are afterthoughts no one really takes seriously.

Examples of the fallacies are legion. In one large firm, for example, top management decided to purchase state-of-the-art technology. The board members were confident that the investment would yield a 50 percent reduction in cycle time from receipt of a customer order to product delivery. Faster turnaround would confer a decisive competitive advantage. The strategy was crafted during hours of careful analysis. The new technology was launched with great fanfare. The CEO assured a delighted sales force that it would now have a high-tech competitive edge. After the initial euphoria faded, the sales force realized that its old methods were obsolete—years of experience were useless. Veterans suddenly became virtual neophytes. When the CEO heard that the sales force was shaky about the new technology, he said, "Then get someone in human resources to throw something together. You know, what's-her-name, the new human resources vice president. That's why we hired her." A year later, the new technology had failed to deliver. The training never materialized. The company's investment ultimately yielded a costly, inefficient technology and a demoralized sales force. The window of opportunity was lost to the competition.

The tax division of a major accounting firm, Arthur Andersen & Company, launched a major change initiative at least as ambitious as the one just described. The division had accumulated years of success by adhering to the profession's traditional, conservative mind-set. Clients called with questions. A typical answer was either "Yes, you can do that" or "No, you can't." The new initiative called for a different approach: probing to learn what was behind a client's question. This more proactive approach was designed to define the real problem and, wherever it might help, to link clients with other Andersen services. It was potentially a win-win situation: savings for the client and more billings for Andersen.

Andersen is distinctive in placing a premium on training and education. Its corporate school offers a variety of state-of-the-art courses. Seeing training as a key to the new initiative's success, management appointed a firmwide task force. This group spent two months developing a prototype course with intensive follow-up and coaching from partners who had mastered the new approach. They brought in outside experts to critique their design. They piloted the course with partners from offices worldwide, carefully including both supporters and opponents of the initiative. The instructors were widely respected tax partners.

The course provided ample opportunities for people to examine and debate one another's assumptions, as well as to learn new skills. It was immensely successful. Andersen invested thousands of dollars in developing the prototype and pilot programs, hundreds of thousands more in training partners and associates worldwide. The firm invested heavily in training to ensure that people understood the new approach, supported it, and had the skills to use it.

From a human resource perspective, people have good reason to resist change. No one likes feeling anxious and incompetent. Changes in routine practices and procedures undercut people's ability to perform with confidence and success. When told to do something they don't understand or don't believe in, people feel puzzled, anxious, and insecure. Lacking the skills and confidence to implement the new ways, they resist or even sabotage, awaiting the return of the good old days. Or, like Thomas Lo's subordinates, they may comply in public while covertly dragging their feet. Even if they try to do what they are told, the results are predictably dismal.

Sometimes resistance is sensible—it produces better results than blind obedience. A European bank installed new computer terminals at each teller window, along with a requirement that tellers enter every deposit item into the computer before issuing a receipt. That often meant long waits—annoying for the customers and stressful for the tellers. The tellers quickly learned to bypass the new procedures so they could speed clients on their way. Customers were much happier, and even management eventually realized that the tellers had a point (Pichault, 1993).

Training, psychological support, and participation all increase the likelihood that people will understand and feel comfortable with the new methods.

Change and Realignment

Individual skills and confidence cannot guarantee success unless structure is also realigned to the new initiative. For example, a school system created a policy requiring principals to assume a more active role in supervising classroom instruction. Principals were trained in how to observe and counsel teachers. Morale problems and complaints soon began to surface. No one had asked how changes in principals' duties might affect teachers. Nor had anyone thought to ask if it was legitimate, in teachers' eyes, for principals to spend time in classrooms observing them and making suggestions about ways to improve teaching. Most important, no one asked who would handle routine administrative duties for which principals no longer had time. As a result, supplies were often late, parents came to feel neglected, and discipline deteriorated. By midyear, most principals were back to concentrating on their administrative duties and leaving teachers alone.

Structure provides clarity, predictability, and security. Formal roles prescribe duties and outline how work is to be performed. Policies and standard operating procedures synchronize diverse efforts into well-coordinated programs. Formal distribution of authority lets everyone know who is in charge, when, and over what. Change undermines existing arrangements, creating ambiguity, confusion, and distrust. People no longer know what is expected or what to expect from others. Everyone may think someone else is in charge when in fact no one is.

In the wake of changes in health care, a hospital was experiencing substantial employee turnover and absenteeism, a shortage of nurses, poor communication, and low staff morale. There were rumors of an impending effort to organize a union. A consultant's report identified several structural problems:

> One set related to top management. Members of the executive committee seemed to be confused about their roles and decision-making authority. Many believed all important decisions were made (prior to the meetings) by Frank Rettew, the hospital administrator. Many shared the perception that major decisions were made behind closed doors, and that Rettew often made "side deals" with different individuals, promising them special favors or rewards in return for support at the committee meetings. People at this level felt manipulated, confused, and dissatisfied.
>
> Major problems also existed in the nursing service. The director of nursing seemed to be patterning her managerial style after that of Rettew. . . . Nursing supervisors and head nurses felt that they had little authority, while staff nurses complained about a lack of direction and openness by the nursing administration. The structure of the organization was unclear. Nurses were unaware of what their jobs were, whom they should report to, and how decisions were made [McLennan, 1989, p. 231].

As the school and hospital examples both illustrate, when things start to shift, people become unsure about their duties, how to relate to others, and who has authority to decide what. Clarity, predictability, and rationality give way to confusion, loss of control, and a sense that cutthroat politics rather than clearcut policies now rule. To minimize such difficulties, change efforts must anticipate structural issues and work to realign roles and relationships. In some situations, this can be done informally. In others, structural arrangements need to be renegotiated in a more formal way (through some version of responsibility charting, discussed in Chapter Five).

Change and Conflict

Changing inevitably creates conflict. It spawns a hotly contested tug-of-war to determine winners and losers. Some individuals and groups support the changes; others are dead set against them. Too often, conflicts submerge and smolder beneath the surface. Occasionally, they burst into the open as outbreaks of unregulated warfare.

A case in point comes from a U.S. government initiative to improve rural schools mentioned in Chapter Eleven. The Experimental Schools Project provided funds for making comprehensive changes. It also carefully documented experiences of all ten participating districts over a five-year period. The first year—the planning period—was free of conflict. But as plans were put into action, hidden issues boiled to the surface. A school district in the Northwest illustrates a more general pattern:

> In the high school, a teacher evaluator explained the evaluation process while emphasizing the elaborate precautions to insure the raters would be unable to connect specific evaluations with specific teachers. He also passed out copies of the check-list used to evaluate the [evaluation forms]. Because of the tension the subject aroused, he joked that teachers could use the list to "grade" their own [forms]. He got a few laughs; he got more laughs when he encouraged teachers to read the evaluation plan by suggesting, "If you have fifteen minutes to spare and are really bored, you should read this section." When another teacher pointed out that her anonymity could not be maintained because she was the only teacher in her subject, the whole room broke into laughter, followed by nervous and derisive questions and more laughter.
>
> When the superintendent got up to speak, shortly afterwards, he was furious. He cautioned teachers for making light of the teacher evaluators who, he said, were trying to protect the staff. Several times he repeated that because teachers did not support the [project] they did not care for students. "Your attitude," he

concluded, "is damn the children and full speed ahead!" He then rushed out of the room.

The superintendent's speech put the high school in turmoil. The woman who questioned the confidentiality of the procedure was in tears. Most teachers were incensed at the superintendent's outburst, and a couple said they came close to quitting. As word of the event spread through the system, it caused reverberations in other buildings as well [Firestone, 1977, pp. 174–175].

After a heated exchange, conflict between the administration and teachers intensified. The school board got involved and reduced the superintendent's authority. Rumors that he might be fired undermined his formal clout even more.

Such a scenario is predictable. As changes emerge, camps form: supporters, opponents, and fence-sitters. Conflicts are avoided or smoothed over until they eventually erupt in divisive battles. Coercive force often determines who will win. Often the status quo prevails and change agents lose. From a political perspective, conflict is a natural part of life. It is managed through processes of negotiation and bargaining where settlements and agreements can be hammered out. If ignored, disputes explode into street fights like the one in the school district in the Northwest. Street fights have no rules. Anything goes. People get hurt, and scars last for years.

The alternative to street fights is *arenas*. Arenas provide rules, referees, and spectators. They create opportunities to forge divisive issues into shared agreements. Through bargaining, compromises can be worked out between the status quo and innovative ideals. Welding new ideas onto existing practices is essential to successful change. One hospital administrator said, "The board and I had to learn how to wrestle in a public forum."

Mitroff (1983) describes a drug company facing competitive pressure from generic substitutes for its branded prescription drug. Management was split into three factions: one group wanted to raise the drug's price, another wanted to lower it, and still another wanted to keep it the same but cut costs. Each group collected information, constructed models, and developed reports showing that its solution was correct. The process degenerated into a frustrating spiral. Mitroff intervened to get each group to identify major stakeholders and to articulate each group's assumptions about those stakeholders and their interests. Everyone agreed that the most critical stakeholders were physicians who prescribed the drug. Each group had different suppositions about how physicians would respond to a price change, but no one really knew. The three groups finally agreed to test their assumptions by implementing a price increase in selected markets.

The intervention worked by convening an arena with a more productive set of rules. Similarly, experimental school districts that created arenas for resolving conflict were more successful in bringing about comprehensive change. In the school district in the Northwest, the teachers reacted to administrative coercion with a power strategy of their own.

> Community members initiated a group called Concerned Citizens for Education in response to a phone call from one teacher who noted that parents should be worried about what the [administrators] were doing to their children. The superintendent became increasingly occupied with responding to demands and concerns of the community group. Over time, the group joined in a coalition with teachers to defeat several of the superintendent's supporters on the school board and to elect members who were more supportive of their interests. The turnover in board membership reduced the administrator's power and authority, making it necessary to rely more and more on bargaining and negotiation strategies to promote the intended change [Deal and Nutt, 1980, p. 20].

Change always generates division and conflict among competing interest groups. Successful change requires an ability to frame issues, build coalitions, and establish arenas in which disagreements can be forged into workable pacts. One insightful executive remarked: "We need to confront, not duck, and face up to disagreements and differences of opinions and conflicting objectives. . . . All of us must make sure—day in and day out—that conflicts are aired and resolved before they lead to internecine war."

Change and Loss

In the early 1980s, America's "cola wars"—a battle between Coke and Pepsi—reached fever pitch. The Pepsi Challenge, a head-to-head taste test, was chipping away at Coca-Cola's market share. In blind tests conducted by Pepsi, even avowed Coke drinkers preferred Pepsi. In a Coke counterchallenge, held at its corporate headquarters in Atlanta, Pepsi again won by a slight margin. Later,

Pepsi stunned the industry by signing singer Michael Jackson to a $5 million celebrity advertising campaign. Coca-Cola executives were getting nervous. They decided on a revolutionary strategy. Coca-Cola struck back with one of the most important announcements in the company's ninety-nine-year history. Old Coke was to be replaced by New Coke.

> Shortly before 11:00 A.M. [on Tuesday, April 23, 1985], the doors of the Vivian Beaumont Theater at Lincoln Center opened to two hundred newspaper, magazine, and TV reporters. The stage was aglow with red. Three huge screens, each solid red and inscribed with the company logo, rose behind the podium and a table draped in red. The lights were low: the music began. "We are. We will always be. Coca-Cola. All-American history." As the patriotic song filled the theater, slides of Americana flashed on the center screen—families and kids, Eisenhower and JFK, the Grand Canyon and wheat fields, the Beatles and Bruce Springsteen, cowboys, athletes, the Statue of Liberty—and interspersed throughout, old commercials for Coke. Robert Goizueta [CEO of Coca-Cola] came to the podium. He first congratulated the reporters for their ingenuity in already having reported what he was about to say. And then he boasted, "The best has been made even better." Sidestepping the years of laboratory research that had gone into the program, Goizueta claimed that in the process of concocting Diet Coke, the company flavor chemists had "discovered" a new formula. And research had shown that consumers preferred this new one to old Coke. Management could then do one of two things: nothing, or buy the world a new Coke. Goizueta announced that the taste-test results made management's decisions "one of the easiest ever made" [Oliver, 1986, p. 132].

The rest is history. Coke drinkers rejected the new product. They felt betrayed, and many were outraged: "Duane Larson took down his collection of Coke bottles and outside of his restaurant hung a sign, 'They don't make Coke anymore.' . . . Dennis Overstreet of Beverly Hills hoarded 500 cases of old Coke and advertised them for $30 a case. He is almost sold out. . . . *San Francisco Examiner* columnist Bill Mandel called it 'Coke for wimps.' . . . Finally, Guy Mullins exclaimed, 'When they took old Coke off the market, they violated my freedom of choice—baseball, hamburgers, Coke—they're all the fabric of America'" (Morganthau, 1985, pp. 32–33).

Even bottlers and Coca-Cola employees were aghast: "By June the anger and resentment of the public was disrupting the personal lives of Coke employees, from the top executives to the company secretaries. Friends and acquaintances were quick to attack, and once proud employees now shrank from displaying to the world any association with the Coca-Cola company" (Oliver, 1986, pp. 166–167).

Coca-Cola rebounded quickly with Classic Coke. Indeed, the company's massive miscalculation led to one of the strangest and most serendipitous triumphs in marketing history. All the controversy, passion, and free publicity stirred up by the New Coke fiasco ultimately helped Coca-Cola reassert its dominance in the soft drink industry—a brilliant stratagem, if anyone had planned it.

What led Coke's executives into such a quagmire? Several factors were at work. Pepsi was gaining market share. As the newly appointed CEO of Coca-Cola, Goizueta was determined to modernize the company. A previous innovation, Diet Coke, had been a huge success. Most important, Coca-Cola's founder, Robert Woodruff, had just passed away. On his deathbed, he reportedly gave Goizueta his blessing for the new recipe.

In their zeal to compete with Pepsi, Coke's executives overlooked a central tenet of the symbolic frame. The meaning of an object or event can be far more powerful than the reality. Strangely, Coke's leaders had lost touch with their product's significance to consumers. To many people, old Coke was a piece of Americana. It was linked to cherished memories. Coke represented something far deeper than just a soft drink.

The executives of Coca-Cola underestimated the symbolic meaning of their core product. Symbols create meaning. When a symbol is destroyed or vanishes, people experience emotions almost identical to those felt at the passing of a spouse, child, old friend, or pet. The introduction of New Coke unintendedly announced the passing of an important American symbol. When a relative or close friend dies, we feel a deep sense of loss. We unconsciously harbor similar feelings when a computer replaces old procedures, a logo changes after a merger, or our old leader is replaced by a new one. When these transitions take place in the workplace rather than in a family, feelings of loss are often denied or attributed to other causes.

Any significant change in an organization triggers two conflicting responses. The first is to keep things as they were, to replay the past. The second is to ignore the loss and rush busily into the future. Individuals or groups can get stuck in either form of denial or bog down vacillating between the two. Nurses in one hospital's intensive care unit were caught in a loss cycle for ten years following their move from an old facility. An AT&T executive, four years after divestiture, remarked: "Some mornings I feel like I can set the world on fire. Other mornings I can hardly get out of bed to face another day." Loss is an unavoidable by-product of change. As change accelerates, executives and employees get caught in endless cycles of unresolved grief.

In our personal lives, the pathway from loss to healing is prescribed. Every culture outlines a sequence for transition rituals following significant loss: always a collective experience in which pain is expressed, felt, and juxtaposed against humor and hope. (Think of Irish actor Malachy McCourt, who, as his mother lay dying, said to the distressed physician, "Don't worry, Doctor, we come from a long line of dead people.") In many societies, the sequence of ritual steps involves a wake, a funeral, a period of mourning, and some form of commemoration.

From a symbolic perspective, ritual is the essential companion to significant change. A military change-of-command ceremony is formally scripted. A wake is held for the outgoing commander, and the torch is passed publicly to the new commander in full ceremony. After a period of time, the old commander's likeness or name is displayed in a picture or on a plaque. Transition rituals initiate a sequence of steps to help people let go of the past, deal with the pain of the present, and move into a meaningful future. The form of these rites varies widely, but without them people are blocked from facing loss. They then vacillate between hanging on to the past and plunging into a meaningless future. Disruption of attachment even to negative symbols or harmful symbolic activities needs to be marked by some form of expressive event.

Owen (1987) vividly documents these issues in his description of change at "Delta Corporation." An entrepreneur named Harry invented a product that created enough demand to support a company of 3,500 people. Although the initial public stock offering was successful, the company soon experienced soaring costs, flattened sales, and a dearth of new products. Facing stockholder dissatisfaction and charges of mismanagement, Harry passed the torch to a new leader.

Harry's replacement was very clear about her vision: she wanted "engineers who could fly." But her vision was juxtaposed against a history of "going downhill." And various parts of the company were governed by a complicated array of stories, each representing a different theme in Delta Corporation. The stories in the finance division exemplified the new breed of executives brought in after Harry's departure. The stories in research and development varied by organizational level. At the executive level, "Old Harry" stories extolled the creative accomplishments of the former CEO. Middle-management stories focused on the Golden Fleece award given behind the scenes each month to the researcher who developed the idea with the least bottom-line potential. On the benches, they told of Serendipity Sam, winner of more Golden Fleece awards than anyone else and exemplar of the excitement and innovation of Harry's regime.

Instead of having a common story, Delta had a collection of independent cells, each with its own story. Across the levels and divisions the stories clustered into two competing themes: the newcomers' focus on management versus the company's tradition of innovation. The new CEO recognized the importance of blending old and new to build a company where "engineers could fly." She brought thirty-five people from across the company to a management retreat where she surprised everyone:

> She opened with some stories of the early days, describing the intensity of Old Harry and the Garage Gang (now known as the Leper Colony). She even had one of the early models of Harry's machine out on a table. Most people had never seen one. It looked rather primitive, but during the coffee break, members of the Leper Colony surrounded the ancient artifact, and began swapping tales of the blind alleys, the late nights, and the breakthroughs. That dusty old machine became a magnet. Young shop floor folks went up and touched it, sort of snickering as they compared this prototype with the sleek creations they were manufacturing now. But even as they snickered, they stopped to listen as the Leper Colony recounted tales of accomplishment. It may have been just a "prototype," but that's where it all began [Owen, 1987, p. 172].

After the coffee break, the CEO divided the group into subgroups to share their hopes for the company. When the participants returned, their chairs had been rearranged into a circle with Old Harry's prototype in the center. With everyone facing one another, the CEO led a discussion, linking the stories from the various subgroups. Serendipity Sam's account of a new product possibility came out in a torrent of technical jargon.

> The noise level was fierce, but the rest of the group was being left out. Taking Sam by the hand, the CEO led him to the center of the circle right next to the old prototype. There it was, the old and the new—the past, present, and potential. She whispered in Sam's ear that he ought to take a deep breath and start over in words of one syllable. He did so, and in ways less than elegant, the concept emerged. He guessed about applications, competitors, market shares, and before long the old VP for finance was drawn in. No longer was he thinking about selling [tax] losses, but rather thinking out loud about how he was going to develop the capital to support the new project. The group from the shop floor . . . began to spin a likely tale as to how they might transform the assembly lines in order to make Sam's new machine. Even the Golden Fleece crowd became excited, telling each other how they had always known that Serendipity Sam could pull it off. They conveniently forgot that Sam had been the recipient of a record number of their awards, to say nothing of the fact that this new idea had emerged in spite of all their rules [Owen, 1987, pp. 173–174].

In one intense event, part of the past was buried, yet its spirit was resurrected and revised to fit the new circumstances. Disparaging themes and stories were merged into a company where "engineers could fly" in a profitable way.

Team Zebra: The Rest of the Story

In Chapter Four we examined the successful restructuring of Kodak's black-and-white film division (B&W), an effort that came to be called Team Zebra. The story line there attributed much of the division's success to structural improvements: integrated flows, performance measures and standards, cross-functional teams, lateral coordination, local decision making. These changes contributed substantially to the division's ability to reduce inventory, cut waste, improve relations with suppliers, and speed delivery time. All the improvements paved the way for the division's transformation and return to profitability.

There is more to the Team Zebra story. Structural changes were necessary but not sufficient. Reengineering guru Michael Hammer, noting the disappointing outcomes of many restructuring efforts, acknowledged that there is more to change than redesigning process and structure. Team Zebra exemplifies an integrated multiframe approach to change.

Top-Down, Bottom-Up Structural Design

The division's first structural overhaul in a century was announced at a meeting for all employees. The shock was lessened by assurances that the initial changes were experimental and that more substantive changes would appear gradually over a six-month period. This gave employees an opportunity to shape the initiative to fit local working conditions. Reasons for the changes were clearly explained and reinforced by management, who themselves had learned in very graphic terms of the division's poor performance record some time earlier:

> During a special meeting convened one warm day in September, I rattled off my list of performance shockers to the Zebra managers. The reaction was one of disbelief and anger. "How could we have been kept in the dark so long?" people demanded to know. During my talk I boiled the issue down to the bitter problems that deeply eroded profit margins and made us dinosaurs in the marketplace.
>
> "You know about all the waste problems," I said. "But did you know we can't sell one-third of everything we make? We load up 1,000 dump trucks with wasted products every year."
>
> A whistle of disbelief broke the ensuing silence.
>
> "Imagine a consumer product company or automobile manufacturer tossing out one-third of its product—they'd be out of business in no time flat! Can you think of *any* organization that can survive that level of waste?" "Yeah, the federal government," someone called out from the back of the room.
>
> That started a spate of laughter, and took the edge off the meeting. I wanted people to feel concerned, but not personally threatened [Frangos, 1993, pp. 65–66].

The managers learned that half their finished product sat in inventory, only 10 percent of their products were improved each year, the percentage of work performed during the manufacturing process was about 1 percent, and they were able to deliver products on time in only 66 percent of the cases. At the end of the meeting, someone asked angrily, "How have we managed to stay afloat so long?" (Frangos, 1993, p. 67).

The shared sense of crisis, combined with an opportunity for everyone to fine-tune and tinker with the radical new design, helped realign roles and relationships so that the new structure worked for, rather than against, people's efforts. Responsibility for shaping and implementing change was widely shared (Frangos, 1993, pp. 120–121):

- Mary Cutcliffe, an emulsion-making operator, went to have her foot X-rayed and discovered that her physician was not using Kodak film. She asked him why. He said he didn't think a company the size of Kodak would care about a small-town physician like himself. Upon returning to work, she asked, "Why not?" Her question led to a plan to focus aggressively on doctors with in-house labs.
- Zack Potter, on a family vacation, overheard a photographer complain about Kodak's poor service. When he returned, he spent his morning break and lunch hour trying to find out who was responsible. That afternoon, the photographer received a call with the needed information.

Learning and Training

B&W provided several kinds of training opportunities. Technical training helped people master new skills needed for changes in work patterns. Supervisors, the often overlooked linchpins in transition from old to new, found ample opportunities to meet with colleagues for training and "peer learning":

> In our case we had a hundred year heritage of the drill sergeant model, and many of our first-line supervisors were 20–25 year veterans of the company. We took into account that asking people to

change the way they do their jobs is a threatening proposition, and asking them to relinquish the authority they have "earned" can seem downright outrageous—unless you can offer them something better. In our case, the "something better" was a set of unprece-dented opportunities; the opportunity to have a greater influence over people through enlightened coaching and teaching [Frangos, 1993, p. 200].

Supervisors and other employees were given opportunities to learn new skills in a supportive, psychologically safe environment. "Peer learning is critical, because everyone makes faster gains when they learn from one another. There's also a critical mass phenom-enon—when enough first-line supervisors are reporting about their acts of coaching and facilitating, others will feel safe trying the 'new style'" (Frangos, 1993, p. 200).

First-time supervisors and others were included with the man-agement team in experimental learning and team-building training conducted by Pecos River (a training organization). "The Pecos course turned out to be an ingenious blend of talk, music, [and] high energy exercises, offered in an upbeat and emotionally charged atmosphere. Through experiential learning, the Pecos program helps people to uncover buried layers of creativity, and to relate in new ways to others with whom they might have worked side by side for many years but never have really come to know" (Frangos, 1993, p. 169).

Apart from formal training, the idea that people can learn new skills from their own experience on the job and from others looms as one of Team Zebra's greatest human resource insights. Informal learning groups became "unofficial" resources anyone could turn to for suggestions on how to improve performance. As people mas-tered a particular aspect of the new order of things, a premium was put on sharing or even stealing new ideas from others: "Our catch phrase for this sharing of knowledge was to 'steal shamelessly but to remember to say thank you.' Through B&W Views [a division news-letter] and informal seminars put on by [employees], the flow man-agement made a concerted effort to broadcast our success stories. At the same time, people were encouraged to seek aggressively innovative solutions in one part of the flow and then employ them in their own" (Frangos, 1993, p. 182).

Arenas for Venting Conflict

From the early launching of the project, a variety of occasions provided arenas and forums for airing people's concerns and grievances. The initiatives changed people's roles, relationships, titles, location, and working conditions. They threatened a long Kodak tradition of job security. In 1989, even before anything became operational, Jim Frangos, B&W's manager, convened a series of town meetings to hear all employees' reactions to the planned changes:

> The first of the town meetings was closer to the terrible end of the spectrum than I had hoped. Although I had steeled myself for the worst, I was still taken by surprise by the amount of anger and hostility that erupted like a furious volcano. . . . In hindsight my straight talk sessions were the first opportunity for the shop floor folks to speak their minds since the company began taking a battering in the Spring. Many were suspicious and completely distrustful of another desperate attempt on management's part to save the company. Some were convinced that they were going to be scapegoats for top management's poor judgment. So for the first month of straight talks I just resigned myself to getting skinned alive as I tried to sell the flow and the improvements it would bring [Frangos, 1993, pp. 68–69].

The employees' negativity continued even though they were encouraged to get everything off their chests. Reactions to Frangos after the meetings included "The dude is nuts," "What's he been smoking?" "Turnaround? He probably can't even parallel park," "Does he think we're drunk or something?" and "What's this 'fun' crap he keeps talking about? Glad I don't have to spend *my* day off with him" (Frangos, 1993, p. 69).

Later, in 1990, Frangos scheduled a second round of what were now officially labeled "Straight Talks." His wife asked him if he were a glutton for punishment. But Frangos knew that even though the changes were moving along, there was still some anger. In the twenty-five or so sessions for all fifteen hundred B&W employees, he found people far less concerned about venting and more interested in "how things were going and what they could do to become part of the solution to our problems" (Frangos, 1993, p. 130). In the second round, sessions moved away from politics to encompass the social value of B&W's efforts. As Frangos put it, "I worked hard to reinforce the theme that we were making products important to society. At one meeting, I described Kodak CFT Film, which is used to determine if a patient needs bypass surgery, and Kodak MIN-RH Film, used in the detection of breast cancer. . . . At another I talked about Kodak WL Surveillance Film. Guess what? Every time you use your ATM card, you're being photographed with a camera loaded with 2210 film. Same if you're robbing the bank. Smile for the cameras" (p. 130).

Occasions for Letting Go and Celebrating

Frangos's appeal to the deep purpose of B&W's operation highlights another impressive aspect of the division's turnaround—attention to symbols and culture. A change in physical arrangements was used to symbolize the management team's openness to dialogue: "I think we'd send a strong message to everyone if we got rid of the planning walls and used partitions instead. . . . We've been talking about a cross-functional team—why not make the office a symbol of an organization without walls?" (Frangos, 1993, p. 71).

A central symbolic challenge in any transformation is helping people let go. Team Zebra's mourning rituals centered around humor and fun. Yet the subtext of outwardly zany occasions allowed for sadness as well as playfulness. Humor is a powerful tool in making transitions. The line between laughing and crying is often hard to draw. Frangos understood that people would not let go until they could attach themselves to other symbols. In the liminal state between release and capture, celebration can serve dual purposes: mourning and meaning-making. Team Zebra presents several poignant examples of how symbols and symbolic activity ease the passage from old to new:

- *Keeping an eye on core values.* "Attitudes and morale can't change unless people believe what they're doing has intrinsic worth to the marketplace and makes a contribution to other people's lives" (Frangos, 1993, p. 70).
- *Encouraging rituals.* Forum meetings, breakfast clubs, and other regular gatherings were opportunities for bonding: "The Breakfast Club had become one of the most exciting aspects of the flow. But Team Zebra still needed some kind of 'glue' that would bind the

flow together and create a strong feeling of unity. That 'glue' came in the form of a shared vision and the articulation of a set of values and principles to live and work by" (Frangos, 1993, p. 84).

• *Anchoring vision embodied in metaphor and symbols.* In one meeting, the management team chose animals as metaphorical representatives of B&W's unity. One manager chose the mongoose: "One of its claims to fame is being able to defeat and devour poisonous snakes. In fact, I've thrown a few of our competitors down here . . . those snakes in the corner . . . the mongoose is extremely quick . . . tenacious, too. [It] just keeps chipping away at whatever it's working on, just like us" (Frangos, 1993, p. 86).

Visioning experiences led to the development of a division logo, "Images of Excellence"—a black diamond on one edge with lines passing throughout it. But the 'superglue,' the galvanizing symbol that pulled B&W's fifteen hundred people together, was the zebra as the division mascot. The idea crystallized in 1990, during a Secretaries' Day excursion to the zoo. As the visitors were admiring two adult animals and a baby, the zoo director told them: "Every zebra is unique. No two zebras' stripes are the same—kind of like fingerprints. They also run in herds. Being animals that are preyed upon, they understand that to the extent they can stay together, they can defend themselves from lions and other predators. In fact, predators probably have a hard time distinguishing the individuals from the mass of black and white stripes" (Frangos, 1993, p. 126).

The visitors picked up on the analogy, observing that each B&W employee brings something unique to the herd. "We need to band together as part of a team—when we're operating as such we 'baffle the competition'" (Frangos, 1993, p. 126). The B&W group became Team Zebra, and in following years the zebra image turned up everywhere.

• *Inventing ceremonies to keep team spirit high.* Numerous skits and awards ceremonies were playful occasions featuring music and merriment. The Whirling Dervish award, for example, honored the group with the best success each month in reducing inventory. The award and trophy (a toy pinwheel mounted on a block of wood) were both invented by employees. "Each month, after reviewing the inventory figures, Bill would announce the team with the best improvement and present the pinwheel. After one group won it three times in a row, the group's manager decided not to 'hog the wheel.' He had the machine shop make a permanent, windmill-like whirling dervish, complete with a plaque. He then relinquished the award for others to enjoy" (Frangos, 1993, p. 134).

Another example was a meeting of Zebra's leadership group to review the first year's progress: "The entire workshop was dotted with songs and skits commemorating the first year. Marty, Tim, and Chip had written a number of skits and songs, with Marty playing the keyboard and Rick accompanying her on the banjo. We poked fun at ourselves in a playful way about moving from being victims to being accountable for the results we generated. And as a cap for the event, we donned sweatshirts bearing our new logo and took a team picture. We then had a funeral for the ways of the past" (Frangos, 1993, p. 17).

Summary

Major organizational change inevitably generates four categories of issue. First, it affects individuals' ability to feel effective, valued, and in control. Without support, training, and chances to participate in the change process, people become a powerful anchor, making forward motion almost impossible.

Second, change disrupts existing roles and working relationships, producing confusion and uncertainty. Structural patterns need to be revised and realigned to support the new direction.

Third, change creates conflict between winners and losers—those who benefit from the new direction and those who do not. This conflict requires the creation of arenas where the issues can be renegotiated and the political map realigned.

Finally, change causes a loss of meaning for people on the receiving end of the change. Transition rituals, mourning the past, and celebrations of the future help people let go of old attachments and embrace new ones. Effective change requires a well-orchestrated, integrated design that responds to needs for learning, realignment, negotiation, and grieving.

Chapter Nineteen

Reframing Ethics and Spirit

You can't energize people or earn their support unless the organization they are committing to has soul.
ROBERT HAAS, CEO, LEVI STRAUSS & COMPANY[1]

Soul? In a company that makes denim pants? Not long ago, Haas might have been laughed at for linking spirituality with business. Not anymore. Haas is among a growing number of business leaders who believe that a company with soul is more likely to do the right things and to become successful over the long term.

What does Haas mean when he talks about soul? Dictionaries define it in terms like "immaterial essence" or "essential nature." For organizations, groups, or families, soul is a bedrock sense of who we are, what we care about, and what we believe in.

Who cares? Why should a company, a school, or a public agency be concerned about soul? Many organizations and most management writers ignore the topic. For example, Treacy and Wiersema's strategy best-seller, *The Discipline of Market Leaders* (1995), mentions Southwest Airlines thirteen times, always in glowing terms, to make the case that Southwest attained its market leadership by being a "low total cost" provider. Hamel and Prahalad's influential book *Competing for the Future* (1994) mentions Southwest four times, crediting the carrier's success to its creative departure from the airline industry's hub-and-spoke strategy. Southwest's results were certainly impressive: in the decade from 1985 to 1995, it was the most profitable airline in the U.S. airline industry by a wide margin, and its chief executive, Herb Kelleher, was touted as America's best CEO by *For-*

tune magazine in 1994 (Labich, 1994). Was strategy at the heart of the company's success?

Not in Kelleher's mind. He claimed that the airline industry was tactical, not strategic, because things change so fast. He offered a very different explanation for what makes Southwest work—one that talked about people, humor, love, and soul. "Simply put, Kelleher "cherishes and respects" his eighteen thousand employees, and his "love" is returned in what he calls "a spontaneous, voluntary overflowing of emotion" (Farkas and De Backer, 1996, p. 87).

Kelleher's style is undoubtedly distinctive: "Kelleher has been known to sing 'Tea for Two' while wearing bloomers and a bonnet at a company picnic (featuring a chili cook-off) in front of 4,000 employees. He regularly helps flight attendants serve drinks and peanuts when he flies. One Easter, he walked a plane's aisle clad in an Easter bunny outfit, and one St. Patrick's Day he dressed as a leprechaun. When Southwest started a new route to Sacramento, Kelleher sang a rap song at a press conference with two people in Teenage Mutant Ninja costumes and two others dressed as tomatoes" (Levering and Moskowitz, 1993, p. 413).

Kelleher claimed that the most important group in the company was the Culture Committee, a seventy-person cross section of employees established to perpetuate the company's values and spirit. His charge to the committee: "It's very important that this be continued. And we want you to be a missionary and an ambassador. We want you to carry the spiritual message of Southwest Airlines" (Farkas and De Backer, 1996, p. 93).

Spiritual message? Love? From a CEO who is notorious for his preference for cigarettes and bourbon? Is there any reason to treat this as more than an outlying fluke? There are plenty of skeptics. A competing airline executive grumbled, "Southwest runs on Herb's bullshit" (Petzinger, 1995, p. 284). But there are many other successful leaders who embrace a philosophy much like Kelleher's. Ben Cohen, cofounder of the ice-cream company Ben and Jerry's Homemade, observes: "Businesses tend to exploit communities and their workers, and that wasn't the way I thought the game should be played. I thought it should be the opposite—that because the business is allowed to be there in the first place, the business ought to support the community. What we're finding is that when you support the community, the community supports you back. When you give love, you receive love. I maintain that there is a spiritual dimension to business just as there is to the lives of individuals" (Levering and Moskowitz, 1993, p. 47).

Herb Kelleher and Ben Cohen are colorful, to put it mildly. Organizational success may not require the CEO to dress as the Easter bunny or as an Eastern mystic. (Cohen occasionally appeared at company celebrations in the person of Habeeni Ben Coheeni, whose stomach was the "mound of round" on which partner Jerry Greenfield broke cinder blocks with a sledgehammer.) An understated counterpoint to such hijinks is Aaron Feuerstein, president of the textile manufacturer Malden Mills. The day after a fire destroyed most of his plant in December 1995, Feuerstein announced that all three thousand of his workers would remain on the payroll for the following month. In January, he announced he would pay them for another month, and he extended the offer again in February. "The second time was a shock. It was the third time that brought tears to everyone's eyes" (Ryan, 1996, p. 4). By March, most of his employees were back on the job. Feuerstein's generosity went against the advice of members of his board and cost him several million dollars. But he felt a responsibility to both workers and community. He quoted Hillel, a first-century Talmudic scholar: "Not all who increase their wealth are wise." Said Feuerstein, "If you think the only function of a CEO is to increase the wealth of shareholders, then any time he spends on Scripture or Shakespeare or the arts is wasteful. But if you think the CEO must balance responsibilities, then he should be involved with ideas that connect him with the past, the present and the future" (Ryan, 1996, p. 5).

Despite unusually bad winter weather, Malden Mills was back in production faster than anyone expected. "Our people became very creative," said Feuerstein. "They were willing to work 25 hours a day."

Growing evidence suggests that tapping a deeper level of human energy pays off. Collins and Porras (1994) and De Geus (1995) both found that a central characteristic of corporations that achieved outstanding, long-term success was a core ideology emphasizing "more than profits" (Collins and Porras, 1994, p. 48) and providing "guidance and inspiration to people inside the company" (p. 88). "They need profits in the same way as any living being needs oxygen. It is a necessity to stay alive, but it is not the purpose of life" (De Geus, 1995, p. 29). Merck & Company, America's most successful pharmaceutical firm, states its core purpose as preserving and improving human life. Is this kind of statement more than words? Are such noble sentiments evident in key decisions and everyday behavior? Merck can point to a number of instances in which it sold a drug at a loss, or gave it away, to fulfill the core value of putting patients first. In one famous example, Merck had to decide whether to develop and distribute a drug for river blindness, an affliction of the poor in many Third World countries. Cost-benefit analysis was clear—the drug had little chance of making money. For companies with eyes fixed on the bottom line, such a decision would be a no-brainer. Merck developed the drug anyway and then gave it away free. A stunning outcome from Collins and Porras's research is that companies that emphasize values beyond the bottom line were more profitable in the long run than companies who stated their goals in purely financial terms.

Recent decades have regularly produced scandals in which major corporations were found to have engaged in unethical, if not illegal, conduct. The 1980s in particular were frequently characterized as a decade of remarkable greed, corruption, and dishonesty in business. A movement to do something about the apparently abysmal state of ethics in management has been building momentum. One strand of those efforts has spotlighted ethics as a curriculum topic in professional training programs. A second strand has emphasized corporate ethics statements. A third strand has pushed for stronger legal requirements, such as the Foreign Corrupt Practices Act, which forbids U.S. corporations from bribing foreign officials to get or retain business.

These are important initiatives, but they do not go deep enough. Solomon (1993) calls for an "Aristotelian ethic":

> There is too little sense of business as itself enjoyable (the main virtue of the "game" metaphor), that business is not a matter of vulgar self-interest but of vital community interest, that the virtues on which one prides oneself in personal life are essentially the same as those essential to good business—honesty, dependability, courage, loyalty, integrity. Aristotle's central ethical concept, accordingly, is a unified, all-embracing notion of "happiness" (or, more accurately, *eudaimonia*, perhaps better translated as "flourishing" or "doing well"). The point is to view one's life as a whole and not separate the personal and the public or professional, or duty and pleasure [p. 105].

Table 19.1. Reframing Ethics.

Metaphor	Organizational Ethic	Leadership Contribution
Factory	Excellence	Authorship
Extended family	Caring	Love
Jungle	Justice	Power
Temple	Faith	Significance

Solomon chose the term *Aristotelian* in part "because it makes no pretensions of presenting something very new, the latest 'cutting-edge' theory or technique of management, but rather reminds us of something very old, a perspective and a debate going all the way back to ancient times. . . . The idea is not to infuse corporate life with one more excuse for brutal changes, a new wave of experts and seminars and yet another downsizing bloodbath. It is to emphasize the importance of continuity and stability, clearness of vision and constancy of purpose, corporate loyalty and individual integrity" (p. 104).

Solomon reminds us that ethics and soul are central to both the good life and the good organization. The world's philosophical and spiritual traditions offer much wisdom to guide us in our search for better ways to live life and conduct business. To this point, we have primarily emphasized the frames as lenses for understanding and tools for influencing organizations. The heads and hands of leaders are vitally important. But so are their hearts and souls. In this chapter, we examine the implications of the frames for organizations as ethical communities and for the moral responsibilities of leadership. Table 19.1 summarizes our view.

The Factory: Excellence and Authorship

Our oldest image of organization is as factories engaged in a production process. Raw materials (steel or peanuts or five-year-olds) come in the front end, and finished products (refrigerators or peanut butter or educated citizens) leave at the back. The ethical imperative of the factory is excellence: to ensure that work is done as well and as efficiently as possible to produce outputs of the highest quality. Since the publication of Peters and Waterman's famous book *In Search of Excellence* (1982), almost everyone has claimed to be searching for excellence, though there are more than enough flawed products and mediocre services to make it clear that not everyone's quest has been successful.

One cause of disappointment is overlooking that organizational excellence requires much more than sermons from top management: it requires commitment and autonomy at all levels of the organization. How do leaders foster such commitment? Bolman and Deal (1995, p. 102) maintain that "leading is giving. Leadership is an ethic, a gift of oneself." Crucial for creating and maintaining excellence is the gift of authorship:

> Giving authorship provides space within boundaries. In an orchestra, musicians each develop individual parts within the parameters of a particular musical score and the interpretative challenges posed by the conductor. Authorship turns the pyramid on its side. Leaders increase their influence and build more productive organizations. Workers experience the satisfactions of creativity, craftsmanship, and a job well done. Gone is the traditional adversarial relationship in which superiors try to increase their control while subordinates resist them at every turn. Trusting people to solve problems generates higher levels of motivation and better solutions. The leader's responsibility is to create conditions that promote authorship. Individuals need to see their work as meaningful and worthwhile, to feel personally accountable for the consequences of their efforts, and to get feedback that lets them know the results [p. 106].

Stung by a comment from a company officer—"Our quality stinks!"—Motorola embarked on one of the world's most ambitious and successful quality improvement efforts. The initiative added some $3.2 billion to Motorola's bottom line between 1987 and 1992 (Waterman, 1994, p. 229). Central to the effort was extensive training and empowerment of front-line workers. One of those workers was Hossain Rasoli, a technician, who worked on power transformers. Before the quality program, he wondered how the product was doing in the field but never knew. As part of the new initiative, he was given a level of responsibility he'd never had before: the charge to improve product quality. "I call it my baby," he says, pointing to the power amplifier. "I take pride in this product. If it fails in the field, I feel hurt, or I get depressed" (Waterman, 1994, p. 245). Rasoli used his training in problem solving and statistical-process control to determine the power amplifier's weakest components. He then went to the development engineers and asked them to redesign the parts. The result was a 400 percent improvement in reliability. One manager said of Rasoli, "He is now recognized as Mr. PA [power amplifier]. He knows more about this product than any designer, any vendor, any manager, anyone else" (p. 246).

Southwest Airlines offers another unique image of authorship— its associates are encouraged to be themselves, have fun, and, above all, use their sense of humor. Only on Southwest are you likely to hear required FAA safety briefings sung to the music of a popular song or delivered as a stand-up comedy routine ("Those of you who wish to smoke will please file out to our lounge on the wing, where you can enjoy our feature film, *Gone with the Wind*"). Too frivolous for something as weighty as safety announcements? Just the opposite—it's a way to get passengers to pay attention to announcements they usually ignore. And it is just as surely a way for flight attendants to have fun and feel authorship.

One of the Saturn Company's greatest accomplishments has been giving autoworkers the special feeling that comes from putting their personal signature, as well as a fender or windshield wiper, on a new car. Saturn employees frequently telephone customers to ask how they enjoy their car. If they see a Saturn stopped along a road, they volunteer assistance. Said one Saturn worker in a recent testimonial, "When given a chance, everyone would prefer to build a superior automobile. At Saturn, they give us that chance."

The Family: Caring and Love

Caring—one person's compassion and concern for another—is both the purpose and the ethical glue that hold a family together. Parents care for children and, eventually, children care for parents. A caring family, or community, requires servant-leaders who serve the best interests of the family and its stakeholders. This implies a profound and challenging responsibility for leaders to understand the needs and concerns of family members so as to serve the best interests of individuals and the family as a whole. The gift of servant-leaders is love.

> Love is largely absent in the modern corporation. Most managers would never use the word in any context more profound than their feelings about food, films or games. They shy away from love's deeper meanings, fearing both its power and its risks. Caring begins with knowing—it requires listening, understanding and accepting. It progresses through a deepening sense of appreciation, respect and, ultimately, love. Love is a willingness to reach out and open one's heart. An open heart is vulnerable. Confronting vulnerability allows us to drop our masks, meet heart to heart and be present for one another. We experience a sense of unity and delight in those voluntary, human exchanges that mold "the soul of community" [Whitmyer, 1993, p. 81].

They talk openly about love at Southwest Airlines: they fly out of Love Field in Dallas, their symbol on the New York Stock Exchange is LUV, the employee newsletter is called *Luv Lines,* and their twentieth anniversary slogan was "20 Years of Loving You" (Levering and Moskowitz, 1993). They hold an annual Heroes of the Heart ceremony to honor family members who have gone above and beyond even Southwest's high standards of duty. There are, of course, ups and downs in any family, and the airline industry certainly brings both good days and bad. Through life's peaks and valleys, love holds people together in a caring community. A Southwest employee said, "Herb loves us. We love Herb. We love one another. We love the company. One of the primary beneficiaries of our collective caring is our passengers."

For Levi Strauss, the issue of caring came to a head in trying to apply the company's ethical principles (honesty, fairness, respect for others, compassion, promise-keeping, and integrity) to the thorny dilemmas of working with foreign subcontractors. How should the company balance concerns for domestic employees and overseas workers? Even if pay and working conditions at foreign subcontractors are below those in the United States, are inferior jobs better than no jobs? A task force was set to work to collect data and formulate guidelines for ethical practice. Ultimately, the company wound up making some tough decisions. It pulled out of China because of human rights abuses, despite that nation's enormous long-term market potential. In a factory in Bangladesh employing underage children, Levi's made an arrangement for the children to go back to school while the contractor continued to pay their salaries (Waterman, 1994).

The Jungle: Justice and Power

Let us turn now to a third image of the organization: as a jungle. Woody Allen captured the competitive, predator-prey imagery succinctly with the observation that "the lion shall lie down with the lamb, but the lamb won't get much sleep." As the image implies, the jungle is a politically charged world of conflict and the under-regulated pursuit of self-interest. Politics and politicians are routinely viewed as objects of scorn. Is there any ethical obligation associated with the political frame? We believe that there is: the duty of justice. In a world of competing interests and scarce resources, we are continually compelled to make trade-offs. We cannot give all parties everything they want, but we can honor a value of fairness in making such decisions. Solomon (1993) views justice as the ultimate virtue in corporations because fairness—the perception that employees, customers, and investors are all "getting their due"—is the glue that holds things together.

In a world of people and groups with very different interests and worldviews, justice is never easy to define, and disagreement about criteria is inevitable. The key gift that leaders can offer is power. People with a voice in key decisions are far more likely to feel a sense of justice than those with no seat at the table, whose interests are easily ignored.

Hoarding power produces a powerless organization. People stripped of power look for ways to fight back: sabotage, passive resistance, withdrawal, or angry militancy. Giving power liberates energy for more productive use. When people have a sense of efficacy and an ability to influence their world, they seek to be productive. They direct their energy and intelligence toward making a contribution rather than obstructing progress.

The gift of power enrolls people in working toward a common cause. It also creates difficult choice points. If leaders clutch power too tightly, they activate old patterns of antagonism. If they cave in and say yes to anything, they put the organizational mission at risk (Bolman and Deal, 1995).

Authorship and power are related—autonomy, space, and freedom are at issue in both. Yet there is an important difference. Artists, authors, and craftspeople can experience authorship even working alone. Power, by contrast, is meaningful only in relationship to others: it is the capacity to influence others and get things to happen on a broader scale. Authorship without power is isolating and splintering. Power without authorship can be dysfunctional and oppressive.

The gift of power is important at multiple levels—the individual, the group, and the organization. At the individual level, people want power to influence their immediate work environment and the factors that impinge on them. Many traditional workplaces still suffocate their employees with time clocks, rigid rules, and authoritarian bosses. Consider again Hossain Rasoli, Motorola's "Mr. Power Amplifier." Putting his own signature on the product gave him a sense of authorship. His ability to persuade others in the organization gave him power as well. In one case, Rasoli was so distressed that he went to a vice president to complain because the purchasing department planned to bring in a new vendor for a particular component. Rasoli was very firm: "You're not going to put this in my product." He won (Waterman, 1994, p. 246).

At Saturn, workers' power is symbolized by "the rope"—a rope with a handle, hanging at regular intervals along the assembly line. Anyone who sees the smallest deviation from Saturn's high standards is authorized to pull the rope and stop the line. One Saturn worker remembered with pride the day he pulled the rope: "It wasn't a major thing. Just a broken retainer clip. In the old [General Motors] world it had to be a life or death issue. At Saturn, they've given us the rope to do the job right, to build a car we can all be proud of."

At the group level, a challenge in organizations and societies around the world is responding to ethnic, racial, and gender diversity. Gallos and Ramsey (1996) get to the heart of the complexity: "Institutional, structural and systemic issues are very difficult for members of dominant groups to understand. Systems are most often designed by dominant group members to meet their own needs. It is then difficult to see the ways in which our institutions and structures systematically exclude others who are not 'like us.' It is hard to see and question what we have always taken for granted and painful to confront personal complicity in maintaining the status quo. Privilege enables us to remain unaware of institutional and social forces and their impact" (p. 215).

Thus justice requires that leaders systematically enhance the power of subdominant groups—ensuring access to decision making, creating internal advocacy groups, building diversity into organizational information and incentive systems, and strengthening career opportunities (Cox, 1994; Gallos and Ramsey, 1996; Morrison, 1992). All this will only happen if there is a rock-solid commitment from top management, the one condition that Morrison found to be universal in organizations that were leaders in responding to diversity.

Another version of the justice as power issue can be seen in Southwest Airlines's relationships with its unions. Labor unions' central purpose is to give employees power—a voice in decisions affecting them—but this process is regularly distorted by unproductive labor-management conflict. Herb Kelleher starts from the premise that the purpose of bargaining is to give the workers not as little as possible but rather as much as possible while still enabling the company to prosper over the long term. After all, he says, they help make it work; they should share in the profits.

The Temple: Faith and Significance

A organization, like a temple, can be seen as a sacred place—an expression of human aspirations, a monument to faith in human possibility. A temple is a gathering place for a community of people with shared traditions, values, and beliefs. Members of a community may be diverse in many ways—age, background, economic status, and personal interests. But they are held together by shared faith and a spiritual commitment to one another. In a work organization, faith is strengthened when individuals feel that the organization is characterized by excellence, caring, and justice. But above all, they must feel that it is doing something worth doing—that the work is a calling that adds something of value to the world.

Significance is partly about work itself but even more about how the work is understood. That point is made by an old story about three stonemasons' accounts of their work. The first said he was "cutting stone." The second reported that he was "building a cathedral." And the third said simply that he was "serving God."

Temples need spiritual leaders. *Spiritual* here means not a specific religion or a particular theology but rather a genuine concern for the human spirit. Dictionary definitions of *spirit* include "the intelligent or immaterial part of man," "the animating or vital principle in living things," and "the moral nature of humanity." Spiritual leaders help people find meaning and faith in work and answers to fundamental questions that have confronted humans of every time and place: Who am I as an individual? Who are we as a people? What is the purpose in my life and in our collective life? What ethical principles should we follow? What legacy will we leave?

Spiritual leaders offer the gift of significance, rooted in confidence that the work is worthy of one's efforts, and the institution deserves one's commitment and loyalty. Work is exhilarating and joyful at its best, arduous, frustrating, and exhausting in less happy moments. Many adults embark on their careers with enthusiasm, confidence, and a desire to make a contribution. Some never lose that spark, or calling, but many do. They become frustrated with working conditions and discouraged by how hard it is to make a difference or even to know if they have. Tracy Kidder (1989) put it well in writing about teachers: "Good teachers put snags in the river of children passing by, and over time, they redirect hundreds of lives. There is an innocence that conspires to hold humanity together, and it is made up of people who can never fully know the good they have done" (p. 313). The gift of significance helps people sustain their faith rather than burn out and retire on the job.

Significance is built through the use of many expressive and symbolic forms: rituals, ceremonies, icons, music, and stories. Organizations without a rich symbolic life become empty and sterile. The magic of special occasions is vital in building significance into collective life. Moments of ecstasy are exclamation points that mark life's major passages. Without ritual and ceremony, transitions remain incomplete, a clutter of comings and goings. "Life becomes an endless set of Wednesdays" (Campbell, 1983).

When ritual and ceremony are authentic and attuned, they fire the imagination, evoke insight, and touch the heart. Ceremony weaves past, present, and future into life's ongoing tapestry. Ritual helps us face and comprehend life's everyday shocks, triumphs, and mysteries. Both help us experience the unseen webs of significance that tie a community together. When inauthentic, such occasions become meaningless, repetitious, and alienating. They waste our time, disconnect us from work, and splinter us from one another. "Community must become more than just gathering the troops, telling the stories, and remembering things past. Community must also be rooted in values that do not fail, values that go beyond the self-aggrandizement of human leaders" (Griffin, 1993, p. 178).

Stories give flesh to shared values and sacred beliefs. Everyday life in organizations brings many heartwarming moments and dramatic encounters. Turned into stories, these events fill an organization's treasure chest with lore and legend. Told and retold, they draw people together and connect them with the significance of their work.

Music captures and expresses life's deeper meaning. When people sing or dance together, they bond to one another and experience emotional connections that are otherwise hard to express. Harry Quadrocchi, chief executive officer of Quadgraphics, convenes employees once a year for an annual company gathering. A management chorus sings the year's themes. Quadrocchi himself voices the company philosophy in a solo serenade.

Max DePree, famed as both a business leader and an author of elegant books on leadership, is clear about the role of faith in business: "Being faithful is more important than being successful. Corporations can and should have a redemptive purpose. We need to weigh the pragmatic in the clarifying light of the moral. We must understand that reaching our potential is more important than reaching our goals" (1989, p. 69). Spiritual leaders have the responsibility of sustaining and encouraging faith in themselves and in recalling others to the faith when they have lost it.

Summary

Organizational ethics must ultimately be rooted in soul—an organization's understanding of its deeply held identity, beliefs, and values. Each frame offers a perspective on the ethical responsibilities of organizations and the roles of leaders. Every organization needs to evolve for itself a sense of its own ethical and spiritual core. The frames offer guidelines for that process.

Signs are everywhere that institutions in many developed nations are at a critical juncture because of a crisis of meaning and moral authority. Rapid change, high mobility, globalization, and racial and ethnic conflict tear at the fabric of community. The most important responsibility of managers is not to answer every question or always to make the right decision. They cannot escape their responsibilities to track budgets, motivate people, respond to political pressures, and attend to symbols. As leaders, they serve a deeper, more powerful, and more durable function when they are models and catalysts for such values as excellence, caring, justice, and faith.

Note
1. Quotation from Waterman (1994, p. 140).

Chapter Twenty

Bringing It All Together

Change and Leadership in Action

Life's daily challenges rarely arrive neatly categorized or clearly labeled. Instead, they flow over us in a murky and turbulent stream of experience. The art of reframing, and of leadership, uses knowledge and intuition to make sense of the flow and to find sensible and effective ways to channel the current in productive directions.

In this chapter, we illustrate the process by taking a new principal through his first week in a deeply troubled urban high school. We assume that he is familiar with the frames and reframing and is committed to the view of leadership and ethics described in Chapter Nineteen. How might he mine his experience to figure out what's going on? What strategies would he consider? What will he do?

Read the case thoughtfully. Ask yourself what you think is going on and what options you would consider. Then compare your reflections to his.[1]

Robert F. Kennedy High School

On July 15, David King became principal of Robert F. Kennedy High School, the newest of six high schools in Great Ridge, Illinois. The school had opened two years earlier amid national acclaim as one of the first schools in the country designed and built on the "house system" concept. Kennedy High was organized into four "houses," each with three hundred students, eighteen faculty, and a housemaster. Each house was in a separate building connected to the "core facilities"—cafeteria, nurse's room, guidance offices, boys' and girls'

gyms, offices, shops, and auditorium—and other houses by an enclosed outside passageway. Each had its own entrance, classrooms, toilets, conference
rooms, and housemaster's office.

Hailed as a major innovation in inner-city education, Kennedy High was
featured during its first year in a documentary on a Chicago television station.
The school opened with a carefully selected staff of teachers, many chosen from
other Great Ridge schools. At least a dozen were specially recruited from out of
state. King knew that his faculty included graduates from several elite East
Coast and West Coast schools, such as Yale, Princeton, and Stanford, as well as
several of the very best midwestern schools. Even the racial mix of students had
been carefully balanced so that blacks, whites, and Latinos each comprised a
third of the student body (although King also knew—perhaps better than its
planners—that Kennedy's students were drawn from the toughest and poorest
areas of the city). The building itself was also widely admired for its beauty and
functionality and had won several national architectural awards.

Despite careful and elaborate preparations, Kennedy High School was in
serious trouble by the time King arrived. It had been racked by violence the
preceding year—closed twice by student disturbances and once by a teacher
walkout. It was also widely reported (although King did not know for sure)
that achievement scores of its ninth- and tenth-grade students had declined
during the last two years, and no significant improvement could be seen in the
scores of the eleventh and twelfth graders' tests. So far, Kennedy High School
had fallen far short of its planners' hopes and expectations.

David King

David King was born and raised in Great Ridge, Illinois. His father was one of
the city's first black principals. King knew the city and its school system well.
After two years of military service, King followed in his father's footsteps by
going to Great Ridge State Teachers College, where he received B.Ed. and
M.Ed. degrees. King taught English and coached in a predominantly black
middle school for several years until he was asked to become the school's assistant principal. He remained in that post for five years, when he was asked to
take over a large middle school of nine hundred pupils—believed at the time
to be the most "difficult" middle school in the city. While there, King gained a
citywide reputation as a gifted and popular administrator. He was credited with
changing the worst middle school in the system into one of the best. He had
been very effective in building community support, recruiting new faculty, and

raising academic standards. He was also credited with turning out basketball and baseball teams that had won state and county championships.

The superintendent made it clear that King had been selected for the Kennedy job over several more senior candidates because of his ability to handle tough situations. The superintendent had also told him that he would need every bit of skill and luck he could muster. King knew of the formidable credentials of Jack Weis, his predecessor at Kennedy High. Weis, a white man, had been the superintendent of a small, local township school system before becoming Kennedy's first principal. He had written one book on the house system concept and another on inner-city education. Weis held a Ph.D. from the University of Chicago and a divinity degree from Harvard. Yet despite his impressive background and ability, Weis had resigned in disillusionment. He was described by many as a "broken man." King remembered seeing the physical change in Weis over that two-year period. Weis's appearance had become progressively more fatigued and strained until he developed what appeared to be permanent dark rings under his eyes and a perpetual stoop. King remembered how he had pitied the man and wondered how Weis could find the job worth the obvious personal toll it was taking on him.

History of the School

The First Year

The school's troubles began to manifest themselves in its first year. Rumors of conflicts between the housemasters and the six subject-area department heads spread throughout the system by the middle of the year. The conflicts stemmed from differences in interpretations of curriculum policy on required learning and course content. In response, Weis had instituted a "free market" policy: subject-area department heads were supposed to convince housemasters why they should offer certain courses, and housemasters were supposed to convince department heads which teachers they wanted assigned to their houses. Many felt that this policy exacerbated the conflicts.

To add to the tension, a teacher was assaulted in her classroom in February. The beating frightened many of the staff, particularly older teachers. A week later, eight teachers asked Weis to hire security guards. This request precipitated a debate in the faculty about the desirability of guards in the school. One group felt that the guards would instill a sense of safety and promote a better learning climate. The other faction felt that the presence of guards in the school would be repressive and would destroy the sense of community and trust that was developing. Weis refused the request for security guards because he believed they would symbolize everything the school was trying to change. In April, a second teacher was robbed and beaten in her classroom after school hours, and the debate was rekindled. This time, a group of Latino parents threatened to boycott the school unless better security measures were implemented. Again, Weis refused the request for security guards.

The Second Year

The school's second year was even more troubled than the first. Financial cutbacks ordered during the summer prevented Weis from replacing eight teachers who resigned. Since it was no longer possible for each house to staff all of its courses with its own faculty, Weis instituted a "flexible staffing" policy. Some teachers were asked to teach a course outside their assigned house, and students in the eleventh and twelfth grades were able to take elective and required courses in other houses. Chauncey Carver, one of the housemasters, publicly attacked the new policy as a step toward destroying the house system. In a letter to the *Great Ridge Times,* he accused the board of education of trying to subvert the house concept by cutting back funds.

The debate over the flexible staffing policy was heightened when two of the other housemasters joined a group of faculty and department heads in opposing Carver's criticisms. This group argued that interhouse cross-registration should be encouraged because the fifteen to eighteen teachers in each house could never offer the variety of courses that the schoolwide faculty of sixty-five to seventy could.

Further expansion of the flexible staffing policy was halted, however, because of difficulties in scheduling fall classes. Errors cropped up in the master schedule developed during the preceding summer. Scheduling problems persisted until November, when the vice principal responsible for developing the schedule resigned. Burtram Perkins, a Kennedy housemaster who had formerly planned the schedule at Central High, assumed the function on top of his duties as housemaster. Scheduling took most of Perkins's time until February.

Security again became an issue when three sophomores were assaulted because they refused to give up their lunch money during a "shakedown." The assailants were believed to be outsiders. Several teachers approached Weis and asked him to request security guards from the board of education. Again, Weis declined, but he asked Bill Smith, a vice principal at the school, to secure all doors except for the entrances to each of the four houses, the main entrance to the school, and the cafeteria. This move seemed to reduce the number of outsiders roaming through the school.

In May of the second year, a fight in the cafeteria spread and resulted in considerable damage, including broken classroom windows and desks. The disturbance was severe enough for Weis to close the school. A number of teachers and students reported that outsiders were involved in the fight and in damaging the classrooms. Several students were taken to the hospital for minor injuries, but all were released. A similar disturbance occurred two weeks later, and again the school was closed. The board of education ordered a temporary detail of municipal police to the school against Weis's advice. In protest to the assignment of police, thirty of Kennedy's sixty-eight teachers staged a walkout, joined by over half the student body. The police detail was removed, and an agreement was worked out by an ad hoc subcommittee composed of board members and informal representatives of teachers who were for and against a police detail. The compromise called for the temporary stationing of a police cruiser near the school.

King's First Week at Kennedy High

King arrived at Kennedy High on Monday, July 15, and spent most of his first week individually interviewing key administrators (see Exhibit 20.1). On Friday, he held a meeting with all administrators and department heads. King's purpose in these meetings was to familiarize himself with the school, its problems, and its key people.

His first interview was with Bill Smith, a vice principal. Smith was black and had worked as a counselor and then vice principal of a middle school before coming to Kennedy. King knew Smith's reputation as a tough disciplinarian who was very much disliked by many of the younger faculty and students. King had also heard from several teachers whose judgment he respected that Smith had been instrumental in keeping the school from "blowing apart" the preceding year. It became clear early in the interview that Smith felt that more stringent steps were needed to keep outsiders from wandering into the buildings. Smith urged King to consider locking all the school's thirty doors except for the front entrance so that everyone would enter and leave through one set of doors. Smith also told him that many of the teachers and pupils were scared and that "no learning will ever begin to take place until we make it so people don't have to be afraid anymore." At the end of the interview, Smith said he had been approached by a nearby school system to become its

**Exhibit 20.1.   Administrative Organization
of Robert F. Kennedy High School.**

Principal:	David King, 42 (black) B.Ed., M.Ed., Great Ridge State Teachers College
Vice principal:	William Smith, 44 (black) B.Ed., Breakwater State College; M.Ed., Great Ridge State Teachers College
Vice principal:	Vacant
Housemaster, A House:	Burtram Perkins, 47 (black) B.S., M.Ed., University of Illinois
Housemaster, B House:	Frank Czepak, 36 (white) B.S., University of Illinois; M.Ed., Great Ridge State Teachers College
Housemaster, C House:	Chauncey Carver, 32 (black) A.B., Wesleyan University; B.F.A., Pratt Institute; M.A.T., Yale University
Housemaster, D House:	John Bonavota, 26 (white) B.Ed., Great Ridge State Teachers College; M.Ed., Ohio State University
Assistant to the principal:	Vacant
Assistant to the principal for community affairs:	Vacant

director of counseling but that he had not yet made up his mind. He said he was committed enough to Kennedy High that he did not want to leave, but his decision depended on how hopeful he felt about the school's future.

As King talked with others, he discovered that the "door question" was highly controversial within the faculty and that feelings ran high on both sides of the issue. Two housemasters in particular, Chauncey Carver, who was black, and Frank Czepak, who was white, were strongly against closing the house entrances. The two men felt such an action would symbolically reduce house "autonomy" and the feeling of distinctness that was a central aspect of the house concept.

Carver, master of House C, was particularly vehement on this issue and on his opposition to allowing students in one house to take classes in another house. Carver contended that the flexible staffing program had nearly destroyed the house concept. He threatened to resign if King intended to expand cross-house enrollment. Carver also complained about what he described as "interference" from department heads that undermined his teachers' autonomy.

Carver appeared to be an outstanding housemaster from everything King had heard about him—even from his many enemies. Carver had an abrasive personality but seemed to have the best-operating house in the school and was well liked by most of his teachers and pupils. His program appeared to be the most innovative, but it was also the one most frequently attacked by department heads for lacking substance and ignoring requirements in the system's curriculum guide. Even with these criticisms, King imagined how much easier it would be if he had four housemasters like Chauncey Carver.

During his interviews with the other three housemasters, King discovered that they all felt infringed upon by the department heads, but only Carver and Czepak were strongly against locking the doors. The other two housemasters actively favored cross-house course enrollments. King's fourth interview was with Burtram Perkins, also a housemaster. Perkins, mentioned earlier, was a black man in his late forties who had served as assistant to the principal of Central High before coming to Kennedy. Perkins spent most of the interview discussing how schedule pressures could be relieved. Perkins was currently developing the schedule for the coming school year until a vice principal could be appointed to perform that job (Kennedy High had allocations for two vice principals and two assistants in addition to the housemasters).

Two bits of information concerning Perkins came to King during his first week at the school. The first was that several teachers were circulating a letter requesting Perkins's removal as a housemaster. They felt that he could not control the house or direct the faculty. This surprised King because he had heard that Perkins was widely respected within the faculty and had earned a reputation for supporting high academic standards and for working tirelessly with new teachers. As King inquired further, he discovered that Perkins was genuinely liked but was also widely acknowledged as a poor housemaster. The second piece of information concerned how Perkins's house compared with the others. Although students had been randomly assigned to each house, Perkins's house had the highest absence rate and the greatest number of disciplinary problems. Smith had told him that Perkins's dropout rate the previous year was three times that of the next highest house.

While King was in the process of interviewing his staff, he was called on by David Crimmins, chairman of the history department. Crimmins was a native of Great Ridge, white, and in his late forties. Though scheduled for an appointment the following week, he had asked King if he could see him immediately. Crimmins had heard about the letter asking for Perkins's removal and wanted to present the other side. He became very emotional, saying that Perkins was viewed by many of the teachers and department chairmen as the only housemaster trying to maintain high academic standards; his transfer would be seen as a blow to those concerned with quality education. Crimmins also described in detail Perkins's devotion and commitment to the school. He emphasized that Perkins was the only administrator with the ability to straighten out the schedule, which he had done in addition to all his other duties. Crimmins departed by threatening, if Perkins were transferred, to write a letter to the regional accreditation council decrying the extent to which standards had sunk at Kennedy. King assured Crimmins that such a drastic measure was unnecessary and offered assurance that a cooperative resolution would be found. King knew that Kennedy High faced an accreditation review the following April and did not wish to complicate the process unnecessarily.

Within twenty minutes of Crimmins's departure, King was visited by Tim Shea, a young white teacher. He said he had heard that Crimmins had come in to see King. Shea identified himself as one of the teachers who had organized the movement to get rid of Perkins. He said that he liked and admired Perkins because of the man's devotion to the school but that Perkins's house was so disorganized and that discipline there was so bad that it was nearly impossible to do any good teaching. Shea added, "It's a shame to lock the school up when stronger leadership is all that's needed."

King's impressions of his administrators generally matched what he had heard before arriving at the school. Carver seemed to be a very bright, innovative, and charismatic leader whose mere presence generated excitement. Czepak came across as a highly competent though not very imaginative administrator who had earned the respect of his faculty and students. Bonavota, at twenty-six, seemed smart and earnest but unseasoned and unsure of himself. King felt that with a little guidance and training, Bonavota might have the greatest promise of all; at the moment, however, the young housemaster seemed confused and somewhat overwhelmed. Perkins impressed King as a sincere and devoted person with a good mind for administrative details but an incapacity for leadership.

King knew that he had the opportunity to make several administrative appointments because of the three vacancies that existed. Indeed, should Smith resign as vice principal, King could fill both vice principal positions. He also knew that his recommendations for these positions would carry a great deal of weight with the central office. The only constraint King felt was the need to achieve some kind of racial balance among the Kennedy administrative group. With his own appointment as principal, the number of black administrators exceeded the number of white administrators by a ratio of two to one, and Kennedy did not have a single Latino administrator, even though a third of its pupils were Latino.

The Friday Afternoon Meeting

In contrast to the individual interviews, King was surprised to find how quiet and conflict-free these same people seemed in the staff meeting he called on Friday. He was amazed at how slow, polite, and friendly the conversation was among people who had so vehemently expressed negative opinions of each other in private. After about forty-five minutes of discussion about the upcoming accreditation review, King broached the subject of housemaster–department head relations. There was silence until Czepak made a joke about the uselessness of discussing the topic. King probed further by asking if everyone was happy with the current practices. Crimmins suggested that the topic might be better discussed in a smaller group. Everyone seemed to agree—except for Betsy Dula, a white woman in her late twenties who chaired the English department. She said that one of the problems with the school was that no one was willing to tackle tough issues until they exploded. She added that relations between housemasters and department heads were terrible, and that made her job very difficult. She then attacked Chauncey Carver for impeding her evaluation of a nontenured teacher in Carver's house. The two argued for several minutes about the teacher and the quality of an experimental sophomore English course the teacher was offering. Finally, Carver, by now quite angry, coldly warned Dula that he would "break her neck" if she stepped into his house again. King intervened in an attempt to cool both their tempers, and the meeting ended shortly thereafter.

The following morning, Dula called King at home and told him that unless Carver publicly apologized for his threat, she would file a grievance with the teachers' union and take it to court if necessary. King assured Dula that he would talk with Carver on Monday. King then called Eleanor Debbs, a Kennedy High math teacher whom he had known well for many years and whose judgment he respected. Debbs was a close friend of both Carver and Dula and was also vice president of the city's teachers' union. Debbs said that the two were longtime adversaries but both were excellent professionals.

She also reported that Dula would be a formidable opponent and could muster considerable support among the faculty. Debbs, who was black, feared that a confrontation between Dula and Carver might create racial tensions in the school, even though both Dula and Carver were generally popular with students of all races. Debbs strongly urged King not to let the matter drop. She also told him that she had overheard Bill Smith, the vice principal, say at a party the night before that he felt King didn't have the stomach or the forceful-ness to survive at Kennedy. Smith said that the only reason he was staying was that he did not expect King to last the year, in which case Smith would be in a good position to be appointed principal.

David King inherited a job that had broken his predecessor and could easily destroy him as well. His new staff greeted him with a jumble of problems, demands, maneuvers, and threats. His first staff meeting began with an undercurrent of tension and ended in outright hostility. Sooner or later, almost every manager will en-counter situations this bad—or worse. The results are often dev-astating, leaving the manager feeling confused, overwhelmed, and helpless. Nothing makes any sense, and nothing seems to work. Can King escape such a dismal fate?

There is one potential bright spot. As the case ends, King is talk-ing to Eleanor Debbs on a Saturday morning. He has a supportive colleague. He also has some slack—the rest of the weekend to re-group. Where should he begin? We suggest that he start by active reflection and reframing. A straightforward way to do that is to examine the situation one frame at a time and ask two simple ques-tions: From this perspective, what's going on? And what options does this viewpoint suggest? This reflective process deserves time and careful thought. It requires "going to the balcony" (Heifetz, 1994) to get a fuller perspective on the scene below. Ideally, King would include one or more other people—a valued mentor, prin-cipals in other schools, close friends, his spouse—for alternative perspectives in the diagnostic process. We will present a streamlined version of the kind of thinking that David King might entertain.

Structural Frame: Issues and Options

King sits down at his kitchen table with a cup of coffee, a pen, and a fresh yellow pad. He starts to review structural issues at Kennedy High. He recalls the "people-blaming" approach (Chapter Two)—blaming individuals for everything that goes wrong. He smiles and nods his head. That's it! Everyone at Kennedy High School is blaming everyone else. He recalls the lesson of the structural frame: we blame individuals when the real problems are systemic.

So what structural problems does Kennedy High have? King thinks about the two cornerstones of structure—differentiation and integration. In a flash of insight, he sees that Kennedy High School has an ample division of labor but very little coordination. He scribbles on his pad, trying to draw the school's organization chart. He gradually realizes that the school has a matrix structure—teachers have an ill-defined dual reporting relationship to both department chairs and housemasters. He remembers the downside of matrix structures. They're built for conflict—teachers wonder whom they're supposed to be loyal to, and administrators bicker about who's in charge. There are no integrating devices to link the concerns of housemasters like Chauncey Carver (who wants a coherent, effective program for his house) with those of department chairs like Betsy Dula (who is concerned about the school-wide English curriculum and adherence to district guidelines). It's not just personalities. The structure is pushing Carver and Dula toward each other's throat. Goals, roles, and responsibilities are all vaguely defined. Nor is there a workable structural device (like a task force or standing committee) to diagnose and resolve such problems. If King had been in the job longer, he might be able to rely more heavily on the authority of the principal's office. It helps that he's been authorized to fix the school by the superintendent. But so far, there is little evidence that Kennedy High staff are endorsing his authority with much enthusiasm.

King's musings are making sense, but it isn't clear what to do about the structural gaps. Is there any way to get the school back under control when it is teetering on the edge of chaos? Particularly when his authority is shaky? He is having trouble controlling the staff, and they are having the same problem with the students. The school is an underbounded system screaming for structure and boundaries.

King notes, ruefully, that he made things worse in the Friday meeting. "I knew how these people felt about one another," he thinks. "Why did I push them to talk about something they were trying to avoid? We hadn't done any homework. I didn't give them a clear goal for the conversation. I didn't set any ground rules for how to talk about it. When it started to heat up, I just watched. Why didn't I step in before it exploded?" He stops and shakes his head. "Live and learn, I guess. But I learned these lessons a long time ago—they served me well in turning the middle school around. In all the confusion, I forgot that even good people can't function very well without some structure. What did I do the last time around?"

King begins to brainstorm options. One possibility is responsibility charting (Chapter Five): bring people together to define tasks and responsibilities. It has worked before. Would it work here? He reviews the language of responsibility charting. Who's responsible? Who has to approve? Who needs to be consulted? Who should be informed? As he applies these questions to Kennedy High, the overlap between the housemasters and the department chairs is an obvious problem. Without a clear definition of roles and relationships, conflict and confusion are inevitable. He wonders about a total overhaul of the structure: Is the house system viable in its current form? If not, is it fixable? Maybe we need a process to look at the structure: What if I chaired a small task force to examine it and develop recommendations? I could put Dula and Carver on it—let them see firsthand what's causing their conflict. Get them involved in working out a new design. Give each authority over specific areas. Develop some policies and procedures.

It is clear even from a few minutes' reflection that Kennedy High School has major structural problems that have to be addressed. But what to do about the immediate crisis between Dula and Carver? The structure helped create the problem in the first place, and fixing it might prevent stuff like this in the future. But Dula's demand for an apology didn't sound like something a rational approach would easily fix. King would prefer to try another angle. He turns to the human resource frame for counsel.

Human Resource Frame: Issues and Options

"How ironic," King muses. "The original idea behind the school was to respond better to students. Break down the big, bureaucratic high school. Make the house a community, a family even, where people know each other and care about each other. But it's not going that way. Everyone's stuck at the bottom of Maslow's needs hierarchy: no one even feels safe. Until they do, they'll never focus on caring. The problem isn't personalities. Everyone's frustrated because no one is getting needs met. Not me, not Carver, not Dula. We're all so needy, we don't realize everyone else has the same problem."

King shifts from individual needs to interpersonal relationships. It's hard not to, with the Dula-Carver mess staring him in the face. Tense relationships everywhere. People talking only to people who agree with them. Why? How do I get a handle on it? He remembers reading, "Lurking in Model I is the core assumption that organizations are competitive, dangerous places where you have to look out for yourself or someone else will do you in" (Chapter Eight). "That's it," he thinks. "That's us. Too bad they don't give a prize for the most Model I school in America. We'd win hands down. Everything here is win-lose. Nothing is discussed openly, and if it is, people just attack each other. If anything goes wrong, we blame others and try to straighten them out. They get defensive, which proves we were right. But we never test our assumptions. We don't ask questions. We just harbor suspicions and wait for people to prove us right. Then we hit them over the head. We've got to find better ways to deal with one another.

"How do you get better people management?" King asks himself. "Successful organizations start with a clear human resource philosophy. We don't have one, but it might help. Invest in people? We've got good people. They're paid pretty well. They've got job security. We're probably OK there. Job enrichment? Jobs here are plenty challenging. Empowerment? That's a big problem. Everyone claims to be powerless, yet somehow everyone expects me to fix everything. Is there something we could do to get people's participation? Get them to own more of the problem? Convince them we've got to work together to make things better? The trouble is, if we go that way, people probably don't have the group skills they'd need. Staff development? With all the conflict, mediation skills might be a place to start." Conflict. Politics. Politics is normal in organizations. He's read it, and he knows it is true. "But we don't seem to have a midpoint between getting along and getting even."

Political Frame: Issues and Options

King reluctantly turns his attention to the political frame. It isn't easy for him. He knows it is relevant—he's never seen a school with more intense political strife. His old school is beginning to seem tame by comparison. He's tackled some things head on there. But Kennedy is a lot more volatile, with a history of explosions. Coercive force seems to be the power tactic of choice.

Things might get even more vicious if he tackled the conflict openly. He mulls over the basic elements of the political frame: enduring differences, scarce resources, conflict, power. "Bingo! We've got 'em all—in spades. We've got factions for and against the house concept. Housemasters want to run their houses and guard their turf. Department chairs want to run the faculty and expand their territory. One group wants to close the doors and bring in guards. Another wants to keep out the guards and throw open the doors. We've got race issues simmering under the surface. No Latino administrators. This Carver-Dula thing could blow up the school. Black male says he'll break white female's neck. A recipe for disaster. We need some damage control.

"Then we've got all those outside folks looking over our shoulder. Parents worry about safety. The school board doesn't trust us. The media are looking for a story. Accreditation is coming in the spring. Maybe there's some way to get people thinking about the enemies outside instead of inside. A common devil might pull people together—for a little while anyway.

"Scarce resources? They're getting scarcer. We lost 10 percent of our teachers—that got us into the flexible staffing mess. Housemasters and department chairs are fighting over turf. Bill Smith wants my job. It's a war zone. We need some kind of peace settlement. But who's going to take the diplomatic lead? We don't seem to have any neutral parties. Eleanor Debbs would respond to the call. People respect her. But she's not an administrator."

King's thoughts turn to the two faces of power. "Power can be used to do people in. That's what we're doing right now. But you can also use power to get things done. That's the constructive side of politics. Too bad no one here seems to have a clue about it. If I'm going to be a constructive politician, what can I do? First, I need an agenda. Without that, I'm dead in the water. Basically, I want everyone working in tandem to make the school better for kids. Most people could rally behind that. I also need a strategy. Networking—I need good relationships with key folks—like Smith, Carver, and Dula. The interviews were a good start. I learned a lot about who wants what. The Friday meeting was a mistake, a collision of special interests with no common ground. It's going to take some horse trading. We need a deal the housemasters and the department chairs can both buy into. And I need some allies—badly."

He smiles as he remembers all the times he's railed against analysis paralysis. But he feels he's getting somewhere. He turns to a clean sheet on his pad. "Let's lay this thing out," he thinks. Across the top he labels three columns: allies, fence-sitters, and opponents. At the top left, he writes "High power." At the bottom left, "Low power." Over the next half-hour, he creates a political map of Kennedy High School, arranging individuals and groups in terms of their interests and their power. When he finishes, he winces. Too many powerful opponents. Too few allies. A bunch of people waiting to choose sides. He begins to think about how to build coalitions and reshape the school's political map.

"No doubt about it," King thinks, "I have to get on top of the political mess. Otherwise they'll carry me out the same way they did Weis. But it's a little depressing. Where's the ray of hope?" He smiles. He's ready to think about symbols and culture. "Where's Dr. King when I need him?" He recalls the famous words from 1963: "For even though we face the difficulties of today and tomorrow, I still have a dream." What happened to Kennedy High's dream?

He decides to take a break, get some fresh air. Moonlit night. Crowded sidewalks. Young and old, poor and affluent, black, white, and Latino. Merchandise pours out of stores into sidewalk bins: clothes, toys, electronic gear, fruits, vegetables—you name it. King runs into some students from his old school. They're at Kennedy now. "We're tellin' our friends we got a *good* principal now," they say. He thanks them, hoping they're right.

Symbolic Frame: Issues and Options

Back to the kitchen and the yellow pad. Fortified by the walk and another cup of coffee, he reviews the school's history. "Interesting," he thinks. "That's one of the problems: the school's too new to have much history. What we have is mostly bad. We've got a hodgepodge of individual histories people brought from someplace else. Deep down, everyone is telling a different story. Maybe that's why Carver is so attached to his house and Dula to her English department. There's nothing schoolwide for people to bond to. Just little pockets of meaning."

He starts to think about symbols that might create common ground. Robert Kennedy, the school's namesake. He had vague images of Bobby Kennedy's speeches. Anything there? He remembers the man. What was he like? What did he stand for? What were the founders thinking when they chose his name for the school? What signals were they trying to send? Any unifying theme? Then it comes to him—words from Bobby Kennedy's eulogy for his brother. "Some people see things as they are, and say why? I dream things that never were, and say why not?"

"That's the kind of thinking we need at Kennedy High," King realizes. "We need to get beyond all the factions and divisions. We need a banner that we all can rally around. Celebrate Kennedy now? Can we have a ceremony in the midst of chaos? It could backfire—make things worse. But it seems the school never had any special occasions—even at the start. No rituals, no traditions. The only stories are bad ones. The high road might work. We've got to get back to the values that launched the school in the first place. Rekindle the spark. What if I pull some people together? Start from scratch—this time with more sensitivity to symbols and ceremony. We need some glue to weld this thing together."

Meaning. Faith. He rolls the words around in his mind. Haunting images. Ideas start to tumble out. "We're supposed to be pioneers, but somehow we got lost. A lighthouse where the bulb burned out. Not a beacon anymore. We're on the rocks ourselves. A dream became a nightmare. People's faith is pretty shaky. There's a schism —folks splitting into two different faiths. Like a holy war between the church of the one true house system and the temple of academic excellence. We need something to pull both sides together.

Why did people join up in the first place? How can we get them to sign up again—renew their vows?" He smiles at the religious overtones in his thoughts. His mother and father would be proud.

He catches himself. "We're not a church; we're a school, in a country that separates religion and state. But maybe the symbolic frame bridges the gap. Organizations as temples. A lot of it is about meaning. What's Kennedy High School really about? Who are we? What happened to our spirit? What's our soul, our values? That's what folks are fighting over! Deep down, we're split over two different versions of what we stand for. Department chairs promoting excellence. Housemasters pushing for caring. We need both. That was the original dream. Bring excellence and caring together. We'll never get either if we're always at war with one another."

He thinks about why he got into public education in the first place. It was his calling. Why? Growing up in a racist society was tough, but his father had it a lot tougher—he'd been a principal when it was something black men didn't do. King had always admired his dad's courage and discipline. More than anything, he remembered his father's passion about education. The man had been a real champion for kids—high standards, deep compassion. Growing up with this man as a role model, there had never been much question in King's mind. As far back as he could remember, he wanted to be a principal too. It was a way to give to the community and to help young people who really needed it. To give everyone a chance. In the midst of a firefight, it was easy to forget this. It felt good to remember.

Before going further, King senses that it is a good time for a review. Over another cup of coffee, he goes back over his notes. They strike him as stream of consciousness, with some good stuff and a little self-pity. He smiles as he remembers himself in graduate school, fighting against all that theory. "Don't think, do! Be a leader!" Now, here he is, thinking, reflecting, trying to pull things together. In a strange way, it feels natural.

He organizes his ideas into a chart (see Table 20.1). He's starting to feel better now. The picture is coming into focus. He feels that he has a better sense of what he's up against. It's reassuring to see that he has lots of options. There are lots of pitfalls, too, but also some real possibilities. He knows he can't do everything at once. He needs to set priorities. He needs a plan of action, an agenda

Table 20.1. Reframing Robert F. Kennedy High School.

Frame	What's Going On?	What Options Are Available?
Structural	Weak integration—goals, roles, responsibilities, linkages undefined; ill-defined matrix structure; weak authority; underbounded structure	Responsibility charting; task force to look at structure
Human resource	Basic needs not met (safety, etc.); win-lose interpersonal dynamics; ineffective conflict management; feelings of disempowerment	Improve safety, security; training in communication, conflict management; participation, teaming
Political	House-department conflict; doors and guards issue; Carver-Dula and racial tensions; outside constituents—parents, board, media, etc.	Arenas for negotiating; damage control; unite against external threats; network, build coalitions; negotiate
Symbolic	No shared symbols (history, ceremony, ritual); loss of faith—religious schism; lack of identity (What is RFK's soul?)	Hoist a banner (common symbol: RFK?); develop symbols, ceremony, stories; gifts

anchored in basic values. Where to begin? Soul? Values? He has to find a rallying point somewhere.

He had already embraced two values: excellence and caring. He thought about leadership as gift-giving. "I've mostly been waiting for others to initiate. What about me? What are my gifts? If I want excellence, the gift I have to offer is authorship. That's what people want. They don't want to be told what to do. They want to put their signature on this place. Make a contribution. They're fighting so hard because they care so much. That's what brought them to Kennedy in the first place. They wanted to be a part of something better. Create something special. They all want to do a good job. How can I help them do it without tripping over each other?

"What about caring? The leadership gift is love. No one's getting much of that around here." He smiles. A song fragment comes to mind: "Looking for love in all the wrong places." "I've been waiting for someone else to show caring and compassion," he realizes. "I've been holding back."

The thought leads him to pick up the phone. He calls Betsy Dula. She is out, but he leaves a message on the machine: "Betsy, Dave King. I've been thinking a lot about our conversation. One thing I want you to know is that I'm really glad you're part of the Kennedy High team. You bring a lot, and I sure hope I can count on your help. We can't do it without you. We need to finish what we started out to do. I care. I know you do, too. I'll see you Monday."

He senses he's on a roll. But it's one thing to leave a message on someone's machine and another to deliver it in person—particularly if you don't know how receptive the other person will be.

On his next call, to Chauncey Carver, he gets through immediately. "Chauncey? Dave King. Sorry to bother you at home, but Betsy Dula called me this morning. She's upset about what you said yesterday. Particularly the part about breaking her neck."

King listens patiently as Carver makes it clear that he was only defending himself against Dula's unprovoked and inappropriate public attack. "Chauncey, I hear you. . . . Yeah, I know you're mad. So is she." King listens patiently through another one-sided tirade. "Yes, Chauncey, I understand. But look, you're a key to making this school work. I know how much you care about your house and the school. The word on the street is clear—you're a terrific housemaster. You know it, too. I need your help, man. If this thing with Betsy blows up and goes public, what's it going to do to the school? . . . You're right, we don't need it. Think about it. Betsy's pushing hard for an apology."

He had feared that the word *apology* might set Carver off again, and it does. This is getting tough. He reminds himself why he made the call. He shifts back into listening mode. After several minutes of venting, Chauncey pauses. Softly, King tries to make his point. "Chauncey, I'm not telling you what to do. I'm just asking you to think about it. I don't know the answer. Two heads might be better than one. Let me know what you come up with. Can we meet first thing Monday? . . . Thanks for your time. Have a good weekend."

King puts down the phone. This is even harder than he expected. Things are still tense, but maybe he's made a start. Carver is a loose cannon with a very short fuse. But he's also smart, and he cares deeply about the school. Get him thinking, King figures, and he'll see the enormous risks in his comment to Dula. Push him too hard, and he'll fight like a cornered badger. Give him some space—he might just figure out something on his own. The gift of authorship. Would Chauncey bite? Or would the problem wind up back on the principal's doorstep—with prejudice?

After the conversation with Chauncey, King needs another breather. He goes back to his yellow pad, which has become something of a security blanket. More than that, it's helping him find his way to the balcony. It has given him a better view of the situation. He had made notes about excellence and caring. Was he making progress or just musing? It doesn't matter. He feels better, and the situation seems to be getting clearer.

King's thoughts move on to justice. "Do people feel the school is fair?" he wonders. "I'm not hearing a lot of complaints about injustice. But it wouldn't take much to set off another war. The Chauncey-Betsy thing is scary. A man physically threatening a woman could send a terrible message. There's too much male violence in the community already. Make it a black man and a white woman, and it's really heavy. The fact that both Chauncey and I are black men is both an asset and a liability: it made for a better chance of getting Chauncey's help—brothers united and all that. But it could be devastating if people think I'm siding with Chauncey against Betsy—sisters in defiance. It's like being on a tightrope—one false step and I'll be history. So would the school—a dismal prospect. All the more reason to encourage Chauncey and Betsy to work this out. If I could get the two together, what a symbol of unity that would be! Maybe just what we need. A positive step at least."

Finally, King thinks about the ethic of faith and the gift of significance. Symbols again, revisited in a deeper way. "How had Kennedy High gone from high hopes to no hope in two years? How do we rekindle the original faith? How do we recapture the dream that launched the school? Well," he tells himself, "I've been around this track before. My last school was a snakepit when I got there. Not as bad as Kennedy, but pretty awful. We turned that one around, and I learned some things in the process—including be patient, but hang tough. It's gonna be hard. But fun, too. And it *will* happen.

That's why I took this job in the first place. So what am I moaning about? I knew what I was getting into. It's just that knowing it in my head is one thing. Feeling it in my gut is another."

By Sunday night, King has twenty-five pages of notes. They help—but not as much as his inner conversation. Going to the balcony, getting a fresh look, reflecting instead of just fretting. The inner dialogue has led to new conversations with others, and on a different level than before. He's made a lot of phone calls—talked to almost every administrator in the building. A lot of them have been surprised—a principal who calls on the weekend is something new.

He is making headway. He needs to hear from Betsy but has some volunteers for a task force on structural issues. He's done some relationship building. A second call to Chauncey to commend him for devotion to the mission. A deeper connection. Crediting Frank Czepak for excellent counsel, even if the principal wasn't smart enough to pay attention—a frank admission.

Some has been pure politics. Negotiating a deal with Bill Smith: "I *could* help you Bill, next time the district needs a principal, but only if you help me. You scratch my back, I'll scratch yours." Gently persuading Burt Perkins that his calling was scheduling, not running a house. A call to Dave Crimmins to tell him Perkins had decided to make a change. An encouraging conversation with Luz Hernandez, a stalwart in his previous school. She is at least willing to think about coming to Kennedy High as a housemaster. Planting seeds with everyone about ways to resolve the door problem.

Above all, King has worked on creating symbolic glue—renewing the hopes and dreams people felt at the time the school was founded. A cohesive group pulling together for a school everyone can feel proud of. His to-do list is ambitious. But at least he has some options. A month and a half until the first day of school and a lot to accomplish. He isn't sure what the future will bring, but he feels just a little more hope in the air. The knots in his stomach are pretty much gone. So are the images of being carried off like his predecessor—a broken man with a shattered career.

The phone rings. It's Betsy Dula. She's been away for the weekend but wants to thank King for his message. It was important to know he cared, she told him. "By the way," she says, "Chauncey Carver called me. Said he felt bad about Friday. Told me he'd lost his temper and said some things he didn't really mean. He invited me to breakfast tomorrow."

"Are you going?" King asks, as nonchalantly as possible. He holds his breath, thinking, "If she declines, we could be back to square one."

"Yes," she says. "Even a phone call is a big step for Chauncey. He's a proud and stubborn man. But we're both professionals. It's worth a try."

A sigh of relief. "One more question," King says. "When you came to the school, you knew it wouldn't be easy. Why did you sign up for this trip in the first place?"

She is silent for a long time. He can almost hear her thinking.

"I love English and I love kids," she says. "And I want kids to love English."

"And now?" he asks.

"Can't we get past all the bickering and fighting? That's not why we launched this noble experiment. Let's get back to why we're here. Work together to make this a good school for our kids. They really need us."

"How about a great school we can all be proud of?" he asks.

"Sounds even better," she says. Maybe she didn't grasp what he meant. But they were beginning to read from the same page. It would take time, but they could work it out.

At the end of a very busy weekend, David King is still a long way from solving all the problems of Kennedy High. "But," he tells himself, "I made it through the valley of confusion and I'm feeling more like my old self. The picture of what I'm up against is a lot clearer. I'm seeing a lot more possibilities than I was seeing on Friday. In fact, I've got some exciting things to try. Some may work; some may not. But deep down, I think I know what's going on. And I know which way is west. We're now moving roughly in that direction."

He can't wait for Monday morning.

The Reframing Process

A different David King would likely have raised different questions and seen different choices. Reframing, like management and leadership, is much more art than science. Every artist brings a different optic and produces unique works. King's reframing process necessarily built on a lifetime of skill, knowledge, intuition, and wisdom. Reframing guided him in accessing what he already knew. It helped him feel less confused and overwhelmed by the uncertainty and disorder around him. A cluttered jumble of impressions and experiences gradually evolved into a manageable picture. His reflections helped him see that he was far from helpless—he had a rich array of actions that he might take. He also rediscovered a very old truth: reflection is a spiritual discipline, much like meditation or prayer. A path to faith and heart. He knew the road ahead was still very long and difficult. There was no guarantee of success. But he felt far more confident and more energized than when he started. He was starting to dream things that never were and saying, "Why not?"

Note

1. Adapted from Case No. 9–474–183, *Robert F. Kennedy High School* © 1974 by the President and Fellows of Harvard College. Used by permission of the Harvard Business School. The case was prepared by John J. Gabarro as a basis for class discussion rather than to illustrate the effective or ineffective handling of an administrative situation.

Chapter Twenty-One

Epilogue

Artistry, Choice, and Leadership

We hope this book will inspire both inventive management and wise leadership. Both managers and leaders require high levels of personal artistry to respond to challenge, ambiguity, and paradox. They need a sense of choice and personal freedom that lets them find new patterns and possibilities in everyday thoughts and deeds. They need the kind of versatility in thinking that fosters flexibility in action. They need the capacity to act inconsistently when consistency fails, diplomatically when emotions are raw, nonrationally when reason makes no sense, politically when confronted by parochial self-interests, and playfully when fixation on task and purpose seems counterproductive.

They face a leadership paradox: how to maintain integrity and mission without making their organizations rigid and intractable. Leading means walking the tightrope between rigidity and spinelessness. Rigidity saps energy, stifles initiative, misdirects resources, and leads ultimately to catastrophes—seen equally in the decline of great corporations and chronic ethnic violence. In a world of "permanent white water" (Vaill, 1989) where nothing is solid and everything is changing, it is tempting to follow familiar paths and to use the same old solutions, regardless of how much the problems have changed. Doing what we have always done is comforting. It lets us feel that our world is orderly and that we are in control. But when the old ways fail, as they eventually must, managers often make the mistake of flipping to the opposite extreme: they begin to agree to anything and everything and try to appease everyone. The result is aimlessness, anarchy, and systems so disorganized that concerted, purposeful action becomes impossible. This is the same lesson that Collins and Porras (1994) drew. "Visionary" companies combine the paradoxical capacity to stimulate change and pursue high-risk new ventures while maintaining their commitment to core ideology and values.

The best managers and leaders create and sustain a tension-filled balance between the two extremes. They combine core values with elastic strategies. They get things done without being done in. They know what they stand for and what they want, and they communicate their vision with clarity and power. But they also know they must understand and respond to the complex array of forces that push and pull organizations in so many conflicting directions. They think creatively about how to make things happen. They develop strategies with enough give to respond to the twists, turns, and potholes that they are sure to encounter on the way to the future.

There is a common but misguided notion that a leader who takes risks and moves into uncharted terrain can somehow see all, know all, and control everything. Keller (1990b) comes closer to the reality: "The greatest leaders are often, in reality, skillful followers. They do not control the flow of history, but by having the good sense not to stand in its way, they seem to. So it is with Mikhail S. Gorbachev. Mr. Gorbachev's achievement was having the vision to see the inevitable, and adopting it as his program rather than applying the repressive apparatus at his command to suppress it" (p. 1).

Gorbachev's extraordinary rise to world leadership and his stunningly rapid fall from grace illustrate many of the complexities that leaders face in the late twentieth century. Leaders need the confidence to confront tangled problems and deep divisions. They must anticipate that they will be buffeted by conflict and that they may unleash forces they cannot fully control. They need the courage to follow uncharted paths, knowing they will often be taken by surprise, events will sometimes outrun them, and the ultimate destination is only dimly foreseeable.

Commitment to Core Beliefs

Poetry and philosophy are rarely included in managerial training, and few business schools have asked themselves whether spiritual development is central to their mission. It is no wonder that managers are often viewed as chameleons who can adapt to any setting or as dispassionate maneuverers guided only by expediency. Analysis and agility are necessary, but they are not enough. Organizations need leaders who can provide a persuasive and durable sense of purpose and direction, rooted deeply in human values and the human spirit. "We have a revolution to make, and this revolution is not political, but spiritual" (Guéhenno, 1993, p. 167).

Leaders need to be deeply reflective, actively thoughtful, and dramatically explicit about their core values and beliefs. Many of the world's legendary corporate heroes articulated their philosophies and values in such a striking way that they still live on in the behavior and operations of their companies. In government, Franklin Delano Roosevelt, Charles de Gaulle, Margaret Thatcher, and Lee Kuan Yew were all as controversial as they were durable, but each espoused a stable and coherent set of values and beliefs. These in turn served as a means of formulating their visions for the direction their respective nations should take.

Multiframe Thinking

Commitment to both durable values and elastic strategies involves a paradox. Franklin Roosevelt's image as lion and fox and Mao's reputation as tiger and monkey were not so much contradictions as signs that they could embrace paradox. They intuitively recognized the multiple dimensions of social organizations and moved flexibly to implement their visions. The use of multiple frames permits leaders to see and understand more—*if* they are able to employ the different logics that accompany different frames.

Leaders fail when they take too narrow a view of the context in which they are working. Unless they can think flexibly about organizations and see them from multiple angles, they will be unable to deal with the full range of issues that they will inevitably encounter. Jimmy Carter's preoccupation with details and rationality made it hard for him to marshal support for his programs or to capture the hearts of most Americans. Even FDR's multifaceted approach to the presidency—he was a superb observer of human needs, a charming persuader, a solid administrator, a political manipulator, and a master of ritual and ceremony—miscarried when he underestimated the public reaction to his plan to enlarge the Supreme Court.

Multiframe thinking is challenging and often counterintuitive. To see the same organization *simultaneously* as machine, family, jungle, and theater requires the capacity to think in different ways at the same time about the same thing. Like surfers, leaders must always ride the waves of change. If they get too far ahead, they will be crushed. If they fall behind, they will become irrelevant. Success requires artistry, skill, and the ability to see organizations as organic forms in which needs, roles, power, and symbols must be integrated to provide direction and shape behavior. The power to reframe is vital for modern leaders. The ability to see new possibilities and to create new opportunities enables leaders to discover alternatives when options seem severely constrained and to find hope amid fear and despair. Choice is at the heart of freedom, and freedom is essential to achieving the twin goals of commitment and flexibility.

Organizations everywhere are struggling to cope with a shrinking planet and a global economy. The accelerating pace of change continues to produce grave political, economic, and social discontinuities. A world ever more dependent on organizations now finds that their form and function often evolve too slowly to meet pressing social demands. Without wise leaders and artistic managers to help close the gap, we will continue to see misdirected resources, massive ineffectiveness, and unnecessary human pain and suffering. All these afflictions are already with us, and there is no guarantee that they will not get worse.

We see prodigious challenges for organizations of the future and for those who will guide them, yet we remain optimistic. We want this volume to help lay the groundwork for a new generation of managers and leaders who recognize the importance of poetry and philosophy, as well as analysis and technique, and who embrace the fundamental values of human life and the human spirit. Such leaders and managers will be playful theorists who can see organizations through a complex prism. They will be negotiators able to design elastic strategies that simultaneously shape events and adapt to changing circumstances. They will understand the importance of knowing and caring for themselves and the people with whom they work. They will be architects, catalysts, advocates, and prophets who lead with soul.

References

"The ABB of Management." *Economist,* Jan. 6, 1996, p. 56.

Adams, S. *The Dilbert Principle.* New York: HarperBusiness, 1996.

Adler, P. S., and Borys, B. "Two Types of Bureaucracy: Enabling and Coercive." *Administrative Science Quarterly,* 1996, *41,* 61–89.

Alderfer, C. P. *Existence, Relatedness, and Growth.* New York: Free Press, 1972.

Alderfer, C. P. "Consulting to Underbounded Systems." In C. P. Alderfer and C. Cooper (eds.), *Advances in Experiential Social Processes,* Vol. 2. New York: Wiley, 1979.

Allison, G. *Essence of Decision: Explaining the Cuban Missile Crisis.* New York: Little, Brown, 1971.

Alterman, E. "Wrong on the Wall, and Most Else." *New York Times,* Nov. 12, 1989, p. E-23.

Argyris, C. *Personality and Organization.* New York: HarperCollins, 1957.

Argyris, C. *Interpersonal Competence and Organizational Effectiveness.* Homewood, Ill.: Irwin, 1962.

Argyris, C. *Integrating the Individual and the Organization.* New York: Wiley, 1964.

Argyris, C., and Schön, D. A. *Theory in Practice: Increasing Professional Effectiveness.* San Francisco: Jossey-Bass, 1974.

Argyris, C., and Schön, D. A. *Organizational Learning: A Theory of Action Perspective.* Reading, Mass.: Addison-Wesley, 1978.

Argyris, C., and Schön, D. A. *Organizational Learning II: Theory, Method, and Practice.* Reading, Mass.: Addison-Wesley, 1996.

Associated Press. "McDonald's Opens Up in India." *Kansas City Star,* Oct. 14, 1996, p. A-4.

Aubrey, B., and Tilliette, B. *Savoir faire savoir: L'apprentissage de l'action en entreprise* [Knowing and teaching: Action learning in the enterprise]. Paris: InterÉditions, 1990.

Axelrod, R. "More Effective Choice in the Prisoner's Dilemma." *Journal of Conflict Resolution,* 1980, *24,* 379–403.

Baldridge, J. V. *Power and Conflict in the University.* New York: Wiley, 1971.

Baldridge, J. V., and Deal, T. E. (eds.). *Managing Change in Educational Organizations.* Berkeley, Calif.: McCutchan, 1975.

Bales, F. *Personality and Interpersonal Behavior.* Austin, Tex.: Holt, Rinehart and Winston, 1970.

Barber, B. R. *Jihad vs. McWorld: How the Planet Is Both Falling Apart and Coming Together—and What This Means for Democracy.* New York: Times Books, 1995.

Bardach, E. *The Implementation Game: What Happens After a Bill Becomes Law.* Cambridge, Mass.: MIT Press, 1977.

Barley, S. R. "The Alignment of Technology and Structure Through Roles and Networks." *Administrative Science Quarterly,* 1990, *35,* 61–103.

Barnes, L. B., and Kriger, M. P. "The Hidden Side of Organizational Leadership." *Sloan Management Review,* Fall 1986, pp. 15–25.

Bartlett, C. A., and Elderkin, K. W. "General Electric: Reg Jones and Jack Welch." Case No. 9–391–144. Boston: Harvard Business School Case Services, 1991.

Bass, B. M. *Stogdill's Handbook of Leadership: A Survey of Theory and Research.* New York: Free Press, 1981.

Bass, B. M. *Leadership and Performance Beyond Expectations.* New York: Free Press, 1985.

Bass, B. M. *Bass & Stogdill's Handbook of Leadership: Theory, Research, and Managerial Application.* (3rd ed.) New York: Free Press, 1990.

Bateson, G. *Steps to an Ecology of Mind.* New York: Ballantine, 1972.

Beam, A. "Michael Porter vs. McGraw-Hill." *Boston Globe,* Sept. 20, 1989, p. 40.

Bell, T. E., and Esch, K. "The Fatal Flaw in Flight 51-L." *IEEE Spectrum,* Feb. 1987, pp. 36–51.

Bellow, G., and Moulton, B. *The Lawyering Process: Cases and Materials.* Mineola, N.Y.: Foundation Press, 1978.

Bennis, W. G. *Why Leaders Can't Lead: The Unconscious Conspiracy Continues.* San Francisco: Jossey-Bass, 1989.

Bennis, W. G., and Nanus, B. *Leaders: Strategies for Taking Charge.* New York: HarperCollins, 1985.

Bensimon, E. M. "The Meaning of 'Good Presidential Leadership': A Frame Analysis." *Review of Higher Education,* 1989, *12,* 107–123.

Bensimon, E. M. "Viewing the Presidency: Perceptual Congruence Between Presidents and Leaders on Their Campuses." *Leadership Quarterly,* 1990, *1,* 71–90.

Bergquist, W. H. *The Four Cultures of the Academy: Insights and Strategies for Improving Leadership in Collegiate Organizations.* San Francisco: Jossey-Bass, 1992.

Bernstein, A. "Why ESOP Deals Have Slowed to a Crawl." *Business Week,* Mar. 18, 1996, pp. 101–102.

Bettelheim, B. *The Uses of Enchantment.* New York: Vintage Books, 1977.

Bion, W. R. *Experiences in Groups.* London: Tavistock, 1961.

Birnbaum, R. *How Colleges Work: The Cybernetics of Academic Organization and Leadership.* San Francisco: Jossey-Bass, 1988.

Birnbaum, R. *How Academic Leadership Works: Understanding Success and Failure in the College Presidency.* San Francisco: Jossey-Bass, 1992.

Blake, R., and Mouton, J. S. *Building a Dynamic Corporation Through Grid Organizational Development.* Reading, Mass.: Addison-Wesley, 1969.

Blake, R., and Mouton, J. S. "A Comparative Analysis of Situationalism and 9,9 Management by Principle." *Organizational Dynamics,* Spring 1982, pp. 20–42.

Blake, R., and Mouton, J. S. *Managerial Grid III.* Houston, Tex.: Gulf, 1985.

Blanchard, K., and Johnson, S. *The One-Minute Manager.* New York: Morrow, 1982.

Blank, W., Weitzel, J. R., and Green, S. G. "A Test of the Situational Leadership Theory." *Personnel Psychology,* 1990, *43,* 579–597.

Blau, P. M., and Scott, W. R. *Formal Organizations: A Comparative Approach.* Novato, Calif.: Chandler & Sharp, 1962.

Block, P. *The Empowered Manager: Positive Political Skills at Work.* San Francisco: Jossey-Bass, 1987.

Blum, A. "Collective Bargaining: Ritual or Reality." *Harvard Business Review,* Nov.–Dec. 1961, pp. 63–69.

Blumberg, P. *Industrial Democracy: The Sociology of Participation.* New York: Schocken Books, 1968.

Blumer, H. *Symbolic Interaction: Perspective and Method.* Upper Saddle River, N.J.: Prentice Hall, 1969.

Bok, S. *Lying: Moral Choice in Public and Private Life.* New York: Vintage Books, 1978.

Bolman, L. "The Client as Theorist." In J. Adams (ed.), *New Technologies in Organization Development.* La Jolla, Calif.: University Associates, 1975.

Bolman, L. G., and Deal, T. E. *Modern Approaches to Understanding and Managing Organizations.* San Francisco: Jossey-Bass, 1984.

Bolman, L. G., and Deal, T. E. "Leadership and Management Effectiveness: A Multi-Frame, Multi-Sector Analysis." *Human Resource Management,* 1991, *30,* 509–534.

Bolman, L. G., and Deal, T. E. "Leading and Managing: Effects of Context, Culture, and Gender." *Education Administration Quarterly,* 1992a, *28,* 314–329.

Bolman, L. G., and Deal, T. E. "Reframing Leadership: The Effects of Leaders' Images of Leadership." In K. E. Clark, M. B. Clark, and D. Campbell (eds.), *Impact of Leadership.* Greensboro, N.C.: Center for Creative Leadership, 1992b.

Bolman, L. G., and Deal, T. E. *Leading with Soul: An Uncommon Journey of Spirit.* San Francisco: Jossey-Bass, 1995.

Bower, J. L. *Managing the Response Allocation Process.* Boston: Division of Research, Harvard Business School, 1970a.

Bower, J. L. "Planning Within the Firm." *American Economic Review,* 1970b, *19,* 186–194.

Bower, M. *The Will to Manage: Corporate Success Through Programmed Management.* New York: McGraw-Hill, 1966.

Bradford, D. L., and Cohen, A. R. *Managing for Excellence.* New York: Wiley, 1984.

Briand, M. "People, Lead Thyself." *Kettering Review,* Summer 1993, pp. 38–46.

Brief, A. P., and Downey, H. K. "Cognitive and Organizational Structure: A Conceptual Analysis of Implicit Organizing Theories." *Human Relations,* 1983, *36*(12), 1065–1090.

Brown, L. D. *Managing Conflict at Organizational Interfaces.* Reading, Mass.: Addison-Wesley, 1983.

Brown, L. D. "Power Outside Organizational Paradigms: Lessons from Community Partnerships." In S. Srivastva and Associates, *The Functioning of Executive Power: How Executives Influence People and Organizations.* San Francisco: Jossey-Bass, 1986.

Bunker, B. B., and Alban, B. T. *Large Group Interventions: Engaging the Whole System for Rapid Change.* San Francisco: Jossey-Bass, 1996.

Burns, J. M. *Leadership.* New York: HarperCollins, 1978.

Burrell, G., and Hearn, J. "The Sexuality of Organization." In J. Hearn, D. L. Sheppard, P. Tancred-Sheriff, and G. Burrell (eds.), *The Sexuality of Organization.* London: Sage, 1989.

Burrough, B., and Helyar, J. *Barbarians at the Gate: The Fall of RJR Nabisco.* New York: HarperCollins, 1990.

Byrne, J. A. "The Shredder: Did CEO Dunlap Save Scott Paper—or Just Pretty It Up?" *Business Week,* Jan. 15, 1996, pp. 56–61.

Campbell, D. "If I'm in Charge, Why Is Everyone Laughing?" Paper presented at the Center for Creative Leadership, Greensboro, N.C., 1983.

Campbell, J. *The Power of Myth.* New York: Doubleday, 1988.

Campbell, J. P., and Dunnette, M. D. "Effectiveness of T-Group Experiences in Managerial Training and Development." *Psychological Bulletin,* 1968, *70,* 73–104.

Carlson, S. *Executive Behavior.* Stockholm: Strombergs, 1951.

Carlzon, J. *Moments of Truth.* New York: Ballinger, 1987.

Chaize, J. *La porte du changement s'ouvre de l'interieur: Les trois mutations de l'entreprise* [The door to change opens from the inside: The three transformations of the corporation]. Paris: Calmann-Lévy, 1992.

Chandler, A. D., Jr. *Strategy and Market Structure.* Cambridge, Mass.: MIT Press, 1962.

Chandler, A. D., Jr. *The Visible Hand: The Managerial Revolution in American Business.* Cambridge, Mass.: Harvard University Press, 1977.

Chandler, S. "United We Own." *Business Week,* Mar. 18, 1996, pp. 96–100.

Clark, B. R. "The Organizational Saga in Higher Education." In J. V. Baldridge and T. E. Deal (eds.), *Managing Change in Educational Organizations.* Berkeley, Calif.: McCutchan, 1975.

Cleveland, H. *The Knowledge Executive: Leadership in an Information Society.* New York: Dutton, 1985.

Clifford, D. K., and Cavanagh, R. E. *The Winning Performance.* New York: Bantam Books, 1985.

Cohen, M., and March, J. G. *Leadership and Ambiguity.* New York: McGraw-Hill, 1974.

Cohen, P. S. "Theories of Myth." *Man,* 1969, *4,* 337–353.

Collins, B. E., and Guetzkow, H. *A Social Psychology of Group Processes for Decision Making.* New York: Wiley, 1964.

Collins, J. C., and Porras, J. I. *Built to Last: Successful Habits of Visionary Companies.* New York: HarperBusiness, 1994.

Collinson, D. L., and Collinson, M. "Sexuality in the Workplace: The Domination of Men's Sexuality." In J. Hearn, D. L. Sheppard, P. Tancred-Sheriff, and G. Burrell (eds.), *The Sexuality of Organization.* London: Sage, 1989.

Conger, J. A. *The Charismatic Leader: Behind the Mystique of Exceptional Leadership.* San Francisco: Jossey-Bass, 1989.

Corwin, R. "Organizations as Loosely Coupled Systems: Evolution of a Perspective." Paper presented at the Conference on Schools as Loosely Coupled Organizations, Stanford University, Nov. 1976.

Cox, H. *The Feast of Fools.* Cambridge, Mass.: Harvard University Press, 1969.

Cox, T., Jr. *Cultural Diversity in Organizations: Theory, Research, and Practice.* San Francisco: Berrett-Koehler, 1994.

Cronshaw, S. F. "Effects of Categorization, Attribution, and Encoding Processes on Leadership Perspectives." *Journal of Applied Psychology,* 1987, *72*(1), 91–106.

Crosby, P. *Let's Talk Quality.* New York: McGraw-Hill, 1989.

Crozier, M., and Friedberg, E. *L'acteur et le système* [The actor and the system]. Paris: Points/Politique Seuil, 1977.

Cusumano, M. A., and Selby, R. W. *Microsoft Secrets: How the World's Most Powerful Software Company Creates Technology, Shapes Markets, and Manages People.* New York: Free Press, 1995.

Cyert, R. M., and March, J. G. *A Behavioral Theory of the Firm.* Upper Saddle River, N.J.: Prentice Hall, 1963.

Dalton, M. *Men Who Manage.* New York: Wiley, 1959.

Davis, M., and others. "The Structure of Educational Systems." Paper presented at the Conference on Schools as Loosely Coupled Organizations, Stanford University, Nov. 1976.

Deal, T. E., and Jenkins, W. A. *Managing the Hidden Organization: Strategies for Empowering Your Behind-the-Scenes Employees.* New York: Warner Books, 1994.

Deal, T. E., and Kennedy, A. A. *Corporate Cultures.* Reading, Mass.: Addison-Wesley, 1982.

Deal, T. E., and Nutt, S. C. *Promoting, Guiding, and Surviving Change in School Districts.* Cambridge, Mass.: Abt Associates, 1980.

De Geus, A. "Companies: What Are They?" *RSA Journal,* June 1995, pp. 26–35.

Delbanco, A. "Scholarships for the Rich." *New York Times Magazine,* Sept. 1, 1996, pp. 36–39.

Deming, W. E. *Out of the Crisis.* Cambridge, Mass.: MIT Center for Advanced Engineering Study, 1986.

DePree, M. *Leadership Is an Art.* New York: Dell, 1989.

DePree, M. *Leadership Jazz.* New York: Dell, 1992.

Dittmer, L. "Political Culture and Political Symbolism: Toward a Theoretical Synthesis." *World Politics,* 1977, *29,* 552–583.

Doktor, J. "The Early Implementation of the Family Resource and Youth Services Centers of Kentucky: Multi-Frame Perspective." Unpublished doctoral dissertation, Vanderbilt University, 1993.

Dornbusch, S., and Scott, W. R. *Evaluation and the Exercise of Authority.* San Francisco: Jossey-Bass, 1975.

Downer, Lesley. *The Brothers: The Hidden World of Japan's Richest Family.* New York: Random House, 1994.

Drucker, P. F. "Peter Drucker's 1990s: The Futures That Have Already Happened." *Economist,* Oct. 21, 1989, pp. 19–20, 24.

Drucker, P. F. *Managing the Future: The 1990s and Beyond.* New York: Plume, 1993.

Dunford, R. W. *Organizational Behavior: An Organizational Analysis Perspective.* Sydney: Addison-Wesley, 1992.

Dunford, R. W., and Palmer, I. C. "Claims About Frames: Practitioners' Assessment of the Utility of Reframing." *Journal of Management Education,* 1995, *19,* 96–105.

Dunlop, J. T. *Industrial Relations Systems.* Carbondale, Ill.: Southern Illinois University Press, 1958.

Dwyer, P., Engardio, P., Schiller, Z., and Reed, S. "Tearing Up Today's Organization Chart." *Business Week,* 1994 (21st Century Capitalism Special Issue), pp. 80–90.

Edelfson, C., Johnson, R., and Stromquist, N. *Participatory Planning in a School District.* Washington, D.C.: National Institute of Education, 1977.

Edelman, M. J. *Politics as Symbolic Interaction: Mass Arousal and Quiescence.* Orlando, Fla.: Academic Press, 1971.

Edelman, M. J. *The Symbolic Uses of Politics.* Madison: University of Wisconsin Press, 1977.

Elden, M. "Client as Consultant: Work Reform Through Participative Research." *National Productivity Review,* Spring 1983, pp. 136–147.

Elden, M. "Sociotechnical Systems Ideas as Public Policy in Norway: Empowering Participation Through Worker-Managed Change." *Journal of Applied Behavioral Science,* 1986, *22,* 239–255.

Elmore, R. F. "Organizational Models of Social Program Implementation." *Public Policy,* 1978, *26,* 185–228.

Enderud, H. G. "The Perception of Power." In J. G. March and J. Olsen (eds.), *Ambiguity and Choice in Organizations.* Bergen, Norway: Universitetsforlaget, 1976.

Engardio, P., and DeGeorge, G. "Importing Enthusiasm." *Business Week,* 1994 (21st Century Capitalism Special Issue), pp. 122–123.

Farkas, C. M., and De Backer, P. *Maximum Leadership: The World's Leading CEOs Share Their Five Strategies for Success.* New York: Henry Holt, 1996.

Fayol, H. *General and Industrial Management.* (C. Stours, trans.) London: Pitman, 1949. (Originally published 1919.)

Fiedler, F. E. *A Theory of Leadership Effectiveness.* New York: McGraw-Hill, 1967.

Fiedler, F. E., and Chemers, M. *Leadership and Effective Management.* Glenview, Ill.: Scott, Foresman, 1974.

Fiedler, K. "Casual Schemata: Review and Criticism of Research on a Popular Construct." *Journal of Personality and Social Psychology,* 1982, *42,* 1001–1013.

Fine, G. A. "Justifying Work: Occupational Rhetorics as Resources in Restaurant Kitchens." *Administrative Science Quarterly,* 1996, *41,* 90–115.

"Fire and Forget." *Economist,* Apr. 20, 1996, pp. 51–52.

Firestone, W. A. "Butte–Angels Camp: Conflict and Transformation." In R. Herriot and N. Gross (eds.), *The Dynamics of Planned Educational Change.* Berkeley, Calif.: McCutchan, 1977.

Fisher, R., and Ury, W. *Getting to Yes.* Boston: Houghton Mifflin, 1981.

Fiske, S. T., and Dyer, L. M. "Structure and Development of Social Schemata: Evidence from Positive and Negative Transfer Effects." *Journal of Personality and Social Psychology,* 1985, *48*(4), 839–852.

Fleishman, E. A., and Harris, E. F. "Patterns of Leadership Behavior Related to Employee Grievances and Turnover." *Personnel Psychology,* 1962, *15,* 43–56.

Floden, R. E., and Weiner, S. S. "Rationality to Ritual." *Policy Sciences,* 1978, *9,* 9–18.

Foucault, M. *Surveiller et punir* [Supervise and punish]. Paris: NRF-Gallimard, 1975.

Frangos, S. *Team Zebra.* New York: Wiley, 1996.

French, J.R.P., and Raven, B. H. "The Bases of Social Power." In D. Cartwright (ed.), *Studies in Social Power.* Ann Arbor, Mich.: Institute for Social Research, 1959.

Frensch, P. A., and Sternberg, R. J. "Skill-Related Differences in Chess Playing." In R. J. Sternberg and P. A. Frensch (eds.), *Complex Problem Solving.* Hillsdale, N.J.: Lawrence Erlbaum Associates, 1991.

Frost, P. J. *Organizational Culture.* Thousand Oaks, Calif.: Sage, 1985.

Frost, P. J. "Power, Politics, and Influence." In L. W. Porter and others (eds.), *The Handbook of Organizational Communication.* Thousand Oaks, Calif.: Sage, 1986.

Fulghum, R. *From Beginning to End: The Rituals of Our Lives.* New York: Villard Books, 1995.

Fullan, M., Miles, M., and Taylor, G. *Organization Development in Schools: The State of the Art.* Washington, D.C.: National Institute of Education, 1981.

Galbraith, J. R. *Designing Complex Organizations.* Reading, Mass.: Addison-Wesley, 1973.

Galbraith, J. R. *Organization Design.* Reading, Mass.: Addison-Wesley, 1977.

Galbraith, J. R. *Designing Organizations: An Executive Briefing on Strategy, Structure, and Process.* San Francisco: Jossey-Bass, 1993.

Gallos, J. V., Ramsey, V. J., and Associates. *Teaching Diversity: Listening to the Soul, Speaking from the Heart.* San Francisco: Jossey-Bass, 1997.

Gamson, W. A. *Power and Discontent.* Florence, Ky.: Dorsey Press, 1968.

Gardner, J. W. *Handbook of Strategic Planning.* New York: Wiley, 1986.

Gardner, J. W. *The Moral Aspects of Leadership.* Washington, D.C: Independent Sector, 1987.

Gardner, J. W. *On Leadership.* New York: Free Press, 1989.

Garland, H. "Throwing Good Money After Bad: The Effect of Sunk Costs on the Decision to Escalate." *Journal of Applied Psychology,* 1990, *75,* 728–731.

Gaventa, J. *Power and Powerlessness: Quiescence and Rebellion in an Appalachian Valley.* Urbana: University of Illinois Press, 1980.

Gegerenzer, G., Hoffrage, U., and Kleinbölting, H. "Probabilistic Mental Models: A Brunswikian Theory of Confidence." *Psychological Review,* 1991, *98,* 506–528.

Gertz, D., and Baptista, J.P.A. *Grow to Be Great: Breaking the Downsizing Cycle.* New York: Free Press, 1995.

Ghoshal, S., and Bartlett, C. A. "The Multinational Corporation as an

Interorganizational Network." *Academy of Management Review,* 1990, *15,* 603–625.

Gibb, J. R. "A Research Perspective on the Laboratory Method." In K. D. Benne, L. P. Bradford, J. R. Gibb, and R. O. Lippitt (eds.), *The Laboratory Method of Changing and Learning.* Palo Alto, Calif.: Science and Behavior Books, 1975.

Goffman, E. *Frame Analysis.* Cambridge, Mass.: Harvard University Press, 1974.

Goodman, D. "Doctor Fights Order to Quit Maine Island." *Boston Globe,* Oct. 15, 1983, pp. 1, 8.

Gordon, M. R. "Ex-Soviet Pilot Still Insists KAL 007 Was Spying." *New York Times,* December 9, 1996, p. A6.

Graeff, C. L. "The Situational Leadership Theory: A Critical View." *Academy of Management Review,* Apr. 1983, pp. 321–338.

Greenleaf, R. K. "The Servant as Leader." Newton Center, Mass.: Robert K. Greenleaf Center, 1973.

Gregory, K. L. "Native View Paradigms: Multiple Cultures and Cultural Conflict in Organizations." *Administrative Science Quarterly,* 1983, *28,* 359–376.

Greiner, L. E. "Evolution and Revolution as Organizations Grow." *Harvard Business Review,* July–Aug. 1972, pp. 37–46.

Greising, D. "Quality: How to Make It Pay." *Business Week,* Aug. 8, 1994, pp. 54–59.

Griffin, E. *The Reflective Executive: A Spirituality of Business and Enterprise.* New York: Crossroad, 1993.

Guéhenno, J.-M. *La fin de la démocratie* [The end of democracy]. Paris: Flammarion, 1993.

Gulick, L., and Urwick, L. (eds.). *Papers on the Science of Administration.* New York: Columbia University Press, 1937.

Hackman, J. R. (ed.). *Groups That Work (and Those That Don't): Creating Conditions for Effective Teamwork.* San Francisco: Jossey-Bass, 1989.

Hackman, J. R., and Oldham, G. R. *Work Redesign.* Reading, Mass.: Addison-Wesley, 1980.

Hackman, J. R., Oldham, G. R., Janson, R., and Purdy, K. "A New Strategy for Job Enrichment." In L. E. Boone and D. D. Bowen (eds.), *The Great Writings in Management and Organizational Behavior.* New York: Random House, 1987.

Hackman, J. R., and Wageman, R. "Total Quality Management: Empirical, Conceptual, and Practical Issues." *Administrative Science Quarterly,* 1995, *40,* 309–342.

Hakim, C. *We Are All Self-Employed.* San Francisco: Berrett-Koehler, 1994.

Hall, R. H. "The Concept of Bureaucracy: An Empirical Assessment." *American Journal of Sociology,* 1963, *49,* 32–40.

Hall, R. H. *Organizations: Structures, Processes, and Outcomes.* (4th ed.) Englewood Cliffs, N.J.: Prentice Hall, 1987.

Hambleton, R. K., and Gumpert, R. "The Validity of Hersey and Blanchard's Theory of Leader Effectiveness." *Group and Organization Studies,* June 1982, pp. 225–242.

Hamel, G., and Prahalad, C. K. *Competing for the Future: Breakthrough Strategies for Seizing Control of Your Industry and Creating the Markets of Tomorrow.* Boston: Harvard Business School Press, 1994.

Hammer, M., and Champy, J. *Reengineering the Corporation.* New York: HarperCollins, 1993.

Hampden-Turner, C. *Creating Corporate Culture: From Discord to Harmony.* Reading, Mass.: Addison-Wesley, 1992.

Hamper, B. *Rivethead: Tales from the Assembly Line.* New York: Warner Books, 1992.

Hampton, W. J., and Norman, J. R. "General Motors: What Went Wrong— Eight Years and Billions of Dollars Haven't Made Its Strategy Succeed." *Business Week,* Mar. 16, 1987, p. 102.

Handlin, H. C. "The Company Built upon the Golden Rule: Lincoln Electric." In B. L. Hopkins and T. C. Mawhinney (eds.), *Pay for Performance: History, Controversy, and Evidence.* Binghamton, N.Y.: Haworth Press, 1992.

Handy, C. *The Age of Unreason.* Boston: Harvard Business School Press, 1989.

Handy, C. *Understanding Organizations.* New York: Oxford University Press, 1993.

Handy, C. *The Age of Paradox.* Boston: Harvard Business School Press, 1995.

Hansell, S. "Citibank: The Ante Rises in East Asia." *New York Times,* July 14, 1996, sec. 3, pp. 1, 12–13.

Hansot, E. "Some Functions of Humor in Organizations." Unpublished paper, Kenyon College, 1979.

Harragan, B. L. *Games Mother Never Taught You: Corporate Gamesmanship for Women.* New York: Rawson, Wade, 1977.

Heath, C., and Gonzalez, R. "Interaction with Others Increases Decision Confidence but Not Decision Quality." *Organizational Behavior and Human Decision Processes,* 1995, *61,* 305–326.

Hedberg, B.L.T., Nystrom, P. C., and Starbuck, W. H. "Camping on Seesaws: Prescriptions for a Self-Designing Organization." *Administrative Science Quarterly,* 1976, *21,* 41–65.

Heffron, F. *Organization Theory and Public Organizations: The Political Connection.* Upper Saddle River, N.J.: Prentice Hall, 1989.

Heifetz, R. A. *Leadership Without Easy Answers.* Cambridge, Mass.: Belknap Press, 1994.

Heimovics, R. D., Herman, R. D., and Jurkiewicz Coughlin, C. L. "Executive Leadership and Resource Dependence in Nonprofit Organizations: A Frame Analysis. *Public Administration Review,* 1993, *53,* 419–427.

Heimovics, R. D., Herman, R. D., and Jurkiewicz Coughlin, C. L. "The Political Dimension of Effective Nonprofit Executive Leadership." *Nonprofit Management and Leadership,* 1995, *5,* 233–248.

Helgesen, S. *The Web of Inclusion: A New Architecture for Building Great Organizations.* New York: Currency/Doubleday, 1995.

Henderson, R. M., and Clark, K. B. "Architectural Innovation: The Reconfiguration of Existing Product Technologies and the Failure of Established Firms." *Administrative Science Quarterly,* 1990, *35,* 9–30.

Hersch, S. M. *The Target Is Destroyed: What Really Happened to Flight 007 and What America Knew About It.* New York: Random House, 1986.

Hersey, P. *The Situational Leader.* New York: Warner Books, 1984.

Hersey, P., and Blanchard, K. H. *The Management of Organizational Behavior.* (3rd ed.) Upper Saddle River, N.J.: Prentice Hall, 1977.

Herzberg, F. *Work and the Nature of Man.* Cleveland, Ohio: World, 1966.

Hogan, R., Curphy, G. J., and Hogan, J. "What We Know About Leadership." *American Psychologist,* 1994, *49,* 493–504.

Holland, J. H. *Hidden Order.* Reading, Mass.: Addison-Wesley, 1995.

Hollander, E. P. *Leadership Dynamics.* New York: Free Press, 1978.

Holusha, J. "No Utopia, but to Workers, It's a Job." *New York Times,* Jan. 29, 1989, sec. 3, p. 1.

House, R. J. "The Path-Goal Theory of Effectiveness." *Administrative Science Quarterly,* 1971, *16,* 321–338.

Iacocca, L., and Novak, W. *Iacocca.* New York: Bantam Books, 1984.

Ishikawa, K. *What Is Total Quality Control? The Japanese Way.* Upper Saddle River, N.J.: Prentice Hall, 1985.

Jackall, R. *Moral Mazes: The World of Corporate Managers.* New York: Oxford University Press, 1988.

Jehn, K. A. "A Multimethod Examination of the Benefits and Detriments of Intragroup Conflict." *Administrative Science Quarterly,* 1995, *40,* 256–282.

Jensen, C. *No Downlink: A Dramatic Narrative About the* Challenger *Accident and Our Time.* New York: Farrar, Straus & Giroux, 1995.

Johnson, K. "Divorced from the Job, Still Wedded to the Culture." *New York Times,* June 16, 1996, p. F-11.

Juran, J. M. *Juran on Leadership for Quality: An Executive Handbook.* New York: Free Press, 1989.

Kahneman, D., and Tversky, A. "Prospect Theory: An Analysis of Decisions Under Risk." *Econometrica,* 1979, *47,* 263–291.

Kamens, D. H. "Legitimating Myths and Education Organizations: Relationship Between Organizational Ideology and Formal Structure." *American Sociological Review,* 1977, *42,* 208–219.

Kanter, R. M. *Men and Women of the Corporation.* New York: Basic Books, 1977.

Kanter, R. M. *The Change Masters: Innovations for Productivity in the American Corporation.* New York: Simon & Schuster, 1983.

Kanter, R. M. *When Giants Learn to Dance.* New York: Simon & Schuster, 1989.

Katzell, R. A., and Yankelovich, D. *Work, Productivity, and Job Satisfaction.* New York: Psychological Corporation, 1975.

Katzenbach, J. R., and Smith, D. K. *The Wisdom of Teams: Creating the High-Performance Organization.* Boston: Harvard Business School Press, 1993.

Kaufer, N., and Leader, G. C. "Diana Lam (A)." Case. Boston University, 1987a.

Kaufer, N., and Leader, G. C. "Diana Lam (B)." Case. Boston University, 1987b.

Kauffman, E. M. "Creating the Uncommon Company." In R. W. Smilor and D. L. Sexton (eds.), *Leadership and Entrepreneurship: Personal and Organizational Development in Entrepreneurial Values.* Westport, Conn.: Quorum/Greenwood, 1996.

Keidel, R. W. "Baseball, Football, and Basketball: Models for Business." *Organizational Dynamics,* Winter 1984, pp. 5–18.

Keller, B. "Of Famous Arches, Beeg Meks, and Rubles." *New York Times,* Jan. 28, 1990a, pp. 1, 12.

Keller, B. "While Gorbachev Gives In, the World Marvels at His Power." *New York Times,* Feb. 11, 1990b, sec. 4, p. 1.

Kidder, T. *The Soul of a New Machine.* New York: Little, Brown, 1981.

Kidder, T. *Among School Children.* Boston: Houghton Mifflin, 1989.

Kleinfeld, N. R. "The Company as Family No More." *New York Times,* Mar. 4, 1996, sec. A, pp. 1, 8–10.

Kohlberg, L. "The Claim to Moral Adequacy of a Highest Stage of Moral Judgment." *Journal of Philosophy,* 1973, *70,* 630–646.

Kopelman, R. E. "Job Redesign and Productivity: A Review of the Evidence." *National Productivity Review,* 1985, *4,* 237–255.

Korten, D. C. *When Corporations Rule the World.* San Francisco: Berrett-Koehler, 1995.

Kotter, J. P. *The General Managers.* New York: Free Press, 1982.

Kotter, J. P. *Power and Influence: Beyond Formal Authority.* New York: Free Press, 1985.

Kotter, J. P. *The Leadership Factor.* New York: Free Press, 1988.

Kotter, J. P., and Heskett, J. L. *Corporate Culture and Performance.* New York: Free Press, 1992.

Kouzes, J. M., and Posner, B. Z. *The Leadership Challenge: How to Get Extraordinary Things Done in Organizations.* San Francisco: Jossey-Bass, 1987.

Kristof, N. "China Update: How the Hardliners Won." *New York Times Magazine,* Nov. 12, 1989, pp. 38–71.

Kühberger, A. "The Framing of Decisions: A New Look at Old Problems." *Organizational Behavior and Human Decision Processes,* 1995, *62,* 230–240.

Kuhn, T. S. *The Structure of Scientific Revolutions.* (2nd ed.) Chicago: University of Chicago Press, 1970.

Labich, K. "Is Herb Kelleher America's Best CEO? *Fortune,* May 2, 1994, pp. 44–52.

Langer, E. *Mindfulness.* Reading, Mass.: Addison-Wesley, 1989.

Lawler, E. E., III. *High-Involvement Management: Participative Strategies for Improving Organizational Performance.* San Francisco: Jossey-Bass, 1986.

Lawler, E. E., III. *From the Ground Up: Six Principles for Building the New Logic Corporation.* San Francisco: Jossey-Bass, 1996.

Lawler, E. E., III, and Shuttle, J. L. "A Causal Correlation Test of the Need Hierarchy Concept." *Organizational Behavior and Human Performance,* 1973, *7,* 265–287.

Lawrence, A. T., and Weckler, D. A. "Can NUMMI's Team Concept Work for You? Part I: A Bicultural Experiment." *Northern California Executive Review,* Spring 1990, pp. 12–17.

Lawrence, P., and Lorsch, J. *Organization and Environment.* Boston: Division of Research, Harvard Business School, 1967.

Lax, D. A., and Sebenius, J. K. *The Manager as Negotiator.* New York: Free Press, 1986.

Leavitt, H. J. *Managerial Psychology.* (4th ed.) Chicago: University of Chicago Press, 1978.

Leavitt, H. J. "The Old Days, Hot Groups, and Managers' Lib." *Administrative Science Quarterly,* 1996, *41,* 288–300.

Ledford, G. E. "Employee Involvement: Lessons and Predictions." In J. R. Galbraith, E. E. Lawler III, and Associates (eds.), *Organizing for the Future: The New Logic of Managing Complex Organizations.* San Francisco: Jossey-Bass, 1993.

Lee, A. *Call Me Roger.* Chicago: Contemporary Books, 1988.

Lesgold, A., and Lajoie, S. "Complex Problem Solving in Electronics." In R. J. Sternberg and P. A. Frensch (eds.), *Complex Problem Solving.* Hillsdale, N.J.: Lawrence Erlbaum Associates, 1991.

Levering, R., and Moskowitz, M. *The 100 Best Companies to Work for in America.* New York: Plume, 1993.

Levine, D. I., and Tyson, L. D. "Participation, Productivity, and the Firm's Environment." In A. S. Blinder (ed.), *Paying for Productivity: A Look at the Evidence.* Washington, D.C.: Brookings Institution, 1990.

Levinson, H. *The Exceptional Executive.* Cambridge, Mass.: Harvard University Press, 1968.

Levinson, H., and Rosenthal, S. *CEO: Corporate Leadership in Action.* New York: Basic Books, 1984.

Lewin, K., Lippitt, R., and White, R. "Patterns of Aggressive Behavior in Experimentally Created Social Climates." *Journal of Social Psychology,* 1939, *10,* 271–299.

Lewis, N. A. "This Mr. Smith Gets His Way in Washington." *New York Times,* Oct. 12, 1996, pp. 17, 30.

Lifson, T., and Takagi, H. *Mitsubishi Corporation: Organizational Overview.* Boston: Harvard Business School Case Services, 1981.

Likert, R. *New Patterns of Management.* New York: McGraw-Hill, 1961.

Likert, R. *The Human Organization.* New York: McGraw-Hill, 1967.

Lipsky, M. *Street-Level Bureaucracy.* New York: Russell Sage Foundation, 1980.

Longworth, R. C. "Old Rules of Economics Don't Work the Way Textbooks Say They Should." *Kansas City Star,* Oct. 27, 1996, sec. K, pp. 1, 4.

Loomis, C. J. "Dinosaurs?" *Fortune,* May 3, 1993, pp. 36–42.

Lord, R. G., and Foti, R. J. "Schema Theories, Information Processing, and Organizational Behavior." In H. P. Sims, Jr., D. A. Gioia, and Associates (eds.), *The Thinking Organization.* San Francisco: Jossey-Bass, 1986.

Love, J. F. *McDonald's: Behind the Arches.* New York: Bantam Books, 1986.

Lukes, S. *Power: A Radical View.* New York: Macmillan, 1974.

Lynch, P. "In Defense of the Invisible Hand." *Worth,* June 1996, pp. 86–92.

Lynn, L. E., Jr. *Managing Public Policy.* New York: Little, Brown, 1987.

Maccoby, E. E., and Jacklin, C. N. *The Psychology of Sex Differences.* Stanford, Calif.: Stanford University Press, 1974.

Maccoby, M. *The Leader.* New York: Ballantine, 1981.

Machan, D. "DEC's Democracy." *Forbes,* Mar. 23, 1987, pp. 154, 156.

Machiavelli, N. *The Prince.* New York: Penguin Books, 1961. (Originally published 1514.)

Maier, N. "Assets and Liabilities in Group Problem Solving." *Psychological Review,* 1967, *74,* 239–249.

Malavé, J. *Gerencia en salud: Un modelo innovador* [Health management: An innovative model]. Caracas: Ediciones IESA, 1995.

Manes, S., and Andrews, P. *Gates.* New York: Touchstone, 1994.

Mangham, I. L., and Overington, M. A. *Organizations as Theater: A Social Psychology of Dramatic Appearances.* New York: Wiley, 1987.

Manning, P. *Police Work: The Social Organization of Policing.* Cambridge, Mass.: MIT Press, 1979.

March, J. G. "The Technology of Foolishness." In J. G. March and J. Olsen (eds.), *Ambiguity and Choice in Organizations.* Bergen, Norway: Universitetsforlaget, 1976.

March, J. G., and Olsen, J. (eds.), *Ambiguity and Choice in Organizations.* Bergen, Norway: Universitetsforlaget, 1976.

Markels, A., and Murray, M. "Call It Dumbsizing: Why Some Companies Regret Cost-Cutting." *Wall Street Journal,* May 14, 1996, p. 1.

Marshall, M. V. "An Introduction to the Marketing Concept of Managing an Institution's Future." Cambridge, Mass.: Institute for Educational Management, 1984.

Marx, K. *Capital: A Critique of Political Economy.* (S. Moore and E. Aveling, trans.). London, 1887.

Marx, R., Stubbart, C., Traub, V., and Cavanaugh, M. "The NASA Space Shuttle Disaster: A Case Study." *Journal of Management Case Studies,* 1987, *3,* 300–318.

Maslow, A. H. *Motivation and Personality.* New York: HarperCollins, 1954.

McCaskey, M. B. *The Executive Challenge: Managing Change and Ambiguity.* Marshfield, Mass.: Pitman, 1982.

McClelland, D. C. *Human Motivation.* Glenview, Ill.: Scott, Foresman, 1985.

McConnell, M. *Challenger: A Major Malfunction.* New York: Doubleday, 1987.

McGrath, J. E. *Groups: Interaction and Performance.* Upper Saddle River, N.J.: Prentice Hall, 1984.

McGregor, D. *The Human Side of Enterprise.* New York: McGraw-Hill, 1960.

McLennan, R. *Managing Organizational Change.* Upper Saddle River, N.J.: Prentice Hall, 1989.

Meredith, R. "New Blood for the Big Three's Plants: This Hiring Spree Is Rewarding Brains, Not Brawn." *New York Times,* Apr. 21, 1996, sec. 3, pp. 1, 3.

Meyer, J. W., and Rowan, B. "The Structure of Educational Organizations." In M. W. Meyer and Associates, *Environments and Organizations: Theoretical and Empirical Perspectives.* San Francisco: Jossey-Bass, 1978.

Meyer, J. W., and Rowan, B. "Institutionalized Organizations: Formal Structure as Myth and Ceremony." In J. W. Meyer and W. R. Scott (eds.), *Organizational Environments: Ritual and Rationality.* Beverly Hills, Calif.: Sage, 1983a.

Meyer, J. W., and Rowan, B. "The Structure of Educational Organizations." In J. W. Meyer and W. R. Scott (eds.), *Organizational Environments: Ritual and Rationality.* Beverly Hills, Calif.: Sage, 1983b.

Miller, D., and Friesen, P. H. *Organizations: A Quantum View.* Upper Saddle River, N.J.: Prentice Hall, 1984.

Mintzberg, H. *The Nature of Managerial Work.* New York: HarperCollins, 1973.

Mintzberg, H. *The Structuring of Organizations.* Upper Saddle River, N.J.: Prentice Hall, 1979.

Mintzberg, H. *The Rise and Fall of Strategic Planning: Reconceiving Roles for Planning, Plans, Planners.* New York: Free Press, 1994.

Mirvis, P. H. "Organization Development, Part I: An Evolutionary Perspective." *Research in Organizational Change and Development,* 1988, *2,* 1–57.

Mirvis, P. H. "Organization Development, Part II: A Revolutionary Perspective." In W. A. Passmore and R. W. Woodman (eds.), *Research in Organizational Change and Development,* Vol. 2. Greenwich, Conn.: JAI Press, 1990.

Mirvis, P. H., and Hall, D. T. "New Organizational Forms and the New Career." In D. T. Hall and Associates, *The Career Is Dead: Long Live the Career.* San Francisco: Jossey-Bass, 1996.

Mitroff, I. I. *Stakeholders of the Organizational Mind: Toward a New View of Organizational Policy Making.* San Francisco: Jossey-Bass, 1983.

Mitroff, I. I., and Kilmann, R. H. "Stories Managers Tell: A New Tool for Organizational Problem Solving." *Management Review,* July 1975, pp. 18–28.

Moeller, J. "Bureaucracy and Teachers' Sense of Power." In N. R. Bell and H. R. Stub (eds.), *Sociology of Education.* Florence, Ky.: Dorsey Press, 1968.

Moore, J. F. "Predators and Prey: A New Ecology of Competition." *Harvard Business Review,* May–June 1993, pp. 75–86.

Morgan, A. *Prescription for Success: The Life and Values of Ewing Marion Kauffman.* Kansas City, Mo.: Andrews & McMeel, 1995.

Morgan, G. *Images of Organization.* Thousand Oaks, Calif.: Sage, 1986.

Morgan, G. *Imaginization: The Art of Creative Management.* Thousand Oaks, Calif.: Sage, 1993.

Morganthau, T. "Saying 'No' to New Coke." *Newsweek,* June 23, 1985, pp. 32–33.

Morris, B. "The Wealth Builders." *Fortune,* Dec. 11, 1995, pp. 80–94.

Morrison, A. M. *The New Leaders: Guidelines on Leadership Diversity in America.* San Francisco: Jossey-Bass, 1992.

Murphy, J. T. *Managing Matters: Reflections from Practice.* Monograph. Cambridge, Mass.: Graduate School of Education, Harvard University, 1985.

Myers, I. *Introduction to Type.* Palo Alto, Calif.: Consulting Psychologists Press, 1980.

Nadler, D. A., Gerstein, M. S., and Shaw, R. B. *Organizational Architecture: Designs for Changing Organizations.* San Francisco: Jossey-Bass, 1992.

Nussbaum, B., and Dobrzynski, J. H. "The Battle for Corporate Control." *Business Week,* May 18, 1987, pp. 102–109.

Ohmae, K. *The Borderless World: Power and Strategy in the Interlinked Economy.* New York: HarperBusiness, 1990.

Oliver, T. *The Real Coke, the Real Story.* New York: Random House, 1986.

Olsen, J. "The Process of Interpreting Organizational History." In J. G. March and J. Olsen (eds.), *Ambiguity and Choice in Organizations.* Bergen, Norway: Universitetsforlaget, 1976a.

Olsen, J. "Reorganization as a Garbage Can." In J. G. March and J. Olsen (eds.), *Ambiguity and Choice in Organizations.* Bergen, Norway: Universitetsforlaget, 1976b.

"On a Clear Day You Can Still See General Motors." *Economist,* Dec. 2, 1989, pp. 77–78, 80.

O'Reilly, C. A., III, and Chatman, J. A. "Working Smarter and Harder: A Longitudinal Study of Managerial Success." *Administrative Science Quarterly,* 1994, *39,* 603–627.

Orgogozo, I. *Les paradoxes du management* [The paradoxes of management]. Paris: Les Éditions d'Organisation, 1991.

Ortner, S. "On Key Symbols." *American Anthropologist,* 1973, *75,* 1338–1346.

Oshry, B. *Seeing Systems: Unlocking the Mysteries of Organizational Life.* San Francisco: Berrett-Koehler, 1995.

Osterman, P. "Work-Family Programs and the Employment Relationship." *Administrative Science Quarterly,* 1995, *40,* 681–700.

O'Toole, J. *Leading Change: Overcoming the Ideology of Comfort and the Tyranny of Custom.* San Francisco: Jossey-Bass, 1995.

O'Toole, P. *Corporate Messiah: The Hiring and Firing of Million-Dollar Managers.* New York: Morrow, 1984.

Owen, H. *Spirit: Transformation and Development in Organizations.* Potomac, Md.: Abbott, 1987.

Owen, H. *Open Space Technology.* Potomac, Md.: Abbott, 1993.

Owen, II. *Tales from Open Space.* Potomac, Md.: Abbott, 1995.

Palumbo, G. *Gerencia participativa: Un caso exito en el sector salud* [Participative management: A successful case in the health sector]. Caracas: Fundación Antonio Cisneros Bermudez, 1991.

Paré, T. P. "Jack Welch's Nightmare on Wall Street." *Fortune,* Sept. 5, 1994, pp. 40–48.

Pennar, K. "Economic Anxiety." *Business Week,* Mar. 11, 1996, pp. 50–52.

Perrow, C. *Complex Organizations: A Critical Essay.* (2nd ed.) Glenview, Ill.: Scott, Foresman, 1979.

Perrow, C. *Complex Organizations: A Critical Essay.* (3rd ed.) New York: Random House, 1986.

Peters, T. J., and Austin, N. *A Passion for Excellence.* New York: Random House, 1985.

Peters, T. J., and Waterman, R. H. *In Search of Excellence.* New York: Harper-Collins, 1982.

Petzinger, T. *Hard Landing: The Epic Contest for Power and Profits That Plunged the Airlines into Chaos.* New York: Times Business, 1995.

Pfeffer, J. *Organizational Design.* Arlington Heights, Ill.: AHM Publishing, 1978.

Pfeffer, J. *Managing with Power: Politics and Influence in Organizations.* Boston: Harvard Business School Press, 1992.

Pfeffer, J. *Competitive Advantage Through People: Unleashing the Power of the Work Force.* Boston: Harvard Business School Press, 1994.

Pichault, F. *Ressources humaines et changement stratégique: Vers un management politique* [Human Resources and Strategic Change: Toward a Political Approach to Management]. Brussels, Belgium: DeBoeck, 1993.

Port, O. "Quality." *Business Week,* Nov. 30, 1992, pp. 66–72.

Porter, E. "Notes for the Looking for Leadership Conference." Paper presented at the Looking for Leadership Conference, Graduate School of Education, Harvard University, Dec. 1989.

Powell, W. W., Koput, K. W., and Smith-Doerr, L. "Interorganizational Collaboration and the Locus of Innovation: Networks of Learning in Biotechnology." *Administrative Science Quarterly,* 1996, *41,* 116–145.

Pressman, J. L., and Wildavsky, A. B. *Implementation.* Berkeley: University of California Press, 1973.

Quinn, R. E. *Beyond Rational Management: Mastering the Paradoxes and Competing Demands of High Performance.* San Francisco: Jossey-Bass, 1988.

Quinn, R. E., and Cameron, K. "Organizational Life Cycles and Shifting Criteria of Effectiveness." *Management Science,* 1983, *29,* 33–51.

Quinn, R. E., Faerman, S. R., Thompson, M. P., and McGrath, M. R. *Becoming a Master Manager: A Competency Framework.* New York: Wiley, 1996.

Rallis, S. "Different Views of Knowledge Use by Practitioners." Unpublished paper, Graduate School of Education, Harvard University, 1980.

Rappaport, C. "A Tough Swede Invades the U.S." *Fortune,* Jan. 29, 1992, pp. 76–79.

Reddin, W. J. *Managerial Effectiveness.* New York: McGraw-Hill, 1970.

Reichheld, F. F. "Loyalty-Based Management." *Harvard Business Review,* Mar.–Apr. 1993, pp. 64–73.

Reichheld, F. F. *The Loyalty Effect: The Hidden Force Behind Growth, Profits, and Lasting Value.* Boston: Harvard Business School Press, 1996.

Ridout, C. F., and Fenn, D. H. "Job Corps." Boston: Harvard Business School Case Services, 1974.

Rifkin, J. *The End of Work: The Decline of the Global Labor Force and the Dawn of the Post-Market Era.* Los Angeles: Tarcher/Putnam, 1995.

Ritti, R. R., and Funkhouser, G. R. *The Ropes to Skip and the Ropes to Know.* (2nd ed.) Columbus, Ohio: Grid, 1982.

Rosenthal, R., and Jacobson, L. *Pygmalion in the Classroom: Teacher Expectations and Pupils' Intellectual Development.* Austin, Tex.: Holt, Rinehart and Winston, 1968.

Rossiter, C. *1787: The Grand Convention.* New York: New American Library, 1966.

Russ, J. *Les théories du pouvoir* [Theories of power]. Paris: Librairie Générale Française, 1994.

Ryan, M. "They Call Their Boss a Hero." *Parade,* Sept. 8, 1996, pp. 4–5.

Salancik, G. R., and Pfeffer, J. "An Examination of Need-Satisfaction Models of Job Attitudes." *Administrative Science Quarterly,* 1977, *22,* 427–456.

Sapolsky, H. *The Polaris System Development.* Cambridge, Mass.: Harvard University Press, 1972.

Schein, E. H. *Process Consultation.* Reading, Mass.: Addison-Wesley, 1969.

Schein, E. H. *Organizational Culture and Leadership.* (2nd ed.) San Francisco: Jossey-Bass, 1992.

Schelling, T. *The Strategy of Conflict.* Cambridge, Mass.: Harvard University Press, 1960.

Schemo, D. J. "Is VW's New Plant Lean, or Just Mean?" *New York Times,* Nov. 19, 1996, p. C1.

Schlesinger, L., Eccles, R., and Gabarro, J. *Managerial Behavior in Organizations.* New York: McGraw-Hill, 1983.

Schlesinger, J. M. "NUMMI Keeps Promise of No Layoffs by Setting Nonproduction Workdays." *Wall Street Journal,* Oct. 29, 1987, p. 30.

Schneider, B., and Alderfer, C. "Three Studies of Measures of Need Satisfaction in Organizations." *Administrative Science Quarterly,* 1973, *18,* 498–505.

Schwartz, H. S. "The Clockwork or the Snakepit: An Essay on the Meaning of Teaching Organizational Behavior." *Organizational Behavior Teaching Review,* 1986, *11,* 19–26.

Scott, W. R. *Organizations: Rational, Natural, and Open Systems.* Upper Saddle River, N.J.: Prentice Hall, 1981.

Scott, W. R. "The Organization of Environments: Network, Cultural, and Historical Elements." In J. W. Meyer and W. R. Scott (eds.), *Organizational Environments: Ritual and Rationality.* Beverly Hills, Calif.: Sage, 1983.

Seeger, J. A., Lorsch, J. W., and Gibson, C. F. "First National City Bank Operating Group (A) and (B)." Boston: Harvard Business School Case Services, 1975.

Selznick, P. *Leadership and Administration.* New York: HarperCollins, 1957.

Semler, R. *Maverick: The Success Story Behind the World's Most Unusual Workplace.* New York: Warner Books, 1993.

Senge, P. M. *The Fifth Discipline: The Art and Practice of the Learning Organization.* New York: Doubleday/Currency, 1990.

Sennett, R. *Authority.* New York: Knopf, 1980.

Sérieyx, H. *Le big bang des organisations* [The organizational big bang]. Paris: Calmann-Lévy, 1993.

Sherman, J. *The Rings of Saturn.* New York: Oxford University Press, 1994.

Shu Li and Adams, A. S. "Is There Something More Important Behind Framing?" *Organizational Behavior and Human Decision Processes,* 1995, *62,* 216–219.

Simmel, G. *The Sociology of Georg Simmel.* New York: Free Press, 1950.

Simon, H. *Hidden Champions: Lessons from 500 of the World's Best Unknown Companies.* Boston: Harvard Business School Press, 1996.

Sloan, A. P., Jr. *My Years with General Motors.* New York: Macfadden, 1965.

Smith, H. *The Power Game.* New York: Random House, 1988.

Smith, R. "It's No Fun Running No. 1 When You're Taking the Heat." *Fortune,* Aug. 3, 1987, pp. 26–27.

Solomon, R. C. *Ethics and Excellence: Cooperation and Integrity in Business.* Oxford, England: Oxford University Press, 1993.

Spector, R., and McCarthy, D. *The Nordstrom Way: The Inside Story of America's #1 Customer Service Company.* New York: Wiley, 1995.

Staw, B. M., and Hoang, H. "Sunk Costs in the NBA: Why Draft Order Affects Playing Time and Survival in Professional Basketball." *Administrative Science Quarterly,* 1995, *40,* 474–494.

Stern, R. N., and Barley, S. R. "Organizations and Social Systems: Organization Theory's Neglected Mandate. *Administrative Science Quarterly,* 1996, *41,* 146–162.

Steward, T. A. "Managing in a Wired Company." *Fortune,* July 11, 1994, pp. 44–56.

Stogdill, R. *Handbook of Leadership.* New York: Free Press, 1974.

Stross, R. E. "Microsoft's Big Advantage—Hiring Only the Supersmart." *Fortune,* Nov. 25, 1996, pp. 159–162.

Taylor, F. W. *The Principles of Scientific Management.* New York, 1911.

Thompson, J. D. *Organizations in Action.* New York: McGraw-Hill, 1967.

Thorsrud, E. "Democracy at Work: Norwegian Experiences with Nonbureaucratic Forms of Organization." *Journal of Applied Behavioral Science,* 1977, *13,* 410–421.

Thorsrud, E. "The Scandinavian Model: Strategies of Organizational Democratization in Norway." In B. Wilpert and A. Sorge (eds.), *International Perspectives on Organizational Democracy.* New York: Wiley, 1984.

Tomsho, R. "How Greyhound Lines Re-Engineered Itself Right into a Deep Hole." *Wall Street Journal,* Oct. 20, 1994, p. A1.

Topoff, H. R. "The Social Behavior of Army Ants." *Scientific American,* Nov. 1972, pp. 71–79.

Treacy, M., and Wiersema, F. *The Discipline of Market Leaders: Choose Your Customers, Narrow Your Focus, Dominate Your Market.* Reading, Mass.: Addison-Wesley, 1995.

Trost, A. H. "Leadership Is Flesh and Blood." In L. Atwater and R. Penn (eds.), *Military Leadership: Traditions and Future Trends.* Annapolis, Md.: Naval Institute Press, 1989.

Uchitelle, L. "We're Leaner, Meaner and Going Nowhere Faster." *New York Times,* May 12, 1996, sec. 4, pp. 1, 4.

Uchitelle, L., and Kleinfeld, N. R. "On the Battlefields of Business: Millions of Casualties." *New York Times,* Mar. 3, 1996, pp. 1, 13–15.

Urwick, L. "Organization as a Technical Problem." In L. H. Gulick and L. Urwick (eds.), *Papers on the Science of Administration.* New York: Columbia University Press, 1937.

Useem, M. *Investor Capitalism: How Money Managers Are Changing the Face of Corporate America.* New York: Basic Books, 1996.

Vaill, P. B. "The Purposing of High-Performance Systems." *Organizational Dynamics,* Autumn 1982, pp. 23–39.

Vaill, P. B. *Managing as a Performing Art: New Ideas for a World of Chaotic Change.* San Francisco: Jossey-Bass, 1989.

Vaughn, D. "Autonomy, Interdependence, and Social Control: NASA and the Space Shuttle *Challenger." Administrative Science Quarterly,* 1990, *35,* 225–257.

Vaughn, D. *The* Challenger *Launch Decision: Risky Technology, Culture, and Deviance at NASA.* Chicago: University of Chicago, 1995.

Voss, J. F., Wolfe, C. R., Lawrence, J. A., and Engle, R. A. "From Representation to Decision: An Analysis of Problem Solving in International Relations." In R. J. Sternberg and P. A. Frensch (eds.), *Complex Problem Solving.* Hillsdale, N.J.: Lawrence Erlbaum Associates, 1991.

Vroom, V. H., and Yetton, P. W. *Leadership and Decision Making.* Pittsburgh: University of Pittsburgh Press, 1973.

Waldrop, M. M. *Complexity: The Emerging Science at the Edge of Order and Chaos.* New York: Simon & Schuster, 1992.

Waterman, R. H., Jr. *What America Does Right: Learning from Companies That Put People First.* New York: Norton, 1994.

Weatherford, J. M. *Tribes on the Hill: The United States Congress—Rituals and Realities.* Westport, Conn.: Bergin & Garvey, 1985.

Weber, M. *The Theory of Social and Economic Organization.* (T. Parsons, trans.). New York: Free Press, 1947.

Weick, K. E. "Educational Organizations as Loosely Coupled Systems." *Administrative Science Quarterly,* 1976, *21,* 1–19.

Weick, K. E. "Cognitive Processes in Organizations." In B. E. Staw (ed.), *Research in Organizational Behavior.* Greenwich, Conn.: JAI Press, 1981.

Weick, K. E., and Bougon, M. G. "Organizations as Cognitive Maps." In H. P. Sims, Jr., D. A. Gioia, and Associates (eds.), *The Thinking Organization.* San Francisco: Jossey-Bass, 1986.

Weiner, S. S. "Participation, Deadlines, and Choice." In J. G. March and J. Olsen (eds.), *Ambiguity and Choice in Organizations.* Bergen, Norway: Universitetsforlaget, 1976.

Weisbord, M. R. *Discovering Common Ground.* San Francisco: Berrett-Koehler, 1992.

Weisbord, M. R., and Janoff, S. *Future Search: An Action Guide to Finding Common Ground in Organizations and Communities.* San Francisco: Berrett-Koehler, 1995.

Weiss, C. H. *Social Science Research and Decision Making.* New York: Columbia University Press, 1980.

Westerlund, G., and Sjostrand, S. *Organizational Myths.* New York: Harper-Collins, 1979.

White, R. W. "Competence and the Psychosexual Stages of Development." In M. R. Jones (ed.), *Nebraska Symposium on Motivation, 1960.* Lincoln: University of Nebraska Press, 1960.

Whitmyer, C. *In the Company of Others.* New York: Putnam, 1993.

Whyte, W. F. *Money and Motivation.* New York: HarperCollins, 1955.

Wimpelberg, R. K. "Managerial Images and School Effectiveness." *Administrators' Notebook,* 1987, *32,* 1–4.

Witkin, R. "Downing of KAL 007 Laid to Russian Error." *New York Times,* June 6, 1993, p. A7.

Woodward, J. (ed.). *Industrial Organizations: Behavior and Control.* Oxford, England: Oxford University Press, 1970.

WuDunn, S. "When Lifetime Jobs Die Prematurely." *New York Times,* June 12, 1996, sec. D, pp. 1, 8.

Zachary, G. P. "Climbing the Peak: Agony and Ecstasy of 200 Code Writers Beget Windows NT." *Wall Street Journal,* May 26, 1993, pp. A1, A6.

Zachary, G. P. *Showstopper! The Breakneck Race to Create Windows NT and the Next Generation at Microsoft.* New York: Free Press, 1994.

Name Index

Thompson, J. D., 143
Thompson, M. P., 17n.2
Thorsrud, E., 131
Tilliette, B., 9, 126, 311
Tomsho, R., 74
Topoff, H. R., 40
Traub, V., 162
Treacy, M., 340
Tsongas, P., 224, 225
Tsutsumi, Y., 227
Tun, W., 319
Tversky, A., 31
Tyson, L. D., 129

U

Uchitelle, L., 114, 115
Updike, J., 89
Urwick, L., 38
Ury, W., 179, 187–188
Useem, M., 209–210

V

Vaill, P. B., 261, 297, 377
Vaughn, D., 162
Veres, J., 256
Voss, J. F., 17n.1
Vroom, V. H., 300, 308

W

Wageman, R., 134
Waldrop, M. M., 54, 55
Wallach, S., 253, 254, 258
Wallin, C., 232
Waterman, R. H., 11, 14, 101, 105, 117, 122,
    123, 126, 134, 274–276, 308, 309, 310,
    345, 346, 348, 349, 353n.1

Weatherford, J. M., 224, 228
Weber, M., 38, 294–295
Weckler, D. A., 135
Weick, K. E., 17n.1, 216
Weigl, H., 194–195
Weiner, S. S., 241, 245
Weis, J., 356–357, 358
Weisbord, M. R., 138
Weiss, C. H., 245
Weitzel, J. R., 301
Welch, J., 139, 204
West, T., 251, 253, 254, 255–256, 258, 260
Westerlund, G., 53
White, R., 74–76, 104, 150
Whitmyer, C., 347
Whyte, W. F., 128
Wiersema, F., 340
Wildavsky, A. B., 9
Wilson, T., 196
Wimpelberg, R. K., 278
Witkin, 19
Wolf, D., 70
Wolfe, C. R., 17n.1
Woodruff, R., 329
Woodward, J., 238
WuDunn, S., 113
Wyman, T., 185–186

Y

Yankelovich, D., 129
Yetton, P. W., 300, 308

Z

Zachary, G. P., 55, 176, 177, 180

Subject Index

Monocratic bureaucracy, 38
Moral discourse, 193. *See also* Ethics
Moral judgment, principles of, 192. *See also*
    Ethics
Morale: and downsizing, 116–117; and par-
    ticipation, 129, and structure, 39. *See also*
    Spirit
Morton Thiokol Corporation, 161–162, 163,
    174, 182, 184, 186
Motivation: and human needs, 103–106; im-
    portance of, and choice of frame, 271;
    and job enrichment, 130; multiple frame
    perspective on, 268; and organizational
    culture, 251
Motorola, 126, 345–346, 349
Multiframe thinking, 12–13, 16–17, 379–
    380
Music, 352
Mutual gains bargaining, 246
Mutuality, 147, 156, 167, 192
Myers-Briggs Type Inventory, 151
Myths, 220–221. *See also* Symbolic frame

N

Nabisco, 195–198
National Aeronautics and Space Admin-
    istration (NASA), 7–8, 161–162, 163–
    164, 182, 184
National Committee to Improve the Qual-
    ity of Working Life, 119
National Health Service Corps (NHSC),
    269–270
National Labor Relations Board, 240
Nature/nurture controversy, 103–104
Needs: human, 103–106; and job enrich-
    ment, 130–131; Maslow's hierarchy of,
    104–105, 106, 191. *See also* Motivation
Negotiation: for goal setting, 163, 165; man-
    agerial skill of, 186–190; and political
    leadership, 312–313; strategies of, 187–
    190. *See also* Bargaining; Conflict man-
    agement; Political frame; Politics
Networking, 182, 184–186, 312
Networks, 45–46; circle, 86–87; developing,
    182, 184–186; electronic, 54–55, 158;
    power of, 170; star, 87, 88; team, 86–87,
    88
New Patterns of Management (Likert), 139
New United Motors Manufacturing, Inc.
    (NUMMI), 4, 5, 307, 134–137
New York Times, 197
Newcomers, 223–226

Nonprofit executives, 278
Nordstrom, 232–233, 310
Norms, informal, 154–155. *See also* Culture
Northwest Airlines, 61
Norway, 133

O

Obedience, 295
Old-timers, 224–226
Olympic Games, 81
One-best-way leadership model, 297–299
One-boss team design, 84
"Open Space," 138
Open systems, 235–236
Operating core, 62, 63
Operating procedures, standard, 42–43
Organization development (OD): evolution
    of, 139–140; sensitivity training and, 137–
    139
Organization theory, 10–17; frames in,
    12–17. *See also* Theories
Organizational change. *See* Change
Organizational design. *See* Structure
Organizational diagnosis: and belief sys-
    tems, 29–31; common fallacies in, 31–34
Organizational learning, 24–28, 126
Organizational processes: multiple per-
    spectives on, 267–270; as theater, 241–
    248.
Organizational structure. *See* Structural
    frame; Structure
Organizations: ambiguity in, 23–24, 25; as
    coalitions, 163–164, 166–167; complex-
    ity of, 7–8, 22; complexity of, coping
    with, 28–31; complexity of, and failure,
    18–24; complexity of, and human re-
    sources, 113–114; complexity of, and
    organizational learning, 24–28; com-
    plexity of, and task complexity, 83; con-
    flict in, 172–173; deceptiveness of, 23;
    ecosystems of, 202–210; effective, 274–
    275; ethics in, 344–353; factory meta-
    phor for, 344–346; failure of, 18–24,
    149–150, 161–166; family metaphor for,
    344, 346–348; frames for, 12–17; high-
    performing, 274–275; improvement
    strategies for, theory base of, 10–17; im-
    provement strategies for, track record
    of, 8–10, 149–150; jungle metaphor for,
    344, 348–350; as multiple realities, 267–
    270; new models of, 9–10; as open sys-
    tems, 235–236; and people, 101–120;